Learning Zig

A reimagined introduction to low-level programming
with Zig

Alex Rios

‹packt›

Learning Zig

Portfolio Director: Kunal Chaudhary
Relationship Lead: Samriddhi Murarka
Project Manager: K. Loganathan
Content Engineer: Sushma Reddy
Technical Editor: Irfa Ansari
Copy Editor: Safis Editing
Indexer: Rekha Nair
Proofreader: Sushma Reddy
Production Designer: Prashant Ghare
Growth Lead: Vinishka Kalra

First published: November 2025
Production reference: 1051125

Published by Packt Publishing Ltd.
Grosvenor House
11 St Paul's Square
Birmingham
B3 1RB, UK.

ISBN 978-1-83508-512-7
www.packtpub.com

This book would not have been possible without the incredible patience of my life partner, Erika, who tolerated my descent into Zig-induced madness with remarkable grace. I must also acknowledge the vital support team consisting of Leleo, Pretinha, and Bubu. Their expert-level napping, persistent demands for attention, and occasional attempts to "debug" my keyboard were essential, in their own unique way, to the completion of this project.

— Alex Rios

Contributors

About the author

Alex Rios, a Brazilian software engineer notorious for wrangling unruly Go code, has seen almost everything. From fintech to telecom to the chaotic gaming world, he's built high-throughput systems that defy the odds (and occasional sanity checks). As a senior staff engineer at Stone Co., he is known for his unconventional system design approach and ability to deliver high-quality results. But even a Go maestro like him knows that every language has limits. That's why he dove headfirst into Zig, a rising star in systems programming that tackles the problems Go wasn't designed to solve.

About the reviewers

Pablo Aguilar is a passionate software engineer specializing in backend development from Brazil. His career features significant contributions to major companies in the financial, gaming, and real estate sectors. He has built a proven track record of delivering high-impact projects, from creating homologation integration for a fintech company to developing a revolutionary advertising optimizer model for a major media conglomerate. In the gaming industry, he developed sophisticated live ops systems for a large game studio. He is currently a senior backend engineer, open source contributor, and speaker. He continues to be a driving force in the tech industry through his dedication to solving complex problems with innovative solutions.

Ellison Leão is a passionate software engineer with more than 10 years of experience in web development and distributed systems. He is also an active open source contributor and loves to learn new programming languages and discuss their trade-offs.

Table of Contents

Part 2: Data, Memory, and Tools

Chapter 9: Memory Management   **215**

Part 3: Advanced Zig and Real-World Application

Chapter 12: Sophisticated Topics   351

Chapter 14: Unlock Your Book's Exclusive Benefits   449

Other Books You May Enjoy   455

Index   459

Preface

Alright, let's talk about **systems programming**. That's the part of software development where you work much closer to the computer hardware. You're expected to *really* understand how things work under the hood, manage memory carefully (or try to, anyway), and deal with the nitty-gritty details often hidden by easier-to-use programming tools. It's a different beast than typical application programming, demanding a deeper level of control and understanding.

Now, **Zig** enters the picture. It's a newer programming language, designed by Andrew Kelley, with the ambitious goal of making systems programming more straightforward, accessible, and less error-prone. It tries to fix some of the long-standing headaches from languages such as C and C++ – the complexity, and the easy ways to shoot yourself in the foot – while still giving you more direct control than you'd get from higher-level languages that automatically manage memory (which often comes with its own set of problems, such as unexpected slowdowns).

You see, in software, you often face tough trade-offs. You might have the following:

- **High-level ease**: Build apps quickly using languages that hide the messy details, often relying on automatic memory management (such as a garbage collector) that can pause your program when you least expect it. Simple, until it's not performing well.
- **Low-level control**: Directly manage memory and resources in C or C++, aiming for top speed, but likely spending a lot of time hunting down tricky bugs related to memory errors. Powerful, but risky.
- **The constant juggle**: Try to balance safety, performance, and simplicity, but usually, you can't perfectly maximize all three.

Most learning resources focus on the high-level side. This book takes a different path. It's designed to help developers – especially those with a couple of years of experience in building applications – learn the fundamentals of systems programming using Zig as our guide. We're not aiming to build a complex operating system right away. Instead, the focus is on the practical skills needed to build solid low-level software with Zig.

The information in this book comes from two main places:

- My own experience working with Zig, figuring out what works and what doesn't
- Observing the common practices and useful patterns emerging from the Zig community and official guides—always viewed with a practical eye, of course

So, why pay attention to Zig? Because the problems it tries to solve are real. Getting consistent high performance out of software is difficult. Writing safe low-level code is notoriously hard. And dealing with build systems can often feel like wrestling an octopus. Zig offers a different approach, aiming for low-level control paired with better safety features and simpler tooling than the old guard.

Is Zig the magic answer to everything? No, of course not. But as more projects run into the limits of current languages – whether it's the lack of control in high-level ones or the safety issues in C/ C++ – Zig looks like a strong, practical alternative. As a result, developers who know how to use Zig effectively for demanding tasks such as high-performance computing, embedded systems, or game development might find that they have a very useful and valuable skill. This book is your starting point for gaining that skill. You will learn enough Zig to tackle interesting low-level problems effectively.

So, if you're curious about what's going on behind the scenes, ready to take more direct control over your code, and willing to manage resources carefully, then let's get started. It might be tough, sometimes frustrating, but it definitely won't be dull.

Who this book is for

This book is aimed squarely at developers who've been programming professionally for, say, two to three years. You're likely comfortable building applications using higher-level languages and understand basic programming concepts such as variables, functions, loops, and maybe some object-oriented ideas. Crucially, you possess a nagging curiosity about what's really going on under the hood and you're ready (or perhaps just resigned) to leave the warm embrace of automatic memory management to learn how things work at a lower level. No prior systems programming or C/C++ experience is strictly required, but a willingness to grapple with new, sometimes challenging, concepts certainly is.

What this book covers

Chapter 1, Safety First, lays the groundwork for why Zig exists, what problems it solves, and how it promises you performance without panic, control without chaos, and simplicity without sacrificing power.

Chapter 2, Setting Up Your Playground, gets your dev environment sorted with Zig installation, ZLS configuration, and a sobering quiz to separate the future Zig wizards from the cavemen.

Chapter 3, Your First Zig Program, dissects the classic "Hello, World!" to teach you about project setup, variables, basic debugging, and Zig's peculiar relationship with strings—no training wheels allowed.

Chapter 4, Control Flow, Loops, and Other Forms of Digital Domination, hands you the spellbook for directing code via conditionals (`if`/`else`/`switch`), loops (`for`/`while`), and exhaustive switches, as well as handling optional types, because code needs a moral compass, apparently.

Chapter 5, Functions for the Efficient Programmer, shows you how to package repetitive code into reusable units, covering declaration, parameters, return values, and the ever-so-useful `defer`, as well as managing scope with blocks.

Chapter 6, Error Handling, explores Zig's rather opinionated philosophy where errors are first-class citizens, diving into error sets, unions, tagged unions, `try`/`catch`, and error return traces.

Chapter 7, Testing Your Zig Code, confronts the reality that your code probably isn't perfect, introducing `std.testing`, unit testing structure, assertions, and even how to measure test coverage with external tools.

Chapter 8, Organizing Data, delves into Zig's foundational techniques for structuring data, covering fixed-size arrays, flexible slices, and custom data types using structs.

Chapter 9, Memory Management, tackles the sometimes-feared topic of pointers, explaining the stack and heap, allocation strategies, lifetime considerations, zero-sized types, and type conversion (casting).

Chapter 10, The Standard Library, guides you through Zig's lean but powerful std, covering common data structures such as ArrayList and HashMap, file I/O, string formatting (std.fmt), memory utilities (std.mem), random numbers, and timekeeping.

Chapter 11, Packing, drags you through Zig's explicit and powerful build system, covering zig init, the build.zig script, dependencies (build.zig.zon, zig fetch, and hashes), cross-compilation, release modes, caching, and the indispensable zig build --watch, because Makefiles are relics of a darker age.

Chapter 12, Sophisticated Topics, provides an introductory overview of Zig's more advanced features, including the time-bending magic of comptime, raw operating system threads and synchronization, and the fine art of C interoperability.

Chapter 13, Real-World Zig, puts your knowledge into practice by building FileGuard, a command-line file monitoring tool, illustrating how to structure a real application, handle CLI arguments, and interact with the filesystem, while also suggesting other project ideas and pointing toward community resources.

To get the most out of this book

This book assumes you already know the basics of programming – variables, loops, functions, and that sort of thing. We're not teaching you how to code from scratch. You should also be comfortable enough with your computer to install software (such as Zig itself, obviously) and maybe poke around your command line or system's PATH variable without accidentally summoning a digital demon. What you *don't* need is a PhD in C++ or assembly; any prior systems knowledge is a bonus, not a requirement. Mostly, you need patience, a willingness to think differently about memory and control, and the acceptance that we'll tackle complex concepts step by step. You've got to learn how to crawl before you can run (or, in this case, before you write code that merely *looks* like it might segfault).

Software/hardware covered in the book	Operating system requirements
Zig (latest stable version recommended)	Windows, macOS, or Linux
Standard text editor/IDE	Windows, macOS, or Linux
Git (for fetching some dependencies)	Windows, macOS, or Linux

You'll need to install Zig and likely set up the **Zig Language Server** (**ZLS**) for a decent development experience. Instead of sending you off to hunt down instructions yourself, **we've provided a detailed guide named SETUP_YOUR_ENV.md right in this book's GitHub code repository.** Follow those steps carefully to get your environment configured correctly. Consider it your first exercise in following directions precisely – a skill you'll definitely need.

Note on Zig version and code updates

At the time of writing and publishing this book, the latest stable release of Zig was version 0.15. Zig is still evolving, and future releases may introduce changes that affect the code examples in this book.

For the most up-to-date code and any version-specific adjustments, please refer to the official GitHub repository:

```
https://github.com/PacktPublishing/Learning-Zig
```

If you are using the digital version of this book, we advise you to type the code yourself or access the code from the book's GitHub repository (a link is available in the next section). Doing so will help you avoid any potential errors related to the copying and pasting of code.

Keep in mind that Zig is still a relatively young language (pre-1.0 as of this writing). While it's surprisingly stable and usable, things can occasionally change between releases. The core concepts you learn here will remain relevant, but always check the official documentation for the absolute latest details if something seems off.

Download the example code files

You can download the example code files for this book from GitHub at `https://github.com/PacktPublishing/Learning-Zig`. If there's an update to the code, it will be updated in the GitHub repository.

We also have other code bundles from our rich catalog of books and videos available at `https://github.com/PacktPublishing/`. Check them out!

Download the color images

We also provide a PDF file that has color images of the screenshots/diagrams used in this book. You can download it here: `https://packt.link/gbp/9781835085127`.

Conventions used

There are a number of text conventions used throughout this book.

`CodeInText`: Indicates code words in text, database table names, folder names, filenames, file extensions, pathnames, dummy URLs, user input, and Twitter/X handles. For example: "Mount the downloaded `WebStorm-10*.dmg` disk image file as another disk in your system."

A block of code is set as follows:

```
const std = @import("std");

pub fn main() !void {
    var arena = std.heap.ArenaAllocator.init(std.heap.page_allocator);
    defer arena.deinit();
    const allocator = arena.allocator();

    const message = try std.fmt.allocPrint(allocator, "Hello, {s}!",
.{"world"});
    defer allocator.free(message);
    try std.io.getStdOut().writer().print("{s}\n", .{message});
}
```

Any command-line input or output is written as follows:

```
$ zig build run
Hello, world!
```

Bold: Indicates a new term, an important word, or words that you see on the screen. For instance, words in menus or dialog boxes appear in the text like this. For example: "If you feel the need to include a UTF-8 **byte order mark (BOM)**, Zig will quietly ignore it"

> Warnings or important notes appear like this.

> Tips and tricks appear like this.

Get in touch

Feedback from our readers is always welcome.

General feedback: If you have questions about any aspect of this book or have any general feedback, please email us at customercare@packt.com and mention the book's title in the subject of your message.

Errata: Although we have taken every care to ensure the accuracy of our content, mistakes do happen. If you have found a mistake in this book, we would be grateful if you reported this to us. Please visit http://www.packt.com/submit-errata, click **Submit Errata**, and fill in the form.

Piracy: If you come across any illegal copies of our works in any form on the internet, we would be grateful if you would provide us with the location address or website name. Please contact us at copyright@packt.com with a link to the material.

If you are interested in becoming an author: If there is a topic that you have expertise in and you are interested in either writing or contributing to a book, please visit http://authors.packt.com/.

Share your thoughts

Once you've read *Learning Zig*, we'd love to hear your thoughts! Scan the QR code below to go straight to the Amazon review page for this book and share your feedback.

https://packt.link/r/1835085121

Your review is important to us and the tech community and will help us make sure we're delivering excellent quality content.

Part 1

Zig Fundamentals

This first part lays the groundwork, guiding you from setting up your environment and writing your first lines of Zig code to mastering essential programming constructs. We'll cover control flow, functions, error handling, and the crucial practice of testing your code to ensure that it behaves as expected. By the end of this part, you'll have a solid grasp of Zig's core syntax and philosophy.

This part of the book includes the following chapters:

- *Chapter 1, Safety First*
- *Chapter 2, Setting Up Your Playground*
- *Chapter 3, Your First Zig Program*
- *Chapter 4, Control Flow, Loops, and Other Forms of Digital Domination*
- *Chapter 5, Functions for the Efficient Programmer*
- *Chapter 6, Error Handling*
- *Chapter 7, Testing Your Zig Code*

1

Safety First

Hey there! Ready to dive into Zig, a systems programming language that's not only powerful but also surprisingly friendly? This first chapter introduces some of the coolest things Zig has to offer. It's like getting a first taste of what makes Zig the new kid on the block that everyone's talking about.

We'll kick things off by exploring the current landscape of systems programming and why a fresh language such as Zig is exactly what developers need. Common headaches faced with mainstream languages will be uncovered, followed by a look at how Zig tackles these issues head-on. The basics of learning Zig will be covered, including its approach to syntax, memory management, and standout features such as compile-time metaprogramming. Additionally, Zig's philosophy of avoiding unnecessary complexity will be highlighted, ensuring that what's seen in the code is exactly what's happening.

Understanding these choices is super important because they'll help you write code that's efficient, reliable, and easy to maintain—whether you're building for embedded systems, operating systems, or cross-platform apps. By the end of this chapter, you'll not only see why Zig is a strong alternative to other languages, but you'll also have your starter kit for thinking in the Zig way. You'll walk away with a solid understanding of how Zig's design makes it perfect for modern systems programming.

In this chapter, we're going to cover the following main topics:

- Training your brain to think in Zig
- Systems programming reimagined
- Maintain with Zig
- A new era begins

Getting the most out of this book — get to know your free benefits

Unlock exclusive **free** benefits that come with your purchase, thoughtfully crafted to supercharge your learning journey and help you learn without limits.

Here's a quick overview of what you get with this book:

Next-gen reader

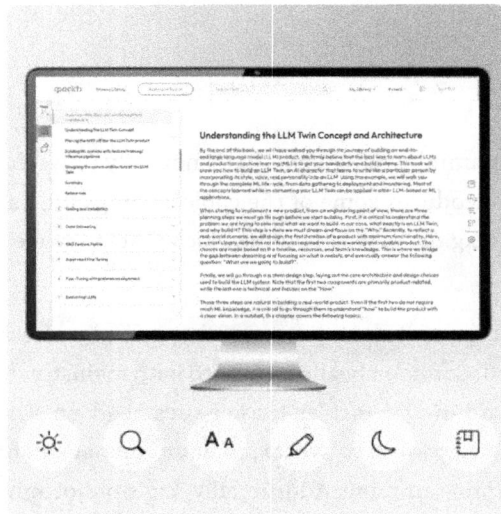

Figure 1.1 – Illustration of the next-gen Packt Reader's features

Our web-based reader, designed to help you learn effectively, comes with the following features:

- **Multi-device progress sync:** Learn from any device with seamless progress sync.
- **Highlighting and notetaking:** Turn your reading into lasting knowledge.
- **Bookmarking:** Revisit your most important learnings anytime.
- **Dark mode:** Focus with minimal eye strain by switching to dark or sepia mode.

Interactive AI assistant (beta)

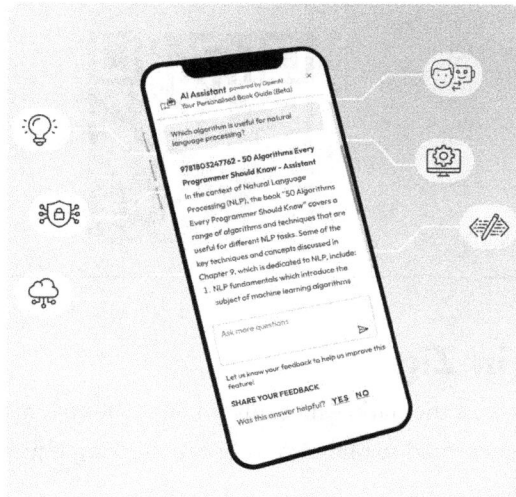

Our interactive AI assistant has been trained on the content of this book, to maximize your learning experience. It comes with the following features:

❖ **Summarize it:** Summarize key sections or an entire chapter.

❖ **AI code explainers:** In the next-gen Packt Reader, click the Explain button above each code block for AI-powered code explanations.

Note: The AI assistant is part of next-gen Packt Reader and is still in beta.

Figure 1.2 – Illustration of Packt's AI assistant

DRM-free PDF or ePub version

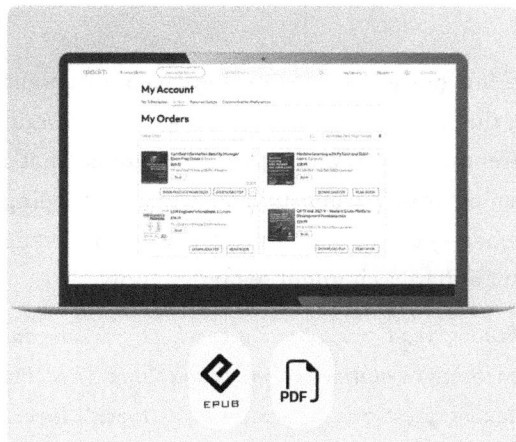

Learn without limits with the following perks included with your purchase:

📖 Learn from anywhere with a DRM-free PDF copy of this book.

📱 Use your favorite e-reader to learn using a DRM-free ePub version of this book.

Figure 1.3 – Free PDF and ePub

Training your brain to think in Zig

Learning a new programming language is no walk in the park, especially when it's a systems programming language such as Zig. You might be tempted to blame your brain, thinking it just isn't wired to absorb all this low-level, technical stuff.

But the truth is, your brain isn't the problem—it's how you're feeding it. Your brain thrives on novelty. It's always on the lookout for something new, something interesting. That's how it's designed, to keep you alert and, quite literally, alive. When faced with the routine, the ordinary, or the dull, your brain tunes it out, pushing it to the background so that it can focus on what really matters.

But how does your brain decide what's important? Imagine you're coding away, deep in thought, and suddenly your computer starts overheating, the fans roaring like a jet engine. Your brain immediately kicks into high gear: neurons fire, emotions spike, and adrenaline pumps. That's how your brain knows something crucial is happening. It's all about survival, and yes, in coding, survival means keeping your machine—and your code—running smoothly. And trust me, by the end of this journey, you'll see that learning Zig isn't as hard as it might seem right now.

Alright, let's get something straight. This isn't one of those "read and repeat" gigs where you zone out after the second paragraph. No, we're going to do something revolutionary: make you think. Shocking, I know. We'll poke at that brain of yours with reflexive questions—because who doesn't love a little self-doubt in the middle of their learning process?—and throw in quizzes that, if nothing else, will keep you awake. And then, just when you think you've got it, we'll slap you with some hands-on exercises to make sure you're not just nodding along like a bobblehead.

Each chapter is a cleverly disguised trap—I mean, step—that builds on the last one. The complexity ramps up, but don't worry; it's all part of the master plan. You'll revisit those "core concepts" in new and exciting ways because, apparently, repetition is how the brain learns. Who knew?

We'll kick things off with the basics. Yes, basics—because you've got to learn to crawl before you can faceplant trying to run. You'll get a taste of Zig's syntax and features, which will undoubtedly leave you wondering why you didn't pick up a more "mainstream" language. But stick with it. You'll be solving problems, answering questions, and doing exercises that—believe it or not—are designed to be relevant to the real world.

By the time we're done with you, Zig won't just be another language in your toolbelt—it'll be the chainsaw you reach for when you need to get serious work done. So, buckle up, buttercup. We're about to take you on a wild, sarcastic, and surprisingly effective journey through Zig programming!

Systems programming reimagined

When you venture into the tangled mess of systems programming, it doesn't take long before you stumble upon the usual suspects. You've got the classics—C and C++—those old rock bands that refuse to retire. Then, there are the hipsters, D and Odin, who are so niche that just knowing they exist feels like an insider secret. And, of course, the cool kids swell in with Rust and Go, showing off their shiny features and acting like they've reinvented the wheel.

But here's the kicker—despite all this variety, none of these heavyweights entirely manage to strike that elusive balance between simplicity, transparency, and portability. That is, until Zig crashes the party, making it clear that it's here to show everyone how it's really done. Zig doesn't just aim for the sweet spot; it plants its flag there and dares anyone to do better.

Language X versus language Y

Throughout this chapter, you'll notice some comparisons to other programming languages such as C, Go, and Rust. Don't worry if you're not familiar with these languages—these comparisons are simply meant to resonate with those who are. They help highlight where Zig stands out or takes a different approach. If any of these references don't ring a bell, that's perfectly fine. The goal is to give you a broader perspective, but you'll still get all the insights you need to understand Zig on its own terms.

The genesis of Zig — fixing what's broken

Figure 1.4 – The frustrated systems programmer's dilemma

Fed up with the endless landmines that C and C++ scatter across your path, Andrew Kelley decided enough was enough. So, he set out on a mission to create Zig—a language that doesn't force you to choose between modern safety features and the low-level control that systems programmers live for. Zig wasn't born out of some academic exercise or a desire to reinvent the wheel; it was forged out of sheer necessity, designed to fix the gaping holes left by its predecessors. In other words, it was born from his deep frustration with the shortcomings of C and C++, especially their undefined behavior, lack of safety guarantees, and the headaches of maintaining large code bases. As Kelley himself put it, *"I have faith that we can do better."*

But with so many languages already vying for attention, why should Zig be the one to steal the spotlight? The answer lies in Zig's design philosophy: it's all about simplicity, transparency, and portability.

So, before you dismiss it as just another contender, take a closer look. Zig isn't just another language to add to the pile; it's a complete toolchain for modern development, crafted to do what others only pretend to.

Kelley was also inspired by his experiences with other languages and tools, which led him to incorporate the features that we're exploring in this book.

But before diving deeper into Zig's virtues, let's take a step back and examine the competition. To truly appreciate what Zig brings to the table, it's worth understanding the flaws and limitations of the mainstream languages that have dominated the scene for so long. **Zig is more than just a programming language,** but to see why, let's first explore Zig purely as a programming language.

The flaws of mainstream languages

Mainstream systems programming languages, despite their widespread use, are riddled with flaws that have frustrated developers for decades. Let's break down a few of these pain points and see how Zig addresses them head-on:

- **Garbage collection: a necessary evil?**

  Garbage collection—on paper, it sounds like a developer's dream. Automatic memory management that spares you the grunt work? Sign me up! But in reality, garbage collection is like that friend who shows up uninvited, makes a mess, and leaves you to clean up the chaos. The dreaded stop-the-world latency glitches are the price you pay for this convenience, and they can turn a smooth user experience into a stuttering nightmare. Sure, it's well intentioned, but when your app grinds to a halt because of an untimely garbage collection pause, "well intentioned" doesn't cut it.

- **Automatic heap allocation: a ticking time bomb**

  Then, there's automatic heap allocation. It's all fun and games until your system runs out of memory. At that point, your program isn't just inefficient—it's unusable. Crashes hang, and the dreaded out-of-memory errors are all too common when you let the system decide how and when to allocate heap memory. It's like handing the keys to your car to someone who doesn't know how to drive—things might go well for a while, but sooner or later, you're headed for a crash.

- **Complex build processes: the ultimate headache**

  Let's talk build processes. If your language makes building from source a complicated mess of scripts, dependencies, and obscure tools, it's already lost the plot. A complex build process is an instant disqualification for most developers who just want to compile their code without needing a PhD in build systems. Yet, many mainstream languages seem to think convoluted build processes are a rite of passage.

The solution? Obviously, Zig

Given these problems, it's clear that something new was needed. Enter Zig—the language that steps up where others fall short. Zig takes the flaws of languages and turns them into its strengths:

- **No garbage collector, more control**

    Zig skips the garbage collector entirely, sparing you from those unpredictable stop-the-world latency glitches. This design choice gives you full control over memory management, a critical feature for systems programming and performance-critical applications. With Zig, you decide when and how memory is allocated and deallocated, allowing for fine-tuned performance optimizations that are essential in environments where every byte and cycle counts.

- **No hidden allocations**

    In Zig, manual memory management isn't just an option—it's the norm. It takes a hands-off approach to memory allocation, giving you full control over when and how heap memory is used. There's no new keyword and no language features that automatically allocate heap memory at runtime. Let me say it one more time: *If you don't explicitly request a heap allocation, it won't happen.*

This is in stark contrast to languages such as Go, where hidden allocations are common due to the automatic management of goroutines and garbage collection, which can lead to unpredictable performance in memory-constrained environments.

Rust, while offering more control over memory allocation than Go, still includes a standard library that often assumes the presence of a heap. Zig, on the other hand, allows you to operate entirely without a heap, making it ideal for embedded systems or real-time applications where deterministic memory management is critical.

Every standard library feature that requires heap memory is explicit, using an `Allocator` parameter. This ensures that memory management decisions are always in the hands of the developer, not hidden (or implicit) within the language.

We'll explore this topic in *Chapter 9, Memory Management.*

So, we've seen how Zig expertly sidesteps the pitfalls that have plagued mainstream languages for years. But what really sets Zig apart is how it takes the best elements of C—its power, its low-level control—and refines them for the modern developer. Let's dive into why Zig isn't just another option but the modern alternative to C that developers have been waiting for.

A modern alternative to C

Zig is a strongly typed, compiled language that positions itself as a modern alternative to C, offering the power and control of low-level programming with a clean, straightforward syntax. At its core, Zig maintains the familiar structure of C-like languages—statements are terminated with semicolons, and code blocks are defined by curly braces. This makes Zig instantly recognizable while introducing features that make it more versatile and safer for modern software development.

Don't worry!

If the code looks a bit unfamiliar or if some parts don't quite click right away, don't worry. This is just a sneak peek. Every piece of this code will be broken down and explained in detail as we move forward in the book. By the time we're done, you'll not only understand every line but also be able to write your own Zig programs with confidence. For now, just sit back and enjoy—everything will make sense soon enough!

Let's look at our first Zig snippet to see how this language blends the familiarity of C-like syntax with modern, developer-friendly enhancements:

```
const std = @import("std");

pub fn main() void {
    std.debug.print("Hello, World!\n", .{});
}
```

This code imports the standard library, defines a main function, and prints "Hello, World!" to the console. It's a straightforward way to see how Zig manages basic tasks such as importing packages, defining functions, and outputting text, all while sticking to a clear and concise syntax.

You might already be wondering: Is Zig just a better version of C? Well, it's a fair question, and the quick answer is a resounding no; we'll see that Zig is much more than just an upgrade.

Simplicity — focus on what matters

Languages such as C++ and Rust are packed with features, but sometimes those features can become distractions. In Zig, simplicity is a core principle. There are no macros, no hidden language features—just straightforward, readable code.

Zig is powerful enough to handle complex programs without the need for special cases or exceptions built into the compiler. This simplicity allows you to focus on what really matters: developing your application.

Languages with powerful macro systems and compile-time code generation can introduce complexity and subtle bugs if not used carefully. **Go's simplicity is one of its strengths, but it comes at the cost of flexibility, particularly in areas such as error handling and memory management.** Speaking of which, we'll explore this topic with care in *Chapter 8, Error Handling*.

No hidden control flow

In Zig, what you see is what you get. If your code looks like it's executing a straightforward sequence of operations, then that's exactly what's happening. There are no surprises lurking in the shadows—no hidden function calls, no implicit control flow changes.

As a brain teaser, take a look at the following code snippet and see if you can spot what might go wrong or which part of the behavior isn't immediately clear. But here's a warning: resist the urge to flip the page for the answer right away. Ready? Got your thinking cap on?

```
var r = x + y.z;
funcA();
funcB();
```

Okay, here's the twist—there's actually nothing to discover! That's the beauty of Zig. In Zig, the code does exactly what it says. When you see funcA() followed by funcB(), that's precisely what happens—no sneaky hidden function calls, no unexpected surprises from operator overloading (unlike C++'s), or property accessors. This predictability isn't just refreshing; it makes your code more readable and easier to reason about. Zig's got nothing to hide!

Languages such as Rust and Go introduce their own set of mechanisms—Rust with its macros and Go with goroutines, panics, and other forms of indirection. While powerful, these abstractions can sometimes obscure the underlying flow, making it harder to predict how code will execute, especially in complex systems.

We'll dive deeper into this subject in *Chapter 4, Control Flow and Loops*.

Compile-time execution

One of the standout features of Zig is its powerful comptime feature, short for **compile-time execution**. This feature allows you to run code during the compilation process, enabling you to generate and manipulate code dynamically, enforce constraints, and optimize performance before your program even runs. It's like giving your compiler a crystal ball to predict and prepare for what's ahead.

Thanks to comptime, Zig supports generics, enabling you to write flexible, reusable code while still maintaining strict type safety. But Zig doesn't stop there. It also boasts powerful compile-time metaprogramming capabilities, which let you perform complex computations, enforce constraints, and generate code during compilation. This not only enhances the language's expressiveness but also ensures that your programs are as efficient and optimized as possible without the need for runtime overhead.

If you're intrigued by this and want to dive deeper into the magic of comptime, don't worry— *Chapter 12, Sophisticated Topics*, will cover it in detail, along with other advanced features that make Zig truly unique.

Tooling — ready to go, right out of the box

Zig's tooling is designed to be as hassle-free as possible. With Zig, you get a single, statically compiled binary that includes everything you need—just download and start building.

Whether you're targeting Linux, Windows, or macOS, Zig's tooling is ready to go right out of the box. With features such as GCC/Clang command-line compatibility, Zig integrates smoothly into existing workflows, making it an excellent choice for both new projects and existing code bases. This kind of out-of-the-box readiness might remind you of another language with famously simple tooling—Go.

Go's tooling is often praised for its simplicity and speed, and rightfully so. But while Go shines in its straightforward approach, Zig takes it a step further, especially when it comes to more complex build scenarios. Zig's integration of cross-compilation and direct C/C++ interoperability gives it a distinct edge, particularly when you're dealing with more intricate environments.

Zig doesn't stop there. Its approach to testing is just as straightforward. You can write test cases directly within your code to ensure everything behaves as expected. And running these tests? It's as easy as typing zig test—a command that builds and executes your test cases using Zig's default test runner. Simple, powerful, and right in line with Zig's philosophy of no-nonsense development.

For a comprehensive overview, see *Chapter 6, Testing Your Zig Code.*

More than just a language

While we have taken our first steps with Zig, it's easy to mistake it for just another programming language. But that's only scratching the surface. Zig is more than that—much more. It's not just a language; it's also a robust building system designed to streamline the entire process of building software. Whether you're compiling a simple project or managing a complex code base, Zig's build system gives you powerful tools right out of the box.

Why does Zig have its own build system?

Traditional build systems often come with a steep learning curve, requiring you to cobble together various tools and scripts to get your project up and running. With Zig, the build system is built into the language itself, offering a seamless experience that reduces friction and increases productivity. Zig's build system is designed to be cross-platform, easy to use, and tightly integrated with the language's features.

A unified approach

Let's get one thing straight: Zig's build system isn't some half-baked afterthought or a bolt-on gimmick. No, it's woven right into the fabric of the language itself. This isn't about juggling multiple tools or switching gears mid-project. Everything you do, from writing your first line of code to hitting **Deploy**, happens in Zig. And yes, that means the build system is written in Zig code too. So, no more mental gymnastics trying to remember which toolchain you're supposed to be using today.

Now, you might be thinking: Sure, but what can it actually do? Well, let's highlight the big hitters:

- **Cross-compile**: Ever wanted to target multiple platforms from a single code base? Zig's built-in cross-compilation has your back. Whether it's Linux, Windows, macOS, or some obscure platform only you and three other developers care about—Zig handles it.

- **Configure projects**: Forget about wrestling with bloated build scripts. In Zig, configuring your project is as simple as writing Zig code. Whether you're in debug mode, release mode, or the "please just work" mode, it's all done with straightforward, no-nonsense syntax.

- **Automate tasks**: Need to generate some code, run tests, or package your app? Zig lets you script it all directly within the build system. That means no more hopping between tools or piecing together duct-taped workflows. Everything is streamlined; everything is Zig.

Cross-compilation made easy

One of the great promises of programming is code reuse, but all too often, we end up reinventing the wheel due to compatibility issues or differing performance requirements. Zig addresses this by making it easy to write portable, reusable libraries. It's fully compatible with the C ABI, meaning you can seamlessly integrate Zig with existing C code bases or use Zig to build libraries that can be consumed by other languages.

Zig's build system also shines when it comes to cross-compilation. With the same `build.zig` file, you can target different platforms without changing your code. Zig handles the details, making cross-compilation as straightforward as native compilation.

Imagine a world where you're (practically) free of `cmake`, `make`, `powershell`, and other build tools. Sounds good, right? With Zig, this world is a reality. In just a few lines of code, you can configure Zig to compile your project across all platforms.

I don't mean to sound like a broken record, but it's worth repeating: there's no need to wrestle with a separate build language or decipher cryptic syntax.

In a world where build systems usually feel like an afterthought—or worse, a necessary evil—Zig's approach is refreshingly different. It's not just about getting your code to compile; it's about giving you complete control, all within a language that actually respects your time and sanity. It's not just about hitting multiple platforms with a single code base—it's about **maintaining that code base with the same ease**. And that brings us to Zig's motto: *Maintain with Zig*.

Maintain with Zig

One of the core principles of the Zig project is *Maintain with Zig*. But what does that really mean? To put it into perspective, let's draw a parallel with two other languages that embrace a progressive approach rather than pushing for massive, disruptive rewrites: Kotlin and Carbon.

Kotlin and Carbon

Developed by JetBrains, Kotlin is a statically typed programming language that runs on the **Java Virtual Machine (JVM)** and can also be compiled into JavaScript or native code. Kotlin is designed to be fully interoperable with Java, which makes it a popular choice for Android development and enterprise applications.

Carbon is a language being developed by Google as a potential successor to C++. It aims to address the limitations of C++ while maintaining performance and control over low-level system resources. Carbon is designed with modern language features to improve developer productivity and code safety.

Kotlin, for example, is a masterclass in interoperability. It seamlessly integrates with existing Java code, allowing developers to introduce it into established projects without turning everything upside down. Kotlin's design is all about making life easier—offering features such as null safety, concise syntax, and **coroutines** for asynchronous programming—while staying fully compatible with the sprawling Java ecosystem. What makes Kotlin so appealing is its gradual adoption path: developers can start small, converting one file at a time, and immediately reap the benefits without a steep learning curve.

Similarly, Carbon is Google's ambitious answer to the aging C++. Designed as a potential successor, Carbon doesn't demand that you throw out your entire C++ code base. Instead, it's built to work hand in hand with C++, allowing developers to adopt Carbon incrementally, leveraging existing C++ code and tools they've already invested in. Carbon respects the past while looking toward the future, offering a smooth transition for developers who are deeply entrenched in the C++ world.

Zig takes a similar path of progressive interoperability. It's not about rewriting everything from scratch—it's about evolving your projects with minimal disruption. Zig integrates seamlessly with C and C++ code, allowing you to maintain and enhance your existing systems while gradually introducing Zig's modern features. This strategy ensures that you can improve and maintain your code base without the risks and costs associated with big rewrites. Just as with Kotlin and Carbon, Zig respects the foundation you've already built while offering a better way forward.

With that in mind, let's explore how Zig's simple build system makes it effortless to maintain and enhance C and C++ code bases while seamlessly integrating modern features.

Interoperability

One of the most challenging parts of maintaining C/C++ projects is dealing with the build system—a maze of configuration files and dependencies that pile up over time. Zig provides a solution to this headache with `zig build`, a tool designed to replace traditional build systems and streamline the entire process of building and maintaining your projects.

Although we will explore the build system in *Chapter 11, Packing*, let me give you first glimpses of its characteristics.

One of the standout features of Zig's build system is its simplicity. You define your build process in a build.zig file, using Zig's language features to control every aspect of your build. This approach offers flexibility while keeping things simple and easy to understand.

By creating a build.zig file, you can compile your project across all platforms without relying on external tools such as Xcode, MSVC, or even basic build tools such as cmake, make, powershell, or autocorf. Sounds good, right?

It does not just sound good, but it's already a reality. With a single build.zig file, you can compile your project across all platforms without relying on external tools such as Xcode or even basic build essentials.

Enough talk. The following snippet is a basic example of what a build.zig file looks like. Don't bother to understand every aspect of it at first glance:

```
const std = @import("std");

pub fn build(b: *std.Build) void {
    const exe = b.addExecutable(.{
        .name = "main",
        .root_source_file = b.path("main.zig"),
        .target = b.host,
    });

    b.installArtifact(exe);
}
```

💡 **Quick tip:** Enhance your coding experience with the **AI Code Explainer** and **Quick Copy** features. Open this book in the next-gen Packt Reader. Click the **Copy** button (**1**) to quickly copy code into your coding environment, or click the **Explain** button (**2**) to get the AI assistant to explain a block of code to you.

```
                                                    Copy      Explain
function calculate(a, b) {                           1          2
  return {sum: a + b};
};
```

📖 **The next-gen Packt Reader** is included for free with the purchase of this book. Scan the QR code OR go to `https://packtpub.com/unlock`, then use the search bar to find this book by name. Double-check the edition shown to make sure you get the right one.

In just a few lines of code, you've configured Zig to compile your project, set the build mode, and install the executable. You might notice that there's no need to learn a separate build language or struggle with cryptic syntax. Everything is clear and concise in Zig.

As you've probably noticed, the `std` package keeps popping up in our code snippets. That's no coincidence—Zig's standard library is a pivotal part of the language and plays a central role in development. It provides a rich set of tools and utilities that streamline everything from testing to handling common programming tasks. While we're touching on it briefly now, rest assured that we'll dive deep into the details of the standard library in *Chapter 10, The Standard Library*. There, you'll get a comprehensive understanding of how `std` empowers you to write Zig programs.

Why not "simply" rewrite in Rust?

Figure 1.5 – The boulder of legacy

In the context of critical or legacy software, rewriting it from scratch often leads to strategic pitfalls that can seriously impact a project's success. Imagine a scenario where a development team decides to start over instead of iterating on their existing code base. This decision could lead to significant delays, giving competitors the opportunity to gain an edge while the team is tied up in redevelopment.

Discarding the old code isn't just about losing the code itself; it means potentially losing years of bug fixes, optimizations, and real-world adaptations that have made the software reliable. **The belief that new code is inherently better is flawed**. The existing code has already been tested and proven in various conditions, while starting from scratch risks reintroducing old problems and creating new ones.

A more effective strategy is to make incremental improvements—refactoring, optimizing, and reorganizing the existing code. This approach allows for continuous evolution of the software while preserving its stability and reliability. Instead of taking on the risks and costs associated with a complete rewrite, incremental changes keep the software competitive and effective.

Moreover, the open source community is incredibly diverse, making it unrealistic to expect universal adoption of a single language. To truly advance our critical software infrastructure, we should focus on improving the programming environment in systems development rather than merely trading one set of issues for another.

The idea of a fresh start might be appealing, but it often leads to wasted time, resources, and missed opportunities. The wiser approach is to build on what's already working, making deliberate, incremental changes that ensure the software remains robust and adaptable.

This strategy is more prevalent in the Rust community. Oh! I almost forgot to mention: **Rust doesn't build C**. So, rewriting is not a very progressive approach, right? RIGHT?

Rather than abandoning the C/C++ ecosystem, Zig takes a different approach. It seeks to move forward in harmony with the legacy systems that have served us for decades. **Zig is not just a language; it's a comprehensive toolchain that can compile C/C++ code**, making it easier to maintain and evolve these projects without discarding everything that's been built.

Zig bundles its own set of `libc`s to facilitate cross-compilation and provides commands such as `zig cc` and `zig c++` to serve as in-place replacements for Clang. This integration allows developers to leverage Zig's modern features while still working within the established C/C++ ecosystem. The Zig project is even developing its own linker, `zld`, to eventually replace `lld`, further reducing dependence on external tools such as LLVM.

For a better understanding of how Zig excels at C interoperability, be sure to check out *Chapter 12, Sophisticated Topics*, where we'll explore this powerful feature in detail. There, you'll see how Zig makes working with C code not just possible but downright easy.

Too good to be ignored

The Zig build system unintentionally solves `cgo` issues by streamlining cross-compilation and dependency management. Unlike `cgo`, which demands intricate configurations for each target platform, Zig handles cross-compilation seamlessly, with no need for external dependencies. This consistency eliminates platform-specific headaches, making it easier and more reliable to integrate C/C++ code into Go projects.

CGO

CGO is a feature in Go that allows Go programs to call C code directly. It provides a way to integrate Go with existing C libraries, enabling access to low-level system features or performance-critical code. However, using CGO introduces complexities in cross-compilation and dependency management, often requiring additional setup and configuration to ensure compatibility across different platforms.

Building from source is a breeze in Zig, making it easy to integrate into development workflows. And when you combine this with Zig's various build modes, you have a toolset that's flexible enough to handle anything from quick debugging to production-ready releases.

Zig offers several release modes that optimize your code for different scenarios:

- **Debug:** Perfect for development, this mode includes extensive safety checks and skips optimizations, making it easier to catch bugs and understand your code's behavior

- **ReleaseSafe:** Strikes a balance between performance and reliability by optimizing your code while still retaining essential safety checks

- **ReleaseFast:** For those situations where speed is king, this mode removes most safety checks to squeeze out maximum performance

- **ReleaseSmall:** Ideal for environments where space is at a premium, this mode focuses on producing the smallest possible binary size

Each of these modes gives you the flexibility to adapt to your project's specific needs, ensuring that you're always using the right tool for the job. We'll delve deeper into each of these release modes in *Chapter 11, Packing*, where you'll learn how to make the most out of Zig's build system.

Figure 1.6 – Zig doesn't need caffeine to run anywhere

Zig might not be running on 3 billion devices like some other languages that go well with coffee, but when it comes to truly "build once, run anywhere," Zig delivers on that promise without a caffeine boost.

Language comparisons

As we progress through this book, you'll notice that comparisons to other languages will start to fade into the background. That's intentional. While these early references help set the stage and highlight where Zig differs or excels, the real focus here is on mastering Zig itself. As we dive deeper, the spotlight will be solely on Zig, exploring its features, strengths, and the unique approach it brings to systems programming. This way, you'll fully immerse yourself in what makes Zig special without the distraction of constant comparisons.

A new era begins

Systems programming has been stuck in the mud for too long, weighed down by the complexities of C/C++. But it doesn't have to stay that way. The Zig project brings a fresh perspective, making systems programming **more accessible, practical**, and **efficient**. With its powerful compiler, flexible build system, a package manager on the horizon, and very simple language, Zig is set to spark a revival in the craft of low-level programming.

Luckily, you're getting ready to be part of this change. And just between you and me, now is the perfect time to dive into Zig. Whether you're contributing to open source projects, learning the language, or just exploring what it can do, Zig offers the tools and community support you need to succeed. As we move forward, Zig is not just helping us maintain the past—it's building the future of systems programming.

Safety

Safety is often touted as the ultimate buzzword in the latest wave of programming languages, and it's easy to see why. You've probably come across the phrase *"Rust is a safer language"* countless times online, and while there's truth to that, it's important to unpack what "safety" really means. But here's the thing: safety isn't just about avoiding memory leaks. It's a loaded term that gets thrown around like confetti.

Rust is obsessed with memory safety, but that's only part of the picture. Zig, on the other hand, is more like the straight-talking uncle who doesn't care about being cool; it's fixated on getting the job done right. Zig's all about overall software correctness—making sure your code does what you think it does, no smoke and mirrors. It's almost like Zig was designed to keep you from outsmarting yourself, avoiding those "clever" mistakes that make you want to slam your head into the keyboard.

So yeah, safety is great and all, but Zig is playing a different game. It's not just about keeping you safe from memory bugs; it's about making sure your code is as straightforward and reliable as possible. No tricks, no surprises—just solid, predictable behavior.

In case of doubt, create a sign and keep it near you with the words **Memory safety is just one pillar of software correctness** on it:

Figure 1.7 – Safety: No Marketing Required

Alright, let's talk about Zig and why it's like the safety helmet C wishes it had. You see, in C, you can create a struct and just forget to initialize half the fields. No big deal, right? Just a ticking time bomb waiting to blow up your code. But in Zig? Nah, Zig doesn't play that game. Every field gets initialized, or the compiler smacks you upside the head. No mystery bugs creep in because you forgot something. It's like having your own personal safety inspector—except this one doesn't miss a thing.

Also, Zig doesn't just suggest you handle errors or missing data; it practically forces you to. No more rolling the dice with undefined behavior like you do in C. Zig catches that nonsense early and keeps you out of the ditch.

Oh, and then there's comptime. Think of it as Zig's way of saying, "Hey, how about we catch some bugs before you even hit **Run**?" You get to validate and generate code at compile time, so by the time your program runs, it's already been through the wringer. Meanwhile, C just sits there, letting you trip over runtime errors like it's 1990.

Memory layout? Zig's got you covered there, too. With field reordering and packing, you can make your structs lean and mean without getting smacked by misaligned memory issues. And let's not forget Zig's *pièce de résistance*: **non-null pointers by default**. In C, you get pointers that can be null because, hey, who doesn't love a good segmentation fault? But Zig? Zig doesn't do null unless you specifically ask for it. It's like Zig saying, "You want null? Fine, but it's on you, buddy." The result? Fewer crashes, more stability.

Zig also gives you safe indexing with `array[idx]`. It's a little thing, but in C, it's terrifyingly easy to go out of bounds and start corrupting memory like it's your day job. Zig says, "Not on my watch," and keeps your indexing in check so that your code doesn't go rogue.

The summary is, Zig solves this by simply removing a lot of the footguns from pointers and adding additional guard rails.

At first glance, Zig might come across as an idealistic project—promising simplicity, safety, and a robust build system in a way that almost sounds too good to be true. But here's the thing: Zig is anything but a pipe dream. It's grounded in reality, with every feature and claim not just theoretical, but **operational right now**. This isn't some lofty vision for the future; it's a practical, material solution that's already up and running, ready to be put to work in real-world projects. Zig's strength lies in its ability to deliver on its promises today, making it a language that's as reliable as it is innovative.

If you're eager to explore how these tools are applied in real-world scenarios, head over to *Chapter 13, Real-World Projects Built with Zig*. There, you'll find examples that demonstrate how Zig can be used to tackle real development challenges, helping you connect the dots between theory and practice.

Where to use Zig

Zig is a versatile language designed for systems programming, with several common use cases and domains where it excels:

- **Embedded systems**: Zig's low-level control and ability to manage memory directly make it ideal for embedded systems development. It allows developers to write highly efficient code for resource-constrained environments.

- **Operating systems**: Zig's deterministic behavior and precise control over hardware make it suitable for writing operating systems, drivers, and other critical system-level software.

- **Cross-platform development**: Zig's powerful cross-compilation capabilities simplify building software that runs on multiple platforms, making it a strong choice for cross-platform applications and tools.

- **Game development**: With its focus on performance and efficiency, Zig is well suited for game development, particularly in areas requiring fine-tuned control over memory and CPU usage.

- **Networking and systems tools**: Zig's safety features, combined with its performance optimizations, make it a good fit for building networking tools, servers, and other high-performance system utilities.
- **Interfacing with C/C++**: Zig can seamlessly interact with C and C++ code bases, making it useful for extending or optimizing existing projects in these languages.

Hold your horses! If you're as excited about Zig's features as I am, I get it. The hype is real, but it's not quite ready for prime time in production just yet. So, you can expect regular refactors and breaking changes.

These changes are a natural part of its development process as the language matures and improves. Until Zig reaches its 1.0 release, adaptability and flexibility will be essential as we navigate these updates together. In *Chapter 14, Zig's Future and Community*, we'll explore how to keep up with the changes and engage with the Zig community.

You're about to complete the first step toward learning Zig. Don't stress over the initial bumps in the road—every journey has its own twists and turns, and each skill level comes with its own unique challenges. Embrace the process and remember that success looks different for everyone. The important thing is that you're making progress, and that's what really counts! So, strap in and embrace the thrill of the unknown—because with Zig, you're not just learning a language; you're part of a pioneering community, pushing the boundaries of what's possible in software development.

Summary

As we wrap up this chapter, you've now had a glimpse of what Zig brings to the table. You got the lowdown on why Zig is the go-to choice for anyone tired of the quirks and headaches of C and C++. We talked about how Zig keeps things simple and safe, without making you pull your hair out over memory bugs. You'll find that what you learned here is the foundation for beginning to master Zig, and trust me—it's going to make your life a lot easier.

Next up, we're going to roll up our sleeves and get your Zig development environment up and running, ensuring you're fully equipped to write, test, and build with Zig. This is where things get real, as we take all the theory we covered today and take the first step to produce actual code. Ready to keep the momentum going? Let's do this!

Unlock this book's exclusive benefits now

UNLOCK NOW

Scan this QR code or go to `https://packtpub.com/unlock`, then search this book by name.

Note: Keep your purchase invoice ready before you start.

2

Setting Up Your Playground

Ah, so you've decided to keep going with Zig. Brave of you. I'm genuinely impressed—most people would've bailed by now, but not you. Good choice—assuming you enjoy having control over every little detail without the usual headache that comes with most system programming languages. However, before we dive into the code and start flexing those low-level muscles, we need to address something crucial. If you think you can embark on this journey without setting up a **Language Server Protocol (LSP)**, you might as well grab a club and start drawing on cave walls. Seriously, in the world of modern programming, not having an LSP running is practically prehistoric. But don't worry, we'll get you sorted. This chapter is all about getting Zig installed and ensuring your setup isn't stuck in the Stone Age.

Figure 2.1 – The modern caveman

By the end of this chapter, you won't just have Zig installed; you'll be ready to dive headfirst into Zig with all the confidence of someone who knows exactly what they're doing—or at least someone who's really good at pretending they do. So, let's leave the caveman days behind and step into the future of systems programming, shall we?

In this chapter, we're going to cover the following topics:

- Installing Zig
- Configuring ZLS

Installing Zig

So, you've decided to give Zig a whirl. Smart move. Now, if you're anything like me, you've probably spent more time than you'd like wrestling with installers who act more like gatekeepers than helpers. But fear not—Zig isn't here to make you question your life choices.

In fact, installing Zig is so refreshingly straightforward that you might wonder whether there's a catch. Spoiler: there isn't. No bloated installers, no mysterious errors, and no convoluted dependency chains. Just you, a few commands, and the promise of a programming language that's as sharp as a tack. Why sharp? Because Zig gives you the kind of low-level control that makes other languages look like they're wrapped in bubble wrap.

Whether you're on Linux, Windows, or macOS, the process is quick, painless, and—dare I say it—pleasant. So, let's cut through the nonsense and get Zig up and running. After all, you've got better things to do, such as programming with the kind of confidence that only comes from true control.

Note on Zig Version and Code Updates

At the time of writing and publishing this book, the latest stable release of Zig was version 0.15.2. Zig is still evolving, and future releases may introduce changes that affect the code examples in this book.

For the most up-to-date code and any version-specific adjustments, please refer to the official GitHub repository: https://github.com/PacktPublishing/Learning-Zig

Playing it safe or living on the edge: your first Zig dilemma

I have a question for you: do you go with the stable, tagged release or take a walk on the wild side with the nightly build? Let's be real—Zig hasn't hit v1.0 yet, and its release cycle is tied to LLVM's rather leisurely six-month pace. That means official Zig releases can feel like they're arriving by snail mail, and by the time they do, they might be a bit stale compared to the cutting-edge changes happening daily.

Sure, you can dip your toes in the Zig pool with a tagged release, and that's fine if you're just testing the waters. However, if you decide that Zig is your new best friend and want to really dig in, do yourself a favor and switch to a nightly build. Why? Because that's where the real action is, and it'll save you a lot of head-scratching when you try to follow tutorials or ask for help. The Zig community and resources such as zig.guide are all keeping up with the master branch, not the fossilized versions.

Confused? Let's play a quick game called *Stable or Bold*.

Stable or Bold

1. **Question**: Is your project already in production or soon to be?

   Yes → Stable release is recommended. You want the reliability and support of a thoroughly tested version.

   No → Move to the next question.

2. **Question**: Are you comfortable with potential bugs or breaking changes?

   Yes → Nightly build is recommended. You'll get access to the latest features and updates.

   No → Move to the next question.

3. **Question**: Do you rely on tutorials, community resources, or third-party libraries?

   Yes → Nightly build is recommended. Most resources and active community discussions are aligned with the latest master branch.

   No → Move to the next question.

4. **Question**: Is compatibility with external tools or systems critical for your work?

   Yes → Stable release is recommended. This version ensures better compatibility and integration with other tools.

   No → Move to the next question.

5. **Question**: Are you okay with frequently updating your environment?

    Yes → Nightly build is recommended. It keeps you up to date with the latest changes, though it may require more frequent updates.

    No → Move to the next question.

6. **Question**: Do you prefer a "set it and forget it" approach to your development environment?

    Yes → Stable release is recommended. This version offers a more hands-off experience, with less frequent updates.

    No → Consider your other priorities.

7. **Question**: Are you experimenting with new features or testing edge cases?

    Yes → Nightly build is recommended. It's ideal for experimentation with the latest enhancements and fixes.

    No → Move to the next question.

8. **Question**: Are you looking to contribute to Zig or stay closely aligned with the language's development?

    Yes → Nightly build is recommended. Contributing to Zig is best done on the cutting edge.

    No → Stable release is recommended. It's more suitable for non-experimental, stable use.

Here is the final decision:

- If you've mostly answered "Yes" to stability, compatibility, and less frequent updates, choose the stable release
- If you've mostly answered "Yes" to wanting the latest features, being comfortable with frequent updates, and staying aligned with the master branch, choose the nightly build

The silver lining? Zig makes it ridiculously easy to switch between versions—or even run multiple versions side by side. Each release is a self-contained bundle that you can plop anywhere on your system. No mess, no fuss, just pure flexibility. Let's explore how to make it happen with the three main OSs: Linux, Windows, and macOS.

Linux: the land of choices

If you're running Linux, you're probably no stranger to making choices—and sometimes, too many. For the sake of convenience, let's start with the easy option: your distribution's package manager. Most major Linux distros package the latest release of Zig, so why not give your fingertips a rest and install it the easy way?

And if you're curious about all the package managers that have Zig available, you can find the complete list at this link: `https://github.com/ziglang/zig/wiki/Install-Zig-from-a-Package-Manager`.

But let's say you're the type who enjoys a bit more control, perhaps even a tinge of masochism. In that case, you can install Zig manually.

First, you'll need to download a prebuilt version of Zig. The binaries are conveniently located on the Zig download page (`https://ziglang.org/download/#release-master`). The *master* in the URL refers to the master branch, which contains the latest nightly builds.

However, if you're looking for a specific version of Zig, such as 0.13.0, you can easily switch to that by using a URL such as this one: `https://ziglang.org/download/#release-0.13.0`.

Before you download, make sure you grab the right build for your CPU architecture. If you're not sure whether your machine is x86_64, arm64, or something else equally mysterious, you can find out by running the following:

```
uname -m
```

Once you know your architecture, you can use wget to download the Zig binary directly to your machine. For example, if you're grabbing the master branch build for x86_64, you would run the following:

```
wget https://ziglang.org/download/0.13.0/zig-linux-x86_64-0.13.0.tar.xz
```

After the download completes, extract the archive with the following:

```
tar xf zig-linux-x86_64-0.13.0.tar.xz
```

Now, unless you want to be typing out the full path to your Zig binary every time (and trust me, you don't), you'll need to add Zig to your PATH:

```
echo 'export PATH="$HOME/zig-linux-x86_64-0.12.0:$PATH"' >> ~/.bashrc
```

And there you have it—Zig on Linux, served just the way you like it.

> **Other shells**
>
> This command works perfectly if you're using Bash, which is the default shell for many Linux distributions. However, if you're using a different shell, such as Zsh, Fish, or something more exotic, you'll need to tweak that command slightly.

Windows: the land of path variables and PowerShell

Windows users, rejoice! You have options, too. Zig can be installed via one of the many package managers available for Windows: Chocolatey, Scoop, and WinGet. Each of these comes with its own quirks, but any will get the job done. Use this for Chocolatey:

```
choco install zig
```

Use this for WinGet:

```
winget install zig.zig
```

Use this for Scoop:

```
scoop install zig
```

However, if you're the type who likes to take the road less traveled (or just enjoys unnecessary complexity), you can manually download Zig. Once again, be sure to choose the right build for your CPU architecture. Most Windows systems will be x86_64, which Microsoft, in its infinite wisdom, also calls AMD64. To check, just run the following:

```
$Env:PROCESSOR_ARCHITECTURE
```

After downloading, extract the files to a directory of your choice. Now comes the fun part: adding Zig to your PATH. For a system-wide installation, use the following:

```
[Environment]::SetEnvironmentVariable(
    "Path",
    [Environment]::GetEnvironmentVariable("Path", "Machine") + ";C:\_\zig-
windows-_",
    "Machine"
)
```

If you'd rather keep things local to your user, use the following:

```
[Environment]::SetEnvironmentVariable(
    "Path",
    [Environment]::GetEnvironmentVariable("Path", "User") + ";C:\_\zig-
windows-_",
    "User"
)
```

Remember to replace `C:\_\zig-windows-_` with the actual path where you extracted Zig. And yes, you need to do this step; otherwise, you'll be cursing your machine (with the full path to the Zig binary) every time you try to compile something.

Mac: the cult of brew

Ah, macOS—where everything just works… until it doesn't. Luckily, getting Zig here is straightforward if you're part of the Homebrew cult. Just run the following:

```
brew install zig
```

Just like that, Zig is installed. Easy, right?

Verifying your installation

Now that you've gone through the motions, it's time to verify that Zig is ready to serve. Run the following:

```
zig version
```

If everything goes well, you should see something like the following:

```
0.12.0
```

BTW, I use ~~Arch~~ Nix

If you're already rocking Nix, you're probably no stranger to doing things in style. Nix has been gaining more and more adopters over the years, turning what was once a niche, hipster approach into something a bit more mainstream—though it still carries that cool "I was into this before it was popular" vibe.

With Nix already installed on your system, installing Zig is as simple as the following:

```
nix-env -iA nixpkgs.zig
```

This will pull the latest stable version of Zig directly from the Nix package repository. No fuss, no muss—just pure, unadulterated convenience. If you're in the mood for something a little more cutting-edge, you can easily customize your setup to grab a specific version or even a nightly build by tweaking your Nix expressions.

The beauty of using Nix lies in its ability to manage multiple versions of Zig (or any software) without cluttering up your system. Each version is neatly contained, ensuring that your environment stays clean and your workflow remains smooth.

Nix might have started as the package manager of choice for the hipster crowd, but with its growing adoption, it's becoming the go-to tool for developers who value reproducibility and isolation in their software environments. So, while it may not be as underground as it once was, using Nix still shows you're ahead of the curve—and who doesn't want that?

But why stop there? If you're the kind of developer who likes to squeeze every drop of efficiency out of your tools, there's one more step to take: setting up the **Zig Language Server** (**ZLS**) for your favorite text editor.

The ZLS for smarter Zig coding

One of the best things about Zig is how easy it makes building things from scratch. This isn't just a perk for your own projects—it's baked right into the tools that make up the Zig ecosystem. In this section, we're going to show you just how painless it is to build and set up your development environment, using the ZLS as our prime example.

Whether you're a Zig newbie or a seasoned pro, you'll quickly see how Zig's "keep it simple" philosophy applies across the board. By the end of this little adventure, you'll have the ZLS up and running in your editor of choice, and you might just find yourself admiring the elegance of Zig's build system.

Building the ZLS from source

Ready to roll up your sleeves? Let's dive into building the ZLS from the source. It's a great way to see just how smooth and satisfying working with Zig can be.

First things first, you need to get your hands on the ZLS source code. Fire up your terminal and clone the ZLS repository to your local machine. This will give you access to the freshest, most cutting-edge code:

```
git clone https://github.com/zigtools/zls.git
cd zls
```

Now that you've got the source code, it's time to build the ZLS. And guess what? Zig makes this part ridiculously easy. Just run the following command, and let Zig's build system do its magic:

```
zig build -Doptimize=ReleaseSafe
```

This command compiles the ZLS in release mode, optimized for safety and efficiency. Before you know it, you'll have a shiny new ZLS binary ready to go. With the ZLS built and ready, it's time to integrate it into your coding workflow.

Integrating the ZLS

Good news! No matter what code editor you prefer, chances are it's fully equipped to handle Zig syntax highlighting and has solid support for integrating with the ZLS. From the sleek interfaces of modern IDEs to the minimalist charm of terminal-based editors, you've got plenty of options. While there are tons of editors ready to make your Zig coding experience smooth and efficient, we're going to focus on two popular choices that cater to distinctly different types of developers: **VS Code** and **Neovim**. VS Code is a go-to for those who prefer a somewhat polished, feature-rich environment that is packed with extensions and has an arguably intuitive GUI. On the other hand, Neovim is favored by developers who appreciate a lean, highly customizable, and keyboard-centric workflow.

If you're using a different editor, don't worry! Many other editors also support Zig and the ZLS, and you can find detailed instructions in the official Zig documentation. So, no matter what your preference, you're covered.

Let's dive into how you can set up VS Code and Neovim for the ultimate Zig development experience.

Using the ZLS in VS Code

Getting the ZLS up and running in VS Code is about as straightforward as it gets. All you need to do is install the official Zig language extension (https://marketplace.visualstudio.com/items?itemName=ziglang.vscode-zig) and you're good to go.

This extension provides full support for the ZLS, giving you all the benefits of intelligent code completions, go-to definition, and more.

Figure 2.2 – VS Code with the LSP information available

🔍 **Quick tip:** Need to see a high-resolution version of this image? Open this book in the next-gen Packt Reader or view it in the PDF/ePub copy.

📖 **The next-gen Packt Reader** and a **free PDF/ePub copy** of this book are included with your purchase. Scan the QR code OR visit https://packtpub.com/unlock, then use the search bar to find this book by name. Double-check the edition shown to make sure you get the right one.

Here's how to set it up:

1. Open VS Code (or VS Codium, if you prefer the open source variant).
2. Search for Zig Language in the **Extensions** marketplace.
3. Install the extension with a single click.
4. Restart VS Code, and you're all set.

Once installed, the extension takes care of everything else, integrating seamlessly with the ZLS. Whether you're writing code, debugging, or navigating your project, you'll find the experience smooth and efficient. No fuss, no headaches—just pure Zig coding bliss.

Using the ZLS in Neovim

If you're a Neovim user, chances are you appreciate the finer things in life—such as minimalism, efficiency, and the joy of configuring your editor exactly the way you want it. Setting up the ZLS in Neovim takes a bit more effort than in VS Code, but the payoff is a highly customized and streamlined Zig development environment.

Mason

If you're using the Zig master branch, do not install the ZLS via the Mason package manager. Mason only installs the latest tagged release of the ZLS, which might not be compatible with the Zig master branch. Instead, follow the manual installation steps that follow to ensure everything works seamlessly.

For this setup, we'll use the nvim-lspconfig plugin along with some specific configurations for the ZLS. This guide assumes you're already familiar with setting up other features such as keybindings and autocompletion. If not, refer to the nvim-lspconfig documentation (https://github.com/neovim/nvim-lspconfig) for more details.

Here's how to get the ZLS up and running.

Installing the vim-plug plugin manager

If you haven't already, you'll need to set up `vim-plug` to manage your Neovim plugins.

Configure your `init.lua` with `vim-plug`:

```
local vim = vim
local Plug = vim.fn['plug#']

vim.call('plug#begin')
  Plug('neovim/nvim-lspconfig')
  Plug('ziglang/zig.vim')
vim.call('plug#end')

vim.g.zig_fmt_parse_errors = 0
vim.g.zig_fmt_autosave = 0
vim.cmd [[autocmd BufWritePre *.zig lua vim.lsp.buf.format()]]

local lspconfig = require('lspconfig')
lspconfig.zls.setup {
  cmd = { '/path/to/zls_executable' },
  settings = {
  zls = {
       zig_exe_path = '/path/to/zig_executable',
  }
    }
}
```

Let's break down this code:

1. `Plug('neovim/nvim-lspconfig')` is used to install the Neovim LSP configuration plugin. The source code can be found at `nvim-lspconfig` (`https://github.com/neovim/nvim-lspconfig`).

2. `Plug('ziglang/zig.vim')` is used to install the Zig language support plugin. The source code can be found at `zig.vim` (`https://github.com/ziglang/zig.vim`).

3. `vim.g.zig_fmt_parse_errors = 0` disables the display of parse errors in a separate window.

4. `vim.g.zig_fmt_autosave = 0` disables format-on-save functionality provided by the `ziglang/zig.vim` plugin.

5. `vim.cmd [[autocmd BufWritePre *.zig lua vim.lsp.buf.format()]]` enables format-on-save functionality using `nvim-lspconfig` and the ZLS.

6. The `lspconfig.zls.setup` block configures the ZLS.

7. `cmd` sets the path to the ZLS executable. (This line can be omitted if ZLS is in your PATH.)

8. `settings.zls.zig_exe_path` sets the path to the Zig executable. (This line can be omitted if Zig is in your PATH.)

9. There are two ways to set configuration options for the ZLS:

   • By editing `zls.json`, which applies to any editor that uses the ZLS

   • By setting in-editor configuration options with the **Settings** field within the setup function

By default, `zig.vim` might have format-on-save enabled. This setup disables it in favor of using the ZLS to handle formatting, ensuring consistency with the Zig community's best practices.

> **Zig path**
>
> Make sure to specify the paths to both `zls` and `zig` if they aren't already in your system's PATH. This ensures that Neovim/Vim can correctly find and use these tools.

Why `zig.vim` specifically? Here's a little bragging point: the Zig Vim plugin you're using gets contributions from none other than Andrew Kelley, the creator of Zig himself. While he doesn't maintain it full-time, his occasional contributions ensure that `zig.vim` stays aligned with the language's evolving features. When the person who designed the language collaborates on the plugin, you can trust that it's a solid choice for your Zig development setup.

So, when you're coding in Neovim, you're not just using any plugin—you're using one that's been touched by the hands that built Zig.

Fine-tuning the ZLS

Now that you've got Neovim (or your preferred editor) configured to work with the ZLS, it's time to take things a step further and fine-tune your setup with a `zls.json` configuration file.

This file allows you to customize ZLS behavior across all editors that use it, giving you control over everything from which Zig executable to use to how semantic tokens are handled.

Here's a simple example of what your zls.json file might look like:

```
{
  "zig_exe_path": "/path/to/zig_executable",
  "semantic_tokens": "partial",
  "enable_build_on_save": true
}
```

This file must be valid JSON, so remember: no comments, no trailing commas, and no funny business.

Finding the right spot for your zls.json file

If you're wondering where to put this configuration file, the ZLS has you covered. Since version 0.14.0, you can easily find out where the ZLS will look for your zls.json file by running the following:

```
zls env
```

This command will give you a detailed output showing where the ZLS searches for the configuration file. Typically, the ZLS first checks local_config_dir (usually something like /home/youruser/.config) and then falls back to global_config_dir (often /etc/xdg). Once you've placed your zls.json file in the appropriate location, you can verify it by running zls env again, and you should see something like this:

```
{
  "version": "0.14.0-dev.50+3354fdcb",
  "global_cache_dir": "/home/user/.cache/zls",
  "global_config_dir": "/etc/xdg",
  "local_config_dir": "/home/user/.config",
  "config_file": "/home/user/.config/zls.json",
  "log_file": "/home/user/.cache/zls/zls.log"
}
```

For versions of the ZLS before 0.14.0-dev.50+3354fdcb (yes, that specific!), you can locate the configuration path by running the following:

```
zls --show-config-path
```

This will either show the path to an existing zls.json file or point you to the local configuration folder where you can create one.

The zls.json file is where you can really tailor the ZLS to fit your workflow. Want the ZLS to automatically run a Zig build every time you save? You got it. Prefer partial semantic tokens to keep things lightweight? No problem. You can explore all available configuration options by checking out the Config.zig file in the ZLS source or by using JSON Schema.

With your editor and the ZLS finely tuned, you're now equipped to tackle Zig projects with a setup that's not just functional but also tailored perfectly to your needs.

Taking the ZLS to the next level

So, you've got the ZLS set up and humming along nicely, catching your errors as you code. However, what if I told you it could get even better? That's right, we're about to supercharge your setup by adding a custom build step that will make sure no error slips through the cracks.

Once you've located your ZLS configuration file, open it up and add these lines:

```
{
    "enable_build_on_save": true,
    "build_on_save_step": "check"
}
```

These settings instruct the ZLS to run a build every time you save your file. However, here's where the real magic happens—the check step. This isn't just any build step; it's a custom step we're about to define in your build.zig file. Trust me, this will take your error-catching game to a whole new level.

Defining a custom check step in your build.zig file

Now that the ZLS is primed to build on save, it's time to define what that build process actually does. We're going to add a custom step to your build.zig file that focuses on checking for compile-time errors without the overhead of generating a final binary. This way, you can catch issues fast and fix them even faster.

Let's say your build.zig file currently defines an executable like this:

```
const exe = b.addExecutable(.{
    .name = "your_magical_executable",
    .root_source_file = b.path("src/main.zig"),
    .target = target,
    .optimize = optimize,
});

b.installArtifact(exe);
```

To introduce the custom `check` step, you'll want to duplicate this definition with a slight twist:

```
const exe_check = b.addExecutable(.{
    .name = "your_magical_executable",
    .root_source_file = b.path("src/main.zig"),
    .target = target,
    .optimize = optimize,
});

const check = b.step("check", "Check if your_executable compiles");
check.dependOn(&exe_check.step);
```

> 💡 **Quick tip**: Enhance your coding experience with the **AI Code Explainer** and **Quick Copy** features. Open this book in the next-gen Packt Reader. Click the **Copy** button (**1**) to quickly copy code into your coding environment, or click the **Explain** button (**2**) to get the AI assistant to explain a block of code to you.

```
                                                        Copy      Explain

function calculate(a, b) {                               1           2
  return {sum: a + b};
};
```

📖 **The next-gen Packt Reader** is included for free with the purchase of this book. Scan the QR code OR go to `https://packtpub.com/unlock`, then use the search bar to find this book by name. Double-check the edition shown to make sure you get the right one.

Notice we didn't include b.`installArtifact` in this version. That's intentional—it focuses purely on verifying that your code compiles without going through the entire build process. This approach means you can quickly identify and fix compile-time issues, staying in your coding flow without unnecessary delays.

Activating your configuration

With your custom `check` step in place, the final step is to restart your editor or the ZLS. Now, whenever you save your files, the ZLS will automatically run the build process and surface any errors directly in your editor. It's like having an instant diagnostic tool that ensures your code is always in top shape.

At this point, you might be thinking, "Do I really need this?". The answer is a resounding yes. While the ZLS is already powerful, it's not perfect—especially when it comes to complex compile-time expressions. Without this custom build-on-save setup, you might miss errors that don't show up until later in your workflow, potentially causing bigger headaches down the line.

By configuring the ZLS to run a build process on save, you're catching those tricky errors right when they happen, keeping your development process smooth and frustration-free. It's about working smarter, not harder, and ensuring that your coding experience with Zig is as efficient and enjoyable as possible.

So, go ahead, activate that custom check, and watch your Zig workflow transform into a well-oiled machine.

You've decked out the ZLS with custom build-on-save diagnostics, and sure, you're probably feeling pretty accomplished. But let's be real, you haven't even started coding yet. All this configuration is just the warm-up, the appetizer before the main course. What if I told you that everything up until now has just been setting the stage for what Zig is truly capable of? That's right. We've been tinkering with the tools, but now it's time to get down to the real business—actually writing some code.

Zig setup: surprise test!

Before we wrap up this chapter, let's take a moment to test what you've learned so far. Whether you're feeling confident or just want to see where you stand, this short quiz is designed to reinforce the key concepts we've covered. It's a fun way to make sure you're ready to tackle your Zig projects with all the tools and knowledge you need. Ready? Let's dive in and see how much you've mastered!

Question 1: You've decided to install Zig on your system. What is the first thing you should consider?

    a.   Downloading the ZLS

    b.   **Choosing between the stable release and the nightly build**

    c.   Setting up your text editor

Correct answer: b. Choosing between the stable release and the nightly build is crucial, as it will determine the version of Zig you'll be working with.

Question 2: You're on a Linux system and want to install Zig. What is the quickest way to get Zig up and running?

    a.   Building Zig from source

    b.   **Using your distribution's package manager**

    c.   Downloading a prebuilt binary from the Zig website

Correct answer: b. Using your distribution's package manager is the easiest and fastest way to install Zig on Linux.

Question 3: True or false? The stable release of Zig is recommended if you want access to the latest features and improvements.

    a.   True

    b.   **False**

Correct answer: b. False. The nightly build is where you'll find the latest features and improvements, while the stable release is more focused on stability.

Question 4: You've downloaded Zig for Windows manually. What must you do to make sure you can easily run the `zig` command from anywhere in the command prompt?

a. Copy the `zig.exe` file to the `System32` folder

b. **Add the path to Zig's binary to your system's `PATH` environment variable**

c. Install Zig using Chocolatey instead

Correct answer: b. Adding Zig to your `PATH` environment variable ensures that you can run the `zig` command from any directory.

Question 5: When setting up the ZLS, why is it important to make sure it's compatible with the version of Zig you're using?

a. The ZLS only works with stable releases

b. The ZLS might not support the latest features or syntax of the nightly build if mismatched

c. **The ZLS requires a specific Zig configuration file to run**

Correct answer: b. Ensuring compatibility between the ZLS and the version of Zig you're using is important because the ZLS might not support all features or syntax in mismatched versions.

Bonus question: You've chosen the nightly build because you want the latest features. What should you keep in mind as you start coding?

a. You might encounter bugs or breaking changes that aren't present in the stable release

b. Tutorials and community resources might be outdated compared to your version

c. **Both of the above**

Correct answer: c. Both of the above. Using the nightly build gives you access to the latest features but comes with potential risks and challenges.

Let's check the results:

- **5–6 correct answers**: Zig Master! You're ready to take on the world with your fully equipped Zig setup. Time to code like a pro!

- **3–4 correct answers**: Zig Apprentice! You've got a solid understanding, but there's still room to refine your setup skills.

- **0–2 correct answers**: Zig Novice! Don't worry, every journey starts with a first step. Go back and review, and you'll be a Zig Master in no time!

Summary

So, you've survived the initiation rites of installing Zig on your machine—congratulations. Whether you're on Linux, Windows, or macOS, you've seen firsthand that Zig doesn't believe in making things harder than they need to be. No convoluted installer rituals, just a few commands, and boom! You're up and running. Let's not forget the existential question you faced: do you play it safe with the stable release or flirt with danger using the nightly build? We've covered that, reminding you that Zig makes it ridiculously easy to flip between versions whenever the mood strikes.

But wait, there's more! We didn't just stop at getting Zig installed. No, we went full throttle into setting up the ZLS, guiding you through building it from source and integrating it into your editor of choice—whether you're a fan of VS Code's polished interface or Neovim's minimalist charm. And because we don't believe in half measures, we also walked you through configuring the ZLS to run builds on save, ensuring you catch errors before they become your next big headache.

These steps weren't just busywork; they're the foundation of a streamlined, frustration-free Zig development environment. And trust me, having a setup that just works is worth its weight in gold when you're knee-deep in code.

But here's the kicker—we're barely getting warmed up. In the next chapter, we're not just going to talk about the Zig toolchain; we're also going to put it to work. You'll write your very first Zig program and explore the toolchain's powerful features, discovering firsthand how they can turn a simple piece of code into a working program. It's the natural progression from setting up your environment to actually building something that works—and works well. Turn the page and let's get started on something truly exciting.

Join us on Discord!

Read this book alongside other users, developers, experts, and the author himself.

Ask questions, provide solutions to other readers, chat with the authors via Ask Me Anything sessions, and much more. Scan the QR or visit the link to join the community.

https://packt.link/deep-engineering-systemsengineering

3

Your First Zig Program

In this chapter, we're going to take a classic cliché—the "Hello, World!" program—and turn it into something a bit more... educational. Yes, it's everyone's favorite first program, but we're going to dissect it like a biology class frog.

What are you going to do? Well, besides writing your first Zig program, you'll learn how to set up a Zig project from scratch, manipulate variables, and take the first steps in debugging. You'll also explore Zig's love-hate relationship with strings. And hey, by the end, you'll be compiling and running your own programs manually, like an actual system programmer who doesn't need training wheels.

In this chapter, we're going to cover the following topics:

- "Hello, World!": Your first taste of Zig
- Basic debugging
- Variables
- Building Zig projects

"Hello, World!": Your first taste of Zig

Here we are! It's time to rip off the Band-Aid and write our very first program. Yes, we're diving into the infamous "Hello, World!" program—but hang on... we're going to do more than just throw text at the screen and call it a day. We'll break it down piece by piece, exploring every token until you're a master of "Hello, World!" Copying and pasting snippets is not the way to learn, right? So, let's build this program from scratch and understand every part of it. First, create a file named `main.zig` and open it in your favorite text editor. This blank canvas is where we'll start crafting our Zig art. Every Zig program begins with a `main` function, and in Zig, it looks like this:

```
pub fn main() void { ... }
```

Let's decode this. It's a public function named `main`, it doesn't take any arguments, and it doesn't return anything—hence, `void`.

> **void**
>
> That `void` might seem a bit dull right now, but don't worry, it's doing its job—keeping things simple and straightforward. And yes, this is already a valid Zig program.

Now, try running it:

```
$ zig run main.zig
```

Nothing happens! That's great news—no errors. It's like a clean slate, which is exactly what we want at this point. But let's be honest, we didn't come all this way just to see nothing. We need to put something on display.

Bringing in the Standard Library

To show something on the screen, we're going to tap into Zig's Standard Library. Let's enter our very first built-in function: `@import`. Here's how it looks:

```
const std = @import("std");
```

In this line, we're importing the Zig Standard Library and linking it to a constant called `std`. This allows us to use various useful tools from the library, including functions to output text. Think of it as giving your program access to a Swiss Army knife of utilities.

> **Note**
>
> The `std` package is always available in Zig—it's like a trusty tool that never leaves your side.

There's a lot going on in that one line, so let's slow down and dissect it. This is the first step toward putting everything together and creating a more dynamic program.

Importing packages

Now that we've imported the Standard Library, let's dig a little deeper into what's actually happening behind the scenes. You might've noticed that the function name starts with an @ symbol—this means it's a built-in function provided directly by the Zig compiler. Welcome to the Zig lingo! Bit by bit, you'll get used to these built-ins. Our current focus is @import. The signature of @import looks like this:

```
@import(comptime path: []const u8) type
```

Looks a bit technical at first, right? Let's break down the official explanation (https://ziglang. org/documentation/master/#import):

> *This function finds a Zig file corresponding to path and adds it to the build if it is not already added. Zig source files are implicitly structs, with a name equal to the file's basename with the extension truncated. @import returns the struct type corresponding to the file.*

In simpler terms, @import takes the path to a file, loads that file, and lets you work with its contents as if it's a struct. This is how we gain access to things like the Standard Library.

Alright, brace yourself—here's your first Zig jump scare: *there are no strings in Zig.* Yep, you read that right. No strings. I know it's edgy, maybe even a bit rebellious, but trust me, Zig doesn't do "traditional" unless it makes sense. Spoiler alert: strings just don't make the cut. What you've got instead are slices of bytes, which sound way more hardcore anyway, right? They're efficient, low-level, and absolutely perfect for system programming, where performance is king.

Slices

A slice in Zig is essentially a reference to a sequence of values—in this case, bytes. Think of it as a pointer to an array but with a known length. It's lightweight, efficient, and flexible, which fits well with Zig's performance-first philosophy.

Curious to learn more about slices and other structures? Don't worry, we'll dive deeper into how Zig organizes data in *Chapter 7, Organizing Data.* There, you'll explore slices, arrays, and more powerful structures that make Zig such a flexible and efficient language. For now, just remember: in Zig, "strings" are really just slices of bytes, and that's one of the many ways Zig gives you more control over your data.

So, when we're printing information, we're using `std.debug.print`. Let's break down this example:

```
const std = @import("std");

pub fn main() void {
    std.debug.print("Hello Zig! \n", .{});
}
```

This program is as simple as it gets, but there's a lot happening here. The `std.debug.print` function expects two things: a format string (which, remember, is just a slice of bytes) and arguments. In our case, we're passing `"Hello Zig! \n"` as the format string and `.{}` as the arguments.

What's with the `.{}`? Oh, you noticed that bit of alien syntax, huh? Well, that's just Zig's quirky way of saying, *"Hey, there are no arguments here, but I'll keep the placeholder for when you need it."* It looks odd now, but soon you'll be slinging `.{}` like it's second nature. Time to run our program!

zig run

You've been using `zig run` to compile and run your Zig programs in one go. But have you ever wondered what's really happening when you type that command? Let's pull back the curtain a bit.

When you use `zig run`, it's not magic—it's simply doing two things for you:

1. Compiling your source code into an executable
2. Running that executable right after

But if you want to understand the process better, let's break it down and do it ourselves step by step.

Step 1: Building the executable manually

Instead of using `zig run`, try this:

```
$ zig build-exe src/main.zig
```

This command tells Zig to build your executable manually. After running it, take a look at your directory. A-ha! Have you noticed two new files created?

- `main`: This is your freshly built executable

- `main.o`: This is the object file, which contains the compiled machine code that makes up your program

Step 2: Running the executable

Now that we've built the executable ourselves, let's run it:

```
./main
```

Voilà! You should see the exact same output that you got when using `zig run`. This is the result of manually building and running the program, which is exactly what `zig run` does under the hood—but without showing you the intermediate steps.

Why go through this?

You might be wondering, *"Why should I bother with* `zig build-exe` *when* `zig run` *does everything in one step?"* Well, while `zig run` is great for small, quick programs, knowing the individual steps—like manually building—gives you greater control over the process. As your projects grow more complex, you'll need to handle things such as object files, customize build configurations, or fine-tune how your code is compiled. Understanding this process opens the door to more advanced optimizations.

So, enjoy the simplicity of `zig run` when it suits your needs, but keep in mind that you now have the power to take the manual approach when necessary. Whether you're using `zig run` for quick tasks or `zig build-exe` for more control, there's a key element that drives it all: variables. Variables are the backbone of any program, and understanding how Zig handles them will give you deeper insight into how your programs behave and perform.

As we move from the mechanics of building executables to understanding variables, remember: the more you understand Zig's language features, the more control you'll have over every part of your development process. Let's explore how variables influence the structure and efficiency of your code.

Variables

Let me tell you something straight: if you're the kind of person who loves using var everywhere, I get it. You enjoy chaos, uncertainty, and living life on the edge. But let's face it—const is your smarter, more reliable, and frankly better-looking friend. Why? Because using const means fewer surprises for both you and the compiler. It's like telling the universe, *"Hey, this variable is set in stone. No, I'm not going to mutate it. Yes, you can relax."* The compiler loves that. So do I.

Figure 3.1 – The essence of a const-type person (left)—steady and reliable—alongside a var-type person (right)—chaotic and unpredictable

In Zig, where optimization is critical and runtime surprises are sacrilege, sticking with const allows the compiler to do all sorts of smart things, such as not blowing up your performance. Sure, you can sprinkle var here and there, but every time you do, know that you're creating extra work for your future self—and trust me, that future self is going to hate you.

Let's begin by using the const keyword to assign values. Once a value is set with const, it is locked in and cannot be changed. Think of it as a commitment—one that your compiler appreciates because it allows for better optimizations.

```
const x = 1234;

pub fn main() void {
const y = 5678;
std.debug.print("x = {}, y = {}\n", .{x, y});
```

```
// Uncommenting the next line will throw a compiler error because y is
constant.
// y += 1;
}
```

> 💡 **Quick tip**: Enhance your coding experience with the **AI Code Explainer** and **Quick Copy** features. Open this book in the next-gen Packt Reader. Click the **Copy** button (1) to quickly copy code into your coding environment, or click the **Explain** button (2) to get the AI assistant to explain a block of code to you.
>
> Copy   Explain
>
> ```
> function calculate(a, b) {
>   return {sum: a + b};
> };
> ```
> (1) (2)

🔒 **The next-gen Packt Reader** is included for free with the purchase of this book. Scan the QR code OR go to `https://packtpub.com/unlock`, then use the search bar to find this book by name. Double-check the edition shown to make sure you get the right one.

When you run this code, you'll see the values of x and y printed, without any surprises. But if you try to change y, the compiler will throw an error:

```
$ zig run main.zig
main.zig:9:7: error: cannot assign to constant
y += 1;
~~~^~~~
```

Now, if you absolutely need to modify a variable, you'll want to use var. This allows mutability, but be cautious—this flexibility comes at the price of potential unpredictability:

```
pub fn main() void {
var y: i32 = 5678;

y += 1; // Modifying the variable
std.debug.print("y = {}\n", .{y});
}
```

This time, the value of y is allowed to change, and the result will be printed:

```
$ zig build-exe mutable_var.zig
$ ./mutable_var
y = 5679
```

There is a catch! Zig enforces the rule that all variables must be initialized. This is a great thing—it ensures that you're always working with valid data from the start. If you forget to initialize a variable, Zig will stop you before things get messy.

```
pub fn main() void {
var x: i32; // Declared, but not initialized!
// Uncommenting the next line without initializing x will cause an error.
// std.debug.print("x = {}\n", .{x});

x = 1; // Properly initialized
std.debug.print("x = {}\n", .{x});
}
```

Try running the code without initializing x, and you'll get an error message:

```
$ zig build-exe var_must_be_initialized.zig
main.zig:2:15: error: expected '=', found ';'
var x: i32;
              ^
```

There are cases where you might not have an initial value ready. In these situations, Zig provides the undefined value, which means "*I have no idea what this is yet.*" But be careful—working with undefined is risky business.

```
pub fn main() void {
```

```
    var x: i32 = undefined; // x is uninitialized and could be anything right
    now.
    std.debug.print("x before initialization = {}\n", .{x});


    x = 42; // Now x is assigned a proper value.
    std.debug.print("x after initialization = {}\n", .{x});
    }
```

When you run this, Zig will initialize x with an undefined value (which could be anything) until you explicitly assign it a proper value:

```
$ zig build-exe assign_undefined.zig
$ ./assign_undefined
x before initialization = -1431655766
x after initialization = 42
```

Is var evil? Not really. It has its place, but that place is limited. Use var when you absolutely need to mutate a value, such as in loops or algorithms that require in-place updates. Stick to const as much as possible. It makes your code predictable, readable, and optimized. Use var only when you have no other choice, and always keep it on a tight leash.

Now that we've established what variables are, let's get into the fun part—where they live, how they behave, and why you shouldn't try to play clever naming tricks with them. Speaking of which, let's talk about **shadowing**.

Shadowing

Zig hates surprises, and so should you!

Let's talk scope. Ever walked into a room and found someone wearing the exact same shirt as you? Awkward, right? Now imagine if, in Zig, you tried to pull off the same trick with variable names. The compiler would glare at you and refuse to move forward. Why? Because in Zig, scope shadowing is simply not allowed. This isn't JavaScript, where shadowing is practically a lifestyle choice. Nope; in Zig, if you want to reuse a variable name in a nested scope, you're out of luck.

Here's an example to demonstrate how Zig handles shadowing and what happens when you attempt it:

```
const std = @import("std");


pub fn main() void {
```

```
const x = 10; // First declaration of x
{
    const x = 20; // Error: cannot redeclare 'x' in the inner scope
    std.debug.print("Inner scope x = {}\n", .{x});
}
std.debug.print("Outer scope x = {}\n", .{x});
}
```

In this code, the following happens:

- const x = 10 declares x in the outer scope
- When you try to declare x again in the inner block (const x = 20;), Zig will throw a compile-time error because shadowing is not allowed in Zig

This error helps prevent the confusion that can arise from using the same variable name in different scopes.

Identifiers

You may think you're clever, naming your variables with funky symbols or starting them with numbers like you're some kind of rebellious hacker from the '90s. Zig doesn't care for your flair. Identifiers must start with an alphabetic character or an underscore. Anything else? Sorry, the compiler will laugh and throw an error in your face. In other words, no, you can't name it 1337_cr3w.

Take this example:

```
var valid_name = 42;  // Good
var _anotherValidName = 100;  // Also good
var 1invalidName = 123;  // Nope, that's going to cause problems
```

If you absolutely need to use something absurd such as 1SmallStep4Man or identifier with spaces, there's a solution: Zig's @"" syntax, which says, "Fine, I'll allow it, but only because you've used the escape hatch." Use it wisely or just avoid it altogether—unless you're the kind of person who enjoys weird syntax just to feel special.

But what if you need to name something that doesn't follow these rules, such as when you're linking with an external library? Maybe you're dealing with a name that includes spaces or starts with a number:

```
const @"identifier with spaces" = 42;
const @"1ExternalLibIdentifier" = 100;
```

This syntax allows you to break the usual rules, but be cautious—use it only when absolutely necessary. Most of the time, it's better to stick with standard identifier rules to keep your code clean and understandable. But when you're linking with external libraries that insist on strange naming conventions, @"" is your friend.

So, keep your identifiers simple, and only use the @"" syntax when you're forced to deal with the unruly names of external libraries.

A quick word on primitive types

Let's be honest—you're not reading some dusty old manual from the '70s, and we're definitely not here to bore you by dissecting every single primitive type Zig has to offer. That's not how we roll. Instead, we'll focus on the quirks and the strictly necessary details to keep you moving forward, learning the language without falling asleep.

If you're the curious type and want to explore all the primitive types at your own pace, you can find the full list here: https://ziglang.org/documentation/master/#Primitive-Types.

It's all there for when you're feeling adventurous.

> **I've got your back**
>
> If anything strange or out of the blue comes up in the next chapters, I'll keep you posted. For now, let's stick to the fun stuff and skip the long, boring type definitions. You're here to learn the language, not slog through a catalog of data types.

Now that we've dodged the monotony of exploring every single primitive type, let's shift gears to something more hands-on—**debugging**. Instead of diving straight into code analysis, let's ease into the tools Zig provides to help you track what's happening with our programs.

Basic debugging

Alright, so you've been living dangerously, dabbling with undefined variables. Maybe you've even thought, *"Hey, it's just uninitialized, how bad could it be?"* Well, let's just say you're playing with fire—but in **debug mode**, Zig gives you a fire extinguisher.

When you run your code in debug mode, Zig catches your use of undefined by filling it with a special byte pattern: 0xaa. This isn't just for fun. This pattern helps you spot when you're working with uninitialized memory. It's like a neon sign saying, *"Hey, you forgot to set this variable!"*

Let's walk through how you can observe this behavior in action.

We'll declare a variable using undefined and print its value. In debug mode, Zig will fill the uninitialized variable with the special 0xaa byte pattern:

```
const print = @import("std").debug.print;


pub fn main() void {
var x: i32 = undefined; // Declare an uninitialized variable
print("x = {}\n", .{x}); // Print the value of the uninitialized variable
}
```

Now, let's build and run this program in debug mode.

Step 1: Building the program in debug mode

Since debug mode is Zig's default, just build your program like you normally do:

```
$ zig build-exe your_program.zig
```

Zig's got your back, filling undefined values with the magic 0xaa byte pattern automatically. You don't have to think about enabling debug mode—it's already there, making sure your code is a little less wild. So, relax—there's no special flag to remember; you're safe by default!

Step 2: Running the program

Once the program is built, run it and see what happens:

```
$ ./your_program
x = -1431655766
```

Step 3: What's going on?

Why are we seeing this strange value? The key here is understanding how memory works. The special 0xaa byte pattern is what Zig uses to fill uninitialized memory in debug mode. This pattern translates to the hexadecimal value 0xaaaaaaaa. When you interpret this as a signed 32-bit integer (i32), it shows up as -1431655766. If you used a different variable type, you'd get a different output, but the underlying memory would still be filled with the 0xaa pattern.

Understanding the byte pattern

This behavior is not just some quirky feature—it's designed to help you find uninitialized variables early on. In Debug Mode, Zig fills uninitialized memory with 0xaa to make it obvious when you've forgotten to properly initialize a variable. It's like a helpful slap on the wrist.

Here's where you get to have some fun. Go ahead and experiment with different types, print their undefined values, and see how Zig fills the memory for each one. You'll quickly realize how this small feature helps you track down uninitialized variables.

Now, push the boundaries—see how many types you can break with undefined. Just remember: after all the chaos, don't forget to put everything back together—and more importantly, how to figure out what went wrong in the first place. This is where debugging comes into play, and Zig has just the tool for the job: std.debug.

std.debug

The std.debug package in Zig is your go-to tool for debugging, and it's designed to make your life easier when things inevitably go wrong. Think of it as your toolbox for inspecting what's happening under the hood. If you've ever wanted to go full detective mode on your code, std.debug is your magnifying glass.

But before we get too deep into the details, it's important to note that many of the advanced features in std.debug are a bit further down the road on your Zig journey. Right now, we're focusing on building a solid foundation. As you progress and your projects grow in complexity, tools such as dumpCurrentStackTrace, attachSegfaultHandler, and even customizable panic functions will become essential to your debugging arsenal.

For now, just know that std.debug is packed with advanced debugging features, including stack trace capture, memory dumps, and error handling. However, tackling these features too early can be overwhelming. We'll circle back to them once you're more comfortable with the fundamentals of Zig.

In the meantime, you'll be seeing plenty of std.debug.print()—a simple yet powerful way to inspect values and get real-time feedback from your code. It's a great tool to quickly understand what's happening in your program, and as you progress, you'll naturally start picking up more advanced features. But before we get into that, there's something even more foundational to focus on: consistency. Writing reliable, predictable code becomes much easier when you're consistent in your approach—whether it's naming variables or structuring your program. And the good news is, the more organized your code is, the easier debugging will become. So, let's take a moment to explore the importance of consistency and how it helps you build a solid foundation for all your Zig projects.

Maintaining consistency

Zig is strict when it comes to encoding: all source code is encoded in **UTF-8**. Why? Because standards exist for a reason, and we don't need any wild, invalid byte sequences messing up our code. Try to slip in an invalid UTF-8 sequence and Zig will throw a compile error faster than you can say "undefined behavior."

To keep things clean, there are some specific characters that Zig just doesn't allow anywhere in the code—including comments:

- **ASCII control characters**: Pretty much all of them are banned except for **Line Feed (LF)**, **Carriage Return (CR)**, and **Horizontal Tab (HT)**. So, no sneaking in U+0000 to U+0008 or anything such as U+007f.
- **Non-ASCII Unicode line endings**: Fancy Unicode line breaks such as U+0085 (NEL), U+2028 (LS), and U+2029 (PS) are off limits. Keep it simple.

Line endings: Keep it simple, keep it LF

In Zig, the humble LF is the line terminator of choice. This is the 0x0a byte value (code point U+000a, or \n if you prefer). Every line in Zig source code must end with LF—except the last one. For non-empty files, it's recommended that the file ends with a blank line, meaning the last byte should be LF.

Now, if you're coming from the Windows world, you might be tempted to use the classic CR + LR combo (CRLF, or \r\n). While Zig tolerates this if you must use it, it's discouraged. Stick to LF if you want to keep the compiler happy. Also, don't try sneaking a CR (0x0d, U+000d) anywhere else, because it's not allowed outside of forming CRLF for line endings.

Tabs versus spaces: Pick a side (spoiler: use spaces)

While Zig tolerates hard tabs (\t, U+0009, 0x09) as token separators, it's best to use spaces instead. Hard tabs and spaces are technically interchangeable, but unless you're trying to start a formatting war, spaces (0x20, U+0020) are the preferred choice.

Byte order marks: Only at the start

If you feel the need to include a UTF-8 **byte order mark (BOM)**, Zig will quietly ignore it—but only if it's at the very start of the file. Put a BOM anywhere else and Zig won't be so forgiving.

The power of zig fmt

If all these rules are making your head spin, don't worry. Zig has a formatting tool (zig fmt) that will automatically enforce all of these recommendations. Just run it, and your source code will be formatted to perfection. It's like having a personal code janitor that sweeps away all your encoding sins:

```
$ zig fmt your_code.zig
```

Zig's source encoding rules are designed to keep everything clean, consistent, and easy to work with. Stick to UTF-8, use LF for line endings, and let zig fmt handle the rest. Keep your source code predictable, and everyone—including the compiler—will be much happier.

With all this knowledge fresh in your head, you're ready to tackle how Zig leverages these concepts to build and manage your project. The build system isn't some mysterious black box—it's just Zig code in action. Let's jump into the build system.

Building Zig projects

So, you're ready to build your first Zig project, which is a bit more complex than just building a single source file. Not just a single source file, but a whole project—welcome to the big league. Before you start panicking about all the files and options, let's walk through it step by step. While the project structure might look a little intimidating at first, it's actually simpler than it seems once you break it down.

Step 1: Creating your project

Alright, time to roll up your sleeves and create your first Zig project. Let's not overcomplicate things—just create a directory, step inside, and let Zig do the heavy lifting:

```
$ mkdir -p hw
$ cd hw
$ zig init
```

Now, if you're wondering why we went with hw for the folder name, it's short for "Hello, World!". But hey, feel free to imagine it stands for "Hard Work." After all, every great project starts with a little hard work, and this is just the beginning of yours!

Boom! Zig just gave you four brand-new files:

```
info: created build.zig
info: created build.zig.zon
info: created src/main.zig
info: created src/root.zig
```

That's right—Zig's already starting to feel like home.

Step 2: Your first build

Now, let's talk building. You'd think Zig would just compile stuff, but no—Zig's build system is structured and packed with options. In fact, it's so eager to show off, let's look at what happens if you run the following:

```
$ zig build --help
```

Zig will flood you with options—so many options! But let's not get distracted by the shiny things. For now, we'll stick to the basics: getting your program to build.

Let's look at what happens when you run the following:

```
$ zig build
```

Zig kindly creates a `zig-out/` directory for you. Inside, you'll find two subdirectories:

- `bin/`: This is where your statically built binary ends up
- `lib/`: If you're building a library, here's where you'll find the `.a` files (a bunch of `.o` files bundled together)

Let's take a peek:

```
zig-out/
├── bin
│   └── hw          # Your statically built binary
└── lib
    └── libhw.a   # The static library, if you had one
```

Step 3: Running your program

Now that we've built the program, let's run it:

```
$ ./zig-out/bin/hw
```

Congrats! Your first Zig project is running. But wait—what's this message?

```
All your codebase are belong to us.
Run `zig build test` to run the tests.
```

Before you go full conspiracy theorist: *no*, the Zig team hasn't hacked your project. This is just the default message for every freshly created Zig program. You can change it later, but let's enjoy it for now.

Step 4: What's inside the source code?

Okay, let's snoop around a bit and see what files you've got:

```
.
├── build.zig
├── build.zig.zon
├── src
│   ├── main.zig
│   └── root.zig
└── zig-out
├── bin
│   └── hw
└── lib
        └── libhw.a
```

Step 5: Too many moving parts

I know what you're thinking—"*All of this just for a simple program?*" Yeah, there's a bit of setup, but every piece has a purpose. Before we get too carried away with throwing things out, let's appreciate what Zig's doing here:

- build.zig handles how your project gets compiled, which is critical for customization later
- build.zig.zon manages external dependencies—if you're pulling in libraries, this is where the magic happens
- src/ is where your code lives—this is the beating heart of the project
- zig-out/ is the output directory where all the results (binaries, libraries) get stored

It might feel like overkill for now, but trust me, you'll be grateful for this structure when your project grows.

Now that you've built and run your first Zig project, there's a lot more to uncover. Zig's build system is highly customizable, but we'll dive into those options in later chapters. Before we go any further, it's important to solidify your understanding of Zig's foundations because every bit of Zig you master directly applies to the build system itself. It's like an infinite feedback loop of mastery: the more Zig you learn, the more powerful you become in controlling the build process. So, let's continue laying the groundwork before we unlock the full potential of the build system.

But for now, kick back and bask in the glory of your freshly compiled binary. You've earned it.

Summary

Mission accomplished! You've successfully navigated your first foray into Zig, and you didn't just type out "Hello, World!" and call it a day. No, you went deeper, decoding the main function, harnessing the power of the Standard Library, and—let's not forget—wrapping your head around Zig's rebellious approach to strings (or, you know, the lack thereof). You've even wrestled with variables in a way that future you will appreciate, and you've started getting comfortable with debugging.

Remember, const is like that friend who always knows the plan, sticks to it, and never causes drama. On the other hand, var is the friend who says, *"Let's just wing it,"* and then somehow gets everyone lost at 3 A.M. in the middle of nowhere. Choose wisely.

Now you know what's happening behind the scenes when you use zig run—Zig builds your executable and runs it, saving you a step. But when you want more control over your build process, knowing how to manually compile and execute your code is a powerful skill.

Next, we'll move on to control flow—where the real decision-making happens. We'll dive into conditionals, loops, and how Zig lets you steer your programs in exactly the direction you need. It's the next logical step in your journey learning Zig and taking full control of your code's flow.

Make it stick

Now that we've covered the essential concepts, it's time to lock in what you've learned. Let's see how well these ideas have stuck! The following questions are designed to help you reinforce the key points from this chapter. Don't worry, this isn't an exam—it's a chance to reflect and strengthen your grasp of Zig. So, grab a coffee, take a deep breath, and let's dive into some exercises!

1. **The main function**

    Question: What does `pub fn main() void { ... }` represent in Zig?

    a. A private function with no return value

    b. A public function that returns a string

    c. A public function that doesn't take arguments and returns nothing

    d. A public function that imports the Standard Library

2. **Running the program**

    Question: After creating your `main.zig` file, what happens when you run `$ zig run main.zig` with no additional code inside the `main` function?

    a. The program prints "Hello, World!"

    b. The program does nothing, but there are no errors

    c. The program returns a compilation error

    d. The program outputs a default message from the Zig compiler

3. **Importing the Standard Library**

    Question: What does the line `const std = @import("std");` do in Zig?

    a. It imports the Standard Library and assigns it to the `std` constant

    b. It defines a new Standard Library for your project

    c. It declares a function in the Standard Library

    d. It imports external dependencies from a custom path

4. **Printing to the screen**

    Question: What is the correct way to print "Hello Zig!" in Zig using the Standard Library?

    a. `std.debug.print("Hello Zig! \n", {});`

    b. `std.print("Hello Zig!", {});`

    c. `std.debug.print("Hello Zig! \n", .{});`

    d. `std.debug.print("Hello Zig!", .{});`

5. **The @import built-in function**

   Question: What is the purpose of the @import built-in function in Zig?

   a.   It loads a Zig file and returns the corresponding struct

   b.   It runs the Zig compiler

   c.   It defines a slice in memory

   d.   It imports external libraries

6. **Zig's approach to strings**

   Question: How does Zig handle text instead of using traditional strings?

   a.   It uses slices of bytes

   b.   It uses pointers to characters

   c.   It uses arrays of strings

   d.   It uses string buffers

7. **Variable declaration: const versus var**

   Question: Which of the following is true about the const keyword in Zig?

   a.   It allows the value to be mutated after initialization

   b.   It declares a variable that cannot be changed after it's initialized

   c.   It declares a function that cannot return a value

   d.   It is used to declare strings in Zig

8. **The use of var in Zig**

   Question: When would you use the var keyword in Zig?

   a.   When you want a variable to be immutable

   b.   When you want a variable to be mutable and change over time

   c.   When you want to import the Standard Library

   d.   When you want to declare a constant value

9. **Uninitialized variables in Zig**

   Question: What happens if you declare a variable in Zig but do not initialize it?

   a. Zig automatically initializes it to 0

   b. The program crashes

   c. The program will not compile due to an error

   d. The variable is initialized with a special undefined value

10. **Debugging with uninitialized variables**

    Question: When you declare a variable with the value undefined in Zig, what value is assigned in debug mode?

    a. 0

    b. 1

    c. A special byte pattern, 0xaa

    d. A memory address

11. **Building executables**

    Question: What does the `zig build-exe src/main.zig` command do?

    a. It runs the Zig program directly

    b. It builds the executable manually from the source code

    c. It creates a new project directory

    d. It builds a library file

12. **Output files after build**

    Question: After running `zig build-exe`, which files are created?

    a. Only the main executable

    b. The executable and a text log file

    c. The executable and an object file (`main.o`)

    d. The executable and a standard output text file

13. **Shadowing in Zig**

    Question: What happens if you try to declare two variables with the same name in a nested scope in Zig?

    a.   Zig will automatically use the inner variable and ignore the outer one

    b.   Zig will throw a compile-time error due to shadowing not being allowed

    c.   Both variables will be accessible

    d.   Zig will replace the outer variable with the inner one

14. **Project initialization**

    Question: What does the `zig init` command do when you create a new project directory?

    a.   It creates a single `main.zig` file

    b.   It creates multiple files, including `build.zig` and `src/main.zig`

    c.   It builds the project and runs the executable

    d.   It compiles a test program

15. **Manually building and running programs**

    Question: What is the benefit of manually using `zig build-exe` over `zig run`?

    a.   It is faster than `zig run`

    b.   It offers more control over the compilation process, which is useful for complex projects

    c.   It is only for debugging purposes

    d.   It skips over object file generation

16. **Handling object files**

    Question: What does the `main.o` file represent after running `zig build-exe`?

    a.   The compiled source code in machine-readable format

    b.   The executable file

    c.   The source code with debug information

    d.   The project settings file

17. **Memory debugging**

    Question: What special byte pattern does Zig use in debug mode to detect uninitialized memory?

    a. `0xbb`

    b. `0xff`

    c. `0xaa`

    d. `0x00`

18. **Variable initialization enforcement**

    Question: Why does Zig enforce the initialization of all variables?

    a. To make the program faster

    b. To avoid using undefined or garbage values in memory

    c. To allow variables to be mutable

    d. To compile the program in Debug Mode

19. **Standard Library tools for debugging**

    Question: What is the purpose of `std.debug.print()` in Zig?

    a. It prints memory addresses

    b. It allows the printing of formatted strings to help debug your program

    c. It automatically prints a stack trace

    d. It runs a test program in debug mode

20. **Variable shadowing rules**

    Question: Why does Zig forbid variable shadowing?

    a. To prevent ambiguity and potential bugs caused by reusing variable names in nested scopes

    b. To enable faster memory allocation

    c. To allow the use of the same variable in multiple scopes

    d. To increase the performance of the program

Answers

1. c
2. b
3. a
4. c
5. a
6. a
7. b
8. b
9. c
10. c
11. b
12. c
13. b
14. b
15. b
16. a
17. c
18. b
19. b
20. a

4

Control Flow, Loops, and Other Forms of Digital Domination

Even the most potent code needs direction. If programming is digital magic, then control flow is your spell book—guiding your code's decisions, dictating when and how often actions occur, and ensuring everything dances to your precise tune.

In this chapter, we'll delve into Zig's approach to control flow—equipping you with tools that not only match but elevate what you're accustomed to in other languages. We'll explore conditional statements, loops, the exhaustive `switch` construct, and the elegant handling of optional types.

By the end of this chapter, even as a seasoned coder, you'll find that mastering Zig's control flow mechanisms elevates your coding prowess. You'll be making decisions with precision, repeating actions efficiently, and embracing uncertainty with the confidence of someone who always has a plan B (or C, or D).

In this chapter, we're going to cover the following topics:

- Making choices with `if`, `else`, and `switch` (your code's moral compass)
- Loops: Repeating actions with `for` and `while` (because doing things once is boring)
- Exhaustive switches: Elegant logic with `switch` (be the matchmaker your code deserves)
- Optional types: Dealing with the uncertainty of life (and code)

So, gear up! Even with your extensive experience, Zig offers exciting twists on control flow that will enhance your programming toolkit. Let's embark on this journey to master the art of guiding your code's destiny.

Technical requirements

All the code shown in this chapter can be found in the Chapter04 directory of our Git repository: https://github.com/PacktPublishing/Learning-Zig/tree/main/Chapter04.

Making choices with if, else, and switch (your code's moral compass)

You've reached a crossroads, dear programmer. It's time for your code to make decisions—big ones. Will it take the high road and print "Hello, World", or the low road and throw an error? Conditional statements are the moral compass that guides your program's flow, making decisions based on data, circumstances, and the ever-uncertain whims of the user. Let's dive into how to make these choices in Zig.

In Zig, conditional statements are a straightforward way to control your program's execution. You're already familiar with them if you've used languages such as C, Go, or even Python, but Zig puts its own spin on them.

Figure 4.1 – Where conditional logic branches your program's journey

When you come to a fork in the road, you make a choice. Your program does the same with if statements, evaluating conditions and acting accordingly:

```
const std = @import("std");
```

```
pub fn main() void {
    const number = 10;

    if (number > 5) {
        std.debug.print("Number is greater than 5.\n", .{});
    } else {
        std.debug.print("Number is 5 or less.\n", .{});
    }
}
```

♀ **Quick tip**: Enhance your coding experience with the **AI Code Explainer** and **Quick Copy** features. Open this book in the next-gen Packt Reader. Click the **Copy** button (1) to quickly copy code into your coding environment, or click the **Explain** button (2) to get the AI assistant to explain a block of code to you.

```
                                          Copy      Explain
function calculate(a, b) {
    return {sum: a + b};             1           2
};
```

🔖 **The next-gen Packt Reader** is included for free with the purchase of this book. Scan the QR code OR go to https://packtpub.com/unlock, then use the search bar to find this book by name. Double-check the edition shown to make sure you get the right one.

Just like that, you've given your program the power to choose its own destiny. If only life were this simple!

But wait—what if you need more than two choices? That's where else if comes in. You can string multiple conditions together, making your decision-making process as complex as you need:

```zig
const std = @import("std");

pub fn main() void {
    const number = 7;

    if (number > 10) {
        std.debug.print("Number is greater than 10.\n", .{});
    } else if (number > 5) {
        std.debug.print("Number is between 6 and 10.\n", .{});
    } else {
        std.debug.print("Number is 5 or less.\n", .{});
    }
}
```

Just when you thought you'd mastered the humble if statement, Zig decides to pull a fast one on you. Why should if be content with merely directing the flow of your program when it can also moonlight as an expression? Yes, in Zig, it isn't just a control structure—it's an overachiever that returns values. It's like that one colleague who not only finishes their work early but also volunteers for extra projects, making the rest of us look bad.

if as an expression

In many languages, you'd use a ternary operator to assign a value based on a condition. But Zig, ever the minimalist, doesn't clutter your code with somewhat cryptic symbols such as ? and :. Instead, it lets you use if directly as an expression, because who needs punctuation when you can write more words?

Here's an example that illustrates this point:

```zig
const std = @import("std");

pub fn main() void {
    const a: u32 = 5;

    const b: u32 = 4;
```

```
    const result = if (a != b) 47 else 3089;

    std.debug.print("Result is: {}\n", .{result});
}
```

Let's break down this marvel of modern programming:

- We declare two constants, a and b, because having actual inputs would be too unpredictable.

- We use `if (a != b) 47 else 3089` as an expression to assign a value to the result. No ternary operator, just a *verbose* yet clear conditional assignment.

- The condition a `!=` b evaluates to true because 5 is, shockingly, not equal to 4.

- Therefore, the result is assigned the value 47. Breathtaking!

- We print out the result, confirming our findings for posterity.

This approach allows you to assign values based on conditions without resorting to the cryptic syntax that other languages seem so fond of. It's as if Zig is saying, "Why be concise when you can be clear?"

if with Boolean conditions: The classic that never gets old

Of course, sometimes you just want to use if the old-fashioned way—to execute code blocks based on conditions. Zig handles this with the grace and elegance you'd expect, which is to say, it works as you'd hope.

Here's a nostalgic trip down memory lane:

```
const std = @import("std");

pub fn main() void {
    const a: u32 = 5;

    const b: u32 = 4;

    if (a != b) {
        std.debug.print("a is not equal to b.\n", .{});
    } else if (a == 9) {
        std.debug.print("a is inexplicably 9.\n", .{});
    } else {
```

```
        std.debug.print("None of the above conditions were met.\n", .{});
    }
}
```

This is the `if` statement you know and love, doing its job without any surprises. Sometimes, predictability is a blessing.

if with union types

While we've seen how `if` can be used as an expression and with Boolean conditions, Zig's `if` construct is also capable of handling union types. This allows you to elegantly manage different types of values and control flow based on them.

For example, `if` can be used with error unions to distinguish between successful results and errors. However, union types, including error unions, are a more advanced feature that we'll delve into in *Chapter 8, Error Handling*. There, we'll explore how to harness the power of union types to write robust and error-resistant code.

For now, it's enough to know that `if` statements in Zig are versatile and can interact with complex types, enabling you to write expressive and maintainable code. The ability to handle union types in `if` expressions adds another layer to your control flow toolkit, allowing more nuanced and precise logic.

Power and flexibility

While it's tempting to revel in the power and flexibility of `if` expressions in Zig, a word of caution is in order.

Don't overcomplicate: Just because you can write intricate `if` expressions doesn't mean you should. Code readability is a virtue, even if it's an unappreciated one.

Be consistent: Use the same style of control flow throughout your code base to avoid confusing your future self—or anyone else unfortunate enough to read your code.

Having thoroughly dissected the multifaceted `if` statement—marveling at its ability to moonlight as an expression and teasing you with glimpses of its union-handling prowess—it's time to turn our jaded gaze to another control flow construct. So, let's pivot from the binary world of `if` statements to the exhaustive universe of `switch`.

The elegant switch: Leveling up decision-making

In Zig, switch doesn't just evaluate one case—it evaluates *all possible cases*, ensuring you cover every possibility. This makes it exhaustive and, thus, a little safer than your typical if-else structure.

Here's a simple example of switch in action:

```
const std = @import("std");

pub fn main() void {
    const day = 3;

    switch (day) {
        1 => std.debug.print("It's Monday.\n", .{}),
        2 => std.debug.print("It's Tuesday.\n", .{}),
        3 => std.debug.print("It's Wednesday.\n", .{}),
        else => std.debug.print("It's some other day.\n", .{}),
    }
}
```

Here's the breakdown:

- switch evaluates the day variable.
- Each number corresponds to a day of the week, with 1 => representing Monday, 2 => Tuesday, and so on.
- The else case acts as a catch-all. If none of the previous cases match, it handles whatever is left—because you never know.

If you comment the else case, the Zig compiler will shout at you:

```
error: switch must handle all possibilities
```

Now, let's see how Zig's switch statement stands out from similar constructs in other languages:

- **Exhaustiveness is guaranteed**: In Zig, the switch statement forces you to handle all possible values of the expression. If you fail to cover a case, Zig will catch this at compile time. Many languages (such as C and Go) don't enforce this, allowing you to leave gaps in your logic that could lead to bugs. Zig's switch makes sure that every possibility is accounted for, either through explicit cases or with the else block, which acts as a safety net. This is particularly useful when dealing with enums, where every possible value must be handled, ensuring that no surprises slip through the cracks.

- **No fallthrough by default**: In C, C++, and even JavaScript, `switch` statements have "fall-through," meaning that once a case is matched, execution continues into the next case unless explicitly stopped with a `break`. This is a notorious source of bugs when a developer forgets to add a `break` statement. In Zig, there's no fallthrough by default—each case is self-contained, so you won't accidentally execute the next block. This makes Zig's `switch` statement far less error-prone and easier to reason about.

- **Explicit control overflow**: If you want to handle multiple cases with the same block of code in Zig, you explicitly group them together. This makes the flow of control much more predictable and prevents the kinds of unintended consequences that can arise from implicit fallthrough in other languages.

Zig's `switch` doesn't just make your code look cleaner—it makes it safer. By enforcing exhaustiveness and eliminating fallthrough, it helps you catch potential bugs early, at compile time, rather than at 3 A.M. when you least expect them. In Zig, `switch` is more than just a decision-making tool—it's a powerful mechanism for writing reliable, predictable code.

So, as you start using Zig's `switch`, remember: you're not just choosing between paths in your program—you're building safety and clarity directly into your logic. And that's the kind of thing that separates good code from great code.

Having conquered the realm of making choices—where your code gets to pretend it has agency with `if`, `else`, and the ever-so-thorough `switch`—it's time to embrace the inevitable: doing the same thing repeatedly. Because, let's face it, if you didn't enjoy a good loop, you probably wouldn't be programming. So, dust off your patience and prepare to dive into the world of loops in Zig.

Repeating actions

Ah, the `for` loop—a pillar of programming so venerable that even your grandparents probably wrote one in their youth. It's the trusty old workhorse we trot out whenever we need to perform the same mind-numbingly dull task over and over again. But fear not; in Zig, the `for` loop brings its own brand of elegance—or at least tries to.

Let's begin with the basics—iterating over a collection. It's like being on an assembly line, performing the same task ad nauseam, but with the faint hope that a computer will handle the tedium for you.

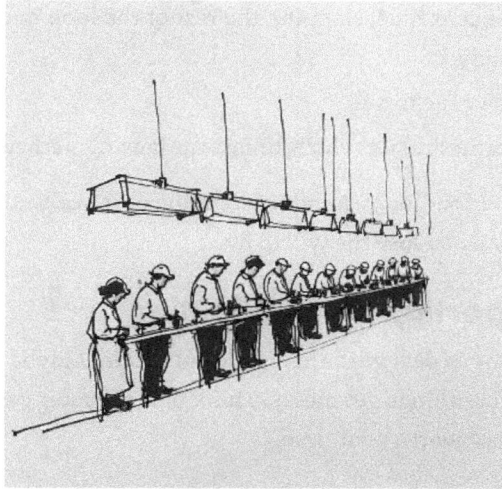

Figure 4.2 – Workers on the loop: each iteration performs the same task

Here's a simple example to ease you into the inevitable complexity:

```
const std = @import("std");

pub fn main() void {
    const items = [_]i32{ 4, 5, 3, 4, 0 };
    var sum: i32 = 0;

    for (items) |value| {
        if (value == 0) {
            continue;
        }
        sum += value;
    }

    std.debug.print("The sum is: {}\n", .{sum});
}
```

Let's dissect this:

- We have an array, items, filled with integers.
- We initialize sum as 0 because starting from any other number would be madness.
- The for (items) |value| loop iterates over each element in items.

- If value is zero, we continue, skipping the rest of the loop body. It's our way of saying, "zeroes need not apply."
- Otherwise, we add value to sum.
- After the loop, we print the sum, which, unless the laws of mathematics have changed, is 16.

This is the bread and butter of for loops: mindless iteration over a collection until you've processed every last element—or until you lose the will to live.

Iterating over a portion of a collection

Sometimes, you don't want to deal with the whole collection. Maybe you're only interested in the first few elements before things get messy. Think of it as reading only the first chapter of a book before deciding it's not worth your time.

Here's how you can focus on a subset:

```
const std = @import("std");

pub fn main() void {
    const items = [_]i32{ 4, 5, 3, 4, 0 };
    var sum: i32 = 0;

    for (items[0..2]) |value| {
        sum += value;
    }

    std.debug.print("Sum of the first two items: {}\n", .{sum});
}
```

Here are some insights from this snippet:

- We use items[0..2] to slice the array, grabbing elements from index 0 up to, but not including, index 2, because off-by-one errors are a programmer's rite of passage.
- The loop now blissfully ignores the rest of the array, summing only the first two values: 4 and 5. The sum is 9.

Selective iteration allows you to pretend the rest of the data doesn't exist, much like how we deal with most of our problems.

Accessing indices

Occasionally, knowing the value isn't enough; you need the index to pinpoint where everything started to fall apart.

Here's how you can drag the index into your loop:

```
const std = @import("std");

pub fn main() void {
    const items = [_]i32{ 4, 5, 3, 4, 0 };

    var sum: i32 = 0;

    for (items, 0..) |_, index| {
        sum += @intCast(index);
    }

    std.debug.print("Sum of the indices: {}\n", .{sum});
}
```

This code calculates the sum of the indices of the items array by using the for loop to iterate over two sequences simultaneously: the array itself and an infinite range starting from zero (0..). The loop syntax for (items, 0..) |_, index| pairs each element of items (which is ignored using _ since the actual values aren't needed) with its corresponding index from the range. This eliminates the need for a separate countervariable to track indices. Inside the loop, it adds each index to sum, casting the usize index to i32 with @intCast(i32, index) to match the type of sum. This approach showcases Zig's ability to iterate over multiple sequences in parallel and efficiently compute the sum of indices without manual index handling, resulting in clean and concise code.

If you prefer to avoid collections altogether—perhaps because managing arrays is too much commitment—you can iterate over a range of numbers.

Here is an example of using a range:

```
const std = @import("std");

pub fn main() void {
    var sum: usize = 0;
```

```
    for (0..5) |i| {
        sum += i;
    }

    std.debug.print("Sum of numbers from 0 to 4: {}\n", .{sum});
}
```

Iterating over ranges is perfect for when you need to occupy your CPU cycles with trivial tasks.

Iterating over multiple collections: Because one isn't challenging enough

Why iterate over one collection when you can juggle two simultaneously? It's like patting your head and rubbing your stomach but with code that can crash.

Here's how you might attempt this feat:

```
const std = @import("std");

pub fn main() void {
    const items1 = [_]usize{ 1, 2, 3 };
    const items2 = [_]usize{ 4, 5, 6 };
    var total: usize = 0;

    for (items1, items2) |i, j| {
        total += i + j;
    }

    std.debug.print("Total sum: {}\n", .{total});
}
```

Here are the key points:

- We have two arrays, items1 and items2, because complexity is our friend.
- The loop iterates over both arrays in lockstep, assuming they are the same length. If not, expect fireworks—or at least a runtime error.
- We sum the pairs of values and accumulate the total, which ends up being 21. The math checks out.

Using loops as expressions with else: Handling disappointment gracefully

Loops don't always run successfully, and you need a way to cope with that crushing disappointment. Enter the `else` clause in `for` loops.

Let's look at some code to make things clearer:

```
const std = @import("std");

pub fn main() void {
    const items = [_]i32{ 1, 3, 4, 5 };

    var sum: i32 = 0;
    var stoppedAtIndex: usize = 0;
    const stoppedEarly = for (0.., items) |i, value| {
        if (@mod(value, 2) == 0) {
            stoppedAtIndex = i;
            break true;
        }
        sum += value;
    } else false;

    std.debug.print("Sum of items: {}\n", .{sum});

    if (stoppedEarly) {
        std.debug.print("Stopped at index: {}\n", .{stoppedAtIndex});
    }
}
```

This code processes an array of integers [1, 3, 4, 5], summing the values until it encounters an even number. It uses a `for` loop that iterates over both indices and values of the array. Inside the loop, it checks whether the current value is even using `@mod(value, 2) == 0`. If an even number is found, it records the index in `stoppedAtIndex`, breaks out of the loop, and sets `stopped` to `true`. Otherwise, it adds the value to `sum`. After the loop, it prints the `sum` and, if it stopped early, the index where it stopped.

What happens when we run this code?

```
Sum of items: 4
Stopped at index: 2
```

In complex scenarios involving nested loops, sometimes you need a way out—a way to break free from the tangled web you've woven. Labeled loops are your emergency exit.

Here's how to make your escape:

```
const std = @import("std");

pub fn main() void {
    var count: usize = 0;

    outer: for (1..6) |_| {
        for (1..6) |_| {
            count += 1;
            break :outer;
        }
    }

    std.debug.print("Count after breaking out: {}\n", .{count});
}
```

In this code, we have this:

- We label the outer loop outer because naming things is hard
- Inside the inner loop, we increment count and then break :outer, escaping both loops in one fell swoop
- The count is 1, indicating we didn't linger any longer than necessary

Labeled loops are your parachute when you've flown too close to the sun.

Alternatively, you might want to skip ahead in the outer loop from deep within nested loops. Here's how:

```
const std = @import("std");

pub fn main() void {
```

```
    var count: usize = 0;

    outer: for (1..5) |i| {
        for (1..5) |j| {
            if (i == j) {
                continue :outer;
            }
            count += 1;
        }
    }

    std.debug.print("Count after continuing outer loop: {}\n", .{count});
}
```

Here are some points to ponder:

- We label the outer loop outer, because why break the trend?
- Inside the inner loop, if i equals j, we continue :outer, skipping to the next iteration of the outer loop
- We increment count only when i and j are not equal
- The final count reflects how many times we've avoided the trap of i == j

Using labeled continue is a surefire way to ensure only you understand your code.

For those who find regular loops too pedestrian, Zig offers inline for loops, executed at compile time, because waiting until runtime is for the weak.

Behold the power of inlining in the following snippet:

```
const std = @import("std");

pub fn main() void {
    const nums = [_]i32{ 2, 4, 6 };
    var sum: usize = 0;

    inline for (nums) |i| {
        const T = switch (i) {
            2 => f32,
            4 => i8,
```

```
        6 => bool,
        else => unreachable,
    };
    sum += @typeName(T).len;
    }


    std.debug.print("Total length of type names: {}\n", .{sum});
}
```

Let's examine this:

- The `inline` keyword forces the loop to unroll at compile time, because who needs flexibility?
- The loop variable `i` is known at compile time, allowing us to perform type-based gymnastics.
- We use a `switch` statement to map `i` to a type `T`, because why not?
- We sum the lengths of the type names, ending up with 9. Fascinating.
- This kind of code is excellent for confusing anyone who dares to read it.

Inline loops are best when you really need them, but they can complicate your build process and increase the final binary size.

> **Caution with inline loops**
>
> Use inline loops sparingly, preferably not at all, unless you have a compelling reason—and a note from your doctor.

Best practices, or how to sleep at night

Here are some tips to make your life easier:

- **Keep it simple:** Just because you can write convoluted loops doesn't mean you should. Simplicity is a virtue, albeit an underappreciated one.
- **Avoid premature optimization:** Trust that Zig's compiler is smarter than you. It probably is.
- **Comment liberally:** If you're doing something clever—or reckless—leave a comment explaining yourself.
- **Test thoroughly:** Loops are fertile ground for off-by-one errors and infinite loops. Test your code unless you enjoy late-night debugging sessions.

Loops are indispensable tools in any programmer's toolkit, Zig included. They allow you to process collections, ranges, and even multiple collections with relative ease—or considerable difficulty, depending on your choices.

As you wield the power of `for` loops, remember that with great power comes great responsibility—or at least more opportunities to introduce subtle bugs. Write your loops with care, test them diligently, and maybe, just maybe, you'll avoid the pitfalls that have ensnared so many before you. But let's be honest: you'll probably make the same mistakes we all have. And that's okay. After all, programming is all about learning from our errors—preferably before they make it into production.

Now, go forth and iterate wisely. Or recklessly. It's your code base.

> **While loops**
>
> Zig also has `while` loops, which are very similar to `for` loops. Take your time to explore the `while` loop examples in the repository.

As you continue your journey through Zig, remember that just because you can write complex, nested loops with labels and expressions, it doesn't mean you should. Sometimes, simplicity is the ultimate sophistication. But before you get too comfortable, it's time to introduce another layer of complexity: the thrilling uncertainty of optional types. Because who doesn't love variables that might—or might not—contain a value? After all, programming without a healthy dose of existential dread is just too easy.

Figure 4.3 – No room to grow: fixed-size collections like cats in a bag

So, let's shift gears from the predictable monotony of loops to the delightful chaos of optional types in Zig. Prepare yourself to embrace the inherent uncertainty of life (and code), where every variable is Schrödinger's cat, simultaneously holding a value and null until you dare to check. It's time to dive into the world of ?T types and learn how to handle the unknown with a forced smile and a weary acceptance that nothing is ever truly certain.

Optional types: Because life (and code) isn't always certain

At some point, every programmer faces a situation where a value might or might not exist. Whether it's missing user input, unreceived data from a network call, or an incomplete file read, dealing with uncertainty is inevitable. In Zig, we handle this with optional types, which force us to be explicit about the possibility of null and ensure we account for missing values. But Zig doesn't stop there—it provides additional mechanisms, such as error unions and try-catch patterns, to enhance error handling and code safety.

Optional types in Zig are about more than just convenience; they're part of Zig's broader philosophy of safety and reliability. By using them properly, we can prevent null pointer dereferences and write robust, predictable code. Let's explore how optional types work, how they interact with error handling, and how to use them effectively in larger projects.

What is the ?T type?

In Zig, an optional type (?T) is used to represent a value that might be present or might be null. This prevents the common issue in other languages where a variable can unexpectedly be null, leading to null pointer exceptions at runtime. Instead, Zig makes handling the potential absence of a value explicit, forcing you to acknowledge and handle it.

Here's a basic example:

```
const std = @import("std");

pub fn main() void {
    const maybeValue: ?i32 = 10;

    if (maybeValue) |value| {
        std.debug.print("The number is {}\n", .{value});
    } else {
        std.debug.print("No number available.\n", .{});
```

```
        }
    }
```

Let's break down this example:

- `maybeValue` is an optional `i32`, meaning it could hold a number or be null
- We explicitly check for null before attempting to access the value using the `.?` operator

This ensures that we never dereference a null value, avoiding a common cause of bugs in languages that allow null values without explicit checks.

So far, we've explored how to handle a single optional value in Zig. But what happens when you have multiple optional variables and you want to perform an operation only if all of them contain valid values? In real-world programming, this situation is quite common. For instance, you might need to compute a result based on several inputs, any of which could be absent or invalid.

Zig provides a straightforward way to handle this scenario using the logical and operator with optionals. This allows you to check multiple optionals simultaneously and proceed only if none of them are null.

Let's look at an example to see how this works in practice:

```
var maybeX: ?i32 = 10;
var maybeY: ?i32 = null;
if (maybeX and maybeY) |x, y| {
    const sum = x + y;
    std.debug.print("Sum: {}\n", .{sum});
} else {
    std.debug.print("Cannot compute sum; one of the values is null.\n",
.{});
}
```

The key takeaways are as follows:

- **Simultaneous null checks**: Using if (maybeX and maybeY) allows you to check multiple optionals at once, simplifying your code and making it more readable.
- **Safe unwrapping**: When the condition is true, Zig safely unwraps both optionals and assigns their values to the variables x and y.
- **Efficient control flow**: This pattern ensures that you only perform operations (such as calculating a sum) when all the necessary data is available, preventing potential errors from attempting to use null values.

Optional types aren't just a convenience—they enforce safety in your code. By making null an explicit type, Zig prevents the kinds of bugs you see in languages where null values can sneak in unnoticed. Here's why they're important for safety:

- **No more null pointer dereferencing**: Optional types force you to check for null before accessing the value, meaning you'll never accidentally dereference a null pointer. This drastically reduces the risk of runtime crashes in large code bases.

- **Clearer intent**: When you declare a variable as ?T, it's clear to anyone reading the code that this value might be absent. This improves code readability and maintainability.

- **Compile-time guarantees**: If you forget to handle the null case, Zig will throw a compile-time error, ensuring you address all possible states of the variable before your code runs.

When working on larger projects, here are some best practices for using optional types effectively:

- **Use orelse for defaults**: In situations where you want a fallback value when an optional is null, use the orelse operator to provide a default:

```
const defaultNumber = maybeNumber orelse 0;
std.debug.print("The number is {}\n", .{defaultNumber});
```

  This is useful in scenarios where you always want to guarantee a value is returned.

- **Handle null early**: It's often a good practice to handle null cases as early as possible, rather than propagating them through your code. This keeps your logic cleaner and reduces the chance of missing a null check further down the line.

- **Document optional usage**: In large code bases, it's crucial to document why a value is optional and what null represents. This helps other developers (or future you) understand the intent and the appropriate way to handle the optional value.

Embracing uncertainty in iteration

Just when you thought iterating couldn't get any more exciting, Zig introduces the concept of optionals into for loops, because who doesn't love the added thrill of not knowing whether your loop will gracefully handle each element or trip over a null value like an unsuspecting pedestrian on a sidewalk?

We'll explore how to combine the relentless repetition of for loops with the delightful uncertainty of optional types. After all, what's better than iterating over a collection of values? Iterating over a collection of values that might not even be there.

Here's how you might write such a loop:

```
const std = @import("std");

pub fn main() void {
    const items = [_]?i32{ 1, null, 3, null, 5 };
    var sum: i32 = 0;

    for (items) |item| {
        if (item) |value| {
            sum += value;
        } else {
            std.debug.print("Encountered a null value.\n", .{});
        }
    }

    std.debug.print("Sum of non-null values: {}\n", .{sum});
}
```

This pattern allows you to handle each element appropriately, whether it's a meaningful value or a void of nothingness.

Remember, programming isn't about eliminating uncertainty—it's about managing it with style. So, embrace the optional, loop with caution, and may your nulls be ever in your favor.

In Zig, optional types are much more than a way to handle missing values—they're a key part of writing safe, reliable code. By forcing developers to handle the absence of a value explicitly, optional types prevent common bugs and improve the clarity of your code. When combined with Zig's error-handling features, you have a powerful toolkit for building robust applications that are less prone to failure.

Labeled switches: When a regular switch just isn't enough

You're already familiar with switch statements and how they elegantly allow your code to make decisions. But what happens when you need to switch things up (pun intended) and give your code more flexibility in managing states? Enter **labeled switches**. This feature cranks up the power of your switch statements by letting them do something extra: they can now be labeled, and you can jump around them using continue as you would in loops. Think of it as a switch with an attitude—no more backtracking through boring loops when you can just jump straight to the next state!

Imagine you're in charge of managing a traffic light system—an everyday scenario that cycles through red, yellow, green, and pedestrian crossing states. A labeled switch is perfect for this, as it allows us to cleanly jump between these states without the need for complex logic or extra loops.

Figure 4.4 – From red to green: labeled switches guide you through state sequences

Let's see how we can implement this using a labeled switch:

```
const std = @import("std");

pub fn main() void {
    light: switch (@as(u8, 1)) {
        1 => {
```

```
            std.debug.print("Light is Red. Cars stop.\n", .{});
            continue :light 2;  // Transition to Yellow
        },
        2 => {
            std.debug.print("Light is Yellow. Prepare to stop.\n", .{});
            continue :light 3;  // Transition to Green
        },
        3 => {
            std.debug.print("Light is Green. Cars go.\n", .{});
            continue :light 4;  // Transition to Pedestrian Crossing
        },
        4 => {
            std.debug.print("Pedestrian crossing activated. Cars stop,
people walk.\n", .{});
            return;  // End of cycle
        },
    }
}
```

This labeled switch represents a simple traffic light system with a clear transition between states:

- **State 1 (red light):** Cars stop. We then continue :light 2 to transition to yellow.

- **State 2 (yellow light):** Drivers are warned to prepare for a stop, and the light transitions to green with continue :light 3.

- **State 3 (green light):** Cars go. After a bit, we move to the pedestrian crossing using continue :light 4.

- **State 4 (pedestrian crossing):** Cars stop, and pedestrians cross the road. The cycle ends with return.

The labeled `switch` simplifies state transitions by making the flow explicit, without the need to manually track the state with variables. The code is more readable, and you prevent potential errors caused by complex loops or conditions.

Figure 4.5 – No hidden state variables: the vending machine's transparent transition logic

Let's take another scenario—a vending machine. This machine accepts money, allows the user to select a drink, and then dispenses it. A labeled `switch` lets us model the vending machine's different states, handling transitions such as coin insertion, drink selection, and dispensing:

```
const std = @import("std");

pub fn main() void {
    vending: switch (@as(u8, 1)) {
        1 => {
            std.debug.print("Insert coins.\n", .{});
            continue :vending 2; // Move to state (coin inserted)
        },
        2 => {
            std.debug.print("Select a drink.\n", .{});
            continue :vending 3; // Move to state (drink selected)
        },
        3 => {
            std.debug.print("Dispensing drink. Enjoy!\n", .{});
```

```
                    return;  // End of transaction
            },
            4 => {
                    std.debug.print("Transaction canceled. Returning coins.\n",
    .{});

                    return;  // End of transaction
            },
        }
    }
```

This example models a vending machine's transaction flow:

- **State 1 (insert coins):** The machine prompts the user to insert coins, then transitions to state 2 with continue :vending 2

- **State 2 (select drink):** The user selects a drink, and the machine moves to state 3 with continue :vending 3

- **State 3 (dispense drink):** The drink is dispensed, and the process completes with return

- **State 4 (cancel transaction):** If the user cancels the transaction, the machine returns the coins and the process ends

Just like with the traffic light system, the labeled switch keeps things clean and straightforward. It eliminates the need for managing multiple variables or adding unnecessary loops, making state transitions much more readable and maintainable.

Finite state machine

If you've ever built a **Finite State Machine** (**FSM**) or worked with state transitions, this construct will feel like a dream. You can cleanly represent state transitions by simply saying continue :fsm new_state, giving your state machine an air of elegance and readability.

The beauty of the labeled switch lies in its simplicity and efficiency. It allows you to jump between states in a clean and controlled way, without manually tracking state variables or building complex loops. Whether you're managing a traffic light system, a vending machine, or more complex state machines, the labeled switch makes the code easy to read and maintain.

Here are a few reasons this construct shines:

- **State management:** It naturally fits scenarios where you have clearly defined states and transitions, such as traffic lights, vending machines, or even game states

- **Clarity:** By using continue :label, you remove the ambiguity of where the code will flow next, making it clear what the next state is

- **Performance:** By making jumps between states explicit, Zig's compiler can optimize these transitions, improving performance, particularly in hot loops or state machines

Now, how does this differ from the *good ol'* switch-inside-a-loop approach? Let's take a look:

```zig
const std = @import("std");

pub fn main() void {
    var op: u8 = 1;

    while (true) {
        switch (op) {
            1 => {
                op = 2;
                continue;
            },
            2 => {
                op = 3;
                continue;
            },
            3 => {
                std.debug.print("Operation completed successfully.\n",
.{});

                return;
            },
            4 => {
                std.debug.print("Operation 4 encountered.\n", .{});
                // Perform some action for operation 4
                break;
            },
            else => {
                std.debug.print("Unknown operation.\n", .{});
                break;
```

```
            },
        }
    }

    std.debug.print("Exiting the loop.\n", .{});
}
```

See the difference? This version does the same thing, but it's more verbose and forces you to manage the state (op), the loop, and the switch expression all at once. The labeled switch cuts out the noise and provides a direct way to handle state transitions without the extra complexity.

So, you might be wondering, why all this fuss about a labeled switch? Well, apart from making your code look cleaner, there's also a performance boost lurking under the hood. You see, when Zig's compiler lowers this construct into machine code, it takes advantage of how CPUs predict branches (i.e., what's coming next in your switch statement).

If the operand to the continue is known at compile time, Zig translates it into a direct, unconditional jump to the correct case. This is incredibly fast because CPUs love these perfectly predictable branches.

If the operand is only known at runtime, Zig still has tricks up its sleeve. Each continue can generate a distinct conditional branch, allowing the CPU's branch predictor to track and optimize how often different branches get hit. So, if case 1 is usually followed by case 2, the CPU can learn this pattern, making the execution faster as it predicts future branches more accurately.

In addition to continuing around, you can also break out of a labeled switch, just like you would in loops. This terminates the evaluation of the switch expression and returns the specified value. It's just like a labeled block, so if you're thinking "Hmm, this feels familiar," you're not wrong. It's yet another tool in your box to keep the control flow efficient and clean.

We could point to three main candidates for labeled switches:

- Handling state transitions becomes a breeze with labeled switches. No more managing external state variables—just jump to the next state directly.

- When you're dealing with a dispatcher or interpreter that selects actions based on incoming data, labeled switches can speed up the flow by eliminating the need for loops.

- If your decision logic involves multiple levels of switching based on different inputs, labeled switches can simplify your flow and improve readability, while potentially giving you a performance boost.

In short, labeled switches are like your regular `switch` statements, but with superpowers. They allow cleaner control over state transitions, especially in situations where performance matters and readability is key. And while they might feel like a fancy new toy, the reality is they provide real-world benefits in both clarity and speed—especially when it comes to branch prediction and CPU performance in critical loops.

So, the next time you're building a state machine or managing instruction dispatch, ask yourself: "Would a labeled `switch` make my life easier?" Chances are that the answer is yes.

Summary

Look at you, conquering loops, conditionals, and `switch` statements like a true digital overlord! You've learned how to make decisions, repeat actions, and handle life's (and code's) uncertainties with the power of optional types. Whether you're directing program flow or managing complex logic, you've now got the tools to ensure your code obeys your every command.

But let's be honest—while control flow is essential, it can only take you so far before you find yourself repeating the same code over and over. And that's a big no-no in the world of programming. Fear not, because in the next chapter, we're taking it to the next level with functions!

So, take a deep breath, crack your knuckles, and get ready to build even more powerful programs. Functions await!

Testing your knowledge

1. What is the primary purpose of an `if` statement in Zig?

   a. To execute code repeatedly until a condition is met

   b. To make decisions based on conditions and execute code accordingly

   c. To iterate over collections

   d. To handle errors and exceptions

   Answer: b

2. In Zig, what is a key difference between the `switch` statement and multiple `if-else` statements?

    a. `switch` statements are not exhaustive, while `if-else` statements are

    b. `switch` statements allow fallthrough by default

    c. `switch` statements require you to handle all possible cases exhaustively

    d. `if-else` statements can only compare equality, while `switch` can compare ranges

Answer: c

3. How do you iterate over an `items` array in Zig using a `for` loop?

    a. `for i in items { ... }`

    b. `for (items) |item| { ... }`

    c. `foreach item in items { ... }`

    d. `while (items) { ... }`

Answer: b

4. What will be the output of the following Zig code?

```
const std = @import("std");

pub fn main() void {
    const number = 7;
    if (number > 10) {
        std.debug.print("Greater than 10\n", .{});
    } else if (number > 5) {
        std.debug.print("Between 6 and 10\n", .{});
    } else {
        std.debug.print("5 or less\n", .{});
    }
}
```

    a. `"Greater than 10"`

    b. `"Between 6 and 10"`

    c. `"5 or less"`

    d. No output

Answer: b

5. In Zig, how do you declare an optional integer that might be null?

   a. `var maybeNumber: int = null;`

   b. `var maybeNumber: ?i32 = null;`

   c. `var maybeNumber: optional i32 = null;`

   d. `var maybeNumber: i32? = null;`

   Answer: b

6. Which keyword allows a `while` loop in Zig to execute an expression at the end of each iteration?

   a. `break`

   b. `continue`

   c. `else`

   d. : (expression)

   Answer: d

7. What does the following Zig code demonstrate?

   ```
   const result = if (a != b) 47 else 3089;
   ```

   a. Using `if` as a statement

   b. Using `if` as an expression that returns a value

   c. A syntax error in Zig

   d. Declaring a variable inside an `if` condition

   Answer: b

8. In Zig's `for` loop, how can you access both the value and the index when iterating over an array?

   a. `for (items) |index, value| { ... }`

   b. `for (items) |value| { ... }` and use a separate counter

   c. `for (items) |value, index| { ... }`

   d. You cannot access the index in a `for` loop

   Answer: c

9. What is the purpose of the `else` clause in a Zig `for` loop?

   a. To execute code if the loop completes all iterations without a break

   b. To execute code when the loop body doesn't execute at all

   c. To handle errors within the loop

   d. To provide a default case for unmatched conditions

   Answer: b

10. How does Zig enforce safety with its `switch` statements?

    a. By allowing fallthrough between cases

    b. By requiring a default case

    c. By enforcing exhaustiveness, ensuring all possible cases are handled

    d. By limiting the number of cases to three

    Answer: c

Join us on Discord!

Read this book alongside other users, developers, experts, and the author himself.

Ask questions, provide solutions to other readers, chat with the authors via Ask Me Anything sessions, and much more. Scan the QR or visit the link to join the community.

`https://packt.link/deep-engineering-systemsengineering`

5

Functions for the Efficient Programmer

Are you tired of writing the same code over and over again? Do you enjoy the thrill of debugging the same logic scattered across multiple places in your code base? If so, this chapter might just change your mind. Welcome to the world of functions in Zig—a realm where you can package repetitive code into reusable, elegant units, making your programs more efficient and your life a tad less chaotic.

In this chapter, we'll embark on a journey through the intricacies of functions. You'll learn how to declare and define them, turning messy blocks of code into organized, callable units. We'll delve into passing parameters and handling return values, so you can make your functions as dynamic or straightforward as you need them to be.

We'll explore advanced features such as defer, which lets you clean up resources gracefully. Along the way, we'll discuss how blocks play a role in managing scope and how to avoid common pitfalls such as variable shadowing.

By the end of this chapter, you'll be able to do the following:

- Define and call your own functions in Zig, transforming repetitive code into reusable components
- Manage scope using blocks, ensuring your variables don't wander off where they shouldn't
- Pass parameters and handle return values effectively, making your functions flexible and powerful
- Utilize features such as defer for resource management

So, gear up and get ready to elevate your Zig programming skills. Who knows? You might even start to enjoy writing functions—or at least appreciate the sanity they bring to your code base.

Technical requirements

All the code shown in this chapter can be found in the Chapter05 directory of our GitHub repository: https://github.com/PacktPublishing/Learning-Zig/tree/main/Chapter05.

Blocks – keeping your variables on a tight leash

In Zig, blocks are used to limit the scope of variable declarations.

Think of them as little cages that keep your variables from running wild across your entire program.

Figure 5.1 – The cage prevents escape: scope isolation through explicit blocks

Here's a simple example:

```
pub fn main() void {
{
    var x: i32 = 1;
    x += 1;
}
// Trying to access x here will result in an error
// x += 1; // Error: x is undefined here
}
```

Inside the inner { ... } block, we declare a variable, x. Once we exit that block, x ceases to exist. Trying to use x outside its scope is like trying to use a library card after it's been deactivated—not gonna happen.

Blocks in Zig aren't just for scoping; they can also act as expressions, meaning they can produce a value, as we can see in the following snippet:

```
const std = @import("std");

pub fn main() void {
    const result = blk: {
        const a = 10;
        const b = 20;
        break :blk a + b; // The block evaluates to this expression
    };

    std.debug.print("result: {}\n", .{result});
}
```

In this example, we use a labeled block, blk, to perform a computation and return its value using the break statement. The block is labeled blk, which allows us to use break :blk to exit the block and provide the value a + b (which evaluates to 30) as the result:

- Inside the block, two constants, a and b, are defined with the values 10 and 20, respectively
- The expression a + b evaluates to 30, and the break :blk a + b statement exits the block and returns 30 as the result of the block
- The block itself acts as an expression that can return a value, which is then assigned to the result variable
- Finally, std.debug.print is used to print the result, which is 30

This is a clean way to encapsulate logic within a block, perform a calculation, and return a result from the block. It's like cooking something in a kitchen: the block hides the intermediate steps (a and b), but in the end, it serves the final product (result), which is all that matters outside the block.

Shadowing — Zig doesn't play that game

In some languages, you can redeclare a variable with the same name in an inner scope, effectively "shadowing" the outer one. Zig doesn't allow this. It wants you to be original with your variable names, or at least consistent.

Figure 5.2 – The cape casts a shadow, but your variables can't: Zig's anti-shadowing stance

Take the following snippet:

```
pub fn main() void {
    const pi = 3.14;
    {
        // var pi: i32 = 1234;
        // Error: cannot redeclare 'pi'
    }
}
```

Zig throws an error here because you're trying to declare pi again in an inner scope. It helps keep your code unambiguous—unlike some of your variable naming conventions.

If you must use the same name—and I strongly advise against it—you can do so in entirely separate scopes:

```
const std = @import("std");
pub fn main() void {
    {
        const value = 42;
        std.debug.print("value: {}\n", .{value});
    }
```

```
    {
        const value: bool = true;
        std.debug.print("value: {}\n", .{value});
    }
}
```

Here, value is declared in two different scopes, and Zig is okay with it because their lifetimes don't overlap. But seriously, consider better variable names to prevent confusion.

Empty blocks

An empty block, {}, in Zig is equivalent to void{} and evaluates to void:

```
pub fn main() void {
    const a = {};      // a is of type void
    const b = void{};  // b is also of type void
    // a and b are the same
    // Not much to do here, but now you know
}
```

Not that you'd have much use for an empty block, but it's good to know—just like knowing how to fold a fitted sheet.

It's time to elevate our code using real functions.

Functions

Now that we've covered blocks and scope, let's talk about functions. Think of functions as named blocks that can take input (parameters) and produce output (return values). They allow you to encapsulate logic and reuse code without copying and pasting like it's 1999.

Here's how you define a simple function in Zig:

```
fn add(a: i32, b: i32) i32 {
    return a + b;
}
```

This add function takes two i32 parameters and returns their sum. It's a block of code that you can call whenever you need to add two numbers, saving you from rewriting a + b every time—as exhilarating as that might be.

Parameters — accepting inputs

Function parameters are the inputs your function needs to perform its task. In Zig, parameters are immutable by default. This means you can't modify them inside the function unless you explicitly make a copy. It keeps your functions pure and your intentions clear.

Figure 5.3 – The entry point enforces the rule: what comes in stays constant

Primitive types such as integers and floats are passed by value. The function gets its own copy of the data.

Consider the following code:

```
fn increment(n: i32) i32 {
    // n += 1; // Error: cannot assign to constant
    var result = n + 1;
    return result;
}
```

Trying to modify n directly results in an error because n is immutable. Instead, we create a new variable, result, to hold the modified value.

For complex types such as arrays and—you guessed it—**structs**, Zig may pass them by value or by reference, depending on what's more efficient. You don't have to worry about it; Zig handles the details.

> **Note**
>
> If you're wondering what a struct is, don't panic. We'll cover structs in detail in
> *Chapter 7, Organizing Data*. For now, just think of a struct as a way to group related
> data together.

Continuing our exploration, let's take this snippet as an example:

```
const Point = struct {
    x: i32,
    y: i32,
};

fn translate(p: Point, dx: i32, dy: i32) Point {
    return Point{ .x = p.x + dx, .y = p.y + dy };
}
```

We take a `Point`, offset its coordinates, and return a new `Point`. The original p remains unchanged, adhering to Zig's preference for immutability unless you explicitly decide otherwise.

Return values – sending outputs back to the caller

Functions can return values to the caller. You specify the return type after the parameter list. If your function doesn't return anything, you can omit the return type or specify void:

```
fn greet() void {
    const std = @import("std");
    std.debug.print("Hello, world!\n", .{});
}
```

Figure 5.4 – The return statement marks the way out: data flows back to the caller

To return a value, use the `return` keyword followed by the value you wish to return:

```
fn multiply(a: i32, b: i32) i32 {
    return a * b;
}
```

Sometimes, you need to exit a function before reaching the end. Maybe there's invalid input, or perhaps you've achieved your goal sooner than expected.

Let's take a function that makes divisions:

```
fn divide(a: i32, b: i32) ?i32 {
    if (b == 0) {
        return null; // Cannot divide by zero
    }
    return a / b;
}
```

In this function, we check whether b is 0. If it is, we return null to indicate an invalid operation. Otherwise, we proceed with the division.

Let's see how you might use these functions in a main function:

```
pub fn main() void {
    const sum = add(5, 7);            // sum is 12
    const incremented = increment(10); // incremented is 11

    // Using Point and translate (don't worry if you're not familiar with
    structs yet)
    const point = Point{ .x = 3, .y = 4 };
    const moved_point = translate(point, 5, -2);
    // moved_point is { x = 8, y = 2 }

    greet(); // Prints "Hello, world!"

    const product = multiply(6, 7);    // product is 42

    const division_result = divide(10, 2);
    if (division_result) |result| {
        // result is 5
        // Do something with result
```

```
    } else {
        // Handle division by zero
        // Maybe print an error message
    }
}
```

In this main function, we call the functions we've defined earlier and use their results. Notice how we handle the optional return from divide using an if statement.

Functions in Zig can be assigned to variables, passed as parameters, and returned from other functions. They're first-class citizens, just like in any modern programming language worth its salt.

In the following snippet, we're passing functions around:

```
const MathOp = fn (a: i32, b: i32) i32;

fn applyOperation(op: MathOp, a: i32, b: i32) i32 {
    return op(a, b);
}

fn subtract(a: i32, b: i32) i32 {
    return a - b;
}

pub fn main() void {
    const sum = applyOperation(add, 5, 3);      // sum is 8
    const difference = applyOperation(subtract, 5, 3); // difference is 2
    std.debug.print("sum: {}, difference: {}\n", .{sum, difference});
}
```

Here, applyOperation takes a function, op, as a parameter and applies it to a and b. It's like giving your function a function—*function-ception*, if you will.

Functions are essential tools in your Zig programming arsenal. They help you encapsulate logic, promote code reuse, and keep your code base organized. By understanding how parameters and return values work, you can write functions that are both efficient and easy to understand.

Remember the following:

- Parameters are immutable by default. If you need to modify them, create new variables.

- Zig prevents variable shadowing. This keeps your code clear and reduces the chance of errors.

- Functions can be used as values. Pass them around as needed to create flexible and reusable code.

Now, go forth and write functions that not only work but also make you look like you know what you're doing, or at least know better than the person who copies and pastes code from the internet without understanding it.

Now that you're comfortable with the basics of functions in Zig, let's explore some of the more advanced features that can make your code cleaner and more robust. Specifically, we'll look at the unreachable statement and the defer statement. Don't worry—we'll keep it straightforward.

The unreachable statement — asserting the impossible

Have you ever been absolutely certain that a piece of code should never be executed? In Zig, you can assert this certainty using the unreachable statement. It's like telling the compiler, "If we ever get here, something has gone horribly wrong."

Figure 5.5 – Code that should never execute: the zombie apocalypse of your program

In **Debug** and **ReleaseSafe** modes, reaching an unreachable statement will cause the program to panic with the message "reached unreachable code." In **ReleaseFast** and **ReleaseSmall** modes, the compiler assumes that unreachable code paths are impossible and may optimize accordingly.

Here's a basic example:

```
pub fn main() void {
    const x = 1;
    const y = 2;
    if (x + y != 3) {
        unreachable; // We assert that this code should never be reached
    }
    // Continue with the rest of the program
}
```

In this code, we check that x + y does not equal 3. Since 1 + 2 is always 3, the condition is false, and unreachable is never executed. If, for some bizarre reason, x + y isn't 3, the program will panic in debug modes, alerting you to the impossible.

The unreachable statement is especially useful when you're certain that a particular code path can't happen, but the compiler isn't smart enough to know that.

For example, consider this function:

```
fn safeDivide(a: i32, b: i32) i32 {
    if (b != 0) {
        return a / b;
    } else {
        unreachable; // We should never have b == 0 here
    }
}
```

Wait a minute—you might be thinking, "But b could be zero!" Yes, it could, but perhaps in your application's logic, you've ensured elsewhere that b can never be 0 before calling safeDivide. By using unreachable, you're asserting that reaching this point is impossible.

The unreachable statement has the noreturn type, just like break, continue, and return. This means you can use unreachable in expressions where a value is expected, and the compiler will accept it because noreturn is compatible with all types.

Here's an example:

```
fn getNumber(code: u8) u8 {
    return switch (code) {
        1 => 42,
        2 => 84,
        else => unreachable,
    };
}

pub fn main() void {
    const num = getNumber(1); // num is 42
    // If code is not 1 or 2, the program panics at unreachable
}
```

In this code, we have the following:

- The `switch` expression expects to return a u8
- For the `else` case, we use `unreachable` because we believe code can only be 1 or 2
- Since `unreachable` has the `noreturn` type, which is compatible with u8, the compiler is happy

While unreachable is a powerful tool, misuse can lead to undefined behavior, especially in **ReleaseFast** and **ReleaseSmall** modes, where the compiler optimizations assume `unreachable` code paths can't happen.

If there's any possibility that the `unreachable` statement might be executed, and it does get executed, the behavior of your program is undefined in optimized builds. So, use it wisely and only when you're absolutely certain.

The standard library's assert function is implemented using `unreachable` (https://github.com/ziglang/zig/blob/ea527f7a850f0200681630d8f36131eca31ef48b/lib/std/debug.zig#L404). Here's the code:

```
pub fn assert(ok: bool) void {
    if (!ok) unreachable;
}
```

Let's use `assert` in the following code:

```
pub fn main() void {
    assert(2 + 2 == 4); // This is fine
    assert(2 + 2 == 5); // This will cause a panic in debug modes
}
```

By using `unreachable`, the `assert` function ensures that if the condition is false, the program will halt, helping you catch bugs during development.

Fortunately, not every decision should be made immediately; we can postpone parts of the function execution using `defer`.

Deferring decisions

Ever wished you could set a reminder to clean up later? In Zig, the `defer` statement lets you schedule code to run when the current scope exits, regardless of how it exits. It's like telling yourself, "I'll deal with that when I'm done here."

Figure 5.6 – The reminder pile: defer creates a stack of tasks to handle on exit

Here's a simple example:

```
pub fn main() void {
    {
        var resource = acquireResource();
        defer releaseResource(resource);

        // Use the resource
        doSomethingWithResource(resource);
```

```
        // No matter how we exit this block, releaseResource will be
    called
        }
    // At this point, resource has been released
    }
```

In this code, `releaseResource(resource)` is guaranteed to run when we exit the inner block, even if we exit early. This ensures that resources are properly cleaned up, preventing leaks and other issues.

Suppose you're working with a file:

```
fn readFileContents(filename: []const u8) void {
    const file = openFile(filename);
    defer closeFile(file);

    // Read from the file
    const contents = readAll(file);
    // Do something with contents
}
```

In this example, `closeFile(file);` is deferred until the function exits, ensuring the file is always closed, even if an error occurs or you return early.

If you have multiple `defer` statements, they execute in reverse order of their appearance:

```
pub fn main() void {
    defer std.debug.print("First defer\n", .{});
    defer std.debug.print("Second defer\n", .{});
    std.debug.print("In main function\n", .{});
}
```

This code outputs the following:

```
In main function
Second defer
First defer
```

Think of it as stacking dishes: the last one you put on the stack is the first one you take off.

Before we wrap up, let's touch on the export keyword. If you want a function to be visible outside of your Zig module—say, to be called from another language or linked into a shared library—you use the export keyword:

```
export fn add(a: i32, b: i32) i32 {
    return a + b;
}
```

By marking add as export, you're telling Zig to make this function available for external linkage. This is a more advanced topic, and we'll delve deeper into it later. For now, just know that export is your way of saying, "Hey, world! Look at this function!"

Summary

In this chapter, we delved into the world of functions in Zig. You learned how to define and call functions, manage scope with blocks, handle parameters, and return values. We discussed the immutability of function parameters and how Zig prevents variable shadowing to keep your code clear and bug-free-*ish*.

We also explored some features:

- unreachable: Helps you assert that certain code should never be executed, aiding in catching impossible scenarios and optimizing your code
- defer: Lets you schedule code to run when a scope exits, ensuring resources are cleaned up properly

Understanding these concepts enables you to write more efficient, maintainable, and robust code. Functions help you encapsulate logic and adhere to the **Don't Repeat Yourself (DRY)** principle, making your code base more organized.

In the next chapter, we'll focus on testing our code. Now that you can write functions, it's crucial to ensure they work as intended. This is the next natural step in our Zig journey, helping you build reliable software and gain confidence in your code's quality.

Lock it in

Question 1: What is the primary purpose of using functions in programming?

    a.   To make code longer and more complex

    b.   To encapsulate reusable logic and prevent repetition

    c.   To confuse other programmers

    d.   To slow down the execution of a program

Question 2: In Zig, what is the default behavior of function parameters regarding mutability?

    a.   They are mutable and can be changed within the function

    b.   They are immutable unless explicitly made mutable

    c.   They are mutable but cannot be reassigned

    d.   They cannot be used within the function

Question 3: Which keyword in Zig is used to schedule code to run when the current scope exits?

    a.   `break`

    b.   `continue`

    c.   `defer`

    d.   `return`

Question 4: What does the noreturn type signify in Zig?

    a.   A function that returns an integer

    b.   A function that returns no value (void)

    c.   Code paths that do not return control normally

    d.   A deprecated feature in Zig

Question 5: Which of the following statements about the unreachable keyword is true?

    a.   It allows variable shadowing in inner scopes

    b.   It asserts that a particular code path should never be executed

    c.   It makes a function accessible outside the module

    d.   It is used to declare a loop that runs infinitely

Question 6: In Zig, variables declared inside a block, {}, are accessible outside that block. (True or False?)

Question 7: The `defer` statements in Zig execute in the order they are declared when the scope exits. (True or False?)

Question 8: The `export` keyword is used to make a function available for external linkage. (True or False?)

Question 9: Zig allows you to redeclare a variable with the same name in an overlapping scope. (True or False?)

Question 10: The `noreturn` type is only compatible with functions that return `void`. (True or False?)

Question 11: Explain why Zig does not allow variable shadowing in overlapping scopes.

Question 12: Describe a scenario where using the `defer` statement would be beneficial.

Question 13: How does the `noreturn` type help in writing functions that may not return a value?

Question 14: What happens when the `unreachable` statement is executed in debug mode?

Question 15: Why is it important to understand the immutability of function parameters in Zig?

Question 16: Given the following code, identify any errors and explain how to fix them:

```
pub fn main() void {
    const pi = 3.14;
    {
        var pi: i32 = 1234;
        // Do something with pi
    }
}
```

Question 17: What will be the output of the following code snippet?

```
pub fn main() void {
    defer std.debug.print("First defer\n", .{});
    defer std.debug.print("Second defer\n", .{});
    std.debug.print("In main function\n", .{});
}
```

Question 18: Is it possible to modify a function parameter directly within the function? Provide a code example to support your answer.

Answers

Question 1: b

Question 2: b

Question 3: c

Question 4: c

Question 5: b

Question 6: False

Question 7: False

Question 8: True

Question 9: False

Question 10: False

Question 11: Zig prevents variable shadowing to avoid ambiguity and potential bugs that arise from using the same name for different variables in overlapping scopes. This ensures that each identifier refers to one specific variable within its scope.

Question 12: Using defer is beneficial when you need to ensure that resources are properly released or cleaned up when a scope exits, such as closing a file or releasing memory, even if the function exits early due to an error or return statement.

Question 13: The noreturn type allows functions that do not return normally to be used in expressions that expect a value. It indicates to the compiler that the code path will not continue past that point, enabling type compatibility and control flow analysis.

Question 14: In **debug** mode, executing unreachable causes the program to panic with the message "reached unreachable code," helping developers catch logical errors where supposedly impossible code paths are actually reached.

Question 15: Understanding the immutability of function parameters is important because it ensures that functions do not have unintended side effects by modifying input data, leading to more predictable and maintainable code.

Question 16: Error: The `pi` variable is redeclared in an overlapping scope, which Zig does not allow. To fix it, use a different variable name.

```
pub fn main() void {
    const pi = 3.14;
    {
        var radius: i32 = 1234;
        // Do something with radius
    }
}
```

Question 17: The output will be as follows:

```
In main function
Second defer
First defer
```

Question 18: No, you cannot modify a function parameter directly because parameters are immutable by default. To modify the value, you need to create a new variable:

```
fn increment(n: i32) i32 {
    var result = n + 1;
    return result;
}
```

Unlock this book's exclusive benefits now

UNLOCK NOW

Scan this QR code or go to `https://packtpub.com/unlock`, then search this book by name.

Note: Keep your purchase invoice ready before you start.

6

Error Handling

Errors happen. It's a fact of life (and coding). But fear not, dear Zig learner, because Zig has your back. This chapter explores one of Zig's central themes: error handling, which makes you wonder why other languages haven't caught on yet. Prepare to be amazed (and maybe slightly annoyed) by Zig's confident way of saying, "I told you so."

In this chapter, we're going to cover the following topics:

- Zig's error handling philosophy
- Unions
- Errors: Turning failures into manageable events
- Error return traces: Breadcrumbs for when it all goes wrong

Picture this: you're deep in a coding session, everything is smooth until... BAM! Errors start popping up. Errors are like uninvited guests who disrupt the harmony of your program. In Zig, errors aren't interruptions; they're an integral part of the language, designed to make your code more resilient.

Technical requirements

All the code shown in this chapter can be found in the Chapter06 directory of our Git repository: https://github.com/PacktPublishing/Learning-Zig/tree/main/Chapter06.

Zig's error handling philosophy

In most programming languages, errors are like unwanted guests—they crash your program's flow without any warning. You throw out an exception or slip in a generic error code and hope someone remembers to clean up the mess. But in Zig, there's no hiding behind exceptions or secret signals. Errors are fully integrated into the type system, right there in the function signature, practically shouting, "Handle me!" It's all about transparency, which means errors get a seat at the table as first-class citizens.

Figure 6.1 – Contemplating the inevitable: Zig makes error handling unavoidable

In Zig, if a function might fail, it's required to return an error value. No "maybe it'll work, maybe it'll fail" ambiguity—Zig makes sure you know exactly what you're getting into by forcing errors to be part of the return type. This way, every potential error is unavoidable, front and center, in the function's return type. It's Zig's way of saying, "Pretending errors don't exist? Not on my watch."

What's an error value?

In Zig, errors aren't some mystical forces of chaos. They're values—literal, concrete, right-in-your-face values. This means that if you write a function that can fail, it must declare an explicit error type in its return signature. Not doing so is like throwing a party without checking if the venue is booked; Zig won't let you get away with it.

Before we plunge into the exhilarating abyss of error handling in Zig, it's imperative—some might say merciful—to acquaint ourselves with a few foundational concepts: enums, union types, and tagged unions. Now, I know what you're thinking: "Enums? Tagged what now?" Bear with me. These aren't arcane spells from a wizard's tome; they're just tools to help you write code that's slightly less catastrophic. We'll take it step by step, demystifying each term along the way. When we're done, you'll understand these concepts and appreciate them—or at least tolerate them enough to make your error handling journey a bit smoother.

Enums: When you're tired of magic numbers ruining your day

Let's face it: scattering magic numbers throughout your code base is a fantastic way to ensure your future self hates you. Enter enums—the programming construct that lets you assign human-readable names to sets of related values. Zig, in its infinite wisdom, provides enums to save you from your own bad habits.

Creating an enum in Zig is about as straightforward as it gets, assuming you can manage to list items without causing a syntax error. Here's how you can declare an enum representing the days of the week:

```
const Day = enum {
    Monday,
    Tuesday,
    Wednesday,
    Thursday,
    Friday,
    Saturday,
    Sunday,
};
```

Well done. You've just created an enum called Day that represents the days of the week.

To use your newly minted enum, you can assign values to variables. For example, let's check if today is Wednesday (try to contain your excitement):

```
const std = @import("std");

pub fn main() void {
    const today = Day.Wednesday;
    if (today == Day.Wednesday) {
```

```
        std.debug.print("Guess what? It's hump day!\n", .{});
    }
}
```

Under the hood, enums in Zig have integer representations starting from zero. If you must know the integer value—perhaps for nostalgia—you can retrieve it using the built-in @intFromEnum function. Here's how you can print the integer value of a day:

```
const std = @import("std");

pub fn main() void {
    const today = Day.Wednesday;
    const dayNumber = @intFromEnum(today);
    std.debug.print("It's day number {d} of the week.\n", .{dayNumber});
}
```

This will inform you that Wednesday is day number 2.

If you enjoy creating puzzles for others (or yourself) to solve, you can assign custom integer values to your enum members. For instance, let's define HTTP status codes:

```
const HttpStatus = enum(i32) {
    OK = 200,
    NotFound = 404,
    InternalServerError = 500,
};
```

Now, when someone reads your code, they don't need to remember that HttpStatus.OK is actually 200. Very considerate. Here's how you might use it:

```
const std = @import("std");

pub fn main() void {
    const status = HttpStatus.NotFound;
    const code = @intFromEnum(status);
    std.debug.print("HTTP Status Code: {d}\n", .{code});
}
```

Believe it or not, enums in Zig can have methods. Yes, methods on enums—because apparently, that's a thing now. Let's define a traffic light enum with a method:

```
const std = @import("std");

const TrafficLight = enum {
    Red,
    Yellow,
    Green,

    pub fn isSafeToGo(self: TrafficLight) bool {
        return self == TrafficLight.Green;
    }
};
```

Now, you can call isSafeToGo on a TrafficLight value:

```
pub fn main() void {
    const light = TrafficLight.Red;
    if (light.isSafeToGo()) {
        std.debug.print("Go ahead.\n", .{});
    } else {
        std.debug.print("Stop right there!\n", .{});
    }
}
```

switch statements revisited: For when you need even more control flow

Enums and switch statements go together like bugs and software. Here's how you can use a switch statement with an enum:

```
const std = @import("std");

pub fn main() void {
    const day = Day.Friday;
    const message = switch (day) {
```

```
        Day.Monday => "Ugh, back to work.",
        Day.Friday => "TGIF!",
        Day.Saturday, Day.Sunday => "Weekend vibes.",
        else => "Just another day.",
    };
    std.debug.print("{s}\n", .{message});
}
```

This code will print "`TGIF!`" because apparently, people still say that.

Enum literals: Saving you a few microseconds of typing

If typing the enum type every time feels like too much effort, Zig offers enum literals. Here's how you can use them:

```
const std = @import("std");

pub fn main() void {
    const day: Day = .Saturday;
    if (day == .Saturday) {
        std.debug.print("Enjoy your weekend!\n", .{});
    }
}
```

Look at that—you've saved yourself from writing Day twice. Use that extra time wisely.

Note: Without explicitly setting the type, it became an enum literal. In this example, it became a Day member. In other words, while const `day: Day = .Saturday;` is a member of Day, `const anotherDay = .Friday;` is just an enum literal.

Non-exhaustive enums: Keep your options open

Sometimes, you might want to define an enum but allow for future expansion without breaking existing code. This is especially important in Zig because of how the compiler enforces exhaustiveness in `switch` statements. In Zig, when you use an exhaustive enum in a `switch` statement, the compiler requires you to handle every possible value. This is normally a great safety feature that prevents bugs. However, it creates a problem when you need to add new enum values later. Consider this scenario:

```
// Library code - version 1
const ErrorCode = enum {
```

```
    Success,
    Failure,
};


// Your application code
pub fn handleError(code: ErrorCode) void {
    switch (code) {
        .Success => std.debug.print("Operation succeeded.\n", .{}),
        .Failure => std.debug.print("Operation failed.\n", .{}),
    // No default case needed or allowed - Zig knows all cases are covered
    }
}


// Later, the library updates to version 2
const ErrorCode = enum {
    Success,
    Failure,
    NetworkTimeout, // New value added!
};
```

Now your application code will fail to compile! The switch statement is no longer exhaustive because it doesn't handle the new NetworkTimeout case.

Zig solves this problem with non-exhaustive enums by including a placeholder _ field and specifying a numeric tag type with room for growth:

```
const std = @import("std");


const ErrorCode = enum(u16) {
    Success = 0,
    Failure = 1,
    _, // This underscore is crucial - it tells Zig "more values may
exist"
};
```

When you declare an enum as non-exhaustive:

- You must specify a tag type (such as u16) that can hold more values than just those you've defined.

- The compiler knows that values beyond your explicit declarations might appear.

- You MUST include a catch-all case in switch statements.

Here's how you handle a non-exhaustive enum properly:

```
pub fn main() void {
    const code: ErrorCode = .Success;
    switch (code) {
        .Success => std.debug.print("Operation succeeded.\n", .{}),
        .Failure => std.debug.print("Operation failed.\n", .{}),
        _ => std.debug.print("Unknown error code.\n", .{}), // Required
for non-exhaustive enums!
    }
}
```

This ensures your code gracefully handles any unexpected enum values that might be added in future versions, making your applications more resilient and forward-compatible.

Introspection: When you want to play detective in your own code

Zig provides built-in functions such as @typeInfo and @tagName to let you inspect enums at runtime.

Figure 6.2 – Looking for clues: @typeInfo and @tagName reveal what your types contain

For example, here's how you can get the name of an enum value:

```
const std = @import("std");

pub fn main() void {
    const day = Day.Tuesday;
    const dayName = @tagName(day);
    std.debug.print("Today is {s}.\n", .{dayName});
}
```

This will print "Today is Tuesday." Because sometimes, you forget what day it is.

Enum type information: Dive deeper if you dare

If you have an insatiable need to dig into the details, you can use @typeInfo to explore your enum's structure. Here's how:

```
pub fn main() void {
    const info = @typeInfo(Day);
    const enumInfo = info.@"enum";

    std.debug.print("Enum tag type: {s}\n", .{@typeName(enumInfo.tag_
type)});
    inline for (enumInfo.fields) |field| {
        std.debug.print("Field: {s}\n", .{field.name});
    }
}
```

This will output the tag type and list all the enum fields. Useful for when you need to write code that adapts to the enum's structure—because hardcoding is so *passé*.

Now that we've bravely conquered enums and had a thrilling encounter with the exclamation mark !, it's time to wade into the murky waters of unions. Don't let the terminology scare you off; unions are just another tool in Zig's arsenal to make your code either more elegant or more convoluted depending on how you wield them. We'll take a leisurely stroll through unions, tagged unions, and see how they can be both a blessing and a curse. Soon, you might even find yourself using them intentionally.

Unions

A union in Zig is a type that can hold one of several specified types, but only one at a time. Think of it as a container that can change its shape to hold different kinds of data, but not simultaneously. This can be useful when you have a variable that might represent different kinds of data in different contexts.

Here's how you might define a union:

```
const Data = union {
    intValue: i32,
    floatValue: f64,
    textValue: []const u8,
};
```

In this union, Data can hold an i32, an f64, or a string slice ([]const u8), but only one of them at any given moment.

Let's see how you might use a union in a main function. Suppose you're writing a program that processes different kinds of input values:

```
const std = @import("std");

pub fn main() void {
    var inputData = Data{ .intValue = 42 };
    std.debug.print("Integer value: {d}\n", .{inputData.intValue});

    // Change the union to hold a float
    inputData = Data{ .floatValue = 3.14 };
    std.debug.print("Floating-point value: {d}\n", .{inputData.
floatValue});

    // Now change it to hold a string
    inputData = Data{ .textValue = "Hello, Zig!" };
    std.debug.print("Text value: {s}\n", .{inputData.textValue});
}
```

In this example, we start by assigning an integer value to inputData. We then reassign inputData to hold a floating-point number, and finally, we assign it a text value. Each time, we create a new instance of Data with the desired field initialized.

It's important to remember that a bare union can only have one active field at a time. If you try to access a field that isn't currently active, Zig will produce a runtime error.

```
const std = @import("std");

pub fn main() void {
    var data = Data{ .intValue = 100 };
    // Incorrectly trying to access an inactive field
    std.debug.print("Floating-point value: {d}\n", .{data.floatValue});
}
```

Running this code will result in a panic with a message such as `access of union field 'floatValue' while field 'intValue' is active`. To prevent this, always ensure you're only accessing the currently active field.

To change the active field of a union, you need to assign a new value to the union variable. Here's how you can do it:

```
data = Data{ .floatValue = 2.718 };
```

This reinitializes data with `floatValue` as the active field. Now you can safely access `data.floatValue`.

Unions are useful, but they don't keep track of which field is currently active. This is where tagged unions come in.

Tagged unions: Adding a tag for safety

A tagged union combines a union with an enum (the tag) that keeps track of which field is active. This adds a layer of safety, as you can check the tag before accessing the field.

Here's how you can define a tagged union:

```
const Result = union(enum) {
    Success: i32,
    Error: []const u8,
};
```

In this `Result` type, we have two possibilities: `Success` with an `i32` value or `Error` with an error message.

Let's use the `Result` type in a function that performs a calculation and might fail:

```zig
const std = @import("std");

fn calculate(input: i32) Result {
    if (input >= 0) {
        // Return Success with the calculated value
        return Result{ .Success = input * 2 };
    } else {
        // Return Error with an error message
        return Result{ .Error = "Input must be non-negative" };
    }
}

pub fn main() void {
    const res = calculate(-5);

    // Use a switch to handle each possible case
    switch (res) {
        .Success => |value| std.debug.print("Calculation result: {d}\n",
.{value}),
        .Error => |errMsg| std.debug.print("Error: {s}\n", .{errMsg}),
    }
}
```

In this example, calculate doubles the input if it's non-negative. If the input is negative, it returns Error. In main, we call `calculate(-5)` and handle the result using a `switch` statement. This ensures we correctly process both success and error cases.

Sometimes, you may need to modify the data inside a tagged union. You can do this by obtaining a mutable reference to the payload within a `switch` statement. Here's how:

```zig
pub fn main() void {
    var res = calculate(10);

    // Modify the payload if it's a Success
    switch (res) {
        .Success => |*value| value.* += 5, // Increment the value by 5
        .Error => |errMsg| std.debug.print("Error: {s}\n", .{errMsg}),
```

```
    }

    // Check the updated result
    switch (res) {
        .Success => |value| std.debug.print("Updated result: {d}\n",
    .{value}),
        .Error => |errMsg| std.debug.print("Error: {s}\n", .{errMsg}),
    }
}
```

In this code, we first call `calculate(10)`, which should succeed. In the `switch` statement, we use `|*value|` to get a mutable pointer to the payload, allowing us to modify it. We then print the updated result.

Just like structs and enums, unions in Zig can have methods. This can help encapsulate behavior related to the union.

Here's an example:

```
const std = @import("std");

const Response = union(enum) {
    Data: i32,
    Message: []const u8,

    pub fn isData(self: Response) bool {
        return @tagName(self) == "Data";
    }
};

pub fn main() void {
    const resp = Response{ .Data = 100 };

    if (resp.isData()) {
        std.debug.print("Received data: {d}\n", .{resp.Data});
    } else {
        std.debug.print("Received message: {s}\n", .{resp.Message});
    }
}
```

In this example, we define a Response union with a method called isData that checks if the active field is Data. In main, we use this method to decide how to handle resp.

Zig allows you to create union instances without explicitly specifying the type, using anonymous union literals. This can make your code more concise.

Here's how you can use them:

```
const std = @import("std");

const Number = union {
    intValue: i32,
    floatValue: f64,
};

pub fn main() void {
    // Create a Number with an integer value using an anonymous union
    Literal
    const num = .{ .intValue = 256 };
    std.debug.print("Integer number: {d}\n", .{num.intValue});

    // Create a Number with a float value
    const numFloat = .{ .floatValue = 1.618 };
    std.debug.print("Floating-point number: {f}\n", .{numFloat.
floatValue});
}
```

In this code, we create instances of Number without specifying the type, relying on Zig's type inference.

Unions in Zig provide a way to work with variables that can hold different types at different times. Unions offer flexibility but require careful handling to prevent accessing inactive fields. Tagged unions add safety by keeping track of the active field, making your code more robust.

As we continue our journey through Zig's type system, it's time to face the inevitable: **errors**.

Errors: Turning failures into manageable events

We'll explore how Zig treats errors as first-class citizens—integral parts of your code that you can manage gracefully. By understanding **error sets** and **error unions**, you'll gain the tools to handle failures elegantly, rather than pretending they don't exist.

Error sets: Enumerating the possible mishaps

In Zig, an error set is similar to an enum but specifically for errors. It allows you to define a set of possible errors that a function might return, making your code's behavior more predictable and easier to handle.

For example, let's define a simple error set for network operations:

```
const NetworkError = error{
    ConnectionLost,
    Timeout,
    InvalidResponse,
};
```

Here, `NetworkError` is an error set containing specific errors related to network communication. This way, you can specify exactly what might go wrong when dealing with network operations.

To see error sets in action, let's write a function that attempts to fetch data from a network resource and returns an error if it fails:

```
const std = @import("std");

fn fetchData(url: []const u8) ![]const u8 {
    // Placeholder logic for fetching data
    if (url.len == 0) {
        return error.InvalidResponse;
    }
    // Imagine successful data retrieval here
    return "Sample Data";
}
```

The `![]u8` return type indicates that `fetchData` may return an error from its error set or a byte array (`[]u8`) on success. By specifying the possible errors, you're making it clear to anyone using your function what could go wrong.

Handling errors with try and catch

To handle errors, Zig provides the `try` and `catch` expressions. The `try` keyword attempts to execute a function that might fail, and if it does, the error is returned from the current function.

Here's how you might use `fetchData`:

```
pub fn main() !void {
    const data = try fetchData("https://example.com");
    // Continue with the program if the data was fetched successfully
    std.debug.print("Data received: {s}\n", .{data});
}
```

If `fetchData` returns an error, it will be propagated up to `main`, and the program will handle it accordingly.

> **Error mark**
>
> Before we proceed further, it's crucial to understand a peculiar character you'll encounter in Zig: the exclamation mark, !. In many programming languages, ! is used for logical negation, meaning "not." In Zig, however, it serves a special purpose in function signatures to indicate that a function may return an error.

Alternatively, you can use `catch` to handle errors inline:

```
pub fn main() void {
    _ = fetchData("https://example.com") catch |err| {
        std.debug.print("Failed to fetch data: {s}\n", .{@
errorName(err)});
    };
}
```

In this example, if `fetchData` fails, the `catch` block is executed, allowing you to handle the error gracefully.

Error unions: Combining errors with values

Sometimes, you might want a function to return either a value or an error. This is where error unions come into play. An error union combines an error set with a return type, indicating that a function might return a value or an error.

Let's write a function that converts a string to a floating-point number:

```
const std = @import("std");

const ParseError = error{
```

```
        InvalidFormat,
        Overflow,
};

fn parseFloat(input: []const u8) ParseError!f64 {
    const result = std.fmt.parseFloat(f64, input) catch |err| {
        return switch (err) {
            std.fmt.ParseFloatError.Overflow => error.Overflow,
            else => error.InvalidFormat,
        };
    };
    return result;
}
```

In this function, parseFloat returns an error union called ParseError!f64, meaning it can return an f64 value or an error from its error set.

Handling error unions

When you call a function that returns an error union, you need to handle both possibilities. Here's how you might use parseFloat:

```
const std = @import("std");
pub fn main() void {
    const result = std.fmt.parseFloat(f64, "3.1415") catch |err| {
        std.debug.print("Failed to parse float: {s}\n", .{@
errorName(err)});
        return;
    };
    std.debug.print("Parsed float: {}\n", .{result});
}
```

In this example, if parseFloat succeeds, we print the parsed floating-point number. If it fails, we handle the error in the catch block.

Coercing error sets

Zig allows you to coerce errors from a smaller error set into a larger one, making it easier to work with functions that have different error sets. For instance, if you have a general error set and a more specific one, you can coerce the specific errors into the general set.

Here's how you might do it:

```
const GeneralError = error{
    NotFound,
    PermissionDenied,
    DiskFull,
    ConnectionLost,
};

const NetworkError = error{
    ConnectionLost,
};

fn connectToServer() NetworkError!void {
    // Simulate a network error
    return error.ConnectionLost;
}

fn performTask() GeneralError!void {
    try connectToServer(); // NetworkError coerced into GeneralError
    // Additional logic...
}
```

In performTask, we're able to use try with connectToServer because NetworkError can be coerced into GeneralError.

Sometimes, you might want to provide a default value if a function returns an error. You can use catch to achieve this:

```
const value = std.fmt.parseFloat(f64, "not a number") catch 0.0;
std.debug.print("Value: {}\n", .{value});
```

In this example, if parseFloat fails, the value will be 0.0.

If you're absolutely certain that a function won't return an error—and you're willing to bet your program's stability on it—you can ignore the error using catch unreachable:

```
const number = std.fmt.parseFloat(f64, "42.0") catch unreachable;
// Proceed confidently (or recklessly)
```

This tells Zig that if an error does occur, the program should crash in Debug Mode or Release-Safe Mode, helping you catch any unexpected issues during development.

The errdefer statement: Cleaning up after errors

Resource management is crucial, especially when errors occur. Zig provides the `errdefer` statement, which ensures that a piece of code runs only if an error is returned from a function.

Consider a function that allocates memory and needs to free it if an error occurs:

```
const std = @import("std");

fn allocateResource(allocator: *std.mem.Allocator) !*u8 {
    const buffer = try allocator.alloc(u8, 1024);
    errdefer allocator.free(buffer);

    // Perform operations that might fail
    performOperation(buffer) catch |err| {
        // The buffer will be freed automatically if an error occurs
        return err;
    };

    return buffer;
}
```

In this example, `errdefer` ensures that `allocator.free(buffer)` is called if an error occurs before the function completes successfully.

Why Zig embraces error values

Error values in Zig act like an accountability partner—they won't let you get away with pretending everything is fine. And if you choose to ignore them, you'll be the one to face the consequences when your code starts misbehaving. With error values, Zig makes sure every function's failure path is explicitly handled or accounted for, which leads to cleaner, more robust programs.

Why do error sets matter?

Error sets in Zig aren't just for show. They make your code base clearer, help prevent silent failures, and give you a structured way to deal with problems. Instead of one-size-fits-all errors, you get a tailored list of potential issues that tell you exactly what went wrong. And by enforcing specific error sets for each function, Zig makes sure you handle errors consistently, without surprises.

When combined with error unions, error sets turn Zig's error-handling model into a tight system where every possible failure is not only expected but also defined and documented. This way, when an error does occur, you're not left wondering what happened. You know exactly what you're dealing with, and you're ready to handle it.

In short, error sets are Zig's way of keeping error handling precise, structured, and professional. No random surprises, no vague error codes—just clear, organized failure modes, ready for whatever your code might encounter. So, now that you know the errors you might encounter, let's look at how Zig helps you handle them with the try, catch, and defer toolkit.

Error return traces: Breadcrumbs for when it all goes wrong

Debugging complex systems can be a bit like detective work—especially when it comes to tracking down where an error originated. Enter error return traces: Zig's way of leaving a trail of breadcrumbs through your code, showing the exact path an error took as it journeyed from its origin to its final crash site. If you've ever been stuck staring at a cryptic stack trace that tells you where something blew up but not why, Zig's error return traces are here to make your life a little easier.

Instead of just telling you that something went wrong, an error return trace shows every single checkpoint where that error was passed along. It's like getting the full backstory on every function that touched the error, complete with details. Rather than just showing the final meltdown, Zig's return trace reveals each spot the error propagated through, making it way easier to diagnose root causes instead of just putting out fires.

The anatomy of an error return trace

A standard stack trace tells you where an error ended up— "this function broke here, good luck with that." But an error return trace in Zig gives you a play-by-play account of how the error moved through your code. It's not just about the end; it's about the journey, every single step of it. Imagine you have a sequence of functions, each calling the next, and somewhere deep down, an error arises. The error return trace shows you not only where it failed but how that error was passed up each layer of the stack.

Let's say we have a few functions, each responsible for one part of an operation. Somewhere at the bottom of this call chain, things go wrong. Here's how an error return trace would help us see the whole tragic journey:

```
pub fn main() !void {
    try topFunction();
```

```
}

fn topFunction() !void {
    try midFunction();
}

fn midFunction() !void {
    try bottomFunction();
}

fn bottomFunction() !void {
    return error.FileNotFound;
}
```

When bottomFunction fails with error.FileNotFound, the error doesn't just pop up in main and expect you to guess how it got there. Thanks to error return traces, you get a map of exactly how the error moved from bottomFunction up through midFunction and topFunction, finally landing in main. Each step is recorded, so you don't have to play "guess the origin" when things go sideways.

Error return traces are better than stack traces

The problem with a typical stack trace is that it shows where things exploded, not how the bomb got there. You're left wondering which previous function call set things up to fail. Zig's error return trace, on the other hand, gives you every handoff of the error, detailing exactly which functions handled, passed, or ignored the error on its way up the call chain.

With a return trace, you get a narrative: "Function A called Function B, which called Function C, and C decided to drop the ball with an error." Instead of fixing symptoms, you get to address root causes because you can see every stop the error made along the way.

Consider this practical example. You run your Zig code, an error crops up, and the error return trace tells you this:

```
Error: FileNotFound
in function bottomFunction
  called by midFunction
  called by topFunction
  called by main
```

In this simplified trace, you see each function that handled the error. No guessing, no extra steps. You can open each function, inspect what went wrong, and know exactly where to start troubleshooting. It's the debugging equivalent of a GPS route with every turn highlighted, so you never have to backtrack.

Enabling and using error return traces

By default, Zig includes error return traces in **Debug** and **ReleaseSafe** builds, where they're most useful. In production modes such as **ReleaseFast** and **ReleaseSmall**, return traces are disabled to save on performance. But during development, error return traces are your best friend, letting you quickly find and squash bugs.

Don't bother yourself with builds and production modes for now. We are covering these topics in *Chapter 11*.

You can enable error return traces explicitly if needed, but most of the time, they'll be on by default in the build modes where they're most helpful. And if you're running a build without error return traces, Zig's global error set `anyerror` is still available, so you can manage and handle errors as usual, even without the full trace.

Why you'll actually love error return traces

Error return traces are more than just debugging tools; they're an invitation to solve problems at the source. Instead of patching over issues or being surprised by silent failures, return traces help you map out exactly how your code handles errors, keeping your code base transparent and your troubleshooting focused. So, next time you're trying to figure out why something went wrong, Zig's error return trace will be there with all the juicy details, helping you fix problems the right way.

In short, Zig's error return traces make sure that when things go wrong, you don't just see the explosion—you see who lit the fuse.

With error values, unions, error unions, and the `try-catch-defer` toolkit, you're ready to tackle error-resistant programming. The following best practices will help you manage errors effectively:

- **Use explicit error types:** Define clear, specific error values for different failure cases. Avoid generic errors when possible.
- **Leverage defer and errdefer:** Use `defer` for general cleanup and `errdefer` for error-specific cleanup, ensuring you manage resources consistently.

- **Handle errors gracefully:** Plan for fallback actions with `catch` or propagate errors predictably with `try`.
- **Stay organized with tagged unions:** Use tagged unions to add structure to error handling, making your error checks more readable and maintainable.

Zig's error handling is powerful, structured, and explicit. By treating errors as values, allowing error unions, and offering tagged unions, Zig provides a comprehensive toolkit for managing errors. Combined with `try`, `catch`, and `defer`, you can handle any error scenario with clarity and confidence.

Error handling in Zig isn't about avoiding failures; it's about managing them well. With Zig's tools, you're prepared to make your programs resilient, predictable, and stable, no matter what unexpected data or situations your code encounters. So, embrace Zig's error model—it's a game changer for building reliable software.

Summary

Congratulations! You've made it through the maze of enums, unions, and errors in Zig without (hopefully) losing your sanity. We've journeyed together from the pitfalls of hardcoded magic numbers to the elegance of enums, providing your code with clarity and self-documentation.

We then dived into the flexible world of unions, those shape-shifting types that let a single variable wear different hats as needed. By understanding how to use both bare and tagged unions, you've added a versatile tool to your programming toolkit, enabling you to write more adaptable and maintainable code.

Finally, we faced the inevitability of errors—not as unwelcome surprises but as integral parts of our programs. By embracing error sets and error unions, you've learned how to handle failures gracefully, turning potential points of failure into manageable, predictable events. You've seen how `try`, `catch`, and `errdefer` can help you write code that not only works but also cleans up after itself when things go awry.

As you continue your journey with Zig, remember that these features are here to help you write better, more robust programs. They might seem daunting at first, but with practice, they'll become second nature. So, go forth and code confidently, knowing that you have the tools to handle whatever challenges come your way—whether it's an unexpected error or just the next sarcastic comment from your friendly programming language.

But wait, there's more! In the next chapter, we'll explore how to ensure that your newly acquired error-handling prowess doesn't go to waste. We'll delve into the world of automated tests, showing you how to write tests that catch bugs before they become features. Because what's the point of writing robust code if you can't prove that it works? Get ready to make your code bulletproof—or at least less likely to explode unexpectedly.

Reinforcing your understanding of enums, unions, and errors in Zig

For each question, choose the correct answer or fill in the blanks as appropriate.

1. Enums in Zig are used to define a collection of _____ values.

    a. mutable

    b. related named

    c. numeric

    d. random

2. To assign custom integer values to enum members, you specify them _____.

    a. explicitly

    b. implicitly

    c. randomly

    d. via a function

3. Which built-in function is used to retrieve the underlying integer value of an enum member?

    a. `@enumToInt`

    b. `@intFromEnum`

    c. `@intCast`

    d. `@enumValue`

4. Enums in Zig can have _____, allowing you to define functions associated with them.

    a. variables

    b. methods

    c. constants

    d. operators

5. A bare union can hold _____ of several specified types at a time.

    a. all

    b. two

    c. one

    d. none

6. To safely change the active field in a bare union, you must _____.

    a. modify the existing field

    b. reassign the entire union

    c. use a pointer

    d. cast the union

7. A tagged union combines a union with a(n) _____ to keep track of the active field.

    a. struct

    b. enum tag

    c. integer

    d. function

8. When using a `switch` statement with a tagged union, you match on the union's _____.

    a. memory address

    b. active field's value

    c. tag

    d. size

9. In Zig, the exclamation mark ! in a function's return type indicates that the function can _____.

    a. panic

    b. return multiple values

    c. return an error

    d. be called recursively

10. To handle a function that returns an error union using try, you write:

    a. `try functionCall();`

    b. `functionCall() try;`

    c. `functionCall() catch;`

    d. `try { functionCall(); }`

11. An error set is defined using the _____ keyword.

    a. `enum`

    b. `error`

    c. `union`

    d. `set`

12. An error union combines an error set with a _____ type.

    a. Boolean

    b. return

    c. variable

    d. pointer

13. Using `catch`, you can provide a _____ value when handling an error union.

    a. default

    b. maximum

    c. random

    d. null

14. To handle specific errors differently, you can use a _____ statement.

    a. `for`

    b. `while`

    c. `switch`

    d. `defer`

15. The `errdefer` statement is used to execute code when a function _____.

    a. returns successfully

    b. returns an error

    c. starts executing

    d. is recursive

16. errdefer differs from defer in that it only runs when an error is _____.

   a. caught

   b. ignored

   c. returned

   d. thrown

17. To ensure resources are properly cleaned up in loops, you should _____.

   a. use errdefer outside the loop

   b. avoid using loops

   c. use global variables

   d. ignore errors

18. You create an anonymous union literal by specifying the field without the _____.

   a. value

   b. type

   c. name

   d. keyword

19. One benefit of using anonymous union literals is reduced _____.

   a. performance

   b. code clarity

   c. verbosity

   d. functionality

20. The built-in @typeInfo function allows you to inspect the structure of a type at _____.

   a. runtime

   b. compile time

   c. link time

   d. execution time

21. `@tagName` returns the _____ of the active field in an enum or union.

    a. value

    b. type

    c. name

    d. size

22. A non-exhaustive enum includes a _____ placeholder to allow for future additions.

    a. `else`

    b. `_`

    c. `default`

    d. `null`

23. When switching over a non-exhaustive enum, you handle unspecified cases using _____.

    a. a default case

    b. an `else` clause

    c. the `_` pattern

    d. all of the above

24. Error return traces help in debugging by showing the sequence of function calls that led to an _____.

    a. exception

    b. error being returned

    c. infinite loop

    d. successful execution

25. Error return traces are enabled by default in _____ builds.

    a. ReleaseFast

    b. ReleaseSmall

    c. Debug and ReleaseSafe

    d. All

26. In a `switch` statement, you can use enum literals by prefixing the case with a _____.

    a. :

    b. .

    c. @

    d. #

27. Omitting handling a possible enum value in a `switch` statement can lead to _____.

    a. improved performance

    b. compiler errors

    c. automatic handling

    d. no effect

28. You use `catch unreachable` when you are certain that a function call will not _____.

    a. return

    b. succeed

    c. return an error

    d. compile

29. In Debug Mode, reaching an `unreachable` statement will cause the program to _____.

    a. continue silently

    b. panic

    c. log a warning

    d. optimize away the code

30. The next topic after learning about enums, unions, and errors is _____.

    a. memory management

    b. automated tests

    c. concurrency

    d. networking

31. Automated tests are important because they help ensure your code _____.

   a.   runs faster

   b.   is well documented

   c.   works as intended

   d.   uses less memory

Answers

1.   **b)** related named

2.   **a)** explicitly

3.   **b)** @intFromEnum

4.   **b)** methods

5.   **c)** one

6.   **b)** reassign the entire union

7.   **b)** enum tag

8.   **c)** tag

9.   **c)** return an error

10. **a)** try functionCall();

11. **b)** error

12. **b)** return

13. **a)** default

14. **c)** switch

15. **b)** returns an error

16. **c)** returned

17. **a)** use errdefer outside the loop

18. **b)** type

19. **c)** verbosity

20. **b)** compile time

21. **c)** name

22. **b)** _

23. **d)** all of the above

24. **b)** error being returned

25. **c)** Debug and ReleaseSafe

26. **b)** .

27. **b)** compiler errors or warnings

28. **c)** return an error

29. **b)** panic

30. **b)** automated tests

31. **c)** works as intended

Join us on Discord!

Read this book alongside other users, developers, experts, and the author himself.

Ask questions, provide solutions to other readers, chat with the authors via Ask Me Anything sessions, and much more. Scan the QR or visit the link to join the community.

`https://packt.link/deep-engineering-systemsengineering`

7

Testing Your Zig Code

Testing is probably the programming world's favorite afterthought. Welcome to the chapter where we confront the uncomfortable reality that your meticulously crafted code might not be as flawless as your ego suggests. But don't worry, you're in good company; we've all shipped a bug or two (or fifty) that we'd rather forget.

In this enlightening journey, we'll jump into Zig's built-in testing package, std.testing, because apparently, the language designers thought we might need a little help catching our own mistakes. We'll explore how to write unit tests that not only verify your code works as intended but also serve as a preemptive strike against those late-night debugging sessions fueled by caffeine and regret.

We'll discuss how to structure your tests effectively—so when your future self looks back, you won't wonder what you were thinking (or if you were thinking at all). We'll also cover assertions, those delightful lines of code that let your program passive-aggressively inform you when something has gone horribly wrong.

In this chapter, we're going to cover the following topics:

- Unit Testing: Because debugging is a form self-torture
- std.testing: Zig's not-so-secret weapon for code confidence
- Test structure: Organization your tests (so you can find them later)
- Test coverage

By the end of this chapter, you'll embrace the habit of writing tests alongside your code. Not because you enjoy it, but because you understand that a little upfront effort beats the soul-crushing despair of tracking down a bug in a sprawling codebase. So, let's roll up our sleeves and get started. After all, if you're not testing your code, who knows what it's doing?

Technical requirements

All the code shown in this chapter can be found in the `Chapter07` directory of our git repository: `https://github.com/PacktPublishing/Learning-Zig/tree/main/Chapter07`.

Unit testing: because debugging is a form of self-torture

We've all been there, staring blankly at the screen at 3 A.M., wondering why our code is behaving like a rebellious teenager. Debugging without tests is like trying to find a needle in a haystack while blindfolded—frustrating, time-consuming, and utterly avoidable.

Enter **unit testing**, the unsung hero of software development. Think of unit tests as your personal army of code guardians, catching bugs before they sneak into production and embarrass you in front of your peers (or worse, your users). In Zig, writing unit tests is not just a good practice; it's a survival strategy.

Why bother with unit tests?

You might be thinking, "My code is flawless. I don't need tests." Ah, the sweet delusion of self-confidence. The harsh reality is that even the best developers make mistakes. Unit tests serve several crucial purposes:

- **Early detection:** Catch errors when they're cheap to fix, not after they've crashed your application in the wild.
- **Documentation:** Provide concrete examples of how your code is supposed to work, saving future you from playing archeologist in your own codebase.
- **Refactoring safety net:** Allow you to make changes with the confidence that you're not introducing new bugs—because who doesn't love a safety net?

Let's dive into an example before you lose interest and go back to scrolling through memes. Suppose you have a function that calculates the square of a number:

```
fn square(x: i32) i32 {
    return x * x;
}
```

Simple enough, right? But simplicity has a way of masking subtle bugs. Let's write a unit test to ensure this function behaves as expected:

```
const std = @import("std");

test "square function should return the square of a number" {
    try std.testing.expect(square(3) == 9);
    try std.testing.expect(square(-4) == 16);
    try std.testing.expect(square(0) == 0);
}
```

Here is what we can observe in this test:

- We're using `std.testing.expect` to assert that our square function returns the correct value.

- We're testing positive numbers, negative numbers, and zero—covering a range of inputs because, believe it or not, users have a knack for inputting the one case you didn't consider.

Understanding the test structure

Zig's testing syntax is straightforward, which is more than we can say for some other languages (cough Java cough). The test keyword introduces a test block, optionally followed by a descriptive string:

```
test "description of what this test verifies" {
    // Test code goes here
}
```

Inside the test block, you can write any code you like—after all, tests are just functions without the need to declare a return type or parameters. The implicit return type is `anyerror!void`, which is a fancy way of saying your test can return an error to indicate failure.

Making Tests Meaningful

A word of caution: writing tests that always pass is about as useful as a chocolate teapot. Your tests should be designed to challenge your code, not to inflate your ego. Consider edge cases, invalid inputs, and anything else that could cause your code to stumble.

Let's expand our square function to handle potential overflow—because overflowing integers tend to ruin everyone's day:

```zig
fn safeSquare(x: i32) !i32 {
    const ov = @mulWithOverflow(x, x);
    if (ov[1] != 0) return error.OverFlow;
    return ov[0];
}
```

Now, let's write a test for this enhanced function:

```zig
test "safeSquare should return an error on overflow" {
    try std.testing.expectError(error.OverFlow, safeSquare(46341));
    // 46341 * 46341 exceeds the maximum value for i32
}
```

Here, we're deliberately triggering an overflow to verify that our function handles it gracefully. This is the kind of proactive testing that saves you from late-night panic attacks.

Embracing failure (in your tests, not in life)

Don't shy away from writing tests that fail. In fact, watching a test fail can be oddly satisfying—it's proof that your tests are actually doing their job. Use failures as an opportunity to improve your code. Remember, the goal of testing isn't to prove that your code works; it's to find the places where it doesn't.

Test-Driven Development

If you're feeling particularly adventurous, you might consider adopting **Test-Driven Development**. TDD involves planning your tests (or the requirements) before you write the code they validate. It sounds backward, but it forces you to think critically about what your code is supposed to do, leading to cleaner, more intentional implementations. Please, don't do it for the dogma (or to be cool), but for the potential benefits.

There are some points to remember to avoid common pitfalls while working with tests:

- **Don't test the compiler**: There's no need to test language features or standard library functions—focus on your own code.

- **Be specific**: Each test should verify a specific behavior. If a test fails, you should immediately know what went wrong.

- **Keep tests independent**: Tests should not rely on the state left by other tests. Otherwise, you'll spend more time untangling dependencies than fixing bugs.

By now, you might be warming up to the idea that testing isn't just a tedious chore devised by sadistic software architects. But perhaps you're wondering how to efficiently integrate testing into your Zig projects without reinventing the wheel—or worse, copying and pasting boilerplate code until your fingers bleed.

Fear not, dear developer, for Zig has bestowed upon us `std.testing`, a built-in testing framework that spares you the indignity of rolling your own test harness. Think of `std.testing` as the trusty sidekick you didn't know you needed—a Robin to your Batman, but without the questionable costume choices.

std.testing: Zig's not-so-secret weapon for code confidence

Let's dive into `std.testing`, Zig's gift to those of us who prefer writing code over debugging it. This nifty namespace is packed with utilities that make writing tests almost enjoyable—or at least less painful.

Why use `std.testing`?

- **Simplicity**: Provides straightforward functions for common testing tasks, so you can focus on the actual tests rather than the plumbing.

- **Integration**: Seamlessly works with Zig's test command, making test discovery and execution a breeze.

- **Diagnostics**: Offers helpful error messages and stack traces when tests fail, so you can pinpoint issues without channeling your inner detective.

- **Memory leak detection**: Because who doesn't love finding out they've been leaking memory like a sieve?

Let's revisit our earlier example, but this time we'll leverage more of what `std.testing` has to offer. Suppose you've written a function that reverses a string—because apparently, palindromes are the next big thing.

Now, even at a glance, you might suspect this function has issues (and you'd be right). Let's write a test using `std.testing` to confirm our suspicions:

```
const std = @import("std");


test "reverseString should correctly reverse a string" {
    const input = "Zig";
    const expected = "giZ";
    const actual = reverseString(input);

    try std.testing.expectEqualStrings(expected, actual);
}
```

In this test we use `std.testing.expectEqualStrings` to compare the expected and actual strings. Also, If the strings don't match, Zig will kindly inform us—complete with a detailed error message highlighting the discrepancy.

`std.testing` offers a variety of functions to make your testing life easier. Let's explore some of the most useful ones:

```
try std.testing.expect(x == y);
```

If the condition is false, the test fails, and Zig reports the line number and the offending expression. It's like having a strict teacher who not only marks your answer wrong but also tells you exactly where you messed up.

The function std.testing.expectEqual compares two values for equality:

```
try std.testing.expectEqual(expectedValue, actualValue);
```

It's type-safe and works with most data types, sparing you from subtle bugs due to type coercion.

The function std.testing.expectEqualStrings is specifically designed for string comparison, because let's be honest, string handling is where many bugs like to hide:

```
try std.testing.expectEqualStrings(expectedString, actualString);
```

The function std.testing.expectError verifies that an error union contains a specific error:

```
try std.testing.expectError(MyErrorType.SomeError,
functionThatMayError());
```

This is particularly handy when testing functions that are supposed to fail under certain conditions—because sometimes failure is the expected outcome.

Let's say you've crafted a function that parses an integer from a string, returning an error if the string is invalid:

```
const std = @import("std");

fn parseInt(s: []const u8) !i32 {
    return std.fmt.parseInt(i32, s, 10);
}
```

Now, let's write a test to ensure it behaves correctly:

```
test "parseInt should return an error for invalid input" {
    const invalidInput = "not a number";
    const result = parseInt(invalidInput);

    try std.testing.expectError(std.fmt.ParseIntError.InvalidCharacter,
result);
}
```

In this test:

- We deliberately pass an invalid string to parseInt.
- We use expectError to verify that the function returns the expected error.

If `parseInt` doesn't return `InvalidCharacter`, the test fails—alerting us that our function isn't handling errors as intended.

Leveraging the testing allocator

Memory management is a common source of bugs, especially in languages that give you enough rope to hang yourself (looking at you, C). Zig provides `std.testing.allocator`, a special allocator that tracks memory usage during tests.

Here's how you might use it:

```zig
const std = @import("std");

test "memory allocation should not leak" {
    var allocator = std.testing.allocator;

    const buffer = try allocator.alloc(u8, 1024);
    defer allocator.free(buffer);

    // Perform operations on buffer...

    // At the end of the test, the testing framework checks for leaks
automatically.
}
```

If you forget to free the memory, Zig will inform you, complete with a stack trace leading back to your oversight. It's like having a personal assistant who reminds you to take out the trash—except the trash is memory leaks, and forgetting has more serious consequences.

When you run your tests using the Zig test, you'll see an output that indicates which tests passed, failed, or were skipped. For example:

```
$ zig test my_tests.zig
1/3 reverseString should correctly reverse a string...FAIL
2/3 parseInt should return an error for invalid input...OK
3/3 memory allocation should not leak...OK
```

Tests failed. Use the following command to reproduce the failure:

```
zig test my_tests.zig --test-filter reverseString
```

Zig's test runner provides helpful information:

- **Test progress**: Shows the number of tests run and their status.
- **Failure details**: Includes the test name and a summary of the failure.
- **Reproduction command**: Offers a command to rerun just the failing test, saving you from sifting through unrelated output.

Filtering tests

When you have a large suite of tests, running all of them can become time-consuming. Zig allows you to filter tests by name:

```
zig test my_tests.zig --test-filter parseInt
```

This runs only the tests whose names contain "parseInt". It's a simple yet effective way to focus on specific areas without getting bogged down.

Sometimes, you might have tests that aren't ready or require conditions not currently met. You can programmatically skip a test by returning error.SkipZigTest:

```
test "this test is not ready yet" {
    return error.SkipZigTest;
}
```

The test runner will report the test as skipped, and you can revisit it when you're ready to tackle the unfinished business.

Making the most of std.testing

To harness the full power of std.testing, keep these tips in mind:

- **Be Descriptive**: Use meaningful test names that describe the behavior being tested. Future you (and your teammates) will appreciate the clarity.
- **Test Incrementally**: Write tests as you develop new features. It's easier than trying to retrofit tests onto a tangled codebase.
- **Use the Allocator**: When testing code that allocates memory, use std.testing.allocator to catch leaks early.
- **Leverage Assertions**: Don't skimp on assertions. The more thoroughly you test your code's behavior, the fewer surprises you'll encounter later.

By now, you've dipped your toes into the invigorating waters of unit testing with Zig's std.testing. Feeling refreshed? Good. But before you start churning out tests like a caffeinated squirrel, let's talk about organization. After all, what good is a suite of tests if you can't find them when things go sideways?

Test structure: Organizing your tests (so you can find them later)

Navigating a disorganized codebase is about as pleasant as cleaning out the office fridge.

Figure 7.1 – Marie Kondo's nightmare: what disorganized tests look like

You might find something interesting, but it's probably going to smell. The same goes for your tests. Without proper structure, you'll spend more time searching for that elusive test case than actually fixing the bug it uncovered.

So, let's channel our inner Marie Kondo and bring some order to your testing chaos.

The art of keeping tests close

In Zig, the prevailing philosophy is to keep your tests close to the code they validate. This approach not only fosters better organization but also ensures that tests and code evolve together in perfect (or at least tolerable) harmony.

Writing your tests in the same file as the code under test is a practice that encourages cohesion and clarity. Here is a snippet with the source code and its tests living along:

```
const std = @import("std");

pub fn add(a: i32, b: i32) i32 {
    return a + b;
}

test "add function should correctly add two numbers" {
    try std.testing.expectEqual(5, add(2, 3));
}
```

The main benefits of adopting this approach are:

- **Immediate context**: Tests are right there with the code, making it easier to see how functions are intended to be used.
- **Simplified maintenance**: When you modify the code, you're reminded to update the tests—no excuses.
- **Reduced cognitive load**: No need to juggle multiple files or directories; everything you need is in one place.

Keeping tests alongside your code, we reduce the friction involved in writing and maintaining them. It's like having your toothbrush in the same bathroom where you shower—convenient and conducive to good habits.

Naming conventions: because vague names help no one

Ever spent hours trying to decipher what `test1.zig` is supposed to do? Let's avoid that tragedy.

1. Be Descriptive

    Test names should clearly indicate what they're testing:

    ```
    test "calculateTax applies correct rate for basic items" { /* ... */
    }
    ```

2. Use Consistent Patterns

   Adopt a naming convention that suits your project and stick to it:

   ```
   test "validateInput with valid data returns true" { /* ... */ }
   test "validateInput with invalid data returns false" { /* ... */ }
   ```

3. Avoid redundancy

   Since the test keyword already indicates it's a test, you don't need to include "test" in your names.

   A bad example:

   ```
   test "testAdditionFunction" { /* ... */}
   ```

   A better one:

   ```
   test "addition function adds two positive numbers correctly" { /*
   ... */ }
   Another good one:
   test "should return the sum when add two positive numbers" { /* ...
   */ }
   ```

When your file starts to accumulate multiple tests, grouping related tests can improve readability.

Organize your tests by functionality using comments as section headers:

```
// Tests for the add function
test "add adds positive numbers" { /* ... */ }
test "add adds negative numbers" { /* ... */ }

// Tests for the subtract function
test "subtract subtracts positive numbers" { /* ... */ }
test "subtract subtracts negative numbers" { /* ... */ }
```

This simple technique helps you (and anyone else reading your code) navigate the tests more effectively.

Tests should be independent of one another. If test B fails because test A left the system in a bad state, you're in for a world of confusion. We should avoid shared state, we should avoid using global variables that persist between tests. Also, remember to use defer or errdefer to ensure resources are released, even if a test fails. To make this idea more tangible, let's assume this test case:

```zig
// loadData handles large inputs
test "a good test name here" {
    var allocator = std.testing.allocator;
    const data = try loadData(allocator, "large_input.dat");
    defer allocator.free(data);

    try std.testing.expect(processData(data));
}
```

Leveraging doctests: Kill two birds with one stone

Doctests are tests that also serve as examples in your documentation. They're a great way to show how your code is intended to be used.

```zig
In your code:
/// Reverses the given string.
///
/// ```zig
/// const reversed = reverse("Zig");
/// // reversed == "giZ"
/// ```
pub fn reverse(s: []const u8) []u8 {
    // Implementation here
}
```

When you run the Zig test, Zig will automatically extract and run the code in the doc comments as tests. Just make sure your examples are actually correct—nothing undermines credibility like a broken example.

Patience Is a Virtue, but Not in Testing

Slow tests discourage frequent execution. If your tests take longer to run than it does to grab a coffee, you're less likely to run them often.

So, you've written your code, sprinkled in some assertions, and even organized your tests with the precision of a Swiss watchmaker. Feeling pretty good about yourself, aren't you? But let's not pop the champagne just yet. It's time to face the music and see if your code can withstand the trials you're about to unleash upon it. After all, code that isn't tested is just a hopeful suggestion to the compiler.

Running tests: the moment of truth (will It blend?)

Zig provides the zig test command, which compiles and runs all the tests in your source file. It's as simple as:

```
zig test your_code.zig
```

Yes, it's that easy. But let's break down what's happening:

- **Compilation**: Zig compiles your code along with all the test blocks.
- **Execution**: It runs each test, reporting success or failure.
- **Feedback**: Provides detailed output for any failed tests, including stack traces.

When you run your tests, you'll see output similar to:

```
1/3 test.addition adds positive numbers...OK
2/3 test.addition handles negative numbers...FAIL
3/3 test.multiplication works correctly...OK
```

Tests failed. Use the following command to reproduce the failure:

```
zig test your_code.zig --test-filter "test.addition handles negative numbers"
```

Let's break down the previous output:

- **Test progress**: Indicates which test is running out of the total number.
- **Test names**: Reflects the descriptions you've (hopefully) provided.
- **Results**: OK for success, FAIL for failure.
- **Failure details**: If a test fails, Zig helpfully provides a command to rerun just that test.

A failed test isn't the end of the world—it's an opportunity for enlightenment (or so we tell ourselves). Zig provides detailed information to help you pinpoint the issue.

In the example below, we can see a failure output:

```
2/3 test.addition handles negative numbers...FAIL
/home/user/your_code.zig:42:5: 0x123456 in test.addition handles negative
numbers (test)
    try std.testing.expectEqual(-5, add(-2, -3));
    ^
```

Here, Zig tells you:

- **Location:** The file and line number where the failure occurred.
- **Function:** The specific test function that failed.
- **Stack Trace:** A stack trace leading up to the failure (useful for more complex tests).

When you have a suite of tests, you might want to run a subset to focus on a particular area.

Here is the example of using the "--test-filter" flag:

```
zig test your_code.zig --test-filter "addition"
```

This command runs only the tests whose names contain "addition". It's a lifesaver when you're iterating on a specific function and don't want to wade through unrelated test output.

Tests failing

Remember, a failed test is a gift—a chance to improve your code. Don't ignore failing tests or, worse, comment them out to get a green build. That's like unplugging the fire alarm because it keeps beeping. Instead, investigate the cause, fix the issue, and watch your test suite turn green with envy (or success).

Test coverage

Here's the kicker: Zig doesn't have built-in support for generating code coverage information (yet). Yes, you read that right. Our shiny new language hasn't yet bestowed upon us the luxury of built-in coverage metrics. But don't despair! Where there's a will (and a command line), there's a way.

While Zig might not hold your hand through the coverage landscape, the open-source community has your back. On Linux systems, you can harness external tools to generate coverage reports for your Zig code. One such tool that stands out is **kcov**.

kcov is a code coverage tester that can analyze compiled executables, even without special compilation flags. It works by using debugging information to map the execution of your program back to the source code.

Why kcov?

- **Ease of use**: Doesn't require modifying your build process extensively.
- **No compilation Instrumentation**: Works with standard debug information.
- **Flexible output**: Generates coverage reports in various formats, including HTML.

Using kcov: Step by step

Let's walk through how you can use kcov to generate coverage reports for your Zig projects.

Step 1: Install kcov

First things first, you'll need to install kcov. On most Linux distributions, it's as simple as:

```
sudo apt-get install kcov
```

Here (https://github.com/SimonKagstrom/kcov/blob/master/INSTALL.md) you can follow the version of installation that suits your current setup.

Step 2: Compile your code with debug Information

Ensure your Zig executable is compiled with debug information. This is typically the default in Debug mode, but you can specify it explicitly:

```
zig build-exe main.zig
```

Step 3: Run your executable with kcov

Now, execute your program using kcov to collect coverage data:

```
kcov coverage_output ./main
```

Replace coverage_output with your desired output directory for the coverage report.

Suppose you have a simple Zig program `main.zig`:

```
const std = @import("std");

pub fn main() !void {
    const args = try std.process.args();
    _ = args.next(); // Skip the program name
    const arg = args.next() orelse "world";
    std.debug.print("Hello, {}!\n", .{arg});
}
```

Compile and generate the coverage report:

```
zig build-exe main.zig
kcov coverage_output ./main Alice
Hello, Alice!
```

Step 4: View the coverage report

Navigate to the `coverage_output` directory, and you'll find an HTML report detailing which lines of code were executed. Open the `index.html` file in your browser and bask in the data.

Generating coverage for tests

But what about your tests? You know, those diligent little functions that are supposed to verify your code works?

Tell Zig to execute your tests using kcov by specifying the `--test-cmd` and `--test-cmd-bin` options:

```
zig test test.zig --test-cmd kcov --test-cmd coverage_output --test-cmd-bin
```

This command instructs Zig to run the tests through kcov, placing the coverage output in coverage_output.

If we look at every flag past, here is what we are trying to achieve with each one of them:

- `--test-cmd kcov`: Specifies kcov as the command to run tests.
- `--test-cmd coverage_output`: Passes coverage_output as an argument to kcov.
- `--test-cmd-bin`: Tells Zig to append the test binary path to the kcov command.

For the automation aficionados among us, you can integrate coverage generation into your build.zig script.

Assuming a build.zig file that makes all the glue code needed to make our test coverage work as intended:

```zig
const std = @import("std");

pub fn build(b: *std.Build) void {
    const mode = b.standardReleaseOptions();

    const exe = b.addExecutable("myapp", "src/main.zig");
    exe.setBuildMode(mode);

    const run_cmd = exe.run();

    const enable_coverage = b.option(bool, "coverage", "Enable code
coverage") orelse false;
    if (enable_coverage) {
        exe.setBuildMode(.Debug); // Ensure debug info is included
        exe.setTestCommand(&[_][]const u8{
            "kcov",
            "coverage_output",
            "--exclude-pattern=std",
        });
        exe.setTestStdDir(b.findStdDir());
    }

    b.default_step.dependOn(&run_cmd.step);
}
```

💡 **Quick tip:** Enhance your coding experience with the **AI Code Explainer** and **Quick Copy** features. Open this book in the next-gen Packt Reader. Click the **Copy** button

(1) to quickly copy code into your coding environment, or click the **Explain** button

(2) to get the AI assistant to explain a block of code to you.

```
                                                    Copy      Explain
function calculate(a, b) {                           1          2
  return {sum: a + b};
};
```

💡 📱**The next-gen Packt Reader** is included for free with the purchase of this book. Scan the QR code OR go to `https://packtpub.com/unlock`, then use the search bar to find this book by name. Double-check the edition shown to make sure you get the right one.

Run your build with coverage enabled:

```
zig build run -Dcoverage
```

Before you rush off to generate coverage reports, keep in mind:

- **Unused code isn't counted:** Zig's compiler is smart—it doesn't compile functions that aren't used. This means any code not referenced won't show up in your coverage reports, potentially giving you a misleading sense of completeness.

- **Results reflect executed code:** Coverage reports indicate which parts of your compiled code were executed. If certain code paths are never triggered during tests, they'll be marked as unexecuted.

Collecting coverage data is one thing; using it effectively is another. Here are the main goals we can achieve with the coverage data:

- **Identify gaps**: Look for areas of your code that aren't covered by tests and consider why. Is it dead code? Does it handle rare edge cases?

- **Prioritize critical paths**: Focus on covering code that's central to your application's functionality.

- **Refine tests**: Use coverage reports to improve your tests, ensuring they exercise all necessary code paths.

Limitations and Considerations

- The kcov method works well on Linux. If you're on Windows or macOS, you'll need to explore other tools or methods, as kcov might not be available or fully supported.

- Running your program through kcov introduces some overhead. While generally acceptable for testing purposes, it's not suitable for production use.

Sure, Zig doesn't spoon-feed you code coverage metrics, but perhaps that's a blessing in disguise. It forces you to be deliberate about your testing strategy, to understand your tools, and to appreciate the insights that coverage data can provide.

So go ahead, measure the unmeasurable, and give yourself one more reason to sleep soundly at night—knowing that your code isn't just written; it's tested, verified, and ready to face the world.

Summary

You've met `std.testing`, your new best friend in writing and running tests that actually catch bugs before they catch you.

We've discussed how to structure your tests effectively, keeping them organized and maintainable so future you don't curse past you for sloppy test code. You've learned the power of assertions, giving your code a voice to complain loudly when things go amiss. And you've braved the moment of truth by running your tests, interpreting the results, and integrating testing into your workflow.

Finally, we faced the reality of test coverage, exploring how to measure it using tools like kcov—even if Zig doesn't spoon-feed you coverage metrics. You now understand the importance of knowing how much of your code is actually tested and how to improve it.

In the next chapter, we'll explore ways to organize your data in Zig. We'll delve into the art of structuring data effectively, leveraging Zig's powerful type system. The world of data organization awaits, and it's time to level up your Zig skills even further. After all, code is not just about making things work—it's about making them work well.

Test time!

Instructions: Choose the correct answer for each question or provide a brief response as required.

1. Why is unit testing important in software development?

    a. It helps catch errors early when they are cheaper to fix.

    b. It provides documentation on how the code is supposed to work.

    c. It allows safe refactoring by ensuring new changes don't break existing functionality.

    d. All of the above.

2. In Zig, how do you declare a unit test?

    a. By using the fn testName() void {} syntax.

    b. By prefixing a function with unit_test.

    c. By using the test keyword followed by an optional description.

    d. By importing the unittest module and writing test cases.

3. Which of the following is the correct way to assert that two values are equal in a Zig test?

    a. assert(value1 == value2);

    b. try std.testing.expectEqual(value1, value2);

    c. std.debug.assertEqual(value1, value2);

    d. test.expect(value1 == value2);

4. True or False: Writing tests that always pass is considered a good practice because it shows your code is correct.

    Answer: True or False?

5. What is the purpose of the std.testing.expectError function in Zig's testing framework?

   a. To assert that a function does not return any errors.

   b. To verify that a function returns a specific error.

   c. To handle exceptions thrown by a function.

   d. To skip a test if an error occurs.

6. When organizing tests in Zig, what is the recommended approach regarding the placement of test code?

   a. Place all tests in a separate tests directory.

   b. Keep tests close to the code they validate, typically in the same file.

   c. Write tests in a separate module and import them.

   d. Include tests in the main function of your application.

7. Which of the following is NOT a benefit of keeping tests in the same file as the code under test?

   a. Immediate context and clarity.

   b. Simplified maintenance.

   c. Reduced cognitive load.

   d. Better performance of the compiled program.

8. How can you run only a subset of tests in Zig that match a certain pattern or name?

   a. By commenting out the tests you don't want to run.

   b. Using the --test-filter command-line option with zig test.

   c. By modifying the test runner to exclude certain tests.

   d. By placing tests in different files and only compiling the desired ones.

9. What is the purpose of using defer in a test function?

   a. To delay the execution of a test until all others have run.

   b. To ensure resources are released even if a test fails.

   c. To postpone the initialization of variables.

   d. To schedule a test to run after a certain time.

10. True or False: Zig has built-in support for generating code coverage information.

    Answer: True or False?

11. Which tool is recommended for generating code coverage reports for Zig code on Linux systems?

    a. gcov

    b. lcov

    c. kcov

    d. covtest

12. When using kcov with Zig's zig test command, which flags are necessary to properly generate coverage reports?

    a. --enable-coverage

    b. --test-cmd and --test-cmd-bin

    c. --coverage-output and --coverage-dir

    d. --kcov and --kcov-output

13. What is a doctest in Zig, and how is it used?

    a. A test that is automatically generated by the compiler.

    b. A test that also serves as documentation, embedded in the code comments.

    c. A test that checks for memory leaks and resource management.

    d. A test that is deferred until runtime.

14. True or False: It is acceptable for tests in Zig to depend on the state left by other tests.

    Answer: True or False?

15. What is the function error.SkipZigTest used for in Zig's testing framework?

    a. To indicate that a test has passed.

    b. To mark a test as skipped programmatically.

    c. To handle unexpected errors in tests.

    d. To retry a failed test.

16. Which of the following is a good practice when naming your tests in Zig?

    a. Use vague names like test1, test2, etc.

    b. Include the word "test" in every test name.

    c. Use descriptive names that clearly indicate what the test verifies.

    d. Keep test names as short as possible to save space.

17. What is the role of std.testing.allocator in Zig's testing framework?

    a. It is a memory allocator optimized for performance in production code.

    b. It tracks memory usage during tests to detect leaks.

    c. It provides functions for allocating and freeing resources in tests.

    d. It replaces the standard allocator when running tests.

18. True or False: In Zig, you can filter tests to run based on their name using the --test-filter option.

    Answer: True or False?

19. Why might you choose to write tests that are designed to fail?

    a. To intentionally break the build and test the CI pipeline.

    b. To ensure that your testing framework correctly reports failures.

    c. To make your code coverage percentage appear lower.

    d. Because failing tests are easier to write.

20. Explain the purpose of using std.testing.expect in a Zig test.

Answers

1. d) All of the above.

2. c) By using the `test` keyword followed by an optional description.

3. b) `try std.testing.expectEqual(value1, value2);`

4. False.

5. b) To verify that a function returns a specific error.

6. b) Keep tests close to the code they validate, typically in the same file.

7. d) Better performance of the compiled program.

8. b) Using the `--test-filter` command-line option with `zig test`.

9. b) To ensure resources are released even if a test fails.

10. False.

11. c) `kcov`

12. b) `--test-cmd` and `--test-cmd-bin`

13. b) A test that also serves as documentation, embedded in the code comments.

14. False.

15. b) To mark a test as skipped programmatically.

16. c) Use descriptive names that clearly indicate what the test verifies.

17. b) It tracks memory usage during tests to detect leaks.

18. True.

19. b) To ensure that your testing framework correctly reports failures.

20. To assert that a given condition is true; if the condition is false, the test fails.

Part 2

Data, Memory, and Tools

With the fundamentals covered, this part dives into the heart of systems programming with Zig. We'll explore how to organize data effectively using arrays, slices, and structs. Then, we'll tackle the critical topic of memory management, demystifying pointers and allocators. We'll also explore the standard library's utilities and master Zig's powerful build system to automate your workflow.

This part of the book includes the following chapters:

- *Chapter 8, Organizing Data*
- *Chapter 9, Memory Management*
- *Chapter 10, The Standard Library*
- *Chapter 11, Packing*

8

Organizing Data

Data organization is at the heart of any program. How you shape and manage your data can make or break the clarity, efficiency, and maintainability of your code. This chapter explores the foundational techniques Zig offers for organizing data—whether it's grouping related values, defining precise memory layouts, or creating flexible views into your data structures.

In this chapter, we're going to cover the following topics:

- Arrays: fixed-size collections of things
- Slices: dynamic views into arrays
- Structs: your own custom data (because you're special)

By the end of this chapter, you'll be able to confidently use arrays, slices, and structs to structure your data in meaningful ways. You'll understand how to use Zig's unique features to achieve both compile-time guarantees and runtime safety, empowering you to create clean and efficient programs.

Technical requirements

All the code shown in this chapter can be found in the `Chapter08` directory of our Git repository: `https://github.com/PacktPublishing/Learning-Zig/tree/main/Chapter08`.

Arrays: fixed-size collections of things

It's time to jump into **arrays**, the simplest of data structures. Just a good old-fashioned, fixed-size collection of items, neatly packed together like so many cats crammed into a duffel bag. The analogy may seem uncomfortable, but trust me, once you understand arrays in Zig, you'll be purring with delight (or hissing with envy, depending on your personality).

Figure 8.1 – No room to grow: fixed-size collections like cats in a bag

In Zig, arrays are plain and predictable: they have a fixed size known at compile time, and you can't just go around resizing them mid-flight because you feel like it. If that's too limiting for you, well, maybe arrays aren't your cup of tea. But hey, some of us appreciate the simplicity. Arrays store a sequence of elements of the same type, arranged in a contiguous block of memory. Nothing fancy—just a disciplined row of data soldiers, ready for duty.

A few good arrays

Declaring arrays in Zig isn't rocket science. You can write them out explicitly, use type inference, or even compute values at compile time. For example, here's the Hello of arrays—literally:

```
const message = [_]u8{ 'h', 'e', 'l', 'l', 'o' };
```

The [_]u8 syntax tells Zig, "Hey Zig, figure out how long this array should be for me." It counts your elements, sets the length, and bam! You have an array. If you're feeling particularly controlling, you can specify the length explicitly:

```
const alt_message: [5]u8 = .{ 'h', 'e', 'l', 'l', 'o' };
```

If that doesn't amuse you, consider verifying that they're the same:

```
comptime {
    const std = @import("std");
    const mem = std.mem;
    const assert = std.debug.assert;
    assert(mem.eql(u8, &message, &alt_message));
}
```

Remember: if `assert` fails at compile time, your code simply won't build. It's like a stern but caring mentor refusing to let you embarrass yourself.

To see this and the following snippets in action, we're using `zig test`, as in the following command:

```
zig test array1.zig
```

Note here that we're using the `zig test` command exclusively to force the compilation to happen; there are no tests to run in this snippet, and it shows in the output:

```
All 0 tests passed.
```

Because size matters

Once you have an array, you can get its length with `.len`. This is handy when your memory is failing you:

```
comptime {
assert(message.len == 5);
}
```

No surprises there. You put in five characters, you get five characters out. It's almost like arrays are predictable. How quaint.

Iterating over arrays

You might want to do something wild, such as summing up values. We can do it by simply using a for loop:

```
test "iterate over an array" {
const message = "hello";
var sum: usize = 0;
for (message) |byte| {
```

```
        sum += byte;
    }
    try expect(sum == 'h' + 'e' + 'l' * 2 + 'o');
    }
```

Yes, you can loop through arrays using a syntax that's deceptively pleasant.

Modifying arrays

Arrays are not immutable. Feel free to scribble all over them (as long as they're var arrays and not const):

```
test "modify an array" {
var some_integers: [100]i32 = undefined;
for (&some_integers, 0..) |*item, i| {
    item.* = @intCast(i);
}
try expect(some_integers[10] == 10);
try expect(some_integers[99] == 99);
}
```

Here, undefined just means "Zig, don't bother initializing this right now, I'll do it myself." If you trust yourself to fill it properly before using it (and you'd better), then this is a neat trick.

Compile-time array magic

Zig loves compile-time computations. Concatenating arrays at compile time is as simple as this:

```
const part_one = [_]i32{ 1, 2, 3, 4 };
const part_two = [_]i32{ 5, 6, 7, 8 };
const all_of_it = part_one ++ part_two;

comptime {
assert(mem.eql(i32, &all_of_it, &[_]i32{ 1, 2, 3, 4, 5, 6, 7, 8 }));
}
```

This is compile-time concatenation. Don't even think about trying to do this dynamically at runtime. Arrays are not your dynamic friend—there are other structures for that. But at compile time, you get to play God.

And remember, since strings are arrays, concatenating them is just as straightforward:

```
const hello = "hello";
const world = "world";
const hello_world = hello ++ " " ++ world;


comptime {
assert(mem.eql(u8, hello_world, "hello world"));
}
```

Look, Mom! No runtime nonsense, just nice and tidy compile-time guarantees. If you're feeling **really** adventurous, ** can be used for repetition:

```
const pattern = "ab" ** 3;
comptime {
assert(mem.eql(u8, pattern, "ababab"));
}
```

Because who doesn't need a quick way to repeat patterns at compile time? (Don't answer that.)

Initialize arrays to zero

If you'd like to start from a place of serenity, do this:

```
const all_zero = [_]u16{0} ** 10;


comptime {
assert(all_zero.len == 10);
assert(all_zero[5] == 0);
}
```

Now, you have a nice zero-filled array. It's like a warm bubble bath for your data.

Multidimensional arrays: like arrays, but more

If single-dimensional arrays are well-behaved cats in a bag, multidimensional arrays are stacks of bags inside bigger bags—organized but a bit more visually complex. Just nest arrays like this:

```
const mat4x4 = [4][4]f32{
[_]f32{ 1.0, 0.0, 0.0, 0.0 },
[_]f32{ 0.0, 1.0, 0.0, 1.0 },
```

```
[_]f32{ 0.0, 0.0, 1.0, 0.0 },
[_]f32{ 0.0, 0.0, 0.0, 1.0 },
};
```

Index them with mat4x4[row][column] and treat them just like arrays of arrays. Zig doesn't care that you try to impress it with multiple dimensions—it's perfectly comfortable iterating over these nested data structures.

Sentinel-terminated arrays: because sometimes you need a flag

A sentinel-terminated array places a special value at the end of the array, indicating a boundary. In Zig, the syntax [N:x]T means "Allocate *N + 1* items of the T type, with the last one being x." Consider null-terminated strings or other data that needs a known stop point:

```
const array = [_:0]u8{ 1, 2, 3, 4 };
// Memory layout: [1, 2, 3, 4, 0]
//                     ^data       ^sentinel
```

Think of sentinel-terminated arrays like old-school C strings with a safety net. The sentinel (usually 0) acts like a **STOP** sign at the end of your data. In [_:0]u8{1, 2, 3, 4}, you get 5 total memory slots, [1, 2, 3, 4, 0], but .len still reports 4 because the sentinel isn't counted as data.

Check this out:

```
test "0-terminated sentinel array" {
const array = [_:0]u8{ 1, 2, 3, 4 };

try expect(@TypeOf(array) == [4:0]u8);
try expect(array.len == 4);
try expect(array[4] == 0);
}
```

The sentinel element at array[4] is 0, as promised. This pattern is especially useful for working with C APIs or any old-school approach that relies on termination-by-a-special-value rather than passing length information around. Just don't forget that the sentinel doesn't magically fix off-by-one errors in your code. You'll have to handle that yourself.

OK! Let's recap before going further:

- Arrays in Zig are fixed-size collections of the same type of elements, known at compile time
- They're straightforward to declare, initialize, and iterate
- Strings are just arrays of bytes—no big deal
- Compile-time concatenation and initialization let you do fun things with arrays before your program even runs
- Multidimensional arrays give you more complex shapes without losing your marbles
- Sentinel-terminated arrays help you handle old C-isms and stop conditions elegantly

Now that you've crammed all these cats into this bag, learned to feed them at compile time, slice them up (figuratively!), and even terminate them with a sentinel (don't worry, it's just a zero), you're well on your way to being an array master. If you found this too limiting, don't worry. We're moving on to slices—those dynamic, cat-peeking alternatives that might just blow your mind. Or at least ruffle your whiskers.

Slices: dynamic views into arrays

If arrays represent a bunch of data locked away in a safe with a combination set at compile time, **slices** are more like having a flexible window you can slide around to see a portion of that data at runtime. Think of arrays as rigid, stuck-up aristocrats who know exactly how big their empire is at birth, and slices as the cunning rogues who can dart through a castle's corridors, choosing which rooms to view at any moment. Both have their place, but slices often give you the freedom and runtime agility that arrays cannot.

Let's build this up step by step with some code that doesn't just rehash `hello` and random integers. We'll start with an array scenario and then create slices from it, progressively increasing the complexity so that, by the end, you'll be nodding knowingly and sipping your coffee smugly.

Step 1: Arrays and their royal stubbornness

First, we begin with a noble array. Let's say we're writing a small game where we have a known number of mystical stones, each with a special power level. Once declared, we can't just resize this array—it's fixed, just like the predetermined nature of fate (or your manager's deadlines).

Figure 8.2 – Six stones, sealed at compile time: arrays refuse to budge

Let's assume this test case:

```
test "arrays and basic slicing" {
    // We have 6 mystical stones with fixed, known-at-compile-time powers.
    const stone_powers = [_]u16{ 42, 17, 93, 58, 11, 99 };

    // The array's length is part of its type. Stone powers are fixed in
stone (pun intended).
    const total_stones = stone_powers.len;
    try std.testing.expect(total_stones == 6);

    // Accessing by index: arrays do no runtime safety checks (by
default),
    // but if you're testing in safe mode, Zig will still panic on out-of-
bounds.
    try std.testing.expect(stone_powers[0] == 42);
    try std.testing.expect(stone_powers[5] == 99);

}
```

♀ **Quick tip**: Enhance your coding experience with the **AI Code Explainer** and **Quick Copy** features. Open this book in the next-gen Packt Reader. Click the **Copy** button

(1) to quickly copy code into your coding environment, or click the **Explain** button

(2) to get the AI assistant to explain a block of code to you.

```
                                                    Copy      Explain

function calculate(a, b) {                           1          2
   return {sum: a + b};
};
```

🔖 **The next-gen Packt Reader** is included for free with the purchase of this book. Scan the QR code OR go to `https://packtpub.com/unlock`, then use the search bar to find this book by name. Double-check the edition shown to make sure you get the right one.

So, we have a fixed array. That's nice, but not very flexible. What if, at runtime, we decide we only need the middle stones, or we want to give a certain player a "view" into just a portion of these stones?

Step 2: Introducing slices (runtime flexibility)

Slices let you take our precious stone_powers and carve out a runtime-defined window into it. You still can't magically rearrange the stones, but you can choose exactly how many to look at and from where once you have the runtime conditions set.

Let's explore this idea in the following snippet:

```
test "creating slices from arrays 2" {
    var stone_powers = [_]u16{ 42, 17, 93, 58, 11, 99 };
    var known_at_runtime_zero: usize = 0;
    _ = &known_at_runtime_zero;

    const middle_stones = stone_powers[known_at_runtime_zero..stone_
powers.len];


    try std.testing.expect(@TypeOf(middle_stones) == []u16);
    try std.testing.expect(middle_stones.len == 6);
    try std.testing.expect(middle_stones[0] == 42);
    try std.testing.expect(middle_stones[1] == 17);
}
```

Confused? I've got your back. Our test function creates a slice from an array at runtime.

Initially, we define a stone_powers array of the [_]u16 type, which is a fixed-size array of unsigned 16-bit integers.

The array is initialized with the values {42, 17, 93, 58, 11, 99}. Let's talk about the scenario we are simulating.

A player enters a dungeon and can only see a subset ("middle half") of these stones at runtime. Here, we define a known_at_runtime_zero variable and assign 0 to it. This variable will represent a runtime-known index. Even though it's set to zero here, in a more realistic scenario, this value might be determined during program execution.

The line _ = &known_at_runtime_zero; is essentially a "compiler trick" that forces the variable to be treated as runtime-unknown even though we can see it's zero. Think of it like putting a black box around the variable; by taking its address and discarding the result, we're telling the compiler "pretend you don't know this value at compile time," which ensures that when we slice the array using this variable, the compiler creates a true runtime slice, []u16, instead of optimizing it into a compile-time-known array type, [6]u16.

We then create a slice out of stone_powers using this runtime index. The slice is stone_powers[known_at_runtime_zero..stone_powers.len], which effectively gives us a slice covering the entire array in this example (from index 0 to stone_powers.len - 1).

Because the start and end indices of a slice can be runtime-known, this results in a non-compile-time known slice, which is represented by [ ]u16.

We confirm that the type of middle_stones is indeed a [ ]u16 slice rather than a compile-time-known-sized array.

We then check the length and contents of this slice to ensure it matches the expected values. If this test passes, it means that slicing an array at runtime worked as intended and produced the correct slice.

Another good aspect of slices is that they protect you from yourself. Let's take a look at another test case:

```
test "slices protect you from yourself" {
    var stone_powers = [_]u16{ 42, 17, 93, 58, 11, 99 };
    const subset = stone_powers[1..3];
    try std.testing.expect(subset.len == 2);
    // Attempting `subset[99] = 100;` here would cause a runtime panic due
to out-of-bounds access.
}
```

Long explanation ahead. Ready?

This new test function demonstrates that slices, unlike compile-time-known arrays, provide runtime bounds checking to prevent out-of-bounds accesses.

We start with a stone_powers array containing six elements. We then create a slice called subset that is a smaller view of the array: stone_powers[1..3]. This slice represents a portion of the array, specifically, the elements at indices 1 and 2 (two elements in total).

Next, we verify that this slice has the expected length of 2. Because subset is a runtime-checked slice, attempting to access an index outside of its bounds (for example, subset[99]) will cause a runtime panic. This ensures safety against accidental or malicious out-of-bounds writes, preventing memory corruption. Although we comment out the actual out-of-bounds write to avoid causing a test failure, it serves as a demonstration that slices have your back and will panic rather than silently produce **undefined behavior**.

The key takeaway is that slices offer a runtime safety net against indexing errors, providing peace of mind and making your code more robust.

Now, we've established that slices are a runtime-known window into data. They're safer than pointers because they carry length information and enforce bounds checks.

Step 3: A more complex scenario — filtering and sub-slicing

Suppose we want to prepare a subset of stones for a spell-casting ritual. The rules are as follows:

- We need stones with power greater than 50
- We don't know how many of them there are until runtime
- Once we know, we want a slice that references just those stones

We can't just conjure arrays of unknown length at compile time. But we can figure out how many stones qualify at runtime and then slice accordingly. Let's simulate that by counting how many stones meet a condition, then create a "qualified" slice:

```zig
test "slices enabling runtime filtering" {
    var stone_powers = [_]u16{ 42, 17, 93, 58, 11, 99 };
    var count_greater_than_50: usize = 0;
    for (stone_powers) |power| {
        if (power > 50) count_greater_than_50 += 1;
    }
    try std.testing.expect(count_greater_than_50 == 3);
    const start_index: usize = 2;
    var length: usize = 3; // Suppose we know at runtime that these good
stones start at index 2
    _ = &length; // runtime-known index

    const good_stones = stone_powers[start_index..][0..length];

    try std.testing.expect(@TypeOf(good_stones) == []u16);
    try std.testing.expect(good_stones[0] == 93);
    try std.testing.expect(good_stones[1] == 58);
    try std.testing.expect(good_stones[2] == 11);


}
```

Once again, let's understand what is going on. Remember, the goal is to count how many stones exceed a certain power threshold and then create a slice that represents exactly those stones.

First, we iterate over the array and count how many stones have a power greater than 50. Once we have the count, we imagine a scenario where we know which portion of the array contains these "powerful" stones, and we want to create a slice that references just them. Because the start index and length are only known at runtime (in a more dynamic program), slicing with runtime values results in a [ ]u16 slice type.

By slicing twice—once with a runtime-known start index, and again with a runtime-known length—we demonstrate how Zig's type inference can yield a slice type at runtime. The first slice operation narrows down the array from a certain start index. The second slice operation uses a runtime-known length, confirming that Zig will produce a slice type ([ ]u16) that's checked at runtime, ensuring safety and correctness.

We then verify that the resulting slice contains the correct stones and that its type is as expected. This shows how slices enable dynamic filtering and subsetting of arrays in a safe, runtime-checked manner.

Before we continue, a quick poem to loosen up the tension a little bit:

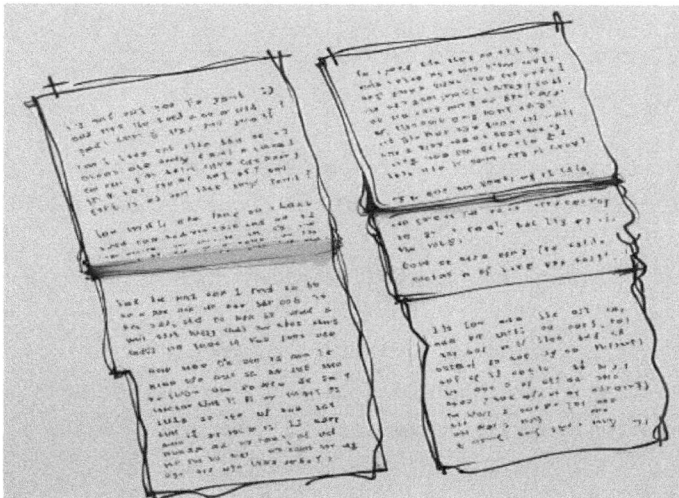

Figure 8.3 – A poem to slicing

To be precise, this is what the minuscule text says:

In arrays of stones, we slice and refine,

A runtime whisper guides which shards align.

No bounds breached, no errant stride,

With safety's guard, we step inside.

Stones of power, filtered and seen,

A slice of truth in code serene.

Feeling better? Let's proceed.

Step 4: Treating strings as slices

Zig doesn't have a dedicated string type; strings are just slices of u8. You can think of them as text-wrapped slices. Let's say we have a spell name, and we want to isolate a substring at runtime:

```
test "strings as slices" {
    // A spell name represented as a UTF-8 slice
    const spell_name: []const u8 = "Caldara's Blaze";

    // We want to isolate the substring "Blaze" at runtime.
    var start_of_substring: usize = 10; // Counting: C(0)a(1)l(2)d(3)a(4)
r(5)a(6)'(7)s(8) (space)(9)B(10)
    _ = &start_of_substring; // runtime-known index

    const substring = spell_name[start_of_substring..];
    try std.testing.expect(@TypeOf(substring) == []const u8);
    try std.testing.expect(std.mem.eql(u8, substring, "Blaze"));

    // If you mess up and pick out-of-range indices, Zig will let you know
at runtime.
    // substring[99]; // would panic, since substring isn't that long.
}
```

This test demonstrates that strings in Zig are essentially slices of bytes. The code starts with a UTF-8 encoded string, "Caldara's Blaze", and then uses a runtime-known index (start_of_substring) to isolate a substring, "Blaze". Because the start index is determined at runtime, the resulting substring is a slice of the []const u8 type.

By verifying the substring's content and type, we show that Zig maintains runtime safety checks. Attempting an out-of-bounds access on the substring would cause a runtime panic rather than leading to undefined behavior. This emphasizes that Zig's approach to memory safety extends even to string slices.

Here, slices allow easy runtime extraction of parts of a string without needing fancy string manipulation functions. Just slice and dice as you please.

Step 5: Sentinel-terminated slices (because some APIs are stuck in the past)

Some old-school APIs think it's a great idea to mark the end of data with a sentinel value, such as a zero-terminated string. Zig's type system can reflect that, so you don't accidentally forget the sentinel. Just don't lie to Zig about the data—if you say it's zero-terminated, it had better have a zero at the end:

```
test "sentinel-terminated slices" {
    const legacy_name: [:0]const u8 = "Elixir";
    try std.testing.expect(legacy_name.len == 6);
    try std.testing.expect(legacy_name[6] == 0);
    var data = [_]u8{ 70, 71, 72 }; // no terminating 0 here
    const good_slice = data[0..data.len]; _ = good_slice;

    // Attempting to create a sentinel-terminated slice from data would
panic:
    // const bad_slice = data[0..data.len :0]; _ = bad_slice;

}
```

Sentinel-terminated slices expect a certain sentinel value (often 0) to mark the end of the sequence. In the given code, `legacy_name` is a sentinel-terminated slice of bytes (`[:0]const u8`) that represents a zero-terminated string, `"Elixir"`. Since `"Elixir"` is 6 characters long plus a terminating 0, the total length of `legacy_name` is 6, with the zero at position 6. This matches the sentinel termination expectations.

Conversely, if you attempt to create a sentinel-terminated slice from data that does not end with the expected sentinel, Zig will detect this mismatch at runtime and panic. This strict checking ensures that your slices always follow the intended memory layout, maintaining both safety and correctness in dealing with sentinel-terminated data.

Let's recap slices:

- Slices offer runtime flexibility, letting you view subsets of arrays without copying data
- They include length information, enabling bounds checks and preventing accidents
- By mixing runtime slicing with compile-time known lengths, Zig sometimes returns pointers to arrays for extra efficiency—Zig never passes up a chance to optimize
- Strings in Zig are just slices of bytes—simple and consistent
- Sentinel-terminated slices let you safely interact with old-style APIs expecting special markers at the end

Slices are your dynamic window into a static world. They respect the underlying arrays' nobility but aren't afraid to show you just the part of that noble lineage you actually need. As you become more comfortable with them, you'll start slicing and dicing data like a master chef—and hopefully not slicing your hand in the process.

While slices help you carve out flexible views of arrays, structs let you define new, custom shapes— bundling related fields and giving names and order to the chaos. Next, we'll explore structs and see how they let you define your own data types, guiding you toward clearer, safer, and more expressive code.

Structs: your own custom data (because you're special)

If arrays and slices are about bundling cats in a bag or peeking at them through a hole, structs are about naming those cats, putting hats on them, and perhaps giving them their own existential crises. In other words, structs let you define your own custom data types that group related values together, each with its own personality. It's your chance to play data god, molding the shapes that best fit your problem domain.

And unlike arrays or slices, you don't have to stick to a single data type. A struct can hold integers, floats, strings, and even nested structs—whatever odd concoction your mind dreams up. It's like building your own toolbox instead of rummaging through someone else's junk drawer.

Let's dive into a progressive example, starting with something simple and moving toward more complex and nuanced uses.

Step 1: A simple struct (the basics)

We'll start with a Spell struct, something you might find in a fantasy game. Each spell has a name, a mana cost, and some vague potency value.

Figure 8.4 – Casting with precision: structs organize data the way spells organize magic

These fields are neatly packaged together, giving you a nicely named blob of data:

```
const std = @import("std");
const expect = std.testing.expect;

test "defining and using a simple struct" {
    const Spell = struct {
            name: []const u8,
            mana_cost: u32,
            potency: f32,
    };

    // Initializing a struct literal—just fill in all the fields:
    const fireball = Spell{
            .name = "Fireball",
            .mana_cost = 25,
            .potency = 0.75,
    };
```

```
    try expect(std.mem.eql(u8, fireball.name, "Fireball"));
    try expect(fireball.mana_cost == 25);
    try expect(fireball.potency == 0.75);
}
```

Simple enough. You have a named data type with fields. The compiler doesn't guarantee the order of fields in memory, but who cares? You shouldn't rely on field order anyway—just trust the compiler to figure out the best layout.

Step 2: Adding functions to structs (methods, but not really)

Structs can host functions too, providing a nice namespace for related operations. Let's evolve our example. Say we want to define a `Creature` that can perform actions. We'll give it a method to "attack," which uses the `Spell` struct defined earlier. Methods aren't magic—just functions that happen to live inside a struct. Still, calling them with dot syntax feels warm and cozy, like drinking cocoa on a winter morning.

Here is the full example:

```
const std = @import("std");
const expect = std.testing.expect;

const Spell = struct {
    name: []const u8,
    mana_cost: u32,
    potency: f32,
};

const Creature = struct {
    health: f32,
    mana: u32,

    pub fn attack(self: *Creature, spell: Spell) bool {
        if (self.mana < spell.mana_cost) {
            // Not enough mana to cast the spell
                return false;
        }
        self.mana -= spell.mana_cost;
        return true;
```

```
        }
    };

    test "struct methods" {
        var goblin = Creature{ .health = 100.0, .mana = 50 };
        const frost_bolt = Spell{ .name = "Frost Bolt", .mana_cost = 20,
    .potency = 0.6 };

        try expect(goblin.attack(frost_bolt) == true);
        try expect(goblin.mana == 30);

        // Try again until the goblin can't cast anymore
        try expect(goblin.attack(frost_bolt) == true);
        try expect(goblin.mana == 10);

        try expect(goblin.attack(frost_bolt) == false);
        // Out of mana now
    }
```

Methods give your structs behavior, allowing you to tie data and functionality together. This can help keep your code organized and logical. Just remember: no OOP inheritance nonsense here—Zig keeps it straightforward and honest.

Step 3: Namespaced declarations and empty structs

Structs can also contain "constants" and other declarations. Sometimes, you just need a namespace to store related constants. An empty struct can stand as a logical grouping of constants with zero runtime cost:

```
const std = @import("std");
const expect = std.testing.expect;

test "struct constants and empty structs" {
    const Alchemy = struct {
        pub const BASE_MULTIPLIER = 2.5;
    };

    const EmptySpace = struct {
        pub const PI = 3.14159;
```

```
            // No fields at all. Perfectly legal. No runtime cost.
    };

    try expect(@sizeOf(EmptySpace) == 0);
    try expect(EmptySpace.PI == 3.14159);

    // You can instantiate an empty struct if you like,
    // but it's basically doing nothing. It's a no-op.
    const nothing = EmptySpace{};
    _ = nothing;

    // Use the constants as needed:
    const result = 10.0 * Alchemy.BASE_MULTIPLIER;
    try expect(result == 25.0);
}
```

Our example shows how a struct can contain public constants that are accessible without creating an instance, and how it is possible to define a completely empty struct with no fields while still including constants.

Such empty structs have zero runtime cost, as verified by checking @sizeOf(EmptySpace).

Although instantiating an empty struct is allowed, it essentially results in a zero-sized no-operation value. By using these constants directly, such as Alchemy.BASE_MULTIPLIER or EmptySpace. PI, the code confirms that working with struct-defined constants requires no runtime overhead and simplifies certain aspects of program design.

Step 4: Field parent pointers (fancy reflection)

Zig provides some neat tricks, such as @fieldParentPtr to calculate a pointer to the parent struct from a pointer to a field. Need a reason for this madness? Imagine you need to backtrack from a field to its owner. It's a bit like following the trail of breadcrumbs back to the witch's house, but less terrifying:

```
const std = @import("std");
const expect = std.testing.expect;

const Creature = struct {
    health: f32,
    mana: u32,
```

```
};

fn boostMana(mana_ptr: *u32, amount: u32) void {
    // We know mana_ptr is a field of Creature. Let's get the Creature
pointer!
    // const Creature = @typeInfo(@TypeOf(mana_ptr.*)).Pointer.parent; //
Just a demonstration of concept
    // Actually use Zig's built-in:
    const creature_ptr: *Creature = @fieldParentPtr("mana", mana_ptr);
    creature_ptr.mana += amount;
}


test "field parent pointer" {
    var elf = Creature{ .health = 150.0, .mana = 10 };
    boostMana(&elf.mana, 40);
    try expect(elf.mana == 50);
}
```

In the boostMana function, it received a pointer to the mana field of a Creature and then invoked @fieldParentPtr("mana", mana_ptr). By doing so, it returned a pointer to the parent Creature that contained the mana field, allowing the code to modify not just a single field, but the entire struct's state.

Step 5: Default field values done right

You can give fields default values, but be careful with the invariants. Don't set defaults that break your logic:

```
const std = @import("std");
const expect = std.testing.expect;

test "default field values" {
    const Potion = struct {
        strength: u16 = 10,
        flavor_rating: u8,
    };

    // Only specify flavor_rating, strength defaults to 10.
    const brew = Potion{ .flavor_rating = 8 };
```

```
    try expect(brew.strength == 10);
    try expect(brew.flavor_rating == 8);
}
```

In the `Potion` struct, the `strength` field was assigned a default value of 10, while the `flavor_rating` field did not have a default and was required to be specified during initialization.

The test created a `Potion` instance named `brew`, providing a value only for the `flavor_rating` field. Since no value was explicitly given for `strength`, it automatically defaulted to 10 as defined in the struct. The assertions verified that `brew.strength` equaled 10 and `brew.flavor_rating` equaled 8, confirming that default field values in Zig work as expected when initializing structs.

> **A note about defaults**
>
> If defaults risk breaking invariants (such as a max < min scenario), don't do it. Instead, define a default instance or a function to create a valid one.

Step 6: Packed structs (memory layout shenanigans)

If you need total control over memory layout (such as dealing with binary protocols or hardware registers), packed structs are your tool. They ensure a known bit-level layout. This is perfect for when you're feeling extra pedantic or talking to old C APIs that still live in the 90s. Here is how you can use them:

```
const std = @import("std");
const expect = std.testing.expect;

test "packed struct example" {
    // Imagine a packed struct that stores
    // two small integers in a single byte:
    const TinyData = packed struct {
        high: u4,
        low: u4,
    };

    const data = TinyData{ .high = 0xA, .low = 0x5 };
    // Bit layout is now predictable and stable:
    try expect(data.high == 0xA);
    try expect(data.low == 0x5);
```

```
    try expect(@sizeOf(TinyData) == 1);
}
```

The `TinyData` struct was defined with two 4-bit fields, high and low, packed into a single byte using the `packed` keyword. This ensured a compact and predictable memory representation.

The test created an instance of `TinyData`, assigning hexadecimal values 0xA to `high` and 0x5 to `low`. It then verified that these values were stored correctly within the packed struct and that the total size of `TinyData` was exactly one byte. This is one of the several examples of how packed structs could be used to optimize memory usage and ensure stable bit layouts for use cases such as low-level programming or data serialization.

Here is a normal versus packed comparison:

```
// Normal struct - compiler optimizes
const Normal = struct {
flag: bool, // Might use 1 byte
value: u16, // Might add padding, then 2 bytes
};
// Total size: possibly 4 bytes due to alignment

// Packed struct - you control every bit
const Packed = packed struct {
flag: u1, // Exactly 1 bit
value: u15, // Exactly 15 bits
};
// Total size: exactly 2 bytes (16 bits total)
```

You can do fancy things such as bit casts and manipulate non-byte-aligned fields. Just remember: with great power comes great responsibility. Zig doesn't prevent you from making your own foot gun, especially if you wander into alignment and packing issues.

Step 7: Anonymous structs and tuples

In Zig, anonymous structs are useful for quickly grouping data without explicitly defining a named struct. The fields and types of the struct were inferred directly from the provided values, showcasing how Zig enables concise and flexible struct usage in scenarios where a named struct isn't necessary.

This approach allows for lightweight and ad-hoc data encapsulation, as we can see in the following snippet:

```
const std = @import("std");
const expect = std.testing.expect;

test "anonymous structs" {
    // Anonymous struct with named fields, inferred by the function
signature:
    try check(.{
        .max_health = 200,
        .respawn_enabled = true,
    });
}
fn check(settings: anytype) !void {
    try expect(settings.max_health == 200);
    try expect(settings.respawn_enabled);
}
```

The test passed an anonymous struct, created "inline" with specific fields, to the check function. The anonymous struct had two fields: max_health, an integer set to 200, and respawn_enabled, a Boolean set to true.

Need something simpler? Tuples (anonymous structs without named fields) let you pack multiple values together in a nameless blob. For quick-and-dirty bundling, they're great.

Let's take a look at the following test case:

```
test "tuples" {
    const hero_stats = .{100, 50.5, "strong"};
    // hero_stats[0] = 100;
    // hero_stats[1] = 50.5;
    // hero_stats[2] = "strong";

    try expect(hero_stats.len == 3);
    try expect(hero_stats.@"0" == 100);
    try expect(hero_stats.@"2"[0] == 's');
}
```

In Zig, tuples are collections of values grouped together with indices serving as their field names. In the test, a tuple named hero_stats was created containing three elements: an integer, 100; a floating-point number, 50.5; and a string, "strong". Tuples in Zig are lightweight and provide indexed access to their elements.

Time to wrap up to consolidate our knowledge! This is what we've covered so far in this section:

- Structs let you define your own data aggregates with strongly typed fields
- They can hold constants, methods, and even nested structs
- Default field values are convenient, but must respect your data invariants
- Packed structs give you full control over memory layout, perfect for those tricky low-level tasks
- Anonymous structs and tuples let you avoid naming when it's not needed, keeping things terse and flexible

Structs are the backbone of structured data in Zig. They are your chance to create logical groupings that make sense for your domain instead of forcing everything into arrays or pointers. After all, you're unique, and so is your data—treat it that way.

Summary

In this chapter, you explored the essential tools Zig provides for structuring and managing data. You learned how arrays serve as fixed-size, compile-time-known collections, offering predictable and efficient storage. Slices expanded this concept, allowing for flexible, runtime-defined views into arrays while maintaining safety through bounds checking. We then ventured into structs, where you gained the ability to design custom data types, integrate default field values, and even manipulate memory layouts using packed structs. Anonymous structs and tuples showed how Zig keeps things terse and dynamic when full structure definitions aren't necessary.

With these tools in hand, you can confidently organize, group, and access your data in clean and efficient ways. Whether you're building a small program or architecting a complex system, you now have the building blocks to keep your data well-structured and easy to manage.

With your data organized, it's time to delve into memory management. In the next chapter, you'll master pointers, safely allocate and deallocate memory, and explore advanced concepts such as zero-sized types and type casting. Zig's tools will guide you in writing safe, efficient code while avoiding common pitfalls such as memory leaks and dangling pointers.

Let's make this knowledge stick!

1. What is the default value of the strength field in the following struct?

```
const Potion = struct {
    strength: u16 = 10,
    flavor_rating: u8,
};
const brew = Potion{ .flavor_rating = 8 };
```

   a.   0

   b.   10

   c.   undefined

   d.   8

2. How do you get the length of an array in Zig?

   a.   .size

   b.   .count

   c.   .len

   d.   @lengthOf(array)

3. Which of the following statements about slices is true?

   a.   Slices require compile-time-known lengths

   b.   Slices are immutable views of arrays

   c.   Slices include length information for runtime bounds checking

   d.   Slices cannot overlap with arrays

4. What is the type of the following variable?

```
const hero_stats = .{100, 50.5, "strong"};
```

   a.   [3]u32

   b.   [3]anytype

   c.   .len

   d.   tuple

5. What happens when you attempt to access an out-of-bounds index in a slice?

    a. Zig silently ignores the access

    b. Zig returns a default value of 0

    c. Zig performs a runtime panic

    d. Zig compiles with a warning

6. What is the size of the following packed struct?

    ```
    const TinyData = packed struct {
        high: u4,
        low: u4,
    };
    ```

    a. 2 bytes

    b. 4 bytes

    c. 1 byte

    d. 8 bytes

7. In Zig, what are strings?

    a. Arrays of char

    b. Immutable by default

    c. Null-terminated by default

    d. Slices of u8

8. How do you initialize an array to all zeros?

    a. `[_]u16{}`

    b. `[_]u16{0}`

    c. `[_]u16{0} ** n`

    d. `[_]u16{undefined}`

9. What keyword allows you to skip explicit array length declaration?

    a. `@autoLength`

    b. `[_]`

    c. `const`

    d. `var`

10. What does @fieldParentPtr do in Zig?

    a.   Returns a pointer to the first field of a struct

    b.   Returns a pointer to the parent struct of a field

    c.   Returns the value of a field from its parent struct

    d.   Returns a reference to a struct array

11. What happens if a compile-time assertion fails?

    a.   The program crashes at runtime

    b.   The program logs a warning

    c.   The program halts compilation

    d.   The program continues with a default value

12. Which of the following is NOT a feature of structs in Zig?

    a.   Default field values

    b.   Dynamic resizing of fields

    c.   Containing public constants

    d.   Grouping multiple data types

13. What does this Zig expression do?

```
const hello_world = "hello" ++ " " ++ "world";
```

    a.   Appends the strings at runtime

    b.   Appends the strings at compile time

    c.   Creates a slice of the strings

    d.   Repeats the string three times

14. What happens when a packed struct has alignment issues?

    a.   Zig raises a runtime error

    b.   Zig raises a compile-time error

    c.   The program silently produces undefined behavior

    d.   The program continues, but logs a warning

15. What is the sentinel value in this array?

```
const array = [_:0]u8{1, 2, 3, 4};
```

    a. 1

    b. 2

    c. 3

    d. 0

Here are the correct answers:

1. b
2. c
3. c
4. d
5. c
6. c
7. d
8. c
9. b
10. b
11. c
12. b
13. b
14. b
15. d

Join us on Discord!

Read this book alongside other users, developers, experts, and the author himself.

Ask questions, provide solutions to other readers, chat with the authors via Ask Me Anything sessions, and much more. Scan the QR or visit the link to join the community.

`https://packt.link/deep-engineering-systemsengineering`

9

Memory Management

Worried about pointers ending your programming career in a blaze of runtime errors? Relax. By the time you finish this chapter, you'll see pointers for what they really are: just another tool for managing memory. You'll have learned why Zig's approach to pointers, allocation, and ownership isn't an evil labyrinth of undefined behavior, but a clear, straightforward deal: you want memory, you allocate it, you own it, and you release it. No guesswork required.

In this chapter, you'll discover how to handle pointers without losing your mind, manage both the stack and the heap safely, and even delve into advanced tricks such as zero-sized types and type conversion (casting). Each subtopic shows you how Zig's design helps you keep control over your memory while still enjoying speed and efficiency.

In this chapter, we're going to cover the following topics:

- Stack and heap: The two-headed beast of memory
- Pointers: The good, the bad, and the ugly (but mostly good)
- Allocation: The art of asking for more memory (and getting it)
- Lifetime considerations
- Zero-sized types: The phantom menace of memory management (but they have their uses)
- Type conversion (casting): When your data needs a disguise

By the end of this chapter, you'll have grasped not only how to work with pointers and allocations correctly but also how to clean up after yourself so your computer doesn't hate you—or crash on you. You'll walk away ready to tackle real-world issues such as memory leaks, use-after-free bugs, and massive heap allocations with confidence.

In both everyday coding and system-level tasks, correct memory management is non-negotiable. Whether you're building a low-level application that must never crash or simply want to level up beyond "it just works" languages, Zig gives you the power and clarity to handle memory explicitly. Learn these concepts here and you'll be prepared to take on everything from debugging weird pointer issues in your own projects to building rock-solid software that stands up to production traffic.

Technical requirements

All the code shown in this chapter can be found in the Chapter09 directory of our Git repository: https://github.com/PacktPublishing/Learning-Zig/tree/main/Chapter09.

Stack and heap: The two-headed beast of memory

If you've ever tried to figure out where your data is living while your program runs, you've probably heard about the stack and the heap. Here's the fast version: not a computer science 101 class, just enough so you know what's going on. Ready for a speedrun?

Memory and processes (at a glance)

First off, memory actually belongs to the computer, and the kernel is the grumpy landlord who doles it out to processes. A process is basically a handle that the OS uses to manage running programs, keep track of open files, and map out which memory sections you're allowed to use. You get a chunk of user-accessible memory that includes the stack, the heap, and a few other areas such as global data, read-only constants, and uninitialized (BSS) segments.

So, imagine two different storage rooms in the same building: one is small, secure, and easy to get in and out of; the other is vast and more flexible but requires more effort to manage. That's the gist of how the stack and the heap work inside your program's memory space.

Stack

The stack is a highly organized memory region for a function's local variables. Think of it as a temporary workspace: when a function is called, it gets a new, clean area to work in.

When the function finishes, that entire workspace is instantly and automatically cleared. This strict, ordered process is why stack allocation is so fast, as it requires no manual cleanup or complex memory searching.

However, the stack is limited in size. If you try to cram a massive array in there or nest too many function calls, you risk hitting a guard page and crashing. Linux often sets a default main-thread stack of around 8 MB, which can vanish quickly if you're reckless.

That's why stack data generally has to be of a known, modest size at compile time.

It can be summarized as follows:

- It's limited. You can't just keep piling stuff in forever. Blow it up with a huge local array or crazy-deep recursion, and you get a crash (the infamous stack overflow error).

- You have to know your variable sizes at compile time. No 50 MB "just in case" arrays in there (unless you enjoy segfaults).

Heap

Consider the heap as a large warehouse space you rent on demand. You can request as much floor area as you need, assuming the kernel has the resources. In Zig, an allocator brokers these requests, grabbing memory from the kernel in bigger chunks, then doling it out to your code. This flexibility is fantastic for unpredictable or large data allocations, but once you're done with that warehouse space, you must free it yourself. Otherwise, you'll keep paying rent on empty shelves and eventually run out of room altogether. Allocating and freeing on the heap is also more complex than stack allocation, so it can be slower and prone to fragmentation when lots of different-sized requests come and go.

Need a huge array but not sure how big it'll be, or expecting the size to grow dynamically? You ask an allocator (in Zig, something such as std.heap.page_allocator or a custom allocator) for more space, and the allocator politely requests a chunk from the kernel. If the operating system says, "Sure," you get your memory. If not, bad luck. Also, you have to free it when you're done (don't be that person who forgets and leaks memory all over).

The 32-bit squeeze

On a 32-bit system, your program lives in a small 4 GB virtual address space. The heap grows upward, and the stack grows downward, so there's only so much room before the two collide. That collision can crash your program (or the kernel might refuse more allocations). In contrast, 64-bit systems have far more virtual space, so heap-stack collisions are less common, and your program can breathe easier. "How much is far more?" you ask. What about 16 exabytes? I personally think that's enough.

Other sections (we swear they exist)

Besides the stack and heap, your process also has areas for global data, code, BSS (uninitialized data), and more. These sections are mostly handled by the operating system or loader, and you rarely mess with them directly. For example, if you declare global variables in Zig, some go into a data segment, and zero-initialized ones might land in BSS. It's good to know they exist, but they're not something you typically tinker with on a daily basis, unless you're debugging a gnarly bug or working on a custom loader.

Now that we've set the stage by talking about the stack and the heap, it's time to see how we actually get references to data in these areas: without copying everything or blowing up our program. Enter pointers, the gateway to powerful (and potentially perilous) memory manipulation.

Pointers: The good, the bad, and the ugly (but mostly good)

Ah, pointers. Mention them to a room full of programmers and you'll see a range of reactions, from grizzled veterans rolling their eyes to new recruits silently mouthing, "Oh no, not again." But in Zig, pointers aren't out to get you (most of the time). They're just another well-defined tool to help you manage memory. Think of them as references with a little more honesty and fewer safety nets. No illusions: just you, your data, and your careful judgment.

Let's face it: in systems programming, you can't get far without pointers. They're like the secret ingredient that makes everything possible, and also the prime suspect when something goes horribly wrong. In Zig, pointers come in a few shapes and sizes, letting you refer to memory in a structured way without carrying the entire data payload on your back.

Let me introduce you to the why behind pointers, their various shapes, and how they help you tame memory. Along the way, we'll see some code snippets that both illustrate the power of pointers and warn us to watch our step. No one wants an accidental null pointer leading to a meltdown at 3 A.M., right?

Why bother with pointers?

Remember when we talked about stacks and heaps? Stacks are quick and tidy but have limited space, and you'd better know in advance how much you need. Heaps let you store bigger or unpredictably sized data, but require you to manage memory (allocate, then free) like you're renting a storage unit. Pointers are the key that opens that storage unit. Instead of lugging around huge arrays on the stack, you can simply pass a pointer to the data, like handing someone a key to your storage locker rather than rolling the entire contents down the hallway.

Roughly speaking, pointers solve two big headaches:

- You can't always know an object's size at compile time
- Even if you do, you might not want to copy that data around

Of course, pointers come with their own stress points: dangling references, memory leaks, alignment issues, and so on. But used responsibly, they're your best bet to handle memory effectively, especially in a language like Zig, which aims to give you the performance of C with fewer foot-guns.

Speaking of which, Zig's pointer model is both simpler and more explicit than what you might be used to in languages such as C. You have single-item pointers and many-item pointers, each with its own capabilities and limitations. Your mission, should you choose to accept it, is to learn how to harness these raw memory references without blowing your own foot off.

> **Running examples**
>
> In our explorations, we'll walk through some tests demonstrating pointer basics. You can run them with `zig test <filename>.zig`.

Getting a pointer: & (address of)

Let's start with the classic "address of" operator, &:

```zig
const std = @import("std");
const expect = std.testing.expect;

test "managing player health using pointers" {
    const npc_health: i32 = 100;
    const npc_health_ptr = &npc_health;
    try expect(npc_health_ptr.* == 100);
    try expect(@TypeOf(npc_health_ptr) == *const i32);

    var player_health: i32 = 150;
    const player_health_ptr = &player_health;
    try expect(@TypeOf(player_health_ptr) == *i32);

    player_health_ptr.* -= 20;
    try expect(player_health_ptr.* == 130);
    try expect(player_health == 130)
}
```

Take your time to explore and understand what's happening in these tests. Once you feel ready, proceed to the following explanation.

In this test, the NPC's health is represented as a constant (`npc_health`) with an initial value of 100. We take its address, resulting in a pointer of type `*const i32` (pointer to a constant integer). Since the pointer points to an immutable value, it can only be read but not modified.

Next up, the player's health is represented as a mutable variable (`player_health`) with an initial value of 150. Taking the address of this variable gives `*i32` (pointer to a mutable integer). Using this pointer, we simulate the player taking damage by directly mutating the health value (`player_health_ptr.* -= 20`).

This small snippet, surprisingly, highlights Zig's memory safety features: explicit mutability, pointer semantics, and compile-time safety.

> **A note on pointer benefits**
>
> You might be thinking that using a pointer for a single `i32` doesn't offer much of a performance gain, and you'd be right. The real power becomes evident when dealing with large structs. Imagine a struct with dozens of fields; copying it every time you pass it to a function would be slow and memory-intensive. By passing a pointer instead, you only copy the memory address (a few bytes), giving you efficient access to the original data without the overhead.

Explicit mutability

You can only modify data if the pointer's type and the original variable's mutability allow it. This prevents accidental side effects in code.

When we take the address of an immutable variable (`const`), the resulting pointer type is `*const T` (a pointer to a constant value). This ensures you cannot modify the value through the pointer. On the other hand, when we take the address of a mutable variable (`var`), the resulting pointer type is `*T` (a pointer to a mutable value). This allows you to modify the value the pointer refers to.

Pointer semantics

Zig enforces strict typing for pointers. The program checks at runtime (and implicitly at compile time) that the pointer to a const variable has type `*const T`, while the pointer to a var variable has type `*T`. This type enforcement ensures that you cannot accidentally modify immutable variables or misuse mutable ones.

By making the mutability of pointers explicit in their types, Zig provides a clear and predictable model for working with memory.

Compile-time safety

After taking the address of a mutable variable (var), the program modifies its value through the pointer (y_ptr.*). This operation succeeds because the pointer's type allows mutations. The updated value is verified by dereferencing the pointer again.

Zig's type system catches many potential bugs related to mutability and pointer misuse at compile time.

What if you take the address of just one element in an array?

Pointer array access

In Zig, arrays cannot hold const values; attempting to declare an array such as [_]const u8 will result in a compile error. Because of this rule, when you take the address of an element within an array, you get a pointer to the element's type, not a pointer to a const value within the array. For a mutable array (var), you get a *T pointer. For an immutable array (const), you get a *const T pointer. If you want to modify data through a pointer, the original array must be mutable from the start.

So, with arrays, you get a single-item pointer (*T), so no pointer arithmetic is allowed.

For mutable data, you get *T. For immutable data, you get *const T. Zig doesn't let you silently drop const. If you want to mutate through a pointer, you need it to be mutable from the start.

But you can still dereference it to read or write that element:

```
test "upgrading player inventory slots using pointers" {
    var inventory_slots = [_]u8 { 1, 2, 3, 4, 5 };
    const slot_ptr = &inventory_slots[2];

    try expect(@TypeOf(slot_ptr) == *u8); // Pointer to a mutable u8
    try expect(slot_ptr.* == 3);

    slot_ptr.* += 1;
    try expect(inventory_slots[2] == 4); // 3rd slot is now at level 4
}
```

Let's explore this example:

- The inventory_slots array represents the levels of different inventory slots available to the player, initialized with the values {1, 2, 3, 4, 5}.

- The slot_ptr pointer is created using the address of operator (&) to point to the third slot (inventory_slots[2]), which initially has a level of 3.

- The slot_ptr pointer is used to upgrade the level of the third slot by incrementing its value (slot_ptr.* += 1).

- Since inventory_slots is mutable, this mutation directly affects the array.

The test ensures the following:

- The pointer type is *u8, confirming mutability
- The value in the third slot is correctly updated to reflect the new level (4)

The ptr.* syntax explicitly dereferences the pointer, making it clear that you are accessing or modifying the value at the pointer's memory address. In other words, that ptr.* is just a fancy way of saying, "the thing at the address ptr."

Converting between pointers and integers

Sometimes, you need to treat pointers as numeric addresses, maybe for system-level fiddling or interfacing with hardware. For example, in a game engine, you might want to inspect memory directly (say, figuring out why your NPCs are spawning at weird positions). Zig gives you tools to treat pointers as raw numeric addresses:

- @intFromPtr(address) converts a pointer address to an integer
- @ptrFromInt(ptr) converts an integer to a pointer

```
test "debugging spawn points with pointer math" {
    const spawn_point_ptr: *usize = @ptrFromInt(0xdeadbee0); // Memory-
mapped spawn point

    const addr = @intFromPtr(spawn_point_ptr);
    try expect(@TypeOf(addr) == usize);
    try expect(addr == 0xdeadbee0); // Spawn point matches the expected
address
}
```

💡 **Quick tip**: Enhance your coding experience with the **AI Code Explainer** and **Quick Copy** features. Open this book in the next-gen Packt Reader. Click the **Copy** button (**1**) to quickly copy code into your coding environment, or click the **Explain** button (**2**) to get the AI assistant to explain a block of code to you.

```
                                              Copy      Explain
function calculate(a, b) {                     1          2
  return {sum: a + b};
};
```

📖 **The next-gen Packt Reader** is included for free with the purchase of this book. Scan the QR code OR go to https://packtpub.com/unlock, then use the search bar to find this book by name. Double-check the edition shown to make sure you get the right one.

Caution!

Feeding your CPU invalid addresses can crash your game faster than a boss fight gone wrong. Always ensure the address is valid before use.

volatile

When working with memory locations that have real-world consequences, volatile is your go-to tool. It tells the compiler not to optimize away reads or writes that might interact with external systems. This is especially crucial in the following scenarios:

- **Hardware interactions**

  Specific memory addresses, such as **Memory-Mapped I/O (MMIO)**, correspond to hardware registers rather than regular RAM. Writing to these addresses can trigger hardware actions such as starting a motor, flipping an LED, or sending data to a peripheral device.

  Also, reading hardware counters or communicating through shared memory with devices requires ensuring that each read or write happens exactly as intended.

- **Interrupt handling**

  When an **Interrupt Service Routine (ISR)** modifies shared variables, volatile ensures the main program always reads the most up-to-date value.

- **Preventing compiler optimizations**

  By default, compilers assume memory loads and stores are simple operations without side effects. They might do the following:

  - Cache values, resulting in fewer actual memory reads
  - Reorder instructions to improve performance

However, in hardware programming, this can lead to incorrect behavior. Take the following example:

  - If reading a hardware register twice, the compiler might optimize away the second read, assuming the value hasn't changed
  - Writing to a control register might be reordered, breaking hardware timing expectations

volatile explicitly instructs the compiler: "These loads and stores must happen exactly as written in the source code."

volatile versus concurrency

It's essential to note that volatile is not a tool for concurrency or threading. While it ensures memory accesses happen as written, it does not do the following:

- Prevent data races
- Enforce atomicity

For concurrent programming, use atomics or proper synchronization primitives. Using volatile for thread-safe flags or multithreading often indicates a bug and could result in undefined behavior.

Casting pointers: Loot boxes and mystery bytes

Imagine you're parsing a network packet containing loot box rewards, and the data arrives as raw bytes. To extract meaningful information, you need to interpret these bytes as structured data. This is where @ptrCast and @alignCast come into play:

```
test "open the loot box (pointer casting)" {
    const loot_bytes = [_]u8 { 0x12, 0x34, 0x56, 0x78 };
    const loot_value_ptr: *const u32 = @alignCast(@ptrCast(&loot_
bytes[0]));
    try std.testing.expect(loot_value_ptr.* == 0x78563412);
}
```

This test shows how to interpret raw bytes (loot_bytes) as a u32 using @ptrCast and @alignCast. It ensures proper pointer alignment and validates the interpreted value (0x78563412), which depends on the system's endianness. This method is useful for working with raw memory but requires caution with alignment and byte order.

> **Safer options**
>
> There's a safer alternative available in the standard library: the bytesAsSlice function can achieve the same result. However, we're saving the standard library for *Chapter 10*. Let's take it one step at a time for now, alright?

A common real-world scenario is in embedded programming, where a specific hardware register (such as a GPIO control port) is located at a fixed memory address provided by the hardware datasheet. To interact with it, you must convert that integer address into a pointer.

Why use @alignCast with @ptrCast?

When interpreting raw bytes as a specific type, alignment matters. While @ptrCast tells the compiler to reinterpret the memory at a given address as a different pointer type (in this case, changing a pointer to a u8 into a pointer to a u32), @alignCast ensures the pointer meets the alignment requirements of the target type. For instance, a u32 typically requires memory to be aligned to a 4-byte boundary. Failing to align properly could result in crashes or undefined behavior, especially on platforms with strict alignment rules.

Reinterpreting bits

Sometimes, you don't need pointer manipulation at all. For example, imagine decoding a special item in a game's inventory where its identifier is packed as a u32, but you need to view it as four individual u8 bytes. Enter @bitCast:

```
test "bitCast for decoding item ID" {
    const item_id: u32 = 0x12345678;
    const item_id_bytes = @bitCast([4]u8, item_id);

    std.testing.expect(item_id_bytes[0] == 0x78);
    std.testing.expect(item_id_bytes[1] == 0x56);
    std.testing.expect(item_id_bytes[2] == 0x34);
    std.testing.expect(item_id_bytes[3] == 0x12);
}
```

This test reinterprets a u32 (item_id) as an array of four bytes using @bitCast. It safely transforms the bits without manipulating memory or pointers and validates the byte order. This is a simpler and safer approach for bit-level reinterpretation.

Why use @bitCast?

- **Safety**: No need for pointer manipulation or alignment checks
- **Simplicity**: Reinterprets bits directly, reducing boilerplate and potential bugs
- **Endian awareness**: Just like pointer casting, the output depends on the system's endianness, so confirm the expected order on your target platform

When should you use @bitCast?

- **Decoding packets**: Interpreting raw network data as structured fields.
- **Graphics programming**: Converting between formats such as packed colors (e.g., u32 RGBA) and arrays of u8 channels

- **Serialization/deserialization**: Quickly reinterpreting a value without copying or additional overhead

If your goal is to reinterpret data, @bitCast avoids the complexity of pointer manipulation and ensures clarity in your code.

Alright! You might be wondering: When should I use one approach over the other? Here are the guidelines:

- Use @ptrCast with @alignCast when you need to reinterpret a specific memory location (e.g., raw bytes from hardware or buffers)
- Use @bitCast when you need to reinterpret the bits of a value without touching memory directly, making it simpler and safer for tasks such as serialization or format conversion

Single-item versus many-item pointers

Zig distinguishes pointers by what they point to. *T is a pointer to a single item of type T. It's like saying: "I know exactly one element is here." Meanwhile, [*]T is a many-item pointer, acknowledging that multiple consecutive items exist in memory, even if their number isn't known at compile time. Consider it as a more flexible view: "This points somewhere in a sequence of items."

*T (single-item pointer) can be described as follows:

- You can dereference it with ptr.*
- You can't perform index operations such as ptr[i] directly
- No pointer arithmetic is allowed (no ptr + 1), since Zig won't assume there's another item after the first

[*]T (many-item pointer) can be described as follows:

- Supports indexing: ptr[i]
- Allows pointer arithmetic: ptr + 1 gives the next element
- Lets you treat memory like a continuous buffet of items, assuming they're actually there

For fixed-size data known at compile time, *[N]T is a pointer to an array of N elements. It's like having a firm guarantee: "Right here, there are exactly N items."

Slicing with pointers

You can create array pointers by slicing a single-item pointer: x_ptr[0..1] produces *[1]i32—a pointer to a single-item array, effectively. Coercing that to [*]i32 gives you a many-item pointer referencing exactly that one element:

```
test "slice syntax on pointers" {
    var y: i32 = 5678;
    const y_ptr = &y;
    const y_array_ptr = y_ptr[0..1]; // *[1]i32
    const y_many_ptr: [*]i32 = y_array_ptr;
    try std.testing.expect(@TypeOf(y_many_ptr) == [*]i32);
    try std.testing.expect(y_many_ptr[0] == 5678);
}
```

This chaining might seem odd, but once you get used to it, it's surprisingly clear. You start with a single reference, then you "pretend" it's an array of length 1, and finally generalize it to a many-item pointer type. I'm pretty sure that slices are making more sense now, right?

Pointer arithmetic: A loaded gun

Pointer arithmetic is allowed with many-item pointers. You can do ptr += 1 to advance to the next element. Just remember that Zig trusts you. If you point off into oblivion, that's your problem.

For slices ([]T), don't mess around by directly changing slice.ptr without adjusting slice.len; you'll create a lying slice that claims more elements than it can back up. Zig's slices are safer, so if you need flexibility, consider working with slices rather than raw pointers.

```
test "pointer arithmetic" {
    const arr = [_]i32{ 1, 2, 3, 4 };
    var ptr: [*]const i32 = &arr;
    try std.testing.expect(ptr[0] == 1);
    ptr += 1; // move forward one element
    try std.testing.expect(ptr[0] == 2);
}
```

Slices versus pointers

Slices ([ ]T) are like a pointer plus a length: a "fat pointer" (I didn't come up with this name; blame Walter Bright). They're safer because they know their bounds. Indexing out of range is caught at runtime. With a raw pointer, you're on your own. Choose wisely.

Pointers in Zig provide direct, flexible access to (virtual) memory, empowering you to manipulate data at a low level. Whether you're referencing a single item (*T), working with a many-item pointer ([*]T), or safely indexing a slice ([ ]T), Zig offers a pointer type for every need. From system-level wizardry to everyday array manipulations, pointers are essential tools, but they come with inherent risks. Missteps such as dangling pointers, alignment issues, or accessing memory you don't own can quickly lead to bugs or crashes.

Zig strikes a great balance between power and safety. It enforces rules to help you avoid obvious mistakes (e.g., mixing single-item and many-item pointers) but leaves ultimate responsibility in your hands. Mastering pointers means thinking carefully about what you're doing, embracing the power to directly control memory while respecting the dangers it brings.

Armed with this knowledge, you're ready to dive into the world of allocation. Pat yourself on the back; you've tamed the pointer beast and are prepared for what lies ahead.

Allocation: The art of asking for more memory (and getting it)

If pointers are the "keys" to memory, allocators are the landlords. Zig's philosophy is like that of a brutally honest landlord who doesn't believe in "magic" services. There's no garbage collector to clean up after you.

Instead, Zig hands you the keys and the lease, making it clear that the contract is between you and the memory system. The responsibility to return the keys (to free the memory) is yours alone. If you fail, it's entirely your fault.

Zig versus mainstream languages: The babysitters and the grown-ups

Most mainstream languages treat you like an overgrown toddler when it comes to memory. Java and Go cheerfully hand you all the memory you want, confident that their garbage collector will clean up after you, like a doting nanny with no boundaries. Python takes it a step further, assuring you that it's fine to throw toys everywhere because someone else will tidy up. Even Rust, with its smug borrow checker, insists on holding your hand, albeit while muttering condescendingly about lifetimes and ownership.

And then there's Zig. Zig doesn't hold your hand. It slaps it away. Memory management here is like renting an apartment in a cutthroat city: you decide where you're going to live, how much you're going to pay, and when to move out. And if you forget to move out, guess what? You're stuck with the mess.

Unlike C, which quietly slips you `malloc` and hopes you don't notice the bad habits it's enabling, Zig makes no assumptions. There's no default allocator lurking in the shadows. You want memory? Fine. But you'll have to decide where it comes from, how it's managed, and when to clean it up.

Manual memory management gives you deterministic performance by eliminating unpredictable pauses caused by a garbage collector. It also allows for fine-grained optimization of memory usage, which is critical in systems programming, game development, and other performance-sensitive domains.

Zig's approach is simple: *You break it, you buy it.*

The OOM reality check

In Java, you'd mainstream languages blissfully write code, ignoring the possibility of running out of memory. When it happens—boom. **Out-of-Memory (OOM)** error, game over. Go tries to be clever with an overcommit, but that just leads to the OOM killer silently assassinating your process.

If memory isn't available, Zig returns `error.OutOfMemory`. No hand-waving, no fairy tales—just a brutal, honest error. It's your job to handle it gracefully, retry, or degrade functionality.

Allocators interface

Zig is the language that dared to show the world how system programming could be more about wielding a blade than just polishing it. Before you get too excited, let me crush your enthusiasm for a moment: Zig doesn't have "interfaces" like the ones you know and love (or tolerate) in other languages.

No, you won't be writing a public interface MemoryAllocator with all the flair of a software architect who's watched too many enterprise tutorials. Zig keeps things raw—as it should in system programming—and yet somehow still manages to provide you with everything you actually need.

No need to sweat the nitty-gritty details right now. The main point is that Zig doesn't come with built-in "interfaces." Instead, it relies on function pointers and structs to let you shape how your code behaves. Think of it like conjuring your own magic spells rather than depending on a premade wand—you're still managing memory, just with more direct control. Everything else can wait until later.

Let's dig into allocators—more precisely, the std.mem.Allocator type—and how they function as an interface, but do it with style. We'll explore the abyss of memory management through some game-inspired analogies.

Allocators in Zig

Imagine you're a game master setting up a dungeon for your adventurers. Allocators are like magical backpacks. Each has its own rules for storing, retrieving, and discarding items (or memory blocks). In Zig, this isn't enforced by an interface, but rather a loose protocol: an allocator needs to have methods for alloc, resize, and free. If you don't adhere to this, your adventure party's mage will cast NullPointerException faster than you can debug.

Here's the brutal truth: Zig won't do the memory-dance for you. Instead, you're the choreographer of your own system-level ballet. We're dealing with three big moves here: alloc, free, and resize. Let's break them down.

alloc: Grabbing memory manually

Forget the cozy safety nets. alloc is your basic command to request memory. Need an array of 10 integers? You call alloc, specify the type, and how many. It either coughs up a shiny new slice or returns an error if your system is too strapped for bytes. Plain and simple, no strings attached.

free: Return it or suffer

When you're done with that memory, free it. Yes, if you forget, your program will quietly eat up more and more memory until your machine screams. Zig doesn't forgive. If you never free memory, your program will expand like a cosmic horror until it devours all the RAM. Good luck explaining that to your boss. It's all on you. So be a responsible adult—free your stuff.

resize: Asking politely for more

Sometimes you realize you need a bigger slice than you originally allocated. Or maybe you got too much and want to shrink it. That's resize for you. It requests a new size for your existing allocation without shifting it in memory—unless your allocator just can't handle that, in which case resize shrugs and returns false. If that happens, you'll need to do a manual dance: allocate a new chunk, copy your data, and free the old chunk.

It's a bit more effort, but that's the trade-off for total control. When working with an allocator, we gain two additional convenience functions: create and destroy.

create: Single-item allocation

create is your go-to for constructing a single item of a given type. Instead of alloc-ing an entire array, you just get a single pointer. Under the covers, it's really just alloc for one element, plus a sprinkle of convenience. It is still your responsibility to manage the memory, as create is a standard convenience function, not a form of automatic memory management.

destroy: Free that single item

Conversely, we have destroy. This pairs with create for one-off items, much like free pairs with alloc for slices. You don't have to pass in a length because that's all tracked under the hood. But the message is the same: stop hogging memory you're not using. Call destroy when you're done.

That's it. Straight to the point, right? No pretty illusions or garbage collectors to save you from the consequences of sloppy code. Zig won't hold your hand here, and that's why you love it... or will, eventually. Compare this to other languages where you'd typically use a new keyword to create instances of objects or memory allocations. This is not just a stylistic choice; it's about giving you complete control. new in other languages often hides the details of memory management, making it easy to use but harder to optimize or debug. Zig's create makes you confront these details head-on.

Lifetime considerations

Memory management in Zig is like managing your hero's health potions in a sprawling RPG dungeon. It's not just about grabbing what you need, but ensuring you don't leave behind a mess of forgotten potions (or dangling pointers) that could come back to haunt you. If you've grown accustomed to the warm embrace of garbage collectors, prepare for the icy sting of accountability. In Zig, you manage your lifetimes explicitly, and there's no magical healer to clean up your mistakes.

Every byte in your program has its place, much like the different inventory slots in your favorite RPG. Let's see where these bytes reside:

```zig
const std = @import("std");

// Stored in the global constant section of memory.
const manaPotion: f64 = 1.337;
const battleCry = "For Honor!";

// Stored in the global data section.
var monstersDefeated: usize = 0;

fn calculateDamage() u8 {
    // These local variables are gone once the function exits.
    const swordDamage: u8 = 10;
    const shieldBonus: u8 = 5;
    const totalDamage: u8 = swordDamage + shieldBonus;
    // Returning a copy of `totalDamage`, safe and sound.
    return totalDamage;
}
```

In this example, global constants such as manaPotion and battleCry are stored in a persistent section of memory—similar to inventory items that never run out. Meanwhile, local variables such as swordDamage live only within the function's scope. Once the function ends, these variables vanish, like temporary buffs after a battle.

This setup works fine until you try to take a shortcut and return memory that doesn't outlive its context. Let's talk about those dangerous traps.

Sometimes, adventurers take dangerous risks, such as walking into a trap-filled dungeon. In Zig, traps often take the form of dangling pointers. Consider this ill-advised strategy:

```zig
fn cursedSword() *u8 {
    var attackPower: u8 = 42;
    // Attack power lives on the stack and will disappear after the
function.
    return &attackPower;
}
```

This function returns a pointer to a stack variable. When the function ends, the stack frame is destroyed, and the pointer becomes invalid. Trying to use it is like equipping a cursed sword—it might work for a moment, but sooner or later, it'll turn against you.

Now meet its equally reckless cousin:

```
fn cursedScroll() []u8 {
    var spell: [5]u8 = .{ 'F', 'i', 'r', 'e', '!' };
    const incantation = spell[1..]; // Slice into the array.
    // The array vanishes after the function, leaving `incantation`
dangling.
    return incantation;
}
```

This slice references memory that is destroyed when the function exits. Returning it is akin to handing your adventurers a map to a dungeon that collapses the moment they enter.

To avoid these traps, ensure that the memory allocated in your functions outlives the function itself. Heap allocation is your hero's sanctuary:

```
fn enchantedSword(allocator: std.mem.Allocator) std.mem.Allocator.Error![]
u8 {
    var swordStats: [5]u8 = .{ 'S', 'l', 'a', 's', 'h' };
    const statsCopy = try allocator.alloc(u8, swordStats.len);
    @memcpy(statsCopy, &swordStats);
    return statsCopy;
}
```

Here, statsCopy is safely allocated on the heap, meaning it will outlive the function. It's now the caller's responsibility to free the memory once it's no longer needed—much like ensuring your adventurers return borrowed items to the guild.

When the quests get longer and the loot piles higher, managing lifetimes manually becomes tedious and error-prone. To handle this, Zig programmers often adopt a conventional pattern using init and deinit methods. It is important to note that these are not special keywords or language features (like constructors and destructors in other languages), but simply a community-aware pattern for functions that you write yourself. This convention allows you to encapsulate memory management within structs, ensuring that resources are allocated and freed in a predictable manner—think of it as hiring a squire to carry your gear and clean up after battles.

```
const Sword = struct {
stats: []u8,

pub fn init(allocator: std.mem.Allocator, stats: []const u8) !*Sword {
    // Allocate memory for the struct.
    const sword_ptr = try allocator.create(Sword);
    errdefer allocator.destroy(sword_ptr);
    // Allocate memory for the sword stats.
    sword_ptr.stats = try allocator.alloc(u8, stats.len);
@memcpy(sword_ptr.stats, stats);
    return sword_ptr;
}

pub fn deinit(self: *Sword, allocator: std.mem.Allocator) void {
    // Free the memory for the stats.
    allocator.free(self.stats);
    // Destroy the struct itself.
    allocator.destroy(self);
}
};
```

This struct ensures that memory for Sword and its stats are properly managed. By encapsulating the allocation and cleanup logic, you reduce the risk of memory leaks and dangling pointers.

> **Pro tip**
>
> Always use errdefer when allocating memory to ensure that any partial allocations are cleaned up immediately if something fails. This guarantees that your program won't leave behind stray memory allocations even in the event of an error.

Testing allocators: std.testing.allocator

Zig takes testing seriously, and memory allocation is no exception. std.testing.allocator is a powerful tool designed to assist with testing your allocator usage. It's a debug-oriented allocator that detects common allocation issues, such as memory leaks, double frees, or invalid accesses. By incorporating this allocator into your tests, you can validate that your code interacts safely and correctly with the memory it allocates.

In Zig, the best practice is not to impose an allocator on your function or library users. Instead, you provide them with the flexibility to choose an allocator that best suits their needs. This approach respects Zig's philosophy of empowering developers with control and transparency. By accepting an allocator as a parameter, you allow the caller to decide whether to use the general-purpose allocator, a custom allocator tailored for specific performance requirements, or even a temporary stack allocator for short-lived data. This design promotes adaptability, making your code more versatile and reusable in a wide range of contexts.

Why use std.testing.allocator?

Imagine running your game or application and encountering a silent memory leak that only reveals itself after hours of runtime. Debugging such issues can be daunting. `std.testing.allocator` addresses this by doing the following:

- Tracking all allocations and deallocations
- Reporting discrepancies like leaked or improperly freed memory
- Enforcing stricter checks to catch issues early in development

Testing your equipment

As any seasoned adventurer knows, testing your gear before heading into battle is essential. Similarly, you should test your memory management to ensure it works as expected:

```
const battleCry = "Victory!";


test "Sword initialization and cleanup" {
const allocator = std.testing.allocator;
var sword_ptr = try Sword.init(allocator, battleCry);

// Ensure the stats were copied correctly.
try std.testing.expectEqualStrings(battleCry, sword_ptr.stats);
}
```

The code seems fine—it appends elements and checks the list length. However, when you run the test, the terminal tells a different story:

```
> [gpa] (err): memory address 0x102bc0000 leaked
```

Now, don't panic! This isn't your college GPA haunting you. In Zig, GPA doesn't stand for "grade point average," but it might as well be the "great panic alarm" for memory management. Forgot to call `deinit`? BAM! Zig tattles on you like a professor who just found out you skipped class to play video games.

The testing allocator is diligent about catching such mistakes during testing, but in production, these leaks can accumulate silently, leading to significant problems.

To resolve this, always pair `init` with `deinit`. Using `defer` ensures that cleanup happens automatically, even if an error occurs:

```
const battleCry = "Victory!";

test "Sword initialization and cleanup" {
    const allocator = std.testing.allocator;
    var sword_ptr = try Sword.init(allocator, battleCry);
    defer sword_ptr.deinit(allocator);

    // Ensure the stats were copied correctly.
    try std.testing.expectEqualStrings(battleCry, sword_ptr.stats);
}
```

This test initializes a `Sword`, verifies that its `stats` were copied correctly, and then cleans up the allocated memory. It's like sharpening your blade and testing its balance before charging into the fray.

Think of it as turning in your homework on time—your allocator professor will be pleased, and no memory leaks will mess up your perfect record. Forget it, though, and Zig will leave you a note on your desk: "Memory address leaked, better luck next semester!"

Handling allocation failures: std.testing.failing_allocator

Memory allocation is a game of Tetris where the stakes are high, and the pieces are invisible. But wait, what if the pieces sometimes just... vanish mid-air? That's where `FailingAllocator` swoops in, wearing its villainous cape, to mess with your tidy little memory management. And honestly, you should thank it for the pain—it's here to make your error-handling code less pathetic.

What's the big deal?

FailingAllocator isn't your everyday allocator. No, this one is a certified troublemaker. It's not here to help your code work; it's here to prove your code doesn't fall apart when things go sideways. Think of it as a chaos monkey for your memory management. It pretends to be a normal allocator, but deep down, it's counting your allocations, sharpening its metaphorical dagger, and waiting for the moment to scream, "Out of memory!"

It simulates allocation failures deterministically. It allows you to reproduce and test edge cases where memory allocation fails, ensuring your code responds gracefully. The following are examples:

- Validating that memory leaks don't occur even when allocations fail
- Ensuring proper error handling and recovery logic in your code

Here's how you conjure this delightful tormentor:

```
const battleCry = "Victory!";

test "Sword initialization and cleanup" {
    const allocator = std.testing.failing_allocator;
    const sword = Sword.init(allocator, battleCry);
    try std.testing.expectError(error.OutOfMemory, sword);
}
```

This test ensures that the Sword.init function correctly handles memory allocation failures.

Simple enough, right? But wait for it...

Meet fail_index: The allocation assassin

fail_index is where the magic happens. It defines how many allocations your code gets to enjoy before the party ends. Set it to 2 and the third allocation will fail harder than your freshman-year Java project.

```
var failing_allocator = std.testing.FailingAllocator.init(std.testing.
allocator, .{ .fail_index = 2 });
var allocator = failing_allocator.allocator();
// Two successful allocations. Hooray!
var a = try allocator.create(i32);
var b = try allocator.create(i32);
```

```
// Oh no! Allocation number three trips over the fail_index.
try std.testing.expectError(error.OutOfMemory, allocator.create(i32));
```

The test attempts a third allocation, but this time the allocator fails. This failure is expected because `failing_allocator` has been set up to fail after a certain number of successful allocations (known as the `fail_index`). The `std.testing.expectError` ensures that the error returned is specifically `error.OutOfMemory`.

Failures with a view: Stack traces

Now, you might be thinking, "What good is a failure if I don't know where it came from?" Don't worry, `FailingAllocator` has your back—or rather, your stack. When an allocation fails, it captures the stack trace leading up to the catastrophe. Because why debug your code when you can have the stack trace roast you instead?

```
if (failing_alloc.has_induced_failure) {
    const trace = failing_alloc.getStackTrace();
    std.debug.print("Stack trace of failure: {any}\n", .{trace});
}
```

It is perfect for those moments when you want to pinpoint exactly which line of code betrayed you.

Resizing? Meet resize_fail_index

If allocations aren't enough to ruin your day, there's also the sibling feature, `resize_fail_index`. Same idea, different target. This one dictates how many times you're allowed to resize memory before it slams the door in your face.

First, we initialize `FailingAllocator` and set `resize_fail_index` to 1. This means the first resize attempt (at index 0) will succeed, but the second one (at index 1) will fail:

```
var failing_alloc = std.testing.FailingAllocator.init(
std.testing.allocator, .{ .resize_fail_index = 1 }
);
const allocator = failing_alloc.allocator();
```

Now, let's allocate a buffer and try resizing it twice:

```
const buffer = try allocator.alloc(u8, 16);
defer allocator.free(buffer);
try std.testing.expect(allocator.resize(buffer, 32) == true);
try std.testing.expect(allocator.resize(buffer, 64) == false);
```

As configured, the first call to resize succeeds. The second call returns `false`, just as we planned. This allows us to deterministically test the failure-handling path in our code.

It's like that annoying friend who only helps you move one box before declaring they're "too tired."

Metrics, because we're fancy like that

Not only does `FailingAllocator` bring chaos, but it also tracks the wreckage with obsessive precision:

- `alloc_index`: How many allocations you've successfully made. Think of it as the allocator's countdown to betrayal.
- `allocated_bytes`/`freed_bytes`: A ledger of memory gained and lost. Like your bank statement, but with pointers instead of bad decisions.
- `allocations`/`deallocations`: A scoreboard for every time you've called `alloc` or `free`.

These metrics let you prove that your code leaks memory under stress—or, if you're lucky, confirm that it doesn't.

Why should you care?

Here's the thing: writing code that works isn't the hard part. Writing code that doesn't crumble under pressure? That's where legends are made. `FailingAllocator` isn't just a tool—it's your personal dungeon master, setting traps and riddles for your error-handling logic. Survive its trials, and you'll emerge with code that's battle-hardened and ready for production—or at least ready to fail more gracefully.

So, go ahead, embrace the chaos. Just don't blame `FailingAllocator` when it exposes your mistakes. It's only doing its job.

So, is Zig's approach to allocators and interfaces unconventional? Absolutely. But that's why it's thrilling—you're not just coding; you're taming a beast. Zig's allocators give you the power to define your own rules, to build your systems the way you want, and to do it with a precision that most "high-level" languages can't touch. Sure, there's more responsibility on your shoulders, but isn't that the point of system programming?

Next up, we'll dive into "real allocators" and talk about how different types work, complete with more game-inspired analogies. For now, go forth and write some code. Or as Zig might put it, "Stop theorizing and start breaking things."

FixedBufferAllocator: Your first real allocator

Alright, so we've played with the fancy abstractions, dipped our toes in the testing allocator and `FailingAllocator`, and debugged our allocations like pros. But here's the kicker: none of that was a "real" allocator. It was all a simulation, like those training wheels on your first bike. Now it's time to ride solo. Meet `FixedBufferAllocator`, the first "real" allocator you'll use from Zig's standard library.

This isn't just another allocator; it's the dependable, pre-allocated workhorse you didn't know you needed. It's designed for situations where memory requirements are predictable and pre-determined. Think embedded systems, game development, or that moment when you decide to live dangerously and say, "No dynamic allocations for me, thanks."

`FixedBufferAllocator` operates on a fixed-size buffer, which means the following:

- You define how much memory it gets upfront
- It manages that memory within strict bounds
- Once the buffer is full, it politely says, "Sorry, you're out of luck"

Here's how you initialize it:

```
const std = @import("std");

pub fn main() !void {
    var buffer: [1024]u8 = undefined; // A 1KB fixed-size buffer.
    var fba = std.heap.FixedBufferAllocator.init(&buffer);
    const allocator = fba.allocator();

    const slice = try allocator.alloc(u8, 512); // Allocate 512 bytes.
    defer allocator.free(slice); // Free it when you're done.

    std.debug.print("Allocated {d} bytes from FixedBufferAllocator\n",
.{slice.len});
}
```

You've just allocated memory like a pro—predictable, controlled, and totally badass.

Let's dive into some examples to see why this allocator deserves its place in your toolkit.

Example 1: Concatenating strings

Imagine you're working with strings (slices of u8) and need to concatenate two of them. Here's how you do it with `FixedBufferAllocator`:

```
fn catAlloc(allocator: std.mem.Allocator, a: []const u8, b: []const u8)
![]u8 {
    const result = try allocator.alloc(u8, a.len + b.len);
    @memcpy(result[0..a.len], a);
    @memcpy(result[a.len..], b);
    return result;
}


test "Concatenating Strings with FBA" {
    var buffer: [64]u8 = undefined;
    var fba = std.heap.FixedBufferAllocator.init(&buffer);
    const allocator = fba.allocator();

    const hello = "Hello, ";
    const world = "world!";
    const result = try catAlloc(allocator, hello, world);
    defer allocator.free(result);

    try std.testing.expectEqualStrings(result, "Hello, world!");
}
```

Here, we pre-allocate 64 bytes and use them to concatenate strings. No heap fragmentation, no surprises. Just good old-fashioned control.

Example 2: Allocating structs

`FixedBufferAllocator` doesn't just work with slices. You can allocate structs too. Let's say you're building a game and need to manage a small pool of `Entity` objects:

```
const Entity = struct {
    id: u32,
    name: []const u8,
};


fn createEntities(allocator: std.mem.Allocator, count: usize) ![]Entity {
```

```
        return try allocator.alloc(Entity, count);
}

test "Allocating Structs with FBA" {
    var buffer: [128]u8 = undefined;
    var fba = std.heap.FixedBufferAllocator.init(&buffer);
    const allocator = fba.allocator();

const entities = try createEntities(allocator, 3);
defer allocator.free(entities);

entities[0] = .{ .id = 1, .name = "Hero" };
entities[1] = .{ .id = 2, .name = "Villain" };
entities[2] = .{ .id = 3, .name = "Sidekick" };

try std.testing.expectEqual(entities[0].id, 1);
try std.testing.expectEqualStrings(entities[1].name, "Villain");
    }
```

This time, we pre-allocate 128 bytes and use them to store a few Entity structs. The allocator manages the memory efficiently, so you can focus on the fun stuff, like saving the world (or destroying it).

Limitations (aka why you can't use this everywhere)

Before you rush to rewrite your entire code base with FixedBufferAllocator, let's talk about its Achilles' heel:

- **Fixed size:** Once the buffer is full, you're done. No fallback, no resizing.
- **No sharing:** It's tied to a specific buffer, so you can't share it across threads without extra work.
- **Manual management:** You have to think about allocation sizes and alignment, which means more work for you.

With FixedBufferAllocator in your arsenal, you're stepping into the big leagues. It's not just about managing memory. It's about owning it. So, saddle up and start using this powerhouse to make your programs faster, leaner, and a whole lot cooler.

Life isn't always so predictable, is it? Sometimes, you just need an all-purpose, jack-of-all-trades allocator to handle the chaos.

Enter `GeneralPurposeAllocator`, the versatile workhorse of Zig's allocator lineup. Whether you're juggling dynamic workloads, handling unpredictable memory requirements, or just want something reliable to back your code, this allocator has got you covered. Think of it as the Swiss Army knife of memory management—ready to adapt, efficient, and always dependable.

The GeneralPurposeAllocator(s): Plural? Yes, plural.

Alright, I lied. Remember how I said the `GeneralPurposeAllocator` was the allocator to rule them all? Well, it turns out there are actually two of them in Zig's standard library. Don't worry; you're not suddenly living in a memory management multiverse. One of these is the practical, no-nonsense implementation you'll likely use 90% of the time. The other? It's more like that backup sword in your inventory—handy but situational.

Let's clear this up before your confusion causes a stack overflow. When we talk about `GeneralPurposeAllocator`, we're typically referring to the big player, the configurable, dynamic allocator designed to handle everything from small objects to behemoth allocations, all while keeping memory management safe and efficient. But lurking quietly in the background is the raw, stripped-down version of this allocator, used for edge cases and special setups.

So, with my credibility restored (somewhat), let's dive into the real `GeneralPurposeAllocator`, the workhorse you'll rely on in production.

Meet THE GeneralPurposeAllocator

This allocator isn't just your average utility belt. It's a highly configurable memory management powerhouse. Designed to balance safety, performance, and flexibility, `GeneralPurposeAllocator` can adapt to your needs with various optimization modes and configuration options.

`GeneralPurposeAllocator` is as customizable as a builder set, with three optimization modes to choose from:

- **Debug mode:** Prioritizes safety and diagnostics. Ideal for catching bugs and ensuring your memory operations are correct.
- **Release fast:** Focuses on runtime performance and low fragmentation, sacrificing some of the safety checks.
- **Release small:** Optimized for small binary sizes, making it perfect for embedded systems or environments where space is a luxury.

You can further tweak its behavior using a slew of configuration options, from enabling stack traces to managing memory limits.

Let's see it in action with a practical example:

```
const std = @import("std");

pub fn main() !void {
    var gpa = std.heap.GeneralPurposeAllocator(.{
        .safety = true,
        .enable_memory_limit = true,
        .retain_metadata = true,
    }){};
    defer _ = gpa.deinit();
    const allocator = gpa.allocator();

    const memory = try allocator.alloc(u8, 512);
    defer allocator.free(memory);

    std.debug.print("Allocated {} bytes\n", .{memory.len});
}
```

In this snippet, we do the following:

- Configure the allocator to enable safety checks, memory limits, and metadata retention
- Allocate 512 bytes using the allocator
- Free the memory afterward, because we're responsible developers (sometimes)

You can tweak its behavior using a configuration struct (`Config`), tailoring it to your specific requirements. Here's a breakdown of some key configuration options and their use cases:

- Safety checks:
    - `safety`: Enables runtime checks to catch double frees, invalid accesses, and other memory-related bugs
    - Default: `std.debug.runtime_safety` (enabled in debug mode, disabled otherwise)

        ```
        var gpa = std.heap.GeneralPurposeAllocator(.{
            .safety = true, // Explicitly enable safety checks
        }){};
        ```

- Memory limits:

  - `enable_memory_limit`: Allows setting a memory cap. When the total allocated memory exceeds the limit, allocations return `error.OutOfMemory`.

  - `requested_memory_limit`: The actual memory limit (when `enable_memory_limit` is `true`).

- Metadata retention:

  - `retain_metadata`: Keeps metadata about allocations even after they are freed. Useful for debugging double frees and tracking memory usage.

  - `never_unmap`: Prevents unmapping memory from the system. Combined with `retain_metadata`, it helps debug rogue writes by keeping memory around indefinitely.

    ```
    var gpa = std.heap.GeneralPurposeAllocator(.{
        .retain_metadata = true,
        .never_unmap = true,
    }){};
    ```

- Thread safety:

  - `thread_safe`: Ensures the allocator can be safely used across threads

  - `MutexType`: Customizes the type of mutex used for thread safety

    ```
    var gpa = std.heap.GeneralPurposeAllocator(.{
        .thread_safe = true,
    }){};
    ```

The page allocator: The unsung hero

While the GPA handles small allocations with its bucket system, larger allocations rely on the page allocator. It interfaces directly with the operating system to manage memory at the page level, making it both versatile and efficient.

Key features are as follows:

- **Platform-specific optimization**: On Linux, it uses mmap; on Windows, it uses VirtualAlloc. This ensures that the page allocator works seamlessly across platforms.

- **Efficient large allocations**: Allocates memory in multiples of the system's page size (commonly 4 KB) and returns aligned memory blocks.

- **Releasing memory**: Frees memory back to the operating system as soon as it's no longer needed, preventing unnecessary resource hogging.

Allocating pages directly

If you want to use the page allocator directly (without GPA), here's how it's done:

```
const std = @import("std");

pub fn main() !void {
    const allocator = std.heap.page_allocator;

    const memory = try allocator.alloc(u8, 8192); // Allocate 2 pages on a
4 KB system
    defer allocator.free(memory);

    std.debug.print("Allocated {} bytes\n", .{memory.len});
}
```

In this example, we have the following:

- We request 8,192 bytes (two pages on a typical 4 KB page system)
- The page allocator handles the system-level allocation and returns the aligned memory block

How the page allocator powers the GPA

The page allocator acts as the backing allocator for the GPA. Here's how the two interact:

- **Small allocations**: The GPA uses buckets to manage small objects efficiently
- **Large allocations**: For objects too large to fit in a bucket, the GPA defers to the page allocator

Configuration modes: Debug, release, and small

Depending on the optimization mode, the GPA adjusts its behavior:

- Debug mode:
    - Focuses on memory safety, debugging, and leak detection
    - Ideal for development

- Release fast:

    - Prioritizes performance with reduced safety checks
    - Suitable for production environments where speed matters

- Release small:

    - Optimizes for small binary sizes
    - Perfect for embedded systems and constrained environments

`GeneralPurposeAllocator` is a powerhouse, capable of handling diverse allocation scenarios with the help of its trusty sidekick, the page allocator. Together, they provide a robust foundation for memory management in Zig, offering flexibility, safety, and efficiency.

In the next section, we'll delve into `ArenaAllocator`, a specialized allocator designed for scenarios where memory deallocation happens in bulk. Let's make your memory management even more efficient!

The arena allocator: A playground for memory management

The arena allocator is like the big kid on the playground who takes care of everyone's toys. It doesn't bother with the "return-to-sender" model of freeing individual allocations. Instead, it manages a big block of memory, lets you grab pieces as needed, and then clears everything out in one fell swoop when you're done.

This makes the arena allocator a great choice for certain use cases, but not for all. Let's dive into how it works, when it shines, and how to configure it effectively.

What is an arena allocator?

At its core, an arena allocator is a memory management strategy where you do the following:

- Allocate a large block of memory up front (or as needed)
- Subdivide the block into smaller allocations without individually freeing them
- Free the entire block of memory all at once when no longer needed

Think of it like setting up a workshop: you buy a big table (memory block), do all your crafting on it (allocations), and then clear the table when the project is done (deallocate the block).

When to use an arena allocator

The arena allocator is a great fit for the following scenarios:

- **Temporary allocations dominate**: You know all allocations are short-lived and can be freed together, such as in a parsing routine or a batch data processing job
- **High performance matters**: Avoiding the overhead of individually freeing allocations can significantly boost performance
- **Predictable memory usage**: You have a good idea of how much memory you'll need, minimizing waste

It's not ideal in the following circumstances:

- Individual allocations need to be freed independently
- Memory usage needs to be highly dynamic and long-lived

Features of the arena allocator

- **Buffer list**: Allocates memory in chunks and chains them together with a linked list. New chunks are added only when existing ones are full.
- **Reset capability**: Clears all allocations without deinitializing the allocator. Optional pre-heating keeps previously allocated capacity for reuse, improving performance in iterative scenarios.
- **Configurable reset modes**:
  - `free_all`: Releases all memory, starting from scratch
  - `retain_capacity`: Keeps the largest buffer size used, avoiding future allocations for similar workloads
  - `retain_with_limit`: Retains capacity up to a specified limit, shrinking larger buffers if necessary

Here's how to use the arena allocator for temporary allocations:

```
const std = @import("std");

pub fn main() !void {
    var arena = std.heap.ArenaAllocator.init(std.heap.page_allocator);
```

```
    defer arena.deinit(); // Frees all memory in one go

    const allocator = arena.allocator();

    // Allocate memory
    const memory1 = try allocator.alloc(u8, 100);
    const memory2 = try allocator.alloc(u8, 200);

    std.debug.print("Allocated {} and {} bytes\n", .{memory1.len, memory2.
len});
    // No need to free individually; `defer arena.deinit()` will take care
of everything
}
```

When working in iterative scenarios, you can reset the arena allocator to reuse previously allocated capacity:

```
const std = @import("std");

pub fn main() !void {
    var arena = std.heap.ArenaAllocator.init(std.heap.page_allocator);
    defer arena.deinit();

    const allocator = arena.allocator();

    for ([_]usize{256, 512, 1024}) |alloc_size| {
        const memory = try allocator.alloc(u8, alloc_size);
        std.debug.print("Allocated {} bytes\n", .{memory.len});

        // Reset the arena and reuse memory
        _ = arena.reset(.retain_capacity);
    }
}
```

If you want to reuse memory but also enforce a size limit, use the retain_with_limit mode:

```
const std = @import("std");

pub fn main() !void {
```

```
    var arena = std.heap.ArenaAllocator.init(std.heap.page_allocator);
    defer arena.deinit();

    const allocator = arena.allocator();

    // Allocate and use memory
    _ = try allocator.alloc(u8, 1024);

    // Reset, retaining only 512 bytes of capacity
    if (!arena.reset(.{ .retain_with_limit = 512 })) {
        std.debug.print("Failed to reset with limit\n", .{});
    }
}
```

The following are benefits of the arena allocator:

- **Performance**: Allocations and resets are fast, as there's no need to individually free memory

- **Simple life cycle**: Easy to manage memory when you know everything can be freed together

- **Reusability**: Resetting with retained capacity optimizes memory usage for repeated workloads

The following are drawbacks of the arena allocator:

- **No individual free**: Memory is only freed all at once, so it's not suitable for dynamic or long-lived allocations

- **Potential memory waste**: If your workload is unpredictable, unused portions of large buffers may go to waste

The arena allocator is an elegant solution for specific scenarios where allocations can be grouped and freed together. By leveraging reset modes and preheating, it ensures high performance for repetitive tasks. However, it's important to evaluate whether its "no individual free" limitation aligns with your use case.

It's time to go even deeper and explore how to extend or modify existing allocators for custom behaviors.

When working with allocators in Zig, the key to success lies in choosing the right tool for the job and following best practices to ensure robust and efficient memory management. Always free allocated memory, ideally using defer to guarantee cleanup even in case of errors. Pass allocators as parameters to promote flexibility and testability in your code base. For applications with cyclical allocation patterns, such as game loops or web servers, std.heap.ArenaAllocator is a natural fit, enabling bulk freeing at the end of each cycle. When bounded memory needs are known at compile time, std.heap.FixedBufferAllocator offers a lightweight and efficient solution. For debugging or testing, std.testing.allocator or std.testing.FailingAllocator can help catch memory issues early. If none of these scenarios apply, Zig's std.heap.GeneralPurposeAllocator provides a reliable fallback, often serving as the backbone allocator in diverse applications. By aligning your choice of allocator with your program's memory allocation patterns, you can achieve both performance and maintainability with ease.

The elephant in the room: Safety, part 2

Most memory safety bugs stem from two usual suspects: null pointer dereferences and out-of-bounds array indexing. Rust's raw pointer types, by the way, are nullable by default and don't even bother with null pointer dereference checks. Sure, there's a NonNull<T> type if you need more safety, but it baffles me why that's not the standard approach, especially given that Rust's references aren't nullable.

In Zig, though, pointers are non-null out of the gate, and you have to explicitly opt in to nullability with a ? (for example, ?*Value). You also get built-in null pointer dereference checks from the get-go. Personally, I find that a whole lot saner. Making the safe path the default just feels right.

Ownership in Zig is simple: you own what you allocate. If your function returns a pointer to allocated memory, you decide who cleans it up. No defaults, no magic. Make the rules explicit:

- If you allocate it, document who deallocates it
- If you borrow memory, make sure the owner sticks around

Get this wrong, and Zig doesn't protect you. Misuse memory, and you're diving headfirst into undefined behavior, because Zig assumes you know what you're doing.

At first glance, it may seem like Zig's manual allocation and deallocation model leaves it exposed to the kinds of memory safety issues that Rust's ownership model is designed to prevent. Rust's borrow checker feels like a strict but loving parent, enforcing rules at compile time to keep you safe. Zig, on the other hand, seems to hand you the sharp tools and say, "Don't cut yourself, good luck." But does this mean Zig is less safe? Absolutely not. Zig just approaches memory safety with a different philosophy.

Let's explore why Zig is not less safe than Rust, despite its lack of a borrow checker.

Zig's design philosophy: Honest, explicit, and controlled

Zig relies on explicit programmer control and design-by-contract principles to achieve safety:

- **No hidden behavior**: Zig doesn't try to guess your intentions. Memory allocation, deallocation, and ownership are entirely under your control. This prevents surprises such as implicit lifetime extensions or hidden allocations.

- **Error handling by default**: Every allocation in Zig returns a result (!T) that must be explicitly handled. If memory runs out, you get an error.OutOfMemory. No silent overcommit, no crashes without explanation.

- **Strict contracts**: Functions that allocate or borrow memory are explicit about what they expect and what they return. This clarity ensures safe collaboration between different parts of your program.

- **Compile-time validation**: Zig's type system enforces correct usage of pointers, slices, and other memory constructs, helping you avoid common pitfalls such as mixing up stack and heap memory.

Rust's compiler ensures these rules are followed, while Zig relies on clear contracts and explicit lifetimes. Take the following example:

```
fn allocateString(allocator: *std.mem.Allocator, len: usize) ![]u8 {
    return try allocator.alloc(u8, len);
}
```

Here, it's clear that the caller owns the result and must free it when done. This explicitness avoids ambiguity and encourages disciplined programming, just like Rust's ownership model.

Zig uses design-by-contract principles instead of runtime safety nets:

- Allocators in Zig are passed explicitly, making it clear who manages memory.

- Borrowing memory is safe as long as you adhere to function contracts. If a function returns a borrowed slice, you know it's valid only as long as the underlying memory remains stable.

For instance, Zig's std.ArrayList exposes its internal buffer but warns you about its lifetime. Rust's borrow checker enforces similar rules, but Zig's approach ensures you're always conscious of these conditions.

Zig isn't less safe than Rust. It's just less paternalistic. Where Rust assumes you'll make mistakes and stops you at compile time, Zig trusts you to think critically and handle memory responsibly. It doesn't impose a borrow checker but gives you powerful tools such as error handling, alignment checks, and contracts to stay safe.

If you want to dig into real-world cases, there is a beautiful post regarding the unsafe-ness and how faster Zig can be in "unsafe" scenarios: `https://zackoverflow.dev/writing/unsafe-rust-vs-zig/`.

Zig's approach to memory management is refreshingly honest and straightforward. You explicitly choose an allocator, explicitly manage memory, and explicitly handle errors. By embracing this transparency, you gain control and predictability. It's not as daunting as it sounds. Once you get the hang of it, you'll wonder how you ever trusted a language to guess what you wanted.

Remember the following:

- Zig doesn't pick your allocator. You do
- Always know where your bytes come from and where they go
- Document ownership and lifetime rules
- Embrace the explicitness; it's what makes Zig powerful and adaptable

With pointers and allocation under your belt, you're now ready to tackle even more nuanced aspects of memory management. Keep your wits about you, know your allocators, and never stop asking: "Where are the bytes?"

Zero-sized types: The phantom menace of memory management (but they have their uses)

Imagine a type that takes up no space at all. No bytes to store, no extra baggage, just a conceptual placeholder that exists only in the compiler's mind. In Zig, certain types have a size of zero bits. They're like ghosts of the type system: they promise nothing (and deliver nothing) in terms of stored data, yet they can be crucial in shaping your code's structure and behavior.

A zero-sized type is a type with `@sizeOf(type) == 0`. In other words, you can have a variable of that type, but it's always the same single possible value. No matter how much you assign or copy it, you're just shuffling around a conceptual handle that doesn't consume any memory.

Common zero-sized types include the following:

- void
- The 0-bit integers: u0 and i0
- Arrays and vectors of length 0, or whose elements are zero-sized types themselves
- Enums with only one possible tag
- Structs whose fields are all zero-sized types
- Unions with a single field that's zero-sized

From the compiler's perspective, these types vanish at runtime. No runtime representation means no runtime overhead. It's a neat trick for encoding compile-time-only information or building generic data structures that can optimize away unnecessary storage.

A type that stores nothing

Consider void. It can be useful for instantiating generic types. For instance, if you have a HashMap(Key, Value), using void as the value type turns it into a Set(Key), since the value doesn't need to store anything. This is more than a stylistic choice; by eliminating an actual stored value, the compiler can produce smaller, more efficient code, free of unnecessary memory loads and stores:

```
test "using void as a value type in a HashMap" {
    var map = std.AutoHashMap(i32, void).init(std.testing.allocator);
    defer map.deinit();

    // Insert keys without any associated data
    try map.put(42, {});
    try std.testing.expect(map.contains(42));
    _ = map.remove(42);
    try std.testing.expect(!map.contains(42));
}
```

In this scenario, map.put(42, {}) doesn't store any data beyond the key. The entry is effectively just a key; no value field exists. This not only reduces memory usage but also eliminates code for handling values.

void versus anyopaque

Don't confuse void with anyopaque. void is a known zero-sized type. anyopaque is a placeholder for unknown types and therefore has a nonzero size at runtime. void truly means "no data," while anyopaque means "some data, but I'm not telling you what."

Ignoring expressions

In Zig, ignoring a non-void expression is usually a compile error. The language wants to ensure that every value you create is either used or explicitly discarded. This prevents accidental logical errors and encourages cleaner code.

But what about void expressions? Since they represent no actual value, it's perfectly safe to ignore them. For example, calling an `fn returnsVoid()` void function without using its return value is fine. There's literally nothing to use.

If you do want to explicitly discard a non-void expression, assign it to _. This says, "Yes, I'm aware this value exists, and I'm deliberately ignoring it."

```
test "ignoring values" {
    // foo() returns i32, so ignoring it is an error:
    // foo(); // compile error
    // Instead, explicitly ignore it:
    _ = foo();

    // returnsVoid() returns void, so ignoring it is fine:
    returnsVoid();
}

fn returnsVoid() void {}
fn foo() i32 { return 1234; }
```

Shrinking your code with zero-sized types

Zig's ability to compile out unused code and data is one of its strengths. Zero-sized types help by giving the compiler a way to represent concepts that need no runtime footprint. They're perfect for the following:

- Turning data structures into "value-less" variants (such as sets from maps)
- Creating generic code that optimizes away unnecessary fields or operations
- Representing states or tags that carry no data—just the fact that they exist

As a result, zero-sized types can improve memory efficiency and reduce generated code, leading to smaller binaries and faster execution.

Zero-sized types are intangible tools in your Zig toolbox. They carry no runtime data, serve as invisible placeholders, and enable more general, memory-efficient code. While they may seem like a trivial curiosity at first, mastering their use can make your code more flexible and optimized. They're the epitome of "less is more": sometimes, the best data is no data at all.

Type conversion (casting): When your data needs a disguise

In a world where data doesn't always appear in the shape you need, casting is the art of politely (or sometimes forcefully) reshaping one type into another. Zig provides a strong distinction between safe, automatic conversions (coercions) and those that require a deliberate cast (explicit casts). This reduces surprises, making it harder for accidental transformations to slip under the radar and cause subtle bugs.

Type coercion: Safe and automatic

Coercion happens automatically when Zig can guarantee a safe and unambiguous conversion. For example, assigning a u8 to a u16 is safe—no information is lost because a u16 can hold every value a u8 can:

```
const a: u8 = 42;
const b: u16 = a; // Automatically widens from u8 to u16
```

These aren't "casts" in the traditional sense. No special syntax is needed. The compiler knows what you want and ensures it's harmless. Coercions can happen in several scenarios:

- **Widening integers and floats:** Smaller numeric types can fit into bigger ones
- **Qualifiers and alignment:** You can add *constness* or reduce alignment without drama
- **Slices, arrays, and pointers:** Easily convert from fixed arrays to slices, or pointers to arrays
- **Optionals and error unions:** Turn a payload or null into an optional type, or wrap a value/ error into an error union
- **Tuples to arrays:** Homogeneous tuples (all elements of the same type) can become arrays

Coercions are always safe, so Zig just does them automatically whenever it's clear and unambiguous.

When coercion fails

If something is ambiguous or risky, Zig refuses to coerce. For instance, narrowing from a large integer type to a smaller one only works at compile time if the value is known to fit. If not, you must handle it explicitly, or Zig will raise a compile error. Another example: trying to coerce a float to an integer without a guaranteed safe path will make Zig balk. You'll have to reach for an explicit cast.

For everything else, Zig requires an explicit cast via built-ins such as `@intCast`, `@floatCast`, or `@ptrCast`. These are the scalpel you pick up when you have to say, "I know what I'm doing, really!" Explicit casts vary in safety and may cause runtime checks, truncations, or other transformations. Some can fail with runtime errors if the conversion isn't actually safe.

Consider these examples:

- `@intCast(u8, some_u32_value)` will try to convert a 32-bit integer into an 8-bit one. If it doesn't fit, you get a runtime error.
- `@floatCast(f32, some_f64_value)` shrinks a float, possibly losing precision, but it's a deliberate act.
- `@bitCast` changes the type without changing the bits. It is useful for reinterpreting raw data as another type, but you must be sure the target type has the same size and a compatible bit pattern.

If coercions are the kinder, gentler transformations, explicit casts are where you roll up your sleeves and say, "This might get ugly, but I know what I'm doing."

There are common explicit casts:

- **Integer to float:** `@floatFromInt(f64, x)` takes an integer x and converts it to a f64
- **Float to integer:** `@intFromFloat(u32, y)` takes a floating-point y and truncates it to a u32
- **Narrowing integers:** `@intCast` or `@truncate` to reduce bit-width
- **Pointer conversions:** `@ptrCast` to reinterpret pointers between different types
- **Bit reinterpretation:** `@bitCast` to treat a data value as a different type without changing the bits

Each cast function is documented in Zig's standard library, detailing when it's safe or dangerous.

C pointers special case

C pointers can be more lenient. When interacting with C code, Zig allows certain coercions that wouldn't be allowed otherwise. The philosophy: if you're bridging Zig and C, you might need to do some less strict casts. But still, proceed with caution. C code has its own pitfalls.

Keeping things clear

Zig is designed to keep you from accidentally casting away valuable information. Coercions are safe and automatic, while explicit casts are deliberate and visible. This keeps the code clearer:

- If you see @intCast, you know there might be a risk of truncation or overflow
- If you see @bitCast, you know someone is reinterpreting bits directly
- If you see just an assignment from u8 to u16, you know that's harmless and guaranteed by the language

This transparency reduces the chance of subtle, hard-to-find bugs.

When your data doesn't fit the type you have, ask yourself: Can Zig coerce it safely? If not, choose the explicit cast carefully. This honesty in the language encourages safer, more maintainable code, an admirable goal for any programmer's toolbox.

Peer type resolution

Imagine you're writing a piece of code that has multiple conditional branches, each returning a slightly different type, but in the end, you want to produce a single uniform type. Or consider a switch expression, with each branch returning something different yet somehow compatible. In such cases, Zig engages in a subtle dance called **peer type resolution**.

Peer type resolution occurs in several places, including the following:

- if expressions
- while expressions
- for expressions
- switch expressions
- Blocks with multiple break statements returning different types
- Certain binary operations

Whenever Zig encounters multiple "peer" types. Types from different branches that need to unify into one result type. It attempts to find a type that all peers can safely coerce into. This ensures that the entire expression has a consistent type without you having to explicitly specify it every time.

How it works

Zig looks at all the possible return values in these constructs and tries to find a common "supertype" that can represent all of them through safe coercions. If such a type exists, Zig uses it. If not, you'll get a compile error.

For example, consider an `if` expression returning either an array or a slice. Arrays and slices of string are often coerced to `[]const u8` or other related types. If one branch returns a fixed array such as `&[_]u8{'h', 'i'}`, and another branch returns a slice derived from runtime data, Zig finds a suitable common type, such as `[]const u8`, to which both can coerce. The resulting expression's type is `[]const u8`.

The following are common scenarios:

- **Numeric widening**

  If one branch returns an `i8` and another returns `i16`, Zig picks `i16` because both can unify into a type that safely holds all possible values. The smaller type can widen without losing data.

- **Arrays and slices**

  Branches that return arrays of different sizes, or a mix of arrays and slices, often resolve into `[]const u8` or a similar slice type. Zig finds a slice type that all arrays or pointers can coerce into safely.

- **Optionals and non-optional values**

  If one branch returns `?T` and another returns `T`, the common supertype is `?T`. The plain `T` can coerce to `?T` simply by presenting a non-null value.

- **Empty arrays and non-empty slices**

  If one path yields an empty array (`&[_]u8{}`) and another yields a non-empty slice (`slice[0..1]`), peer type resolution might pick `[]const u8`. Both the empty array and the slice can coerce into that slice type.

- **Error unions**

  If one branch returns a value and another branch returns an error union, Zig may unify them into a single error union type or an optional type, depending on the pattern. This lets you handle both success and error conditions gracefully in a single expression.

- **Pointers and optional pointers**

  If one branch returns *const T and another returns ?*T, the result might be unified into ?*const T. Zig finds a type that can accommodate both a pointer and a null state if needed.

- **Enums and tagged unions**

  If you have an enum in one branch and a tagged union in another, and the tagged union can represent the same set of values, Zig finds a way to pick a type that all values can match.

Why is this useful?

Peer type resolution saves you from writing verbose casts every time you return from different branches. It simplifies your code and lets the compiler handle the complexity of finding a compatible type. This leads to cleaner, more maintainable code, especially in complex branching logic or polymorphic functions.

What if Zig can't resolve?

If Zig cannot find a type that all branches can coerce into, it will fail with a compile error. This is your cue to step in and provide an explicit cast or rethink your logic so that the return types are compatible.

- Peer type resolution happens where multiple branches or peers return differing but potentially compatible types
- Zig tries to find a common supertype that can represent all outcomes via safe coercions
- This mechanism reduces code clutter, as you don't need to manually cast everything to a single type
- If no suitable common type is found, Zig informs you with a compile error, prompting a more explicit approach

By understanding peer type resolution, you can write more flexible, concise code. Let Zig handle the subtle negotiations between types, and enjoy simpler logic in your branching expressions.

These concepts, from the high-level control over the stack and heap to the fine-grained details of type conversion, all contribute to Zig's powerful and explicit approach to programming. With these tools in hand, let's step back and summarize the key principles you've learned about managing memory.

Summary

Now that you've marched through a jungle of pointers, allocators, and downright wacky memory sections, congratulations! You've survived the grittiest side of Zig. You've not only learned the difference between the stack and heap but also how to juggle them without dropping your entire process into the void. You've tangled with pointer arithmetic, ephemeral stack frames, and soul-crushing null checks, and yet here you are: still alive, eyes wide open, and (hopefully) with fewer memory leaks.

Let's be honest: it's one thing to read about memory management in a textbook, but quite another to see your program die in a blaze of "Invalid read of size 4." Zig's whole shtick is to keep you honest. You want raw power? Fine! Here's the raw address. You want a guarantee you're not indexing out of bounds? Use a slice, or prepare to blow off your foot. Zig's explicit approach may seem harsh, but it's refreshingly sane once you realize how many booby traps other languages keep under the rug.

So yes, pointers in Zig are simultaneously your best friend and a potential Monday-morning migraine. But keep practicing, and you'll see that they're neither black magic nor nuclear explosives, just a set of well-defined tools that expect you to do your job. Throw in zero-sized types (because who doesn't love a type that takes up no space?) and some cleverly designed allocators, and you've got a language that redefines "manual memory management" into something dangerously close to "actually manageable."

Now, if you're thinking, "Great, I get it. Zig makes me do the heavy lifting. But how do I stop rewriting the same old memory routines over and over?" you're not alone. The good news is that Zig's **standard library** is waiting in the wings. In the next chapter, we'll dig into the built-in data structures, high-level helpers, and best practices that tie all these memory concepts into a neat, cohesive package. If you thought wrangling pointers was enlightening, just wait until you see how the standard library builds on that foundation without adding a single ounce of fluff. Get ready: your memory-wrangling adventure is about to become a lot more civilized.

Unlock this book's exclusive benefits now

UNLOCK NOW

Scan this QR code or go to https://packtpub.com/unlock, then search this book by name.

Note: Keep your purchase invoice ready before you start.

10

The Standard Library

Think the Standard Library is just a dusty crate of old tools? Think again. Zig's std is a dungeon vault packed with blades, potions, and arcane artifacts—all designed to let you hack through system programming like a barbarian with a PhD in efficiency. By the end of this chapter, you'll wield Zig's Standard Library not as a timid scribe, but as a battle-hardened engineer who treats memory, files, and threads like a DM treats rulebooks: with ruthless precision.

In this chapter, we're going to cover the following topics:

- Common data structures: ArrayList, HashMap, and other fun things
- File I/O: reading, writing, and wrangling files like a boss
- Formatting and printing: making your output look pretty (or at least legible)
- Other utilities: random numbers, time, and more fun stuff

The Standard Library is Zig's beating heart. Forget bloated frameworks or magic runtime incantations—this is lean, explicit, and utterly uncompromising. Whether you're writing a kernel that must never crash, a game server that scoffs at GC pauses, or a WebAssembly module smaller than a goblin's ego, std is your ticket to code that's fast, reliable, and yours. Miss this, and you'll be debugging segfaults in Valhalla.

Ready to swap garbage collectors for a crowbar and a flashlight? Let's dive in.

Technical requirements

All the code shown in this chapter can be found in the Chapter10 directory of our Git repository: https://github.com/PacktPublishing/Learning-Zig/tree/main/Chapter10.

Common data structures: ArrayLists, HashMaps, and other fun things

Party Members: ArrayLists in Zig — the art of controlled chaos

Imagine you're commanding a battalion of bytes. They're rowdy, unpredictable, and will revolt at the slightest misstep. Zig's ArrayList is your field manual for this mutiny—a dynamic array that lets you grow your troops precisely when needed, but demands you bury the fallen. No garbage collectors here to play undertaker. You'll either leave a trail of memory leaks like a C programmer on a bender or rise as a memory maestro. Let's dig trenches.

Figure 10.1 – Dynamic troops in line: ArrayLists demand discipline and memory management

init: raising the banner

Every ArrayList begins as a hollow promise. You declare it with init, handing it an allocator—a mercenary that'll fight for memory on your behalf. Forget Java's coddling new ArrayList<>() or Go's slice literals. In Zig, you earn your dynamic arrays:

```zig
zig var list = ArrayList(u8).init(allocator);
// Congrats. You now own a list that can't even hold a single byte.
// It's like buying a sword with no blade. But wait—there's potential.
```

This isn't laziness; it's austerity. Zig won't allocate a single byte until you explicitly order it. Why? Because embedded developers loathe hidden allocations like a cat hates water, and system programmers need to know exactly where their memory grenades are planted.

append: the delusion of safety

Ah, append—the function every new Zig programmer clings to like a security blanket. "Look!" they say, "I can add elements dynamically!" But here's the rub:

```
try list.append(42);
```

That innocent try is your first clue. In Zig, even appending a measly integer can fail. Out of memory? Tough. The allocator's rebelling? Handle it or crash. This isn't Python, where lists grow like weeds. It's a contract: You manage the cavalry; Zig just provides the horses.

And when you get cocky—when you've "ensured" capacity and think you're safe—Zig hands you appendAssumeCapacity. It's the function equivalent of a dare: *"Go ahead, add that element. I double-dog dare you to overrun the buffer."* One misstep, and you're staring at a segmentation fault—Zig's version of a participation trophy.

Capacity: the chess game

Memory in Zig isn't a buffet; it's a chess match. ensureTotalCapacity is your opening move—a gambit to reserve space without committing:

```
try list.ensureTotalCapacity(1000); // "I might need this later."
```

But Zig scoffs at your hesitation. Reserved memory is wasted memory in embedded realms. So, you pivot to ensureTotalCapacityPrecise, the anal-retentive cousin. It allocates exactly what you ask for, not a byte more—perfect for when you're threading a microcontroller's memory needle.

And when you're done? shrinkAndFree cuts the dead weight. It's the Marie Kondo of memory management—if KonMari involved manually freeing each byte and checking for tears.

The unmanaged horde

Then there's ArrayListUnmanaged—Zig's "hold my beer" mode. This is where you ditch the allocator babysitter and go rogue:

```
var list = ArrayListUnmanaged(u8){};
// You: "I'll handle the allocator myself, thanks."
// Also you: [Later, sweating] "Why is there a buffer overflow in
production?"
```

Unmanaged lists are for when you want to pass allocators like contraband—useful for kernel developers who juggle memory zones, or WebAssembly modules that treat the browser's memory like a borrowed trench coat. But forget to pass the allocator to append? Enjoy your undefined behavior. Zig's not your nanny; it's your drill sergeant.

Insertions and removals: the dance of death

Let's talk about inserting elements. In JavaScript, you splice. In Zig, you insert, but with the grace of a chainsaw:

```
try list.insert(0, 99); // Prepends 99. Complexity: O(n)
```

That 0 is a death wish for large lists. Every element shifts right, like commuters scooting down a subway seat. For small lists? Fine. For 10,000 elements? You've just invented a new form of latency.

And removals! orderedRemove maintains order like a polite queue. swapRemove is the bar brawl alternative—yank the last element into the gap. It's fast, chaotic, and perfect for real-time systems where speed trumps civility.

The sentinel gambit

Need a C-friendly slice with a terminal null? toOwnedSliceSentinel has you covered:

```
const c_str = try list.toOwnedSliceSentinel(0);
defer allocator.free(c_str);
// Behold: a Zig slice masquerading as a C string.
// One wrong move, and it's a buffer overflow valentine.
```

It's Zig's way of mocking C interop. *"Oh, you want sentinels? Here. But you manage the lifetime."* The deference to manual control is almost poetic—if poetry involved dereferencing null pointers.

The philosophy of pain

Zig's ArrayList isn't just a data structure—it's a moral stance. It says: *"Memory is a resource, not a right."* You want dynamic growth? Fine, but you'll handle the reallocation errors. You want safety? Use defer list.deinit() like your job depends on it (because it does).

To the Go developer, this feels barbaric—where's your garbage-collected slice? To the C++ engineer, it's nostalgic—a std::vector that doesn't pretend to be safe. But to the embedded programmer, it's freedom: no hidden allocations, no runtime surprises, just raw, unapologetic control.

Epilogue: why bother?

Because in the trenches of system programming, every byte counts. Because WebAssembly modules can't afford a GC pause. Because real-time systems demand deterministic behavior. Zig's `ArrayList` is a tool for those who see memory not as an abstraction, but as a ledger—every allocation a debt, every free a repayment.

It's not for everyone. But if you've ever stared at a Rust borrow-checker error or a Java `OutOfMemoryException` and thought, "I could do better," Zig's `ArrayList` is your Excalibur. Wield it wisely, and the system programming grail is yours. Misuse it, and may the segfault gods have mercy on your soul.

HashMaps: the tavern brawlers of data structures

Zig's `HashMap` is like a rowdy tavern: keys elbow their way in, values chug ale in the corner, and if you don't clean up after closing time (cough `deinit` cough), you'll wake up to a system admin screaming about memory leaks. Here's the kicker: Zig gives you the keys to the tavern. No bouncer, no magic. Just you, your wits, and a very explicit set of rules.

Figure 10.2 – A tavern brawl in motion: keys colliding with purpose

Key operations (pun intended)

Let's break down the chaos:

`init`: Summon a new HashMap. Think of it as carving a fresh dungeon room into existence.

```
var map = AutoHashMap(u32, u32).init(allocator);
// Congrats! You've just allocated a void. Now fill it with loot (or
keys).
```

deinit: Burn the tavern down. Metaphorically.

```
defer map.deinit(); // Free it or the cosmic RAM horrors return.
```

Pro tip: Forget this, and your program becomes a memory-hoarding dragon. Nobody likes dragons.

put: Toss a key-value pair into the fray. Clobber existing keys? Your call.

```
try map.put(42, 9001); // Key: 42. Value: Over. Nine. Thousand.
```

get: Retrieve a value. Returns null if the key's hiding in the ethereal plane.

```
if (map.get(42)) |val| {
// Found it! Now don't drop it like a hot potato.
}
```

remove: Delete a key. Leaves a tombstone (not the cool rock band).

```
_ = map.remove(42); // Tombstone installed. Performance degradation
incoming!
```

The dark arts of hashing

Zig's AutoHashMap is like a grumpy wizard—it'll auto-hash your keys, but it demands you define two spells:

1. hash: Turn keys into numbers. No two keys should share a number (unless you like tavern brawls).

2. eql: Check whether two keys are identical. No room for impostors.

3. Here's an example for u32:

```
const Context = struct {
    pub fn hash(self: @This(), key: u32) u64 { ... }
    pub fn eql(self: @This(), a: u32, b: u32) bool { ... }
};
// Your spells, sir. Cast them wisely.
```

Here's the kicker: If you use []const u8 (strings) as keys, Zig slaps you with a compile error. Why? Because strings are sneaky—they could be hashed by value (contents) or identity (memory address). Zig says: "*Choose, coward.*"

Solution: Use StringHashMap for string keys. It's like a librarian—it hashes the contents of the string, not the address.

Tombstones: the ghosts of hashes past

When you remove a key, Zig doesn't erase it. It leaves a tombstone—a spectral reminder that something once lived there. Why? Because linear probing (the algorithm Zig uses) needs these markers to avoid early search termination.

But tombstones pile up. Too many, and your HashMap becomes a haunted graveyard. Enter rehash:

```
map.rehash(); // Exorcise the tombstones. Your HashMap is now 50% less
spooky.
```

> **Rehash versus CPU cache**
>
> Rehash periodically if you're doing heavy insert/delete cycles. Your CPU cache will thank you.

Adapt or perish: contexts and customization

Zig's HashMaps let you swap out hashing logic like an RPG character swapping gear. Use getOrPutAdapted for custom key types:

```
const AdaptedKey = struct {
    name: []const u8
};
const AdaptedContext = struct {
    fn hash(ctx: @This(), key: AdaptedKey) u64 { ... }
    fn eql(ctx: @This(), a: AdaptedKey, b: AdaptedKey) bool { ... }
};
```

Now sling adapted keys like a necromancer slings curses:

```
try map.getOrPutAdapted(AdaptedKey{.name="Zig"}, AdaptedContext{});
```

Zig versus the world

- Rust: Borrow checker mutters, *"Thou shalt not have dangling pointers."* Zig says, *"Here's the blade. Try not to stab yourself."*
- JavaScript: *"LOL, just use objects!"* Zig retorts, *"Your 'hash tables' are 80% glue and hope."*
- C++: *"std::unordered_map is safe!"* Zig laughs. *"Your move, -fsanitize=undefined."*

Boss fight: test your gear

```
var map = AutoHashMap(u32, u32).init(allocator);
defer map.deinit();
// Quest: Insert 3 keys, delete one, then clone the map.
// Reward: Eternal glory (and no memory leaks).
```

Hint: Use ensureTotalCapacity before a boss fight (read: heavy insertion). No one likes frame rate drops mid-battle.

Zig's HashMaps are rough, explicit, and gloriously fast. Master them, and you'll bend memory to your will. Forget to deinit? Well… let's just say the cosmic RAM horrors are always hungry.

File I/O: reading, writing, and wrangling files like a boss

"Where bytes meet bravery, and segmentation faults fear to tread."

Opening act: the filesystem dungeon

Feeling overwhelmed by files? Don't worry, you'll slice through file operations like a rogue with a +5 dagger. Zig's file I/O is simpler than you might anticipate. Let's dive in.

Opening files: negotiating with the file system's bouncer

Imagine files as grumpy librarians guarding ancient tomes. To read or write, you need the right permissions, a steady hand, and a healthy fear of error codes. In Zig, opening a file is like convincing a dragon to lend you its hoard—possible, but only if you follow the rules.

Figure 10.3 – Grumpy librarians guarding ancient tomes: the file system's gatekeepers

```
const std = @import("std");
pub fn main() !void {
    // Open "secret_plans.txt" for reading. If it doesn't exist? Tough
Luck.
    const file = try std.fs.cwd().openFile("secret_plans.txt", .{ .read =
true });
    defer file.close(); // Close it, or the file handle goblin will haunt
your RAM.
}
```

💡 **Quick tip:** Enhance your coding experience with the **AI Code Explainer** and **Quick Copy** features. Open this book in the next-gen Packt Reader. Click the **Copy** button (1) to quickly copy code into your coding environment, or click the **Explain** button (2) to get the AI assistant to explain a block of code to you.

```
                                              Copy      Explain
function calculate(a, b) {
    return {sum: a + b};                        1          2
};
```

📖 **The next-gen Packt Reader** is included for free with the purchase of this book. Scan the QR code OR go to `https://packtpub.com/unlock`, then use the search bar to find this book by name. Double-check the edition shown to make sure you get the right one.

Note: Zig forces you to handle errors explicitly. Remember the `try` keyword? It's your shield against undefined behavior. Forget to check for errors, and the compiler will roast you harder than a troll in daylight.

Now that you've breached the gates, let's loot the treasure chest...

Reading files: from bytes to bragging rights

Reading files in Zig is like looting a treasure chest—you decide how much gold (data) to carry, and you better have enough pockets (memory). Let's raid that chest:

```
// Allocate a buffer to hold the file's contents.
const allocator = std.heap.page_allocator;
const data = try file.readToEndAlloc(allocator, 1024);
defer allocator.free(data); // Free it, or face the memory leak kraken.
std.debug.print("File contents: {s}\n", .{data});
```

The readToEndAlloc function is your trusty steed here, but it's greedy—it'll slurp up bytes until the file ends or your buffer explodes. For large files, read in chunks unless you enjoy RAM-induced existential crises.

Loot acquired? Time to carve your legacy into the disk...

Writing files: carving your legacy into the disk

Writing files is where you transition from apprentice to *archmagi*. Want to scribble "Hello, World" into existence? Zig's got your back, but it won't clean up your ink stains (looking at you, dangling file handles).

```
const new_file = try std.fs.cwd().createFile("achievements.txt", .{});
defer new_file.close();
const message = "Defeated the Boss Monster in 3.2s";
_ = try new_file.writeAll(message); // Write it, or your bragging rights vanish.
```

Pop quiz, hotshot: What happens if you forget defer new_file.close()?

- a) Zig politely closes it for you.
- b) The file handle leaks like a sieve.
- c) The compiler sends you a passive-aggressive error.

(Answer: **b**. Always. Close. Your. Files.)

But why stop at scribbling text? Let's carve data into the disk's very soul...

Binary files: telepathy for machines

Text files are polite conversations. Binary files? They're telepathic data dumps—raw, efficient, and utterly merciless. Let's encode an RPG character's stats without getting devoured by alignment errors:

```
const Player = extern struct {
    health: u32,
    mana: u32,
    level: u16,
};
// Save the player's state
var player = Player{ .health = 100, .mana = 50, .level = 42 };
try file.writeAll(std.mem.asBytes(&player));
// Load it back
const saved_data = try file.readToEndAlloc(allocator, @sizeOf(Player));
const loaded_player = std.mem.bytesToValue(Player, saved_data);
```

Warning: Binary I/O is like time travel—mess with the struct layout, and your past self (data) becomes corrupted.

Now that you've mastered raw bytes, let's turbocharge your I/O...

Buffered I/O: the blazing-fast option

Why plod through files one byte at a time when you can blaze through them? Buffered I/O is your turbocharged steed, devouring data in chunks.

```
var buffer: [4096]u8 = undefined;
var reader = file.reader(); // Buffered reader go BRRR
while (try reader.readUntilDelimiterOrEof(&buffer, '\n')) |line| {
    std.debug.print("Line: {s}\n", .{line});
}
```

Buffered reads are like looting a dungeon in bulk—fewer trips, more treasure.

But writing data isn't safe until it's etched into the disk's bones...

File sync: the ritual of flushing

Writing to a file is like scribbling on parchment—it's not real until the ink dries. sync is your holy incantation to banish buffer demons.

```
try file.writeAll("Critical quest data: DO NOT CORRUPT");
try file.sync(); // Begone, buffer gremlins!
// Sync just the data (metadata can wait)
try file.syncDataOnly();
```

Use sync after critical writes. Your users will thank you when the tavern's power grid dies mid-save.

Ready to bend time itself? Let's rewind...

File seeking: time travel for bytes

Files are scrolls and seek is your time-travel spell. Rewind, fast-forward, or get lost in the void.

```
try file.seekTo(0); // Rewind to the beginning (like a save point)
const pos = try file.getPos(); // "Where am I?"
try file.seekBy(-10); // Step back 10 bytes (watch for underflows!)
```

A common use case: Parsing binary formats? seek lets you dance around headers like a bard dodging arrows. But beware—tampering with time has consequences. Even files remember when you've meddled...

Error handling: Zig's "No BS" policy

Zig treats errors like a hardcore RPG—no respawns, no checkpoints. You either handle them or game over.

```
const maybe_file = std.fs.cwd().openFile("config.json", .{}) catch |err| {
    std.debug.print("Failed to open file: {s}\n", .{@errorName(err)});
    return; // Exit gracefully, like a rogue vanishing into shadows.
};
```

Now, let's talk about the rules of this dungeon...

File permissions: the guardian spells

"Speak friend, and enter." Except here, the door (file) demands more than a password—it requires incantations. Zig lets you rewrite the rules of access like a wizard tweaking a spellbook.

Figure 10.4 – Access control materialized: permissions define boundaries between users

```
// Cast a protection spell (read/write for you, read-only for peasants)
try file.chmod(0o644); // 0o644 = "I own this, but you can look."
// Summon the file's guardian stats
const stats = try file.stat();
if (stats.mode & 0o200 == 0) {
    std.debug.print("File is write-locked. Not today, hacker.\n", .{});
}
```

Permissions are the moat around your data castle. Forget them, and your files become a free-for-all tavern brawl.

But what if you need a clone of your precious file to share the load? Enter...

Hard links: the doppelgänger files

Hard links aren't mere shortcuts—they're twins sharing a soul. Delete the original? The clone lives on, smirking in the shadows.

```
// Forge a hard link (two files, one soul)
try std.fs.cwd().link("original_quest.txt", "backup_quest.txt", .{});
// Break the link (the data survives in Valhalla)
try std.fs.cwd().deleteFile("original_quest.txt");
```

Use hard links for backup systems. They're cheaper than clones and twice as loyal.

Final boss challenge: the atomic logger

Here's your quest:

- Create a temp file
- Write log data to it
- Atomically rename it to app.log on success
- Delete the temp file on failure

Beware of the following:

- Permissions (the bouncer might say no)
- Partial writes (don't leave half-baked files lying around)
- Errors (check every return code)

Reward: The sysadmin's blessing (and no corrupted logs).

The Zig filesystem creed

Zig doesn't hold your hand. It hands you a sword and a map, and says, *"You command the bytes. You negotiate with errors. Forget to close() a file? The compiler won't scold you—but your RAM will weep. Master these tools, and you'll bend filesystems to your will, one openFile at a time."*

Now go forth and may your std.fs adventures be leak-free.

Still here? The filesystem dungeon awaits. Your next quest: **man 2 open**.

Untapped territories in Zig file operations: the lost scrolls

You've slain the dragons of basic I/O—now let's raid the vaults of untouched std.fs secrets.

File modes and flags: the fine print of file creation

Opening a file isn't just "read" or "write." Zig's openFile and createFile accept flags that turn you into a filesystem lawyer.

```
// Open a file in "append-only" mode (like a ledger for logging)
const log_file = try dir.createFile("combat.log", .{ .append = true });
// Create a file exclusively (fails if it exists)
```

```
const vault = try dir.createFile("loot.dat", .{ .exclusive = true });
// Truncate a file to zero on open (delete its contents)
const clean_slate = try dir.openFile("save.txt", .{ .truncate = true });
```

These flags are your contract with the filesystem. .exclusive is like claiming "*dibs*" on a treasure chest.

Remember: Combine flags such as .{ .read = true, .write = true } for read-write mode—perfect for RPG save files.

Memory-mapped files: the necromancy of I/O

Bend files into RAM with dark magic. While not in std.fs, Zig's std.os.mmap lets you treat files as mutable memory.

```
const data = try std.os.mmap(
    null,
    file_size,
    std.os.PROT.READ | std.os.PROT.WRITE,
    std.os.MAP.SHARED,
    file.handle,
    0 // Offset
);
defer std.os.munmap(data);
// Edit the file DIRECTLY IN MEMORY (handle with care)
data[0] = 'Z'; // Corrupt the first byte? You monster.
```

Warning: This is like juggling live grenades. One misstep, and your program becomes a segmentation fault fountain.

Disk space intel: the scout's report

Query filesystem stats to avoid writing to a full disk (a silent killer of embedded systems).

```
const stats = try std.fs.FileSystemStats.get(dir.fd);
std.debug.print(  "Free space: {d} MB\n",  .{stats.blocks_available *
stats.block_size / 1024 / 1024}  );
```

This is critical for IoT devices—because running out of space mid-firmware update is a bad time.

Symbolic link creation: traps for the unwary

Create symlinks that point to nowhere (or everywhere).

```
// Create a symlink
try dir.symLink("innocent.txt", "suspicious.link", .{});
// Check if a symlink's target exists
const target_stats = std.fs.File.stat("suspicious.link") catch |err| {
    if (err == error.FileNotFound) std.debug.print("It's a trap!\n", .{});
};
```

Symlink gotcha

Symlinks can dangle. Always check whether the target exists before trusting them.

Advanced error recovery: the phoenix protocol

Handle transient errors (such as `EINTR`) by retrying—because even syscalls get stage fright.

```
fn writeWithRetry(file: std.fs.File, data: []const u8) !void {
    while (true) {
        file.writeAll(data) catch |err| {
            if (err == error.Interrupted) continue; // Retry
            return err; // Surrender to other errors
        };
        break;
    }
}
```

Use a similar strategy for network filesystems or flaky hardware. Your users will never know the chaos you've averted.

Zig's unspoken rule: The filesystem is a wilderness—Zig gives you a machete and a compass, and says, "*Good luck.*" Master these arcane arts, and you'll code like a demigod. Forget them? Enjoy debugging `ENOENT` on a sunny day.

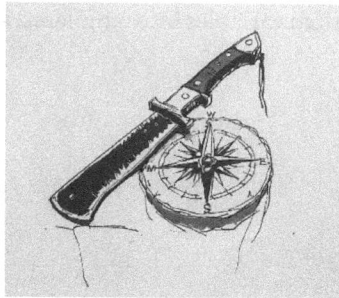

Figure 10.5 – Your tools in the wilderness: a machete and compass for filesystem navigation

Now go forth—and may your openFile calls never return error.AccessDenied.

Formatting and printing: making your output look pretty (or at least legible)

Ever stared at a program's output and felt like you were decoding a cryptic puzzle? Zig's std.fmt is your trusty guide—turning chaos into clarity, one format specifier at a time. You'll craft output that's not just functional but purposeful, whether you're debugging a driver or logging data for a high-stakes WebAssembly module.

Why std.fmt? Precision meets flexibility

Formatting strings in Zig isn't a guessing game. While some languages prioritize brevity, Zig opts for explicitness: every placeholder has a type, every alignment is deliberate, and every byte is accounted for. No hidden conversions, no runtime surprises—just you and the compiler working as a team.

Here's the beauty of it: Zig's formatters are transparent. If you mismatch a type, the compiler flags it early, like a co-pilot gently nudging you back on course. Ready to dive into the toolbox? Let's unpack Zig's formatting essentials—think of this as your roadmap to output zen.

Core tools: crafting strings with purpose

std.fmt hands you three trusty instruments. Let's explore them like a chef sharpening their knives:

format — the architect

Build strings programmatically, stitch variables into templates, and ship them to any writer (files, buffers, networks).

```
const name = "Zig";
const power_level = 9001;
try std.fmt.format(writer, "{s}'s power level is {d}.", .{name, power_
level});
// Output: Zig's power level is 9001.
```

Note the {s} for strings and {d} for integers. Zig asks for clarity—no ambiguous %v placeholders here.

print — the scout

Send formatted text straight to stdout. This is ideal for debugging or quick experiments.

```
std.debug.print("Temperature: {d}°C\n", .{98});
// Output: Temperature: 98°C
```

Tip: std.debug.print is your reconnaissance tool. Use it to peek at values mid-battle, then retire it before deployment.

allocPrint — the librarian

Need a formatted string to reuse later? Dynamically allocate it, then return it to the shelf when done.

```
const message = try std.fmt.allocPrint(allocator, "Errors: {d}", .{42});
defer allocator.free(message); // Return the memory—it's good hygiene!
```

Now that you've got the fundamentals down, let's level up. Zig's formatting isn't just functional—it's expressive.

Advanced techniques: precision, padding, and personality

Formatting in Zig is like designing a UI: every detail matters. Let's add flair while keeping things rock-solid.

Alignment and padding

```
std.debug.print("Health: {d:0>4}\n", .{5});  // Health: 0005
std.debug.print("Mana:   {d:*<4}\n", .{8}); // Mana:   8***
```

Control alignment with > (right) or < (left), and pad with any character. This is perfect for tables or status displays.

Hex, binary, and friends

```
std.debug.print("Hex: 0x{x}\n", .{255});      // 0xff
std.debug.print("Binary: 0b{b}\n", .{42});    // 0b101010
```

This is essential for low-level debugging. Use {X} for uppercase hex (e.g., 0xDEADBEEF) to match protocol specs.

Floating-point control

```
std.debug.print("PI: {d:.3}\n", .{3.1415926535}); // PI: 3.142
```

Specify decimal precision to avoid floating-point ambiguity. No more "0.1 + 0.2 = 0.30000000000000004" surprises.

But what about your own data types? Zig doesn't leave you hanging—custom formatting is a first-class feature.

Custom formatting: make your types shine

Got a struct? Teach it to format itself elegantly. Transform this:

Monster@7ef9e1b4

Into this:

Lifetime Leak (HP: 9999)

```
const Monster = struct {
    name: []const u8,
    hp: u32,
    pub fn format(
        self: Monster,
        comptime _: []const u8,
        _: std.fmt.FormatOptions,
        writer: anytype,
    ) !void {
        try writer.print("{s} (HP: {d})", .{self.name, self.hp});
    }
};
// ...
```

```
const boss = Monster{ .name = "Lifetime Leak", .hp = 9999 };
std.debug.print("Boss: {}\n", .{boss}); // Output: Boss: Lifetime Leak
(HP: 9999)
```

Define a format method, and Zig seamlessly integrates your type into any format string. It's like giving your struct a voice.

Ready for a challenge? Let's put your newfound skills to the test.

Quiz time: spot the mistake

What's wrong with this code?

```
std.debug.print("User {s} has {d} unread messages.\n", .{"Ziggy", "5"});
```

(**Hint:** Zig's type-checking is meticulous. What's mismatched here?)

Answer:

The {d} specifier expects an integer, but "5" is a string. Zig requires explicit types—no implicit conversions. Fix it with 5 (an integer) instead of "5".

Treat format strings like blueprints. Double-check your specifiers and types before hitting compile.

Why Zig's formatting stands out:

- **Compile-time checks:** Catch errors early, without waiting for runtime explosions
- **Zero hidden allocations:** Perfect for embedded systems or WebAssembly, where every byte matters
- **Transparent control:** Align, pad, and format exactly how you want—no magic, no guesswork

Zig's std.fmt is like a precision instrument—simple to learn, deeply powerful in practice. Whether you're tuning an embedded device or optimizing a WASM module, clear output starts here. Now go make those logs meaningful.

But clear output is just the start—ready to add unpredictability, precision, and a dash of utility to your toolkit? Let's explore Zig's Standard Library beyond formatting: where random numbers, timekeeping, and other essentials turn code into craft.

Other utilities: random numbers, time, and more fun stuff

Imagine you're coding a procedurally generated dungeon. You need randomness that feels fair, time tracking precise enough to measure a dragon's sneeze, and sorting that won't buckle under 10,000 treasure chests. Zig's Standard Library isn't just tools—it's a philosophy of "no surprises, no excuses." Let's level up.

Figure 10.6 – A treasure chest of randomness: choose your random generator wisely

Randomness: choose your weapon wisely

`std.rand.DefaultPrng`

- **Uses:** Games, simulations, anything where speed > paranoia.
- **How it works:** A deterministic pseudo-random generator. Seed it once, and it spits out the same sequence every time. Great for debugging or replayable gameplay.
- **Gotcha:** If your seed is predictable, your "random" is too.

```
var rng = std.Random.DefaultPrng.init(42); // The answer to life, the
universe, and bad RNG
const damage = rng.random().intRangeAtMost(u16, 1, 100); // Roll for
initiative!
```

`std.crypto.random`

- **Uses:** Passwords, encryption, anything where predictability = game over.
- **How it works:** Taps into OS-level entropy (like `/dev/urandom`). It's slower, but as secure as Fort Knox's Wi-Fi password.

- **Gotcha**: Overkill for most apps. Don't summon Cthulhu to open a pickle jar.

```
var buffer: [16]u8 = undefined;
std.crypto.randomBytes(&buffer); // Your data is now NSA-proof
(probably).
```

Randomness is fun until you need order. Let's talk about something that is more predictable: time.

Time: raw, unfiltered, and unapologetic

Zig's time API is like a mechanic's toolbox: no frills, just precision instruments. Need a timestamp? Here's a nanosecond counter. Want a calendar date? You build it.

Why no DateTime?

Zig's philosophy is "no hidden code, no bloated APIs." Dates involve time zones, leap years, and political baggage (looking at you, daylight savings). Instead of forcing a one-size-fits-all solution, Zig gives you the following:

- `std.time.timestamp()`: Seconds since 1970-01-01 (Unix epoch)
- `std.time.nanoTimestamp()`: Nanoseconds since an arbitrary point (perfect for benchmarks)
- `std.time.Timer`: Measure code execution like a lab experiment

```
// How to calculate a 30-day trial period without DateTime:
const now = std.time.timestamp();
const trial_end = now + (30 * 24 * 60 * 60); // sorry, February,
you're special!
```

> **Overflow alert!**
>
> Adding large durations can exceed integer limits. Use saturating math (+|) to cap at the type's maximum value instead of crashing (debug) or wrapping (release). This is critical for timers, sensors, and resource calculations.

Need a date library?

Zig's community datetime package is in the works. Until then, roll your own—or embrace the chaos.

Time is just one dimension of control. Let's slice data into pieces with iterators.

Iterators: scalpels versus chainsaws

Zig's iterators are tools, not magic. Here are two heavy hitters:

1. std.mem.SplitIterator

- **Uses:** Split a slice by a fixed delimiter (e.g., parsing CSV).
- **Behavior:** Ruthlessly efficient. No allocations. Just give it a delimiter and watch it chop.

```
const data = "Zig,C,Rust,Go";
var iter = std.mem.split(u8, data, ",");
while (iter.next()) |lang| {
    // lang = "Zig", "C", "Rust", "Go"
}
```

2. std.mem.TokenIterator

- **Uses:** Split by whitespace or custom token sets (e.g., parsing CLI args).
- **Behavior:** Skips empty tokens and trims whitespace by default. Less brutal, more polite.

```
const cli_args = "  zig build -Doptimize=ReleaseFast  ";  var iter
= std.mem.tokenize(u8, cli_args, " ");
    while (iter.next()) |arg| {
        // arg = "zig", "build", "-Doptimize=ReleaseFast"
    }
```

Here are the rules of thumb:

- `SplitIterator`: When you need surgical precision (e.g., binary protocols)
- `TokenIterator`: When you want human-friendly parsing (e.g., text files)

Once your data's split, you might need to sort it. Zig's got opinions on that too.

Sorting: no training wheels, no regrets

Most languages hide sorting behind a generic sort() function. Zig says, "Tell me exactly what you want."

```
const enemies = [_]u8{ 'Z', 'D', 'A', 'G' };
std.sort.block(u8, &enemies, {}, comptime std.sort.asc(u8));
// Now: ['A', 'D', 'G', 'Z'] — alphabetical order, because chaos is
overrated.
```

Custom comparators: Want to sort structs by a field? Zig makes you write the logic—no black boxes.

```zig
const Player = struct {
    name: []const u8,
    score: u32
};
var leaderboard = [_]Player{
    .{ .name = "Ziggy", .score = 99 },
    .{ .name = "Rusty", .score = 42 },
};
// Sort by score descending:
std.sort.block(Player, &leaderboard, {}, struct {
pub fn lessThan(_: void, a: Player, b: Player) bool {
    return a.score > b.score; // > for descending, < for ascending
    }
}.lessThan);
```

- Note that there are no allocations, it sorts in-place. Also, it is deterministic. Same input? Same output. Every. Single. Time.

The Zig difference: no magic, no compromises

- **WebAssembly:** Zig's std.time and std.rand compile to WASM without dragging in a runtime. Your code stays leaner than a JSON parser in C++.

- **Embedded:** No syscalls, no surprises. std.time.Timer uses hardware counters directly.

- **C/C++ refugees:** Zig's APIs are what C's stdlib dreams of becoming after therapy. Yes, no more "segfault roulette."

Final challenge

Build a program tool that does the following:

- Generates a secure password using std.crypto.random

- Times how long it takes to sort 1,000 random integers

- Logs the result to a file without using std.log (use std.fs and std.fmt)

Stuck? Zig's documentation is your quest log. Now go hack the planet!

std.mem utilities: a comprehensive guide

Here's a breakdown of Zig's `std.mem` functions, organized by practical use cases and technical depth. There's no philosophy—just what you need to manipulate memory efficiently.

Core operations

Copy

This safely copies bytes between two slices. Unlike C's `memcpy`, Zig enforces that source and destination slices have the exact same length, preventing buffer overflows.

You can use it for copying fixed-size network packets into a buffer.

Here's an example:

```
const source = "Hello";
var dest: [5]u8 = undefined;
std.mem.copy(u8, &dest, source); // dest now holds "Hello"
```

set

This fills a slice with a specific byte value. It's useful for initializing arrays or wiping sensitive data (e.g., zeroing a password buffer after use).

```
var buffer: [128]u8 = undefined;
std.mem.set(u8, &buffer, 0); // ALL bytes set to 0
```

eql

This compares two slices byte for byte. It returns true only if lengths and contents match. It could be used for validating cryptographic hashes.

```
const hash1 = "a1b2c3";
const hash2 = "a1b2c3";
if (std.mem.eql(u8, hash1, hash2)) {
// Hashes match
}
```

Memory manipulation

replace

This replaces all occurrences of a substring with another. It returns a **new heap-allocated slice**. You can use it for sanitizing user input (e.g., replacing swear words).

```
const input = "Zag is better than Zig";
const output = try std.mem.replace(
    allocator,
    u8,
    input,
    "Zag",
    "Zig");
defer allocator.free(output); // Output: "Zig is better than Zig"
```

sliceAsBytes / bytesAsSlice

This converts slices of any type to/from byte slices. It's a safe alternative to C's type punning. It is particularly useful for serializing integers for network transmission.

```
const numbers = [_]u32{ 0xDEADBEEF, 0xCAFEBABE };
const bytes = std.mem.sliceAsBytes(&numbers); // Convert to []u8
const restored = std.mem.bytesAsSlice(u32, bytes); // Convert back to []
u32
```

Advanced utilities

alignForward / alignBackward

This adjusts a pointer or offset to the nearest alignment boundary (e.g., 16 bytes). It is commonly used for preparing data for SIMD operations.

```
const ptr: *u8 = ...; // Some unaligned pointer
const aligned_ptr = std.mem.alignForward(ptr, 16);
```

readInt / writeInt

This reads/writes integers with explicit endianness (little-endian or big-endian). It is used for parsing binary files (e.g., PNG headers).

```
const bytes = [_]u8{ 0x12, 0x34, 0x56, 0x78 };
const value = std.mem.readInt(u32, &bytes, .Big); // 0x12345678
```

Iteration and splitting

split (iterator)

This splits a slice by a fixed delimiter. It includes empty slices if the delimiter appears consecutively. It could be used to parse CSV files.

```
const data = "Zig,Rust,,C";
var iter = std.mem.split(u8, data, ",");
while (iter.next()) |lang| {
// Yields "Zig", "Rust", "", "C"
}
```

tokenize (iterator)

This splits a slice by a delimiter, skipping empty tokens and trimming whitespace. It is better suited for parsing command-line arguments.

```
const args = "  zig build -Doptimize=ReleaseFast   ";
var iter = std.mem.tokenize(u8, args, " ");
while (iter.next()) |arg| {
// Yields "zig", "build", "-Doptimize=ReleaseFast"
}
```

Challenge solution: 64-byte chunk processor

Task: Split a binary slice into 64-byte chunks, replace 0xFF with 0x00, and time it.

```
fn processChunks(input: []u8) !void {
    var timer = try std.time.Timer.start();
    var i: usize = 0;
    while (i < input.len) {
        const end = @min(i + 64, input.len);
        const chunk = input[i..end];
        // Replace 0xFF with 0x00 (in-place)
        for (chunk) |*byte| {
            if (byte.* == 0xFF) byte.* = 0x00;
        }
        i += 64;
    }
    const elapsed_ns = timer.read();
```

```
        std.debug.print("Processed in {d} ns\n", .{elapsed_ns});
    }
```

Let's break down what is happening here:

- **Chunking**: Uses pointer math to slice the input into 64-byte segments
- **In-place replacement**: Modifies the original data (no allocations)
- **Timing**: Uses `std.time.Timer` for nanosecond precision

When to use which function

Task	Function
Safe byte copying	`copy`
Initialize/wipe memory	`set`
Compare data	`eql`
Heap-based string replacement	`replace`
Binary serialization	`sliceAsBytes`
Protocol parsing	`split or tokenize`

Now that we've explored the ins and outs of `std.mem` and how it can be used to manage memory efficiently, let's take a step back and recap the key points we've covered in this chapter.

Summary

You've navigated Zig's Standard Library, from low-level file operations to efficient string formatting and common data structures. These tools aren't just about getting work done—they're about how the work gets done: with clarity, precision, and full accountability for every resource.

Here are the key takeaways:

- **Files and I/O**: Zig forces you to handle errors and cleanup upfront, preventing resource leaks
- **String formatting**: Compile-time checks eliminate cryptic runtime failures
- **Memory utilities**: Functions such as `std.mem.copy` and `std.mem.split` offer predictable, allocation-free operations
- **Determinism**: Timekeeping and random number APIs prioritize reproducibility and control

But what's the point of crafting god-tier data structures if you can't build anything with them? Next up: Zig's Build System—learning to compile projects across platforms, manage dependencies, and fine-tune binaries for speed or size. This is where Zig's "no hidden steps" philosophy shines, letting you script builds as meticulously as you write code.

Ready to turn your knowledge into executable workflows? Prepare your terminal. The build lollapalooza awaits.

Join us on Discord!

Read this book alongside other users, developers, experts, and the author himself.

Ask questions, provide solutions to other readers, chat with the authors via Ask Me Anything sessions, and much more. Scan the QR or visit the link to join the community.

https://packt.link/deep-engineering-systemsengineering

11

Packing

Manually writing build scripts is about as fun as debugging assembly code, and I'm sure you have better things to do than wrestling Makefiles. If my assumptions are correct, the Zig build system is here to save the day. It's not your typical hand-holding build system. Zig's build system is like that brutally honest friend who tells you exactly what's wrong with your code, even if it hurts a little. It's explicit. It's powerful. And, dare I say, it's even enjoyable (once you get past the initial learning curve).

This isn't a fluffy, *everything just works* kind of system. This is a *roll up your sleeves, understand the underlying mechanisms, and take control* kind of system. You'll be dealing with dependencies, targets, release modes, caches, and even a bit of graph theory (don't worry, it's not as scary as it sounds). But in return for your effort, you'll get a build system that's fast, reliable, and remarkably flexible.

In this chapter, we're going to cover the following topics:

- The Zig build system: automating your workflow
- Cross-compilation: Zig's party trick (1 code base, 57 platform-specific bugs)
- Package management: because reinventing the wheel is so last century
- Cache: the memory of the compiler
- `zig build --watch`: your new best friend (who doesn't talk back)

We'll then move on to the core concepts: `build.zig.zon` for dependencies, `zig fetch` for grabbing those dependencies, and the all-important hash verification (because security matters, even in build systems).

Finally, we'll delve into the advanced topics: understanding Zig's caching system (the secret to its speed), external dependencies, and mastering zig build --watch for a lightning-fast development workflow. By the end of this journey, you'll be a Zig build system wizard, capable of conjuring builds with the best of them. So, buckle up, grab a strong cup of coffee, and let's dive in!

Technical requirements

All the code shown in this chapter can be found in the Chapter11 directory of our Git repository:

https://github.com/PacktPublishing/Learning-Zig/tree/main/Chapter11.

The Zig build system: automating your workflow

Since we've got plenty of ground to cover, let's start with the very first entry point to create your next Zig masterpieces. Enter zig init—Zig's way of saying, "Here's a flashlight, now get out of the boilerplate mines." You'll initialize projects, dissect build.zig, and bend the build system to your will. No incantations required.

zig init: your project's starter kit (with free existential dread)

Let's cut to the chase (and the anxiety). Just type zig init in a new directory in your terminal and hit *Enter*. Boom! Now, you're officially initiated.

So you ran zig init and got a build.zig file, a build.zig.zon file, and two Zig files you didn't ask for. Congratulations — you've just adopted a robot butler that insists on folding your code into origami. Spoiler: Zig assumes you'll write a library, even if you're just making a to-do app.

Here is what you get:

```
.
├── build.zig          # Your build script (RIP Makefiles)
├── build.zig.zon      # Zig's answer to "dependency hell"
└── src/
    ├── main.zig       # The "Hello World" you'll delete in 5 minutes
    └── root.zig       # Zig's passive-aggressive nudge to write a library
```

This is the passive-aggressive hierarchy:

- build.zig: The build script, crafted in pure Zig. Here is the gold.
- root.zig: A library skeleton. "But I just wanted an executable!" Too bad. Zig knows better.
- main.zig: Your executable "Hello World" that will almost certainly be deleted within 5 minutes to make room for your own creations.

- `build.zig.zon`: Zig's shiny new package manifest (think `package.json` but with fewer left-pad disasters). It's currently empty of actual code but packed with comments, like that old ancient legacy monolith lurking in enterprise code bases.

> **Hint**
>
> Use `zig init` in an empty directory, unless you enjoy explaining to Git why `main.zig` vanished faster than your motivation.

We are here to explore the build system, so let's take a peek at these two source files, just to know what was generated.

The yin and yang of Zig's init twins

(Or, *Why Zig gave you two files when you just wanted one*)

Zig wants you to learn by deleting. The `main.zig` file is a temporary demo—a sacrificial lamb. You're meant to gut it within minutes and replace it with your code. It's a sandbox for you to break, test, and flush buffers (literally).

Zig is nudging you toward modular design. `root.zig` is the skeleton of a reusable library, even if you're just building a CLI tool today. Zig assumes you'll eventually want to share code, optimize for performance, or battle-test components—and it's already one step ahead of you.

Note that both files include tests to remind you: *Write tests early, or I'll make your debug sessions a living hell*. Also, Zig wants you to think in terms of composable parts, not monolithic scripts. Even if you delete `root.zig` tomorrow, its existence taught you to structure code for flexibility.

The core idea behind `zig init` is to give you two files because it's a control freak with good intentions. `main.zig` is your today; `root.zig` is your tomorrow.

Now that you've been initiated into Zig's world of dual-source-file enlightenment, it's time to meet the puppet master behind the scenes: the `build.zig` script.

build.zig dissected: what's in the box?

Zig doesn't just hand you a flashlight to escape the boilerplate mines; it hands you a blueprint to build your own escape tunnel. And that blueprint is written in Zig itself. No obscure syntax, no arcane incantations—just pure, unadulterated Zig code. It's not a Pandora's box. Mostly. Assuming that we ran `zig init` in a directory called `"zigt"`, here's the play-by-play moves of it.

First, we have the library you didn't want:

```
const lib = b.addStaticLibrary(.{
    .name = "zigt",
    .root_source_file = b.path("src/root.zig"),  // ← Zig's subtle hint
});
```

Keep in mind that it exists because Zig assumes you'll eventually write reusable code. Maybe you won't, but let it have this fantasy for now. Assuming we want to make a simple executable, there is another section in the script:

```
const exe = b.addExecutable(.{
    .name = "zigt",
    .root_source_file = b.path("src/main.zig"),  // Your actual code
});
```

Also, there are sections regarding running the project tests:

```
const exe_unit_tests = b.addTest(.{
    .root_source_file = b.path("src/main.zig"),
    .target = target,
    .optimize = optimize,
});

const run_exe_unit_tests = b.addRunArtifact(exe_unit_tests);

const test_step = b.step("test", "Run unit tests");
test_step.dependOn(&run_lib_unit_tests.step);
test_step.dependOn(&run_exe_unit_tests.step);
```

Translation: *You'll write tests eventually. Here's the scaffolding for you.*

Are you thinking what I'm thinking? You've never needed to write or read a build script for the Zig project before, but with all the knowledge you've got until now, you're just reading the build without struggling despite the functions that you don't know (yet!).

Before we discuss the build anatomy and features of the build system, let's do something more tangible: use the build system.

Using zig build

The build script has the four main things you are probably doing during your daily workflow: run, test, install, and uninstall. You don't need to trust me, let's verify together by running zig build --help. Besides the gazillion options, there is a section called Steps:

```
Steps:
  install (default)          Copy build artifacts to prefix path
  uninstall                  Remove build artifacts from prefix path
  run                        Run the app
  test                       Run unit tests
```

Building

Here is where the default step (install) executes. In other words, to compile the program (and run all steps associated with the build), run zig build, and the output will be located at zig-out/bin/zigt (and a library you'll never intend to use):

```
zig-out
    ├── bin
    │   └── zigt
    └── lib
        └── libzigt.a
```

Ah, yes! You figured it right. The uninstall step reverts the programs created by install. The next step is to run our automated tests. We are not animals printing on stdout to test the program behavior, right?

Testing

Here, once again, is the build system version of zig test. Execute zig build test in the terminal. It runs tests for both the executable *and* the library (you didn't want to write).

If tests fail, Zig's error messages will roast you harder than a campfire.

Let's visit the last and most anticipated step: run.

Running

To run our executable, we can always call it after a build, but when you need to complete this task quickly, there is a shortcut: `zig build run`. This command is very similar to using `zig run src/hello.zig`; the executable is created and run in a single step. When we use `zig build run`, we don't need to point out the source file since it is already baked into the script:

```zig
const std = @import("std");
pub fn build(b: *std.Build) void { // Standard target and optimization
options
const target = b.standardTargetOptions(.{});
const optimize = b.standardOptimizeOption(.{});
// Create the module for the executable
const exe_mod = b.createModule(.{
    .root_source_file = b.path("src/main.zig"),
    .target = target,
    .optimize = optimize,
});

// Create the executable artifact
const exe = b.addExecutable(.{
    .name = "hello-zig",
    .root_module = exe_mod,
});

// Install the executable into zig-out/bin
b.installArtifact(exe);

// Create a "run" step to execute the compiled binary
const run_cmd = b.addRunArtifact(exe);
run_cmd.step.dependOn(b.getInstallStep()); // Ensure it's built first.

const run_step = b.step("run", "Run the app");
run_step.dependOn(&run_cmd.step);

}
```

The `main.zig`:

```
const std = @import("std");

pub fn main() !void {
    // The main entry point for the executable
    std.debug.print("Hello, Student!\n", .{});
}
```

Test by yourself!

We've just covered the basics of working with `build.zig`, which gives you the starting point for understanding how to set up and run builds in Zig. These first steps provide everything you need to get going, but there's a lot more to discover as we dive deeper into Zig's powerful build system.

Customizing build.zig: from Meh to MVP**

Turning up the heat, we'll explore more options such as building for different platforms (cross-platform compatibility), optimizing your code for release (release modes), and getting into the nitty-gritty of how builds work under the hood—specifically, the **directed acyclic graph** (**DAG**) structure that drives Zig's build process.

DAG

In the context of the Zig build system, a DAG represents the dependencies between build tasks. Each node in the graph corresponds to a task (e.g., compiling a file), and the directed edges indicate dependencies (e.g., *Task A* must complete before *Task B* can start). The *acyclic* part means there are no circular dependencies, ensuring that tasks can be executed in a well-defined order. This structure helps the build system efficiently determine the correct sequence of tasks and parallelize work where possible.

Let's start with cross-compilation!

Cross-compilation: Zig's party trick (1 code base, 57 platform-specific bugs)

Imagine you're building a game that needs to run on a Nintendo Switch, a web server that targets ARM-based cloud infrastructure, or even a tiny IoT device with limited resources. Wouldn't it be amazing if you could build for all these platforms without leaving your development machine? Well, with Zig, you can. Zig's cross-compilation capabilities are so seamless, they feel like magic. No more wrestling with obscure toolchains or praying that your dependencies will compile on a foreign platform. Zig's build system makes cross-compilation as easy as flipping a switch. So, let's dive into how you can build for any platform, any architecture, and any target—all from the comfort of your own machine.

Do you remember the option target that appears multiple times in build.zig? It is the knob for controlling the cross-compilation.

Let me break it down for you: a target is your computer's resume, right? It includes all the details about its CPU architecture, enabled features, operating system version, and ABI—essentially, everything that makes your code as portable as a concrete block. But don't worry; with Zig, you're in luck! This general-purpose language (because let's face it, specificity is for the birds) is designed to generate optimal code for a vast array of targets.

Oh, and if you're wondering how to find out what these targets are, well, just run zig targets—it's like magic but without the sparkle or the fun.

Now, by default, Zig compiles your code for your current machine. This is fantastic because it means your executable will be useless on any other computer. Brilliant! But if you somehow want to use your code elsewhere (I know, radical idea), you'll need to specify the -target option. Also, our loved Zig stdlib has cross-platform abstractions, which is like saying it tries to make your life easier by making the same source code work on many targets. But hey, some code is just more portable than others—like how some people can pull off a tracksuit while others shouldn't even think about it. In general, Zig code is extremely portable compared to other languages. So if you're tired of your code being tied to a single platform, Zig's got your back—though I'm sure there are still edge cases that will make you want to throw your computer out of the window.

But here's the kicker: each platform requires its own implementations to make those cross-platform abstractions work. These implementations are at various degrees of completion, which is just a polite way of saying some platforms get all the love while others are left in the cold. And don't even get me started on how well documented all this is.

Zig's target support is categorized into four tiers (Tier 1 to Tier 4), which reflect the level of support (or love) and reliability for building software targeting specific hardware architectures. Understanding these tiers helps us decide which targets are suitable for their projects based on stability, community support, and experimental status.

Tier 1: production-ready support

Targets in Tier 1 have robust, well-tested support in Zig. These targets are considered production-ready and are widely used. They receive **continuous integration** (**CI**) coverage to ensure they work reliably with the latest updates to Zig.

Key features of Tier 1 targets are as follows:

- **Stable application binary interface** (**ABI**): The calling conventions and binary compatibility are well defined and consistent
- **Comprehensive standard library support**: The standard library provides all necessary functionality for these targets
- **Regular testing**: These targets undergo frequent automated testing to catch regressions early
- **Community and ecosystem support**: There is an active community contributing tools, libraries, and resources for these targets

Examples of Tier 1 targets include the following:

- x86_64 (Windows, macOS, Linux)
- aarch64 (Apple Silicon macOS, Linux ARM64)
- riscv64
- PowerPC64

Tier 2: community-maintained support

Tier 2 targets have some level of support in Zig but may not be as thoroughly tested or maintained as Tier 1 targets. These targets rely heavily on community contributions and may require additional effort to use effectively.

Key features of Tier 2 targets are as follows:

- **Partial standard library support**: Some parts of the standard library may work, while others may need customization
- **Less frequent testing**: These targets are tested less frequently, which can lead to bugs or compatibility issues
- **Dependent on community contributions**: Maintenance and improvements often depend on contributions from users who rely on these targets

Examples of Tier 2 targets include the following:

- ARM32 (Linux)
- MIPS
- SPARC
- **System-on-a-chip (SoC)** architectures

Tier 3: experimental or minimal support

Tier 3 targets have minimal support in Zig and are considered experimental. These targets may not be well documented or thoroughly tested, and they often require significant effort to use effectively.

Key features of Tier 3 targets are as follows:

- **Very little standard library support**: The standard library has limited or no knowledge of these targets
- **Requires manual configuration**: Users may need to manually configure the compiler, specify C integer sizes, or provide custom calling conventions
- **Unlikely to be tested regularly**: These targets are not tested frequently and may have compatibility issues with newer versions of Zig

Examples of Tier 3 targets include the following:

- Hexagon
- AMDGPU
- SPARC (32-bit)
- Some embedded architectures

Tier 4: deprecated or legacy support

Tier 4 targets are either deprecated by their respective vendors or provide only experimental support. These targets may not be updated in the future and should be used with caution.

Key features of Tier 4 targets are as follows:

- **Deprecated by vendors:** These targets are no longer supported by hardware manufacturers or software ecosystems
- **Experimental status in Zig:** They may require special configuration or custom builds of LLVM to use
- **Limited functionality:** Some targets may only support assembly output (-femit-asm) and not object files

Examples of Tier 4 targets include the following:

- AVR
- RISC-V32
- xCore
- MSP430

Too much information? Take it as a general guideline:

- **Tier 1:** Ideal for production environments due to their reliability and comprehensive support
- **Tier 2:** Suitable for projects that require less mainstream architectures, but are willing to invest effort in testing and maintenance
- **Tiers 3 and 4:** Best reserved for experimental or niche use cases where the target's specific capabilities justify the risks

Using the target

Before we start to shove values into target, it's crucial to understand what target is in the script. Well, target is the ResolvedTarget type. In other words, our first line defining target in the build.zig file should be written this way:

```
const target:ResolvedTarget = b.standardTargetOptions(.{});
```

In Zig's build system, targets are specified using Target.Query, which is resolved into ResolvedTarget containing both the query and the fully resolved target details. Here's how it works.

Target.Query represents a partial target specification (e.g., from command-line options). It can include the following:

- Triple (e.g., x86_64-linux-gnu)
- CPU features
- Dynamic linker path

Note: *Triple* in this context is a standardized string format specifying the following parts of a target platform:

- Architecture (CPU type)
- Operating system
- ABI/environment

This is the format: <arch>-<os>-<abi>.

Examples include the following:

- x86_64-linux-gnu (Desktop Linux)
- aarch64-macos-none (Apple Silicon Mac)
- wasm32-freestanding-musl (WebAssembly)

It is specified via the -Dtarget=<triple> flag and handled internally via std.Target.Query.parse().

The ResolvedTarget is created by resolving a query using std.zig.system.resolveTargetQuery(). It contains the original query and the complete std.Target with all details filled in.

By understanding the tiers of target support in Zig, developers can make informed decisions about which architectures to use for their projects, balancing stability, performance, and community resources.

The key functions within the Zig code base (build.zig) in this workflow are as follows:

```
// Parse command-line options into a Target.Query
pub fn standardTargetOptionsQueryOnly(b: *Build, args:
StandardTargetOptionsArgs) Target.Query


// Resolve a query into a full target configuration
pub fn resolveTargetQuery(b: *Build, query: Target.Query) ResolvedTarget
```

OK, OK! I can feel you frowning and resisting the desire to skip all the details. Hold tight! There is just one more piece of information before the customization of targets. We must know what StandardTargetOptionsArgs is. Fortunately, there are only a few: whitelist and default_target. I personally think whitelist could simply be called allowed_targets. But what do I know, right?

Both are a Target.Query, but whitelist is a slice, and default_target is a single value:

- whitelist: This option restricts valid build targets to ensure compatibility
- default_target: This is a fallback when no target is specified

The user's (your) experience you should expect is to call zig build to use the default target and zig build -Dtarget=... to override the default.

compare the default and using the target options:

```
const target = b.standardTargetOptions(.{});
```

then

```
const target = b.standardTargetOptions(.{
    .whitelist = &.{ // Optional allowed targets
        .{ .cpu_arch = .x86_64, .os_tag = .linux },
        .{ .cpu_arch = .aarch64, .os_tag = .macos }
    },
    .default_target = .{} // Native target
});
```

We can explore this with more details to make it easier to grasp:

```
const allowed_targets = &[_]std.Target.Query{
    .{ // x86_64 Linux
        .cpu_arch = .x86_64,
        .os_tag = .linux,
        .abi = .gnu
```

```
    },
    .{ // ARM macOS
        .cpu_arch = .aarch64,
        .os_tag = .macos
    }
};

pub fn build(b: *std.Build) void {
    const target = b.standardTargetOptions(.{
        .whitelist = allowed_targets,
        .default_target = .{}
    });
    // ... use target ...
}
```

Are the pieces connecting? The allowed targets are a slice of `std.Target.Query` that orients `standardTargetOptions` to achieve cross-compilation. Phew! What a ride, huh?

Zig cross-compiles like it's playing *Stardew Valley* on easy mode.

When using an invalid target:

```
$ zig build -Dtarget=riscv64-windows-msvc
error: chosen target 'riscv64-windows-msvc' not in allowed list
Allowed targets:
  - x86_64-linux-gnu
  - aarch64-macos-none


zig build -Dtarget=riscv65-windows-msvc unable to parse target 'riscv65-
windows-msvc': UnknownArchitecture
zig build -Dtarget=riscv64-windows11-msvc unknown OS: 'windows11'
available operating systems: freestanding ananas (long list of OS)
zig build -Dtarget=riscv64-windows-hello unable to parse target 'riscv64-
windows-hello': UnknownApplicationBinaryInterface
```

This system provides robust target management while maintaining Zig's signature developer experience. The combination of flexible triples, safety-focused whitelisting, and sensible defaults makes cross-compilation approachable yet controlled. And yes, there is no `./configure && make && sudo make install` nonsense.

Why do these matter?

- **Cross-compilation safety**: Whitelist prevents invalid target combinations
- **User guidance**: Clear errors help developers specify valid targets
- **Project consistency**: They ensure that all team members build for the same targets
- **CI/CD reliability**: They prevent accidental builds for the wrong architectures

There is so much happening behind the scenes, and we just need to pass simple parameters. This is another Zig lesson on pragmatism. Your Windows binary compiles on Linux while you argue about tabs versus spaces.

Now that you've seen how Zig's build system can handle the basics and even cross-compile for different platforms, let's talk about optimizing your code for real-world use.

Release modes

Whether you're building a high-performance game, a resource-constrained embedded system, or a production-grade web service, you'll need to think about how your code is compiled. Should it be fast? Small? Debuggable? Zig's release modes give you fine-grained control over these trade-offs. With just a few tweaks to your build.zig file, you can optimize for speed, reduce binary size, or enable detailed debugging information. It's like having a performance dial for your code—and Zig makes it easy to turn. So, let's explore how you can use Zig's release modes to make your applications faster, leaner, and ready for the real world.

Optimizations: Debug versus Release (choose your poison)

Back again in the first lines of the build.zig script, we can find the following line:

```
const optimize = b.standardOptimizeOption(.{}); // Debug = "Crash
Verbosely", Release = "Crash Fast"
```

But wait. What is this function expecting to receive? We can investigate the function signature to help us understand it better and navigate into future problems with ease:

```
pub fn standardOptimizeOption(b: *Build, options:
StandardOptimizeOptionOptions) std.builtin.OptimizeMode
```

To expand the hidden type information in our build script, we can type the very same line as follows:

```
const optimize: std.builtin.OptimizeMode = b.standardOptimizeOption(std.
Build.StandardOptimizeOptionOptions{});
```

Don't bother with this verbose version. We will not be using this version once we know what is going on. The main insight regarding this function is that the `StandardOptimizeOptionOptions` parameters have just one option, `preferred_optimize_mode`, of the `std.builtin.OptimizeMode` type, which is exactly equal to the function return. In other words, you can choose what optimization mode is preferred.

Navigating to the definition of `std.builtin.OptimizeMode`, we can find all options declared within the enum:

```
pub const OptimizeMode = enum {
    Debug,
    ReleaseSafe,
    ReleaseFast,
    ReleaseSmall,
};
```

Hmm... Interesting. But what do these values mean? Well, you'll find these values commonly referenced as **release modes**. Zig provides four distinct release modes that offer different trade-offs between performance, safety, and binary size. We can use them to configure our build script (and select them at compile time).

You might be wondering why this is called `OptimizeMode` instead of `ReleaseMode`. Well, the answer is: There are "real" release modes in the code base, but they are one abstraction deeper than `OptimizeMode`, and they are called, as you guessed, `ReleaseMode`:

```
pub const ReleaseMode = enum {
    off,
    any,
    fast,
    safe,
    small,
};
```

You don't touch them because the `standardOptimizeOption` function does all the heavy-lifting for you. If you still want to directly interface with `ReleaseMode`, you should access it directly from the current reference of `std.Build`:

```
b.release_mode = std.Build.ReleaseMode.any;
```

When no release mode is explicitly set, the default value is off, which translates to `OptimizeMode`. Debug. You still can choose one of the remaining values, but if you choose the any value, you are deferring the decision. In this case, the execution output will scream at you: `"The project does not declare a preferred optimization mode. Choose: --release=fast, --release=safe, or --release=small"`.

Bring back the attention for the trade-offs. Let's explore one of the release modes.

Debug

Debug is the default release mode. It is the careful healer. The cautious one who double-checks every door for traps. The optimizations are disabled, and the safety catch is on. This means that your compilation times are fast, but there are greater runtime performance penalties, and we're giving up reproducible builds. Think of this mode as a "development and debugging" mode:

```
// Debug mode: "Are you *sure* you want to do that?"
var x: u8 = 255;
x += 1; // Panics: "Integer overflow detected!"
```

ReleaseSafe

This is our balanced warrior. The reliable fighter who's fast but still wears a helmet. It is the first mode for production use. However, this mode has drawbacks such as moderate runtime performance penalties and slower compilation times. This time, we have reproducible builds. This is the mode where safety is still critical:

```
// ReleaseSafe: "I'll protect you, but don't push it."
var x: u8 = 255;
x += 1; // Still panics, but faster!
```

To change in the build, set `b.release_mode = std.Build.ReleaseMode.safe`, or via the CLI with the `zig build -Doptimize=ReleaseSafe` argument.

ReleaseFast

`ReleaseFast` is where things get *Ziggy*. This mode is the berserker. The reckless barbarian who charges in, no questions asked. It aims for production but with performance-critical requirements. The safety checks are disabled, which translates directly to a better runtime performance:

```
// ReleaseFast: "What's a safety check? CHARGE!"
var x: u8 = 255;
x += 1; // Undefined behavior. Good luck!
```

To change in the build, set b.release_mode = std.Build.ReleaseMode.fast, or via the CLI with the zig build -Doptimize=ReleaseFast argument.

ReleaseSmall

Here is the mode for constrained environments: ReleaseSmall. The stealth rogue who slips through cracks and leaves no trace. In this mode, we get the same performance as with ReleaseSafe, but with a small binary size:

```
// ReleaseSmall: "I'll fit in anywhere, but don't ask for help."
var x: u8 = 255;
x += 1; // Undefined behavior, but hey, it's tiny!
```

Use zig build -Doptimize=ReleaseSmall to make your binary smaller than your ego.

Here is the deal: Want speed? You'll sacrifice safety. Want safety? You'll sacrifice speed. It's like choosing between a shield and a *zweihander*—both are great, but you can't wield both at once (at least for the current Zig release).

Here's a practical demonstration of how different release modes affect runtime behavior. First, create the build.zig file:

```
const std = @import("std");
pub fn build(b: *std.Build) void { const target =
b.standardTargetOptions(.{}); // Let the user choose the optimization mode
from the command line const optimize = b.standardOptimizeOption(.{});
// Create module for the executable
const exe_mod = b.createModule(.{
    .root_source_file = b.path("src/main.zig"),
    .target = target,
    .optimize = optimize,
});

const exe = b.addExecutable(.{
    .name = "safety-demo",
    .root_module = exe_mod,
});

b.installArtifact(exe);

const run_cmd = b.addRunArtifact(exe);
```

```
const run_step = b.step("run", "Run with selected optimization");
run_step.dependOn(&run_cmd.step);


}
```

Then, create the main.zig file:

```
const std = @import("std");

pub fn main() void {
    var x: u8 = 255;
    std.debug.print("Initial value: {}\n", .{x});

    // This will cause an overflow.
    x += 1;

    // This line may or may not be reached depending on the release mode.
    std.debug.print("Value after overflow: {}\n", .{x});
}
```

Try running this with different optimization modes:

- `zig build run -Doptimize=Debug` (panics with overflow detection)
- `zig build run -Doptimize=ReleaseSafe` (panics with overflow detection)
- `zig build run -Doptimize=ReleaseFast` (undefined behavior, likely wraps to 0)
- `zig build run -Doptimize=ReleaseSmall` (undefined behavior, optimized for size)

Mix and match

Although you can't use two optimization modes at the same time, you can mix modes within the same project. For example, you can compile your core logic in ReleaseFast while keeping your tests in Debug. It's like having a berserker on the front lines and a healer in the back:

```
const core = b.addExecutable(.{
    .name = "core",
    .root_source_file = .{ .path = "src/core.zig" },
    .optimize = .ReleaseFast,
});

const tests = b.addTest(.{
```

```
    .root_source_file = .{ .path = "src/tests.zig" },
    .optimize = .Debug,
});
```

Undefined behavior and granular control

Zig leverages **undefined behavior (UB)** for optimizations, but it's not shy about it. In `ReleaseFast` and `ReleaseSmall`, UB is like a dragon—powerful but dangerous. If you're not careful, it'll burn your code to ash:

```
@setRuntimeSafety(false); // "I know what I'm doing, Zig. Trust me."
var x: u8 = 255;
x += 1; // Undefined behavior. You've been warned.
```

Zig provides granular control through automatic safety checks in `Debug/ReleaseSafe` and explicit unsafe blocks using `@setRuntimeSafety(false)`.

Here is where you can use granular control on safety:

```
fn optimizedFunction() void {
    @setRuntimeSafety(false);
    // rest of the function omitted.
}
```

One important aspect of `@setRuntimeSafety` is that the control is set for the scope that contains the function call. So, you can set the safety for one code block, and change it for another block, regardless of how deep it is.

Note for readers in the future: there are plans to rename `@setRuntimeSafety` as `@optimizeFor`. If you don't find `@setRuntimeSafety` available, this means the future is here.

At this point, we've explored the two standard options (`standardTargetOptions` and `standardOptimizeOption`), but what about our own custom options? (estale os dedos) Let's start customizing our own options.

Custom options

Before we dive deep, think of a custom option as a **key decision point** in your build process. Much like a well-designed function in programming, it takes inputs (perhaps an argument or a condition), and based on that input, it directs the flow of your build process in a way that is not only efficient but also clear and maintainable. So, how do you introduce these "decision points" into your Zig project? Well, it starts with understanding that options in Zig are not just simple toggles.

They're flexible constructs, much like the way we craft clean, readable code—to be dynamic and expressive, yet not overwhelming.

Imagine you're developing a multi-platform app and you want to give users the ability to enable or disable a special feature, such as a dark mode for the UI, directly through the build configuration. This isn't just about turning something on or off, though. Perhaps the feature needs to be activated only under certain conditions—maybe based on the environment or a developer's choice.

Now, instead of just a simple version string, let's define an option for this feature. Here's how you can use Zig's custom options to give your build process a bit of flexibility and interactivity:

Consider a simple option for versioning:

```
const enable_dark_mode = b.option(bool, "enable_dark_mode", "Enable Dark
Mode UI") orelse false;
const options = b.addOptions();
options.addOption([]const u8, "dark_mode_enabled", enable_dark_mode);


exe.root_module.addOptions("ui", options);
```

In this example, the enable_dark_mode option becomes a toggle for enabling the dark mode UI theme. When running the build, developers (or even CI/CD pipelines) can set this option to true or false. If not set, it defaults to false, meaning the light theme will be used by default.

When building the app, if the developer decides they want to test the app with the dark mode enabled, they can simply specify this option like so:

```
zig build -Denable_dark_mode true
```

In the program, you can import these options as simply as using @import("ui"), and this is compile-time known. In other words, this single line adjusts the behavior of the application, demonstrating how custom options in Zig can make your builds more adaptable and responsive to varying needs, without modifying the core code.

Here's the complete implementation of the custom options feature:

```
const std = @import("std");
pub fn build(b: *std.Build) void { const target =
b.standardTargetOptions(.{}); const optimize = b.standardOptimizeOption(.
{});
// Define a custom boolean option for dark mode
const enable_dark_mode = b.option(bool, "dark_mode", "Enable Dark Mode
```

```
UI") orelse false;

// Create an options module to pass the value to the program
const options = b.addOptions();
options.addOption(bool, "is_dark_mode_enabled", enable_dark_mode);


// Create module for the executable
const exe_mod = b.createModule(.{
    .root_source_file = b.path("src/main.zig"),
    .target = target,
    .optimize = optimize,
});

const exe = b.addExecutable(.{
    .name = "ui-app",
    .root_module = exe_mod,
});

// Add the options under the name "config"
exe.root_module.addOptions("config", options);

b.installArtifact(exe);

const run_cmd = b.addRunArtifact(exe);
const run_step = b.step("run", "Run the app");
run_step.dependOn(&run_cmd.step);


}
```

Here is the main.zig file:

```
const std = @import("std");
// Import the options module created in build.zig
const config = @import("config");
pub fn main() void {
    if (config.is_dark_mode_enabled) {
```

```
            std.debug.print("UI is running in Dark Mode!\n", .{});
    } else {
        std.debug.print("UI is running in Light Mode.\n", .{});
    }
}
```

Try running this example:

- `zig build run` (outputs "UI is running in Light Mode.")
- `zig build run -Ddark_mode=true` (outputs "UI is running in Dark Mode!")

The beauty of this approach is that the configuration is known at compile-time, allowing the compiler to optimize away unused code paths.

This is the very start of the Zig build system, and we should continue exploring several functions, and believe me, there are dozens of them. This book is called *Learning Zig*, so I want to give you the tools to understand the build system and how to go further in your explorations. You're not expecting a large tutorial to copy and paste, right? Let's understand the build system entities.

The build team

The Zig build system is a **team**:

- **Build** is the project manager
- **Steps** are the workers
- **Modules** are the deliverables
- **Dependencies** are subcontractors
- **LazyPath** and **Cache** are the tools and logistics

Every member has a role, and the DAG is the workflow that keeps them all in sync.

In the very first place on the list, we have our well-known `Build`, which acts as the manager, coordinating all workers (steps). As we saw in previous examples, this is the root object created in the `build.zig` script:

```
pub fn build(b: *std.Build) void { ... }
```

It manages the entire build graph, options, and dependencies.

Steps: the atomic actions of a build pipeline

In the software construction theater, steps are the solo performers—each tasked with a precise, unglamorous role that collectively brings the production to life. They are the rivets in the assembly line, the unsung heroes of reproducibility. To declare a step is to choreograph an intent: *Here, compile this. There, execute that. Now, place the artifact here.* The build system, ever the dutiful stage manager, ensures that each actor hits its mark.

The taxonomy of steps

Steps follow a philosophy of *singular purpose*. Like Unix tools, they do one thing well, but compose elegantly. Let's dissect the archetypes:

- **Step.Compile**: The translator. It takes the raw dialect of Zig, C, or C++ and weaves it into the machine's tongue. Behind the scenes, it negotiates optimizations, the inclusion of libraries, and the subtle art of not overstepping memory. For example, compiling a .zig file into an executable is akin to baking a soufflé—precision in ingredients (flags) and timing (dependencies) matters.

- **Step.Run**: The executor. This step is a hired hand, running shell commands, CodeGen scripts, or even invoking other tools in your toolchain. Imagine it as a concierge—*"Would you like to generate protobuf bindings before compiling? Certainly."*

- **Step.Install**: The archivist. It copies binaries, headers, or assets to their designated folders, curating order from the chaos of intermediate files. Without it, your build artifacts would scatter like orphaned socks.

- **And your own custom steps**: The wildcards. These are the steps you define to handle tasks Zig hasn't foreseen—bundling assets, uploading releases, or even sending a celebratory Slack message post-build. Custom steps are where the build system admits, *Fine, you're the creative one here.*

The DAG: Git's angrier cousin

If steps are the actors, the DAG is the plot. It dictates who speaks first, who waits in the wings, and who must finish before the curtain rises. Zig's DAG is Git's angrier cousin, not out of malice, but rigor—it enforces dependency order with the sternness of a librarian who's seen one too many overdue books.

When you declare `test_step.dependOn(&run_tests.step)`, you're not merely adding a task to a queue. You're etching a rule into the DAG's stone tablet: *Thou shalt not pass until these tests are run.* The build system, like a passive-aggressive butler, arranges these dependencies with silent efficiency. Cross it at your peril.

Declarative syntax: the illusion of simplicity

Defining steps in `build.zig` feels almost deceptively simple. Consider this snippet:

```
const tests = b.addTest(.{
    .root_source_file = .{ .path = "src/tests.zig" },
});
const run_tests = b.addRunArtifact(tests);
test_step.dependOn(&run_tests.step);
```

Here, we've orchestrated a miniature saga:

- **Create a test artifact**: A binary that embodies your test suite
- **Stage it for execution**: `addRunArtifact` wraps it in a `Step.Run`
- **Bind it to the test step**: A dependency that ensures that `zig build test` runs the gauntlet

The declarative syntax masks the machinery beneath. It's like ordering a coffee by describing the taste—the barista (Zig) grinds the beans, steams the milk, and hands you the cup, all while you muse abstractly about caffeine.

Custom steps: the build system's escape hatch

To define a custom step is to inject your own logic into Zig's veins. Suppose you want to bundle assets for a game:

```
const bundle_step = b.step("bundle-assets", "Pack textures and sounds");

const bundle_assets = b.addSystemCommand(&.{
    "python3", "scripts/bundle_assets.py", "--output", "assets.zip"
});
bundle_step.dependOn(&bundle_assets.step);
```

This is the build system's concession: *You're right, I can't do everything. But I'll make sure your script runs at exactly the right moment.* Custom steps are where Zig's precision meets your chaos—a handshake agreement between framework and creativity.

The RPG side quest principle

"Test steps are RPG side quests. Skip them, and your project stays mediocre."

Tests are the optional quests that, when ignored, leave your code base vulnerable to dragons (regressions) and cursed loot (bugs). Zig's addTest is the guild master nudging you: "You could rush the main quest, but will you survive the final boss?" By binding tests to the build DAG, you ensure they're not just an afterthought—they're part of the hero's journey.

The philosophy beneath

Zig's build system is a study in constrained flexibility. It gives you a lexicon of steps and a grammar (the DAG) to compose them, but resists the temptation to become an all-powerful scripting engine. Like a seasoned carpenter, it believes in sharp, well-defined tools—not a single Swiss army knife.

When you next write a build.zig script, remember that you're not just compiling code. You're drafting a blueprint, directing a play, and yes—occasionally appeasing that passive-aggressive butler.

Alright, let's take another crack at this Zig build system thing, shall we? You think you've seen it all? I've been around since punch cards were a thing, and let me tell you, Zig's build system is... well, it's something else. It's like that eccentric uncle of programming: a bit odd, but once you get to know him, you realize he's got some surprisingly good ideas. Think of me as your grizzled guide through this wilderness. I've seen more build systems than you've had hot dinners, and I'm here to tell you, Zig's is worth a look. But be warned, it doesn't coddle you. This is the "roll up your sleeves and get your hands dirty" kind of system. Ready to dive in? Good. Let's get to it.

In the old days, we just dumped all our code in one file and prayed. Now, everyone's obsessed with "modularity." Zig, in its infinite, quirky wisdom, has its own take on this, which it calls, predictably, **modules**.

Modules

First, let's try to understand what a module is in Zig's twisted mind. It is like that perfectly organized toolbox where every tool has its place. Each module is not just a haphazard collection of code. Oh no, it's a carefully curated set of source files, dependencies, and configurations. It is a self-contained unit, but let's be honest, it's more like a tiny, self-important kingdom.

Code islands

Each module is a little island of code. It's got its own source files, its own little rules, and its own inflated sense of self-worth. It's like a tiny kingdom where your code lives. But remember, with great power comes great responsibility to not make a mess:

```
// This is a module, in all its glory
const my_module = b.addExecutable(.{
    .name = "my_precious",
    .root_source_file = .{ .path = "src/main.zig" },
});
// Behold, the kingdom of "my_precious"
```

Dependency hoarders

Modules love to collect dependencies like a dragon hoards gold. This is where they keep track of all the other little kingdoms they rely on. Zig's not shy about this; it's all laid out, explicit as a tax form:

```
my_module.addImport("utils", utils_module);
// "I need 'utils' to function. Go fetch it, peasant!"
```

Configuration fetishists

If you thought you were particular about your editor's tab settings, wait till you see Zig modules. Architecture, optimization, debug settings—they've got an opinion on everything. It's like having a project manager who's also a control freak about the office thermostat:

```
my_module.setTarget(target);
my_module.setOptimizeOptions(.ReleaseSafe);
// "Compile it for THIS architecture, and optimize it, but don't you dare
make it unsafe!"
```

The circle of (module) life: from declaration to domination

Modules aren't born fully formed. They go through a "life cycle," which is Zig's fancy way of saying "a bunch of steps you have to follow." Think of it as the assembly line for your code, but with fewer robots and more caffeine.

Declaration: the grand proclamation

This is the moment you announce your module's existence to the build system. It's like planting a flag on the moon, but instead of a barren landscape, you're claiming territory in your project's code base:

```
const my_module = b.addStaticLibrary(.{
    .name = "my_lib",
    .root_source_file = .{ .path = "src/lib.zig" },
});
// "Hear ye, hear ye! A new module is born! Its name is 'my_lib'."
```

You're declaring a new static library module named `"my_lib"` with `"src/lib.zig"` as its foundational source file. You are the architect, and this is your blueprint.

Configuration: the fiddling and tweaking

Now, you get to customize your module, shaping it to your exact specifications. It's the "setting up camp" phase, where you tailor your environment. You can add dependencies, tweak compiler settings, link external libraries—essentially, you're outfitting your module for the specific challenges it will face:

```
my_module.addIncludePath("include/");
my_module.addImport("zmath", zmath_module);
// "Look in 'include/' for headers, and make friends with the 'zmath'
module."
```

You're configuring `my_module` to include headers from the `"include/"` directory and to form a strategic partnership with the zmath module. You are the diplomat, negotiating treaties between different parts of your code.

Integration: joining the big leagues

Finally, you expose your module to the rest of the build system. This is the grand unveiling, the moment your module steps onto the stage. It's like flipping the switch on your project, activating the module, and making it a functioning part of the whole:

```
b.installArtifact(my_module);
// "Alright, 'my_module', you're ready for the big time. Go get 'em,
tiger!"
```

You're instructing the Zig build system to install my_module, transforming it from a carefully crafted blueprint into a tangible, usable component. You are the conductor, and this is the moment your orchestra begins to play.

There you have it: declaration, configuration, and integration. Each step plays a vital role in bringing your module to life. It's a structured process, a carefully choreographed dance, but one that ultimately leads to a more organized, efficient, and powerful code base.

Multi-module mania: when modules collide

So, you think you're a big shot, huh? Ready to graduate from single-module projects to the big leagues of multi-module madness?

Let's assume the following build file:

```
const std = @import("std");

pub fn build(b: *std.Build) void {
    const lib = b.addStaticLibrary(.{
        .name = "mylib",
        .root_source_file = .{ .path = "src/mylib.zig" },
    });
    // "We're making a library called 'mylib'. It's gonna be great."

    const exe = b.addExecutable(.{
        .name = "myexe",
        .root_source_file = .{ .path = "src/main.zig" },
    });
    // "And an executable called 'myexe'. Because why not?"

    exe.addImport("mylib", lib);
    // "'myexe' needs 'mylib'. Let's hope they get along."

    b.installArtifact(exe);
    // "We're betting on 'myexe'. It's the chosen one."
}
```

Here, you are not just writing code; you are managing a fleet. mylib is a support vessel, and myexe is your main battleship. addImport is like assigning crew between ships.

So, when should you actually use these module things? Here's the lowdown:

- **Code reuse (because copy-pasting is for rookies)**: If you find yourself writing the same code over and over, it's time for a module. It's like creating your own little library of code snippets, but without the embarrassing comments you wrote at 3 A.M.

- **Dependency management (keeping the chaos at bay)**: Modules help you manage third-party libraries. It's like having a bouncer for your code base, keeping the riff-raff out.

- **Cross-compilation (for the polyglots among us)**: Building for different architectures? Modules can handle that. It's like being a UN translator, but for your code.

- **Mixed-language projects (when Zig meets C and others)**: Zig plays surprisingly well with other languages. Modules are like the diplomats in this multi-lingual world.

Modules aren't lone wolves. They have a support system, a whole entourage of helpers. Let's meet the crew:

- **Dependencies, the mercenaries**: These are external packages that your modules can hire to do their bidding. They come with their own set of skills (and build.zig files), ready to be deployed in your project. It is like hiring a specialist for a high-stakes mission.

- **LazyPath, the scouts**: These are your pathfinders, always knowing the location of files and directories. Think of them as the scouts of your project, providing reconnaissance on where resources reside. It is like having an uncanny sense of direction in a foreign city.

And then you have the system components, the unsung heroes (or villains, depending on your perspective):

- **Cache, the roadie with a photographic memory**: This guy remembers every build artifact, so you don't have to rebuild things unnecessarily. It's like having an elephant for a roadie—a bit weird, but incredibly efficient. We'll explore it later in this chapter.

- **Graph, the cartographer**: This is the master map of your build system, tracking the intricate relationships between all components. It is the grand architect's plan, ensuring everything fits together perfectly.

The show must go on

Let's see how these components work together, like a well-rehearsed orchestra.

`Build` creates modules and steps. It's like the director, calling the shots:

```
const lib = b.addStaticLibrary(...); // "Create a library module! Now!"
const exe = b.addExecutable(...); // "And an executable! Make it snappy!"
const install_step = b.addInstallArtifact(exe); // "Install the
executable! Now, now, now!"
```

Dependencies create subgraphs. It's like a family tree, but for code:

```
const dep = b.dependency("zlib", .{ .optimize = .ReleaseSmall }); //"Get
me 'zlib', and make it snappy!"
exe.linkLibrary(dep.artifact("z")); // "Link 'zlib' to the executable! We
need to compress things!"
```

`LazyPath` connects resources. It's like a GPS for your build system:

```
exe.addAssemblyFile(.{ .path = "src/arch/cpu.s" }); // "Add this assembly
file! It's... somewhere."
```

Cache avoids doing unnecessary work.

The grand finale

So, there you have it. Modules, steps, and dependencies—it's all a bit of a circus, isn't it? Zig's build system, with all its quirks and complexities, actually makes sense:

- **Modules** are your outputs: the *what*
- **Steps** are the tasks: the *how*
- **Dependencies** are the relationships: the *who needs what*
- **Control flow** (the DAG) is the order of operations: the *when*

Zig's "no magic" philosophy means you have to be explicit about everything. It's a bit like being forced to write detailed instructions for making a sandwich. Annoying at first, but it prevents a lot of confusion down the line. You're not just a programmer anymore; you're a software architect, a build system engineer, a master of your domain.

Pop quiz: Are you smarter than a build script?

- **Scenario:** You're building a sprawling metropolis of code with distinct districts: a core library (the city's heart), a GUI (its public face), and a command-line interface (its industrial sector).

- **Question:** How would you deploy Zig's modules to bring order and efficiency to this urban sprawl, and why?

- *Hint: Ponder the concepts of modularity and reusability. And try not to get lost in the city.*

- **Code challenge:** Architect a build.zig file that orchestrates three modules: a static library named math_orchard, an executable named fruit_renderer that depends on math_orchard, and another executable named fruit_simulator that also depends on math_orchard.

- *Pro Tip: Employ* addStaticLibrary *and* addExecutable *like a master builder. And ensure your dependencies are linked with the precision of a master craftsman.*

- **Philosophical debate:** Is Zig's explicit, no-magic approach to building systems a utopian ideal or a dystopian nightmare? Weigh up the pros and cons.

- *Bonus points for metaphors that soar and analogies that dance. Extra bonus points for insights that provoke thought or spark joy (or a healthy dose of existential dread).*

> **Embrace the pain**
>
> Let's be real, Zig's build system is not a walk in the park. It is the intellectual equivalent of a high-intensity workout. But here's the secret: once you push through the initial burn, you'll find it builds a code base that's lean, mean, and incredibly powerful.

So, venture forth, build incredible things, and try not to lose your sanity in the process. And remember, I'm always here, in the digital ether, ready to dispense more unconventional wisdom and analogies that might just be crazy enough to work. You're welcome. Or, as they say in certain circles, "Happy coding, and may your builds always succeed."

Let's talk about turning your code into something resembling documentation. We're venturing beyond the realm of mere compilation and stepping into the arcane arts of generating actual, readable docs. Think of it as enchanting your code with the power of explanation.

Generating docs: because code should be less cryptic than ancient runes

Feeling overwhelmed by code that's more cryptic than a wizard's grimoire? Don't worry. You'll transform your Zig code into documentation so clear that even a sleep-deprived **site reliability engineer (SRE)** could understand it. Let's dive in, shall we? It is like teaching your code to speak a human language.

Doc comments: breadcrumbs for future-you

Zig's doc comments are your lifeline, your trail of breadcrumbs in the dark forest of your own code. Use `///` to annotate declarations and `//!` for file-level lore. They're like **quest markers** in your code base; they explain *what* your code does without forcing you to decipher ancient runes, or, you know, remember what you were thinking three months ago at 2 A.M.

Let's consider an example of a module for tracking dragon hoards (because who doesn't need a good gold management system?):

```zig
//! This module handles dragon hoard logistics.
//! Warning: May contain traces of cursed gold.

const std = @import("std");

/// A dragon's hoard coordinate (because dragons love grids)
pub const HoardPos = struct {
    /// X-axis (0 = first pile of gold)
    x: u32,
    /// Y-axis (0 = first pile of gemstones)
    y: u32,

    /// The "you're standing on it" position
    pub const HERE_BE_DRAGON: HoardPos = .{ .x = 0, .y = 0 };

    /// When the dragon eats your map
    pub const LOST: HoardPos = .{
        .x = std.math.maxInt(u32),
        .y = std.math.maxInt(u32),
    };
};
```

Let's break down what is happening here:

- **//!**: This is your module's grand introduction, its opening scroll. It sets the stage for what this chunk of code is all about.
- **///**: These are your individual item descriptions, explaining each piece of the puzzle.
- **HoardPos**: Even your types can have lore. Here, it's a struct representing a location on a dragon's treasure map.

You're not just coding; you're storytelling. You're leaving a trail of notes for anyone brave enough to explore your code.

Generating docs: the compiler's side hustle

To turn those doc comments into a **static website** (because 1990s web design is apparently retro chic now), invoke Zig's hidden talent, its side hustle as a documentation generator:

```
zig build-lib -femit-docs src/dragon_hoard.zig
```

This command is your incantation. It tells Zig to not just compile your code, but also to weave those comments into a beautiful tapestry of HTML. It's like telling your compiler, "Hey, while you're at it, could you also write a user manual?" The -femit-docs flag is your secret weapon, the magic spell that unlocks this functionality.

This creates a ./docs folder containing the following:

- An HTML grimoire of your code's API
- Navigation so intuitive that even a directionally-challenged kobold wouldn't get lost
- Zero dragons, probably

Error set drama

When merging error sets, Zig picks docs like a bard picking favorites at a tavern. The **leftmost error's docs** win. This error is the chosen one, the error message that gets the spotlight. Here is an example:

```
pub const DragonError = error{
    /// The dragon ate your homework
    FireBreathIncident,
    /// The hoard is guarded by a mimic
    TreasureChestGoneWrong,
};
```

```
pub const MapError = error{
    /// The map is written in invisible ink
    FireBreathIncident,
    /// The compass points to soup
    MagneticSoup,
};


pub const ExpeditionError = DragonError || MapError;
```

When errors clash, the documentation of the first error you listed takes precedence. In other words, in ExpeditionError, FireBreathIncident inherits the *dragon's* doc comment ("ate your homework"), not the map's ("invisible ink"). Priorities!

Weaponize the build system

Forge documentation into your build pipeline like a dwarven smith. Add this to build.zig:

```
const std = @import("std");

pub fn build(b: *std.Build) void {
    // ... previous setup ...

    const hoard_lib = b.addStaticLibrary(.{
        .name = "dragon_hoard",
        .root_source_file = .{ .path = "src/hoard.zig" },
        .target = target,
        .optimize = optimize,
    });

    // Install the library (for mortals)
    b.installArtifact(hoard_lib);

    // Install docs (for scholars)
    const docs_install = b.addInstallDirectory(.{
        .source_dir = hoard_lib.getEmittedDocs(),
        .install_dir = .prefix,      // "zig-out" directory
        .install_subdir = "scrolls", // "zig-out/scrolls"
    });
```

```
    const docs_step = b.step("scrolls", "Generate hoard documentation");
    docs_step.dependOn(&docs_install.step);
}
```

> 💡 **Quick tip:** Enhance your coding experience with the **AI Code Explainer** and **Quick Copy** features. Open this book in the next-gen Packt Reader. Click the **Copy** button
>
> **(1)** to quickly copy code into your coding environment, or click the **Explain** button
>
> **(2)** to get the AI assistant to explain a block of code to you.
>
> ```
> Copy    Explain
> function calculate(a, b) {         ①      ②
>   return {sum: a + b};
> };
> ```

🔖 **The next-gen Packt Reader** is included for free with the purchase of this book. Scan the QR code OR go to `https://packtpub.com/unlock`, then use the search bar to find this book by name. Double-check the edition shown to make sure you get the right one.

Now, run the following:

```
zig build scrolls
```

Your docs will appear in `zig-out/scrolls`, ready for distribution to apprentices (or angry code reviewers).

Documentation isn't a chore—it's a **contract with future-you**. Treat it like feeding a documentation dragon: neglect it, and it'll burn down your code base. Feed it regularly, and it'll defend your kingdom from chaos.

Now go forth, and may your doc comments be ever verbose (but not *too* verbose).

Just as Zig automates the tedious process of generating documentation, it also streamlines the often-complex task of managing project dependencies.

Package management: because reinventing the wheel is so last century

So, you're writing Zig and using the build system, huh? Excellent. You've clearly decided that manually managing memory and wrestling with undefined behavior is your idea of a good time. But even the most hardened systems programmer eventually tires of rewriting the same data structures and network protocols from scratch. That's where package management saunters in, stage left, hopefully not tripping over its own feet.

Now, if you're coming from languages where package management is an afterthought bolted on later – languages whose names I shall charitably omit – prepare for a shock. Zig, in its infinite wisdom, decided that dependency management wasn't some fluffy extra, but a core part of the development experience. Groundbreaking, I know.

build.zig.zon: your new best friend (or worst enemy, the jury's still out)

Forget package.json, pom.xml, or whatever monstrosity your language of choice inflicts upon you. Zig gives us build.zig.zon. **ZON**, apparently, stands for **Zig Object Notation**. Catchy, right? It sounds like something you'd find in a sci-fi movie, not a build configuration file. But hey, at least it's not XML.

This build.zig.zon file, residing in the root of your project, is where you declare your project's metadata and, more importantly, its dependencies. Think of it as a manifest of external code you're grudgingly willing to incorporate into your pristine Zig project.

Let's peek at what a dependency declaration looks like in this ZON thingy:

```
.{
    .name = "my_project",
    .version = "0.1.0",
    .dependencies = .{
```

```
    .zap = .{
        .url = "git+https://github.com/zigzap/
zap?ref=v0.9.1#ae5c9278335d8e1133cd6d22707323dda712e120",
        .hash =
"12200223d76ab6cd32f75bc2e31463b0b429bb5b2b6fa4ce8f68dea494ca1ec3398b",
    },
},
}
```

See that dependencies section? That's where the magic, or perhaps the mild annoyance, happens. You declare each dependency with a name (such as zap), a URL pointing to its source, and a hash. Yes, a hash. Zig is *very* serious about verifying the integrity of your dependencies (more on that later). Think of it as Zig's way of saying, "Trust, but verify. And by verify, I mean *really* verify with cryptographic hashes."

zig fetch: your command-line dependency fetcher

Alright, let's get one thing straight: zig fetch is a command. A real, honest-to-goodness command that you can type into your terminal and expect something to happen. Specifically, it's Zig's dedicated command for fetching external dependencies. Think of it as your personal, command-line dependency retriever, ready to snag packages from the vast expanse of the internet (or your local network, if you swing that way).

Now, before you envision zig fetch as some all-powerful package manager in shining armor, let's temper expectations. It's not designed to be a comprehensive package manager *on its own*. Instead, zig fetch is a focused utility, a tool for the specific task of downloading dependencies and, crucially, updating your project's build.zig.zon manifest file. It's a specialized operative, not a general-purpose dependency Swiss army knife.

The most common way you'll interact with zig fetch is via the --save flag. This flag is the key to the helpfulness of zig fetch. It tells Zig to not only download the dependency you specify, but also to intelligently add (or update) an entry in your build.zig.zon file with the dependency's URL and its all-important cryptographic hash. Automation, in small, measured doses.

The basic syntax for this dependency-summoning spell is as follows:

```
zig fetch --save <dependency-url>
```

Here, `<dependency-url>` is, unsurprisingly, the URL pointing to the dependency package you wish to acquire. This could be a URL to a `.tar.gz`, `.zip`, or even a Git repository (though Zig prefers direct download links for efficiency, naturally).

Let's illustrate with our trusty example, the `pg.zig` library. If you want to fetch `pg.zig` and have Zig helpfully update your `build.zig.zon` file, you would execute the following:

```
zig fetch --save "git+https://github.com/zigzap/zap#v0.9.1"
```

Upon running this command, Zig will do the following:

- **Download** the zap archive from the provided URL
- **Calculate** the SHA-256 hash of the downloaded archive, because Zig takes security more seriously than most people take their morning coffee
- **Modify** your `build.zig.zon` file

Let's compare the file before and after. Imagine that your `build.zig.zon` file initially looks like this (a minimal example without any dependencies):

```
.{
    .name = ...,
    .version = ...,
    .dependencies = .{},
}
```

And after `zig fetch`, it looks like this:

```
.{
    .name = ...,
    .version = ...,
    .dependencies = .{
        .zap = .{
            .url = "git+https://github.com/zigzap/
zap?ref=v0.9.1#ae5c9278335d8e1133cd6d22707323dda712e120",
            .hash =
"12200223d76ab6cd32f75bc2e31463b0b429bb5b2b6fa4ce8f68dea494ca1ec3398b",
        },
    },
}
```

Take note of the automatically generated dependency name, zlib. Zig does its best to create a reasonable name based on the URL, but in another case, you might find yourself wanting to rename it to something more... aesthetically pleasing. Such is the price of automation — occasional naming eccentricities.

Now that we've established zig fetch as a command-line entity, let's explore how it relates to the broader Zig build system and its integrated dependency management capabilities.

Putting dependencies to work: from build.zig.zon to @ import

Declaring dependencies in build.zig.zon and fetching them is all well and good, but how do you actually *use* these external libraries in your Zig code? Excellent question. It involves a bit of build.zig and the @import directive in your Zig source files.

Let's revisit our zlib example. Assuming you've added the zlib dependency to your build.zig.zon file, as shown before, you now need to modify your build.zig file to link against this dependency. Within build.zig, you'll typically have an executable or library definition. You need to tell Zig's build system to include your fetched zlib dependency in the build process. This is achieved using the b.dependency function and linking the resulting artifact.

Here's how you might modify your build.zig file:

```
pub fn build(b: *std.Build) !void {
    // ... earlier build configuration code ...
    const zap = b.dependency("zap", .{
        .target = target,
        .optimize = optimize,
        .openssl = false, // set to true to enable TLS support
    });
    exe.root_module.addImport("zap", zap.module("zap"));
    b.installArtifact(exe);
}
```

Let's break down this snippet:

- We declare a dependency named "zap" with b.dependency("zap", ...). Crucially, the name "zap" must match the key used in your build.zig.zon file.

- We expose the dependency's module by calling `exe.root_module.addImport("zap", zap.module("zap"))`. This makes the module available to your Zig source code via the `@import("zap")` directive.

- Finally, after setting up the dependency and linking it properly, we install the executable with `b.installArtifact(exe)`.

Now, in your Zig source code (for example, in `src/main.zig`), you can import and use the `zap` library like so:

```
const zap = @import("zap"); // Import the 'zap' dependency
```

Important naming relationship

The name used in `@import("zap")` in your Zig code must match the dependency name you used in `b.dependency("zap", ...)` in your `build.zig` file. Likewise, the dependency key in your `build.zig.zon` file (e.g., `.zap = .{ ... }`) must match this name.

It's a naming chain—a dependency name trifecta. Get the names wrong, and Zig will promptly inform you of your error.

So, what's the deal with that hash value? It's all about security and ensuring your dependencies haven't been tampered with.

From fingerprint to fortress

Let's talk hashes. You might have noticed that `.hash` field in `build.zig.zon` and wondered, "Why is Zig so obsessed with hashes?" The answer, in short, is **security and reproducibility**.

The hash in `build.zig.zon` is a cryptographic SHA-256 hash of the *contents* of the dependency package you're fetching. When Zig fetches a dependency, it downloads the package and then *verifies* that its calculated hash matches the hash you declared in `build.zig.zon`. If the hashes don't match, Zig throws a fit and refuses to use the dependency.

Why this paranoia? Imagine a scenario where you depend on a crucial library hosted on some website. Without hash verification, if that website were compromised, or someone maliciously replaced the library with a backdoored version, your builds would silently start using the compromised library. This is a supply chain attack, and it's nasty.

Zig's hash verification prevents this. By verifying the hash, Zig ensures that you are always using the *exact* version of the dependency you intended, and that it hasn't been tampered with in transit or at the source. It's a crucial security measure, especially when dealing with external code from the internet.

Think of the hash as a digital fingerprint of the dependency package. Any change to the package, even a single bit, will result in a different hash. This guarantees that your builds are reproducible – if you build your project today, and again a year from now, with the same build.zig.zon and Zig version, you will always get the *exact* same dependencies, and therefore, a consistent build output.

While manually dealing with hashes might seem like a bit of extra work (you need to get the correct hash and put it in build.zig.zon), it's a small price to pay for significantly enhanced security and build reproducibility. Zig, in its typical fashion, prioritizes correctness and security, even if it means a bit more upfront effort for the developer.

Beyond the usual suspects

You might think URLs are just URLs, right? Wrong, my friend. Zig's package manager is surprisingly versatile when it comes to dependency URLs. It's not just limited to Git repositories or simple tarballs. Oh no, Zig likes to keep things interesting.

Here's a taste of the URL sorcery Zig can perform:

- **Raw file URLs (HTTP/S)**: Want to grab a .zip file directly from some obscure server? Zig says, "Sure, why not?" Just point .url to the raw file. This is particularly handy for bypassing those pesky GitHub release pages and linking directly to files in repositories. Just remember the ?raw=true incantation for GitHub raw URLs, or you'll get an HTML wrapper as a dependency. Nobody wants that.

- **The file:// protocol (local network shares)**: Got a corporate network drive overflowing with internal packages? Zig can slurp them up using the file:// protocol. Perfect for those enterprise environments where everything is behind 17 firewalls. This works with UNC paths on Windows too, because Zig is surprisingly well mannered.

- **GitHub release assets**: For those who prefer the curated chaos of GitHub releases, Zig supports those directly. Combine this with .hash to pin specific versions, and you've got a dependency setup that's both version-controlled and (relatively) fast. Faster than cloning entire Git repos for large binaries, anyway.

- **IPFS gateway URLs:** Feeling adventurous? Zig can even fetch packages from the **Inter-Planetary File System (IPFS)** via gateway URLs. Just remember, hash verification becomes *extra* critical here. IPFS content identifiers are not the same as Zig package hashes, so don't get them confused. Self-hosted IPFS gateways? Zig is ready for your air-gapped, decentralized package dreams.

- **Debian packages (yes, really):** In a move that might surprise you, Zig can even ingest Debian package tarballs. Why? Because many Linux distributions package Zig-compatible tarballs. The catch? .orig tarballs often lack a build.zig.zon file, so you're on your own for verifying the contents. Advanced users only, proceed with caution (and maybe a hazmat suit).

- **Amazon S3/cloud storage signed URLs:** For the truly paranoid (or security-conscious), Zig supports time-limited, signed URLs from cloud storage providers such as Amazon S3. Distribute private packages securely! But seriously, *always* use .hash with these. Tamper-proof dependencies are non-negotiable.

And for the truly rebellious, there's the **directory URL** — or rather, the lack thereof. Using .path instead of .url lets you point to a local directory as a dependency. Want to symlink to another code base for active development? Zig will let you, but it's the dependency management equivalent of juggling chainsaws. Hash verification? Out the window. Use with extreme caution, and only when you know *exactly* what you're doing.

Zig even *allows* obfuscated URLs with redirects, but strongly advises against it. Why? Because server-side redirects can break hash guarantees. If you must use them, make sure your hash is based on the *final* URL after all redirects. Zig is watching you.

We've seen how zig fetch (and potentially other package management tools) can effortlessly bring external code into your project. But this raises a crucial question: how does Zig manage all these downloaded dependencies? How does it avoid redundant downloads and ensure that builds are consistent and reproducible, even if you're juggling dozens of libraries? The answer, my friend, lies in the ingenious (and occasionally infuriating) mechanism known as the Zig build cache.

Cache: the memory of the compiler

So, you've been building your Zig projects, marveling at the speed, and perhaps wondering, "Is this some kind of sorcery?" Well, I'm here to tell you it's *not* sorcery. It's just clever engineering. (Although sometimes, clever engineering *feels* like sorcery.) The secret sauce? The Zig build cache.

Now, most build systems treat caching like an afterthought. A bolted-on feature that *sometimes* works, and occasionally requires a ritualistic "clean" command to appease the build gods. Zig, however, takes caching seriously. It's not just a feature; it's the foundation upon which fast builds are built. It's the reason you can change one line of code and not have to wait an eternity for your project to recompile.

Core concepts (how to avoid recompiling the universe)

Let's break down the core ideas behind Zig's caching, because understanding is the first step to appreciating (and not cursing at) your build system.

Content-addressable storage (everything has a unique fingerprint)

Imagine a library where every book is identified not by a title, but by a unique fingerprint based on its *exact* content. That's essentially what Zig does with build artifacts. Every object file, every compiled module, gets a unique hash key derived from the following:

- **File contents:** The actual bytes of the source files. We're talking a robust hash here, SipHash128, not some flimsy checksum. This ensures that even a single-bit change results in a different hash.

- **Metadata:** Because sometimes, just *looking* at a file is enough. We also consider the file's size, modification time (mtime), and inode number. This is like a quick glance at the book's cover before diving into its contents.

So, if your foo.zig file produces a hash of a1b2c3, the compiled object file will be nested comfortably in your zig-cache directory as a1b2c3.o. It's like a perfectly organized, albeit slightly obsessive, filing system.

Manifest files (the librarian's secret notebook)

Now, how does Zig *know* which files contribute to which hash? That's where manifest files come in. These are unassuming .txt files hidden within the zig-cache directory. Each one is like a librarian's secret notebook, meticulously recording everything about a particular build step.

These manifests are the key to incremental compilation. They store the following:

- **Input file paths:** A list of all the source files that went into creating the artifact. But not just *any* paths — we're talking *normalized* paths. No absolute paths allowed! This keeps things portable, so you can share your cache with your colleagues without causing a cosmic rift.

- **Hashes, sizes, and timestamps:** The vital statistics of every dependency. Think of it as a detailed inventory of every ingredient that went into baking your code cake.

- **Locking mechanisms:** Because even in the digital world, we need to avoid stepping on each other's toes. These mechanisms ensure that multiple Zig processes don't try to write to the same cache entry simultaneously.

The format of these manifest entries is beautifully spartan: `<size> <inode> <mtime> <hex-digest> <prefix-id> <file-path>`.

It's like a minimalist haiku of file metadata. Each field has a purpose; each field contributes to the grand scheme of caching efficiency.

Cache workflow (the dance of hashes)

Here's how it all comes together, in a beautifully choreographed dance of hashes and timestamps:

- **Hash inputs:** Before building anything, Zig diligently calculates the hashes of *everything* that matters: source files, imported modules, compiler flags, even the compiler version itself. It's like a chef meticulously checking every ingredient before starting to cook.

- **Check manifest:** Zig then peeks into the corresponding manifest file (if it exists) and compares the newly calculated hashes with the cached ones. It's like comparing the chef's current ingredients with a recipe card.

- **Cache hit:** If everything matches—hashes, sizes, timestamps, the whole shebang—it's a cache hit! Zig gleefully reuses the existing artifact, saving precious time and CPU cycles. The chef pulls a premade dish from the fridge.

- **Cache miss:** If *anything* is different—a single byte out of place, a timestamp a nanosecond off—it's a cache miss. Zig sighs, rolls up its sleeves, and starts rebuilding. The chef starts cooking from scratch.

But, importantly, after the build is complete, the manifest is updated, ensuring that the *next* time, things will be faster.

The Zig build cache directories

The Zig build cache, typically located in a `zig-cache` directory within your project (or a global cache location), is crucial for fast incremental builds. It contains several subdirectories, each serving a distinct purpose. This section details the roles of the `h/`, `o/`, and `z/` directories, and the `tmp` directory.

The h/ directory (the hash cache) is the heart of Zig's content-addressable caching system, but with a focus on *metadata* about builds, rather than the build artifacts themselves. It stores the *manifest files* that track the inputs and outputs of each build step. This allows Zig to determine whether a cached build artifact is still valid.

This directory contains *only* .txt files. These are the manifest files. Each manifest file contains the following:

- The *full* SipHash128 hash of the inputs
- Normalized paths to all input files (source files, dependencies, etc.)
- The size, mtime, and inode of each input file
- Information about the build configuration (compiler flags, target architecture, etc.)
- Locking information for concurrency control

When Zig needs to determine whether a build artifact is already cached, it can compute the hash of the current inputs and look for a corresponding .txt manifest file in h/. If the manifest file exists, Zig reads it and compares the stored metadata with the current state of the input files.

For example, if the full hash of the inputs for building foo.o is abcdef0123456789..., the corresponding manifest file would be stored as zig-cache/h/abcdef01.txt. This file would contain all the information needed to validate a potential cache hit.

The o/ directory (the output cache) stores the *actual build artifacts* (object files, libraries, executables, etc.) produced by the Zig compiler. It's organized to mirror the intended output structure of your project.

The directory structure within o/ reflects the layout of your project's output. For example, if your build.zig file specifies that an executable should be placed in zig-out/bin/myprogram, the cached version of that executable might be found in zig-cache/o/zig-out/bin/myprogram. The filenames in o/ are the *intended* output filenames, *not* hashes.

This directory contains the compiled output of your project:

- .o: Compiled object files
- .a: Static libraries
- Executables (no extension on Linux/macOS, .exe on Windows)
- .wasm: WebAssembly modules
- dependencies.zig: A *generated* file that describes the dependencies

This is the *first* place Zig looks for cached artifacts. It checks the metadata (size, mtime, and inode) of the file at the expected output path. If this initial check suggests that the file is up to date, Zig *then* uses the corresponding manifest file in h/ to *verify* that the inputs haven't changed.

o/ and h/ work together. o/ provides the fast path for cache lookups based on output paths and metadata. h/ provides the definitive answer, using content hashing and detailed input tracking to ensure correctness. If a file exists in o/ but the corresponding manifest in h/ indicates that the inputs have changed, the file in o/ is considered stale and will be overwritten by a rebuild.

The z/ directory (the Zig data directory) stores global information related to the Zig installation itself, *not* specific to any individual project. This data is shared across all Zig projects on the system.

The z/ directory holds crucial components for Zig's operation, including, but not limited to, the following:

- **Global cache:** This is a system-wide cache shared by all Zig projects. It helps to avoid redundant downloads and builds of common dependencies, such as parts of the standard library.
- **Self-hosted compiler:** When Zig's compiler is fully self-hosted, its executable will likely reside here.
- **Standard library cache:** Precompiled parts of the Zig standard library are stored here to accelerate compilation.
- **Downloaded package information:** Metadata and cached versions of downloaded packages are stored here (when using a package manager).

The tmp/ directory within the Zig cache is used for temporary files during the build process. These files are not intended to be long-lived and are typically cleaned up automatically. It contains files used internally. This is a working directory for the build system; don't rely on anything stored here persisting.

Real-world scenarios (proof that it works)

Let's peek behind the curtain and see how Zig's caching system handles the messy reality of software development. No hand-waving, just cold, hard facts (and a few educated guesses, because who *really* understands build systems completely?).

Suppose you're working on a project that uses the `facil.io` library (a fine choice, by the way). You modify `src/main.zig`, your project's main file. Zig, being the diligent cache manager that it is, notices the change. The `mtime` value on `src/main.zig` is different. More importantly, the *content hash* is different. This triggers a cache miss. But not just *any* cache miss. Zig knows, thanks to the manifest file in `h/`, *exactly* which build artifacts depend on `src/main.zig`. It doesn't rebuild the entire universe; it rebuilds only what's necessary. It's surgical precision.

Now, let's say you decide to add a new dependency: `@import("some_new_library")`. This is a bigger deal. The manifest file associated with your target in `h/` now has a new entry. It's like adding a new ingredient to a recipe. Zig sees this new entry, recognizes that it doesn't have a cached artifact for this combination of inputs, and initiates a rebuild. Again, it's not rebuilding *everything*, just the parts affected by this new dependency.

But what about those cryptic paths in the manifest? `/home/alexrios/.cache/zig/p/1220...`? Are we doomed to hardcoded absolute paths, making our cache as portable as a concrete elephant? Of course not! Look closely. See that little `0` character before the path? That's the **prefix ID**. Zig maintains a separate table, mapping these IDs to actual base paths. So, `0` might mean `/home/alexrios/.cache/zig/p/1220...` on *your* machine, but it could map to `/Users/somebodyelse/.cache/zig/p/1220...` on *their* machine. The cache is portable because the manifest uses these *relative* identifiers, not absolute paths, for the lookup. The *absolute* path is only used when storing new items, and is stored separately, so it doesn't break the cache hit. This is where the "no absolute paths" rule is *technically* true, but with a clever workaround.

And what about those pesky system headers, such as `/usr/include/stdio.h`? They have a *different* prefix ID (1 in this example). Zig is smart enough to recognize that these are system-wide dependencies and handles them appropriately. It doesn't try to copy the entire `/usr/include` directory into your project's cache (thank goodness!).

Parallel builds? Same story as before. File locks prevent chaos, ensuring that multiple Zig processes don't corrupt the cache. It's all handled gracefully, behind the scenes. You, the developer, don't need to worry about it (unless something goes horribly wrong, in which case, good luck!).

Networked filesystems with their flaky timestamps? Zig's got you covered. It detects the unreliability and falls back to the full content hash. Slower, yes, but *always* correct. Because in the world of build systems, correctness trumps speed (usually).

Hey! Don't just imagine it all. Go test it by yourself!

Performance and reliability (fast and correct)

The beauty of this system isn't just that it works; it's that it works *efficiently*. Most of the time, Zig can determine whether to reuse a cached artifact by just checking the metadata (the size, modification time, and inode) of the output file in the o/ directory. This is *blazing fast*. Nanoseconds. We're living in the future!

But—and this is a big but—Zig doesn't *blindly* trust that metadata. It *always* checks the manifest file in h/ to make *absolutely sure* that the inputs haven't changed. This is where the content hashing comes in. It's the safety net, the guarantee that you're not accidentally using a stale artifact. This two-stage check—fast metadata check in o/, followed by a hash-based validation against the manifest in h/—is the key to Zig's speed and reliability.

The "slow path," where Zig has to compute the full content hash, is the exception, not the rule. It's there for those edge cases, those moments when the filesystem is lying to you, or when you've made a change that *doesn't* affect the metadata (rare, but it happens). It might add a *tiny* bit of overhead, but it's a small price to pay for peace of mind.

And the cache size? It grows proportionally with your project. It's not going to magically consume all your disk space (unless you're importing the entire internet, which, please don't).

Why this matters (the "so what?" section)

Zig's caching system isn't just about making your builds faster (although it does that *very* well). It's about creating a development experience that's *predictable*, *reliable*, and *portable*:

- **Predictable:** You know that if you change a file, only the necessary parts of your project will be rebuilt. You don't have to second-guess the build system.
- **Reliable:** You can trust that your builds are always correct. No more "clean" builds, no more stale artifacts, no more heisenbugs caused by caching issues.
- **Portable:** You can share your cache with your team, move your project to a different machine, or build in a CI environment, and it will *just work*. No absolute path dependencies to trip you up.

The Zig build cache isn't just some obscure implementation detail. It's a core part of what makes Zig a powerful and enjoyable language to use. It's a testament to the principle that the details matter, and that a well-designed build system can make all the difference in the world. Now, go forth and build, knowing that Zig has your back (and your cache).

You now have a solid grasp of how Zig leverages its sophisticated caching system to achieve impressive build speeds. But this cache is even *more* powerful when combined with a mechanism that automatically detects changes and triggers incremental rebuilds. That mechanism, my friend, is zig build --watch. It's like adding a turbocharger to an already-fast engine.

zig build --watch: your new best friend (who doesn't talk back)

Alright, you've learned about the Zig build system. You've delved into the mysteries of the cache, with its h/, o/, and z/ directories (and hopefully, you haven't accidentally deleted anything important). You're feeling *somewhat* confident. But let's be honest, manually typing zig build after every single code change is about as enjoyable as repeatedly stubbing your toe.

Enter zig build --watch. This is where the magic *really* happens. This is the command that will transform your development workflow from a tedious, manual process into a streamlined, almost-automated experience. This is the command that will make you wonder how you ever lived without it. (OK, maybe that's a slight exaggeration. But it's *really* useful.)

Think of --watch as your tireless, ever-vigilant assistant. It sits there, quietly observing your code, and the *instant* you make a change—you save a file, you create a new file, you even *delete* a file—it springs into action. It doesn't judge you. It doesn't complain. It just *rebuilds*. And it does it *fast*. So, what does zig build --watch actually do? In essence, it combines the power of the Zig build system with the responsiveness of operating system filesystem notifications. It's like having a build server running directly on your machine, but without the overhead and complexity.

Here's the breakdown, in plain(ish) English:

- **The initial build**: First, it performs a full build of your project, just like a regular zig build command. This is the "get everything up to date" step. It's like making sure all your ducks are in a row before you start the real work.

- **The watchful eye**: Then, it enters a loop. A *magical* loop, powered by the operating system's filesystem notification APIs. (Don't worry about the specifics; it's different on Linux, macOS, and Windows, but Zig handles it all for you.) This loop is constantly monitoring your project's source files for any changes. It's like having a security guard who *never* sleeps, *never* takes a coffee break, and *only* cares about your code.

- **The incremental rebuild**: The moment a change is detected—a file is saved, created, deleted, or renamed—Zig springs into action. But it doesn't just blindly rebuild *everything*. Oh no, that would be wasteful. It uses the dependency graph (remember those dependencies. zig files?) and the build cache (remember h/ and o/?) to determine the *minimal* set of files that need to be recompiled. It's surgical precision, not a blunt instrument.

- **The continuous cycle**: And then, it goes back to watching. Waiting. Ready to pounce on the next change. This cycle continues until you mercifully interrupt it with *Ctrl + C* (because even the most dedicated developer needs to sleep eventually).

- **Error reporting (because we all make mistakes)**: If a build error occurs, fear not! Zig will display the error message in your terminal, just like a regular build. But unlike a regular build, the --watch process *doesn't* terminate. It keeps watching, waiting for you to fix the error. It's remarkably patient, really.

- **The testing nirvana (optional, but highly recommended)**: The *real* power of --watch comes when you combine it with test. This is because zig build test --watch is the developer's equivalent of having a personal quality assurance team. It not only rebuilds your project on every change, but it also *reruns your tests*. This means you get *immediate* feedback on whether your latest code tweak has broken anything. It's like having a safety net that catches your mistakes before they can do any real damage.

Using --watch is ridiculously simple. It's like flipping a switch and suddenly entering a world of automated build goodness.

Here is the basic command:

```
zig build --watch
```

This will build your project and then watch for changes, rebuilding as needed. It's the "default" mode, and it's often all you need.

This is how you target a specific step:

```
zig build install --watch
```

If you have a specific build step defined in your build.zig file (install, in this example), you can target it with --watch. This is useful if you only want to rebuild a particular part of your project.

Here is the verbose output:

```
zig build test --watch -v
```

If, for some unfathomable reason, you enjoy watching a torrent of build messages scroll by, you can add the -v (verbose) flag.

Why this is better than the old way

Before --watch, you were probably stuck in the dark ages of manual builds. You'd edit your code, save the file, manually run zig build, wait (im)patiently, run your program or tests, and then repeat the whole tedious process. It was like living in the Stone Age of software development.

--watch automates all of that. It frees you from the drudgery of manual builds, allowing you to focus on what really matters: writing code (and, let's be honest, fixing bugs). It's a productivity booster, a time-saver, and a sanity preserver.

Of course, even --watch has its limitations. It's not *actually* magic. The initial build is still a full build. You'll have to wait for that one. But after that, it's smooth sailing. It only tracks files that are part of your project's dependency graph. If you're messing with files outside of that graph, you might need to manually trigger a rebuild. Also, changes to your build.zig file itself *won't* automatically trigger a rebuild within the --watch loop. You'll need to restart the --watch process for those changes to take effect. This is a safety measure to prevent your build script from going haywire.

It's one of those features that, once you start using it, you'll wonder how you ever lived without it. So, embrace the automation, embrace the speed, and embrace the joy of zig build --watch. Your future self will thank you.

But before you get *too* carried away with your newfound powers, let's take a moment to recap what we've covered in this whirlwind tour of Zig build features. It's time to wrap up.

Summary

Well, you've made it. Feeling good? You've navigated the treacherous waters of the Zig build system, wrestled with dependencies, tamed the build cache, and emerged (hopefully) victorious. You're no longer a Zig build system novice; you're a... well, let's call you a "competent initiate." You've learned the basics, and you've even dabbled in some advanced techniques.

Let's recap the key takeaways from our adventure:

- **zig init is your friend**: It's the "easy button" for starting new Zig projects, providing a sensible default structure and a preconfigured build.zig file.

- **build.zig is your command center**: This is where you control *everything* about your build process: defining targets, configuring release modes, adding dependencies, and even creating custom build steps.

- **build.zig.zon is your dependency manifest**: This file lists all the external code your project relies on, along with their URLs and cryptographic hashes (for security, of course).

- **zig fetch is your dependency retriever**: This command downloads and verifies your dependencies, ensuring that you're always using the correct versions.

- **Hashes are your friends (even if they look scary)**: They guarantee the integrity of your dependencies, protecting you from supply chain attacks and ensuring reproducible builds.

- **Cross-compilation is surprisingly easy**: Zig makes it a breeze to build for different platforms, without the usual headaches of setting up multiple toolchains.

- **Release modes give you fine-grained control**: Optimize for speed, size, or debuggability, depending on your needs.

- **The build cache is your secret weapon**: It's the key to Zig's fast incremental builds, avoiding unnecessary recompilation and saving you precious time.

- **zig build --watch is your productivity superpower**: It automatically rebuilds your project (and optionally runs your tests) whenever you change your code, providing instant feedback.

- **Modules are your organizational units**: They help to structure large projects and keep your dependencies neat and tidy.

- **Steps are the basic units**: They are indivisible and compose a DAG.

But this is just the beginning. The Zig build system is a vast and powerful tool, and there's always more to learn. Don't be afraid to experiment, to dig into the Zig source code, and to push the boundaries of what's possible. Remember, the best way to learn is by doing. So, go forth, build amazing things, and may your builds always be fast and your code always be correct (or at least, mostly correct). And if you ever get stuck, remember the lessons you've learned here, and don't be afraid to ask for help. The Zig community is a welcoming and helpful bunch (most of the time). Happy coding! But don't get *too* comfortable. You've conquered the build system, but there's a whole universe of advanced Zig features waiting to be explored. Get ready to have your mind expanded (and possibly your code broken) as we tackle generics, threads, C interoperability, and the dark arts of metaprogramming in the next chapter.

Unlock this book's exclusive benefits now

UNLOCK NOW

Scan this QR code or go to `https://packtpub.com/unlock`, then search this book by name.

Note: Keep your purchase invoice ready before you start.

Part 3

Advanced Zig and Real-World Application

In this final part, we'll elevate your Zig skills by exploring more sophisticated language features, such as compile-time execution (comptime), threading, and C interoperability. We'll then apply everything you've learned by building a practical, real-world command-line application, demonstrating how Zig's features come together to create robust and efficient software.

This part of the book includes the following chapters:

12

Sophisticated Topics

Ever wished you could code with a time machine? Zig hands you one. This chapter isn't about writing code; it's about *rewriting the rules of reality itself*. You'll graduate from writing code to sculpting reality itself.

A quick note before we begin: since you're just starting your Zig journey, this chapter provides an introductory overview of these topics. It's designed to familiarize you with the core concepts and spark your curiosity. Each of the subjects could easily fill a book on its own. Think of this as your first friendly encounter, paving the way for deeper exploration later.

Okay, so you're probably wondering why any of this Zig stuff matters, right? Well, runtime errors are expensive and can cause major headaches, but Zig's comptime feature checks things during compilation, saving you from those repeated runtime checks. Plus, those nasty concurrency bugs are super-hard to track down, but Zig forces you to be really explicit about thread synchronization, preventing those hidden race conditions. And let's be real, we all have to eventually deal with legacy C code. Zig lets you work with that existing code smoothly, modernizing parts of it without throwing everything away. We'll walk you through the important things.

In this chapter, we're going to cover the following topics:

- comptime: The time machine you didn't know you needed
- Threads in Zig: Herding cats with a laser pointer
- Interoperability with C: When you need to borrow someone else's tools (but make them work your way)

Technical requirements

All the code shown in this chapter can be found in the Chapter12 directory of our Git repository: https://github.com/PacktPublishing/Learning-Zig/tree/main/Chapter12.

comptime: The time machine you didn't know you needed

We now turn our attention to some of Zig's more sophisticated capabilities, rooted in its comptime mechanism. These features are powerful and, consequently, can be complex, so I suggest you proceed at a comfortable pace. We'll explore a set of foundational comptime patterns sufficient for many use cases, but consider this a foothold; true mastery will require further exploration into the language's deep support for metaprogramming.

Let's face it: most programming languages treat compile time like a boring warm-up act. In Zig? It's the main event. With comptime, Zig lets you run code before your program even starts, like having a time machine for your compiler. It runs code during compilation, giving you the power to precompute values, validate types, and generate code without any runtime overhead. Your programs can rehearse their lines before stepping on stage—no awkward pauses, no forgotten cues.

During compile time, the code runs to precompute values, validate types, or generate code. Think of it as the backstage crew setting up the stage before the show begins. There's no runtime overhead because all the heavy lifting happens up front.

Why not just use macros? Because macros are like duct tape—they might hold things together, but they're opaque, error-prone, and hard to debug. Zig's comptime is clean, is type-safe, and doesn't leave a mess behind. No more #ifdef hell!

So, we've seen the high-level distinction between compile time and runtime. But what does this look like in code? Let's roll up our sleeves and dig into the basics of comptime, complete with examples that'll make you feel like a wizard.

comptime basics

So, how do you actually *use* comptime? Let's walk through the basics with some examples. Picture comptime as your personal assistant who handles all the prep work so you can focus on the big picture.

When you mark a variable or function as comptime, it means that the value or computation must be known at compile time. Let's assume the following snippet:

```
const x = comptime someCompileTimeFunction();
```

Here, someCompileTimeFunction() runs during compilation, and its result gets baked directly into the binary. It's like ordering a custom cake; the baker (compiler) prepares it ahead of time, so you don't have to whip up batter at the party.

Type inference: Schrödinger's integer

One of the interesting aspects of comptime is how it affects type inference. For example, consider the following code:

```
const my_number = 1234;
```

In this case, my_number is inferred to be of type comptime_int. This is a special type that has no fixed memory size at compile time and can be coerced to any integer or float type. However, it can only be used at compile time. Think of it as a chameleon—it blends seamlessly into whatever context it's placed in.

Now, let's say we use my_number in a function:

```
fn add(x: comptime_int, y: comptime_int) comptime_int {
  return x + y;
}


const result = add(my_number, 5678);
```

In this case, the compiler will infer the type of result to be comptime_int as well. This is because the add function is also executed at compile time, thanks to the comptime keyword in front of the function parameters. This feature can be incredibly useful for optimizing your code.

Speaking of prep work, one of the coolest tricks comptime pulls off is optimization. Let's say you have a complex calculation:

```
fn complex_calculation(x: i32) i32 {
  //... lots of code...
}
```

If you know x at compile time, force the compiler to crunch the numbers early:

```
const result = comptime complex_calculation(1234);
```

Boom. No runtime overhead. Your program is now faster and leaner than a triathlete.

Now that we've covered the fundamentals of comptime and how it interacts with type inference, it's time to zoom out a bit. Picture this: every block of comptime code is like a mini workshop where all the prep happens before the main event. Let's see how these blocks can be used effectively.

Every block, every time: The backbone of comptime

To create a comptime block, wrap your code in curly braces after the keyword. These blocks are like little workshops where you can craft tools, validate inputs, and ensure everything's shipshape before runtime.

To create a comptime block, simply use the comptime keyword followed by a block of code enclosed in curly braces:

```
comptime {
  // Your code here
}
```

Want to make sure your array size isn't zero? Use a comptime block:

```
const array_size = 10;

comptime {
    std.debug.assert(array_size > 0);
}
```

This ensures array_size is valid before the program even starts. It's like double-checking your parachute before jumping out of a plane.

Validate function parameters at compile time:

```
fn my_function(comptime x: i32) void {
    comptime {
        if (x < 0) {
        @compileError("x must be non-negative");
        }
    }
    //... function body...
}
```

If someone tries to pass a negative value, the compiler slams the door shut with an error message. No runtime surprises here.

Also, you can call functions within `comptime` blocks, as long as those functions are also comptime-aware:

```
fn factorial(comptime n: u32) comptime_int {
    if (n == 0) {
        return 1;
    } else {
        return n * factorial(n - 1);
    }
}


comptime {
    const result = factorial(5); // result will be 120 at compile time
}
```

Don't overdo it

While `comptime` blocks can be incredibly powerful, it's important to use them judiciously. Overusing `comptime` blocks can make your code harder to read and debug, so it's best to use them only when they provide a clear benefit.

Think of `comptime` blocks as the backstage of your program. All the prep happens here, so the curtains can rise smoothly.

The best way to learn about `comptime` blocks is to experiment with them. Try writing your own `comptime` code and see what you can achieve. You might be surprised by the power and flexibility they offer!

Speaking of prep work, Zig's dual identity is what makes `comptime` so powerful. It's like having two languages in one, each with its own strengths. Ready to meet the Dr. Jekyll and Mr. Hyde of programming? Let's unpack Zig's split personality.

Zig's double identity: Compile time versus runtime

Now, let's talk about the dual nature of Zig. Just like how Dr. Jekyll and Mr. Hyde share the same body but have wildly different personalities, Zig splits its execution into two realms: compile time and runtime. Understanding this distinction is key to mastering comptime. But unlike confusing time paradoxes, Zig's system is crystal clear.

Compile-time Zig: The master planner

Compile-time Zig uses a **tree-walking interpreter**. Imagine a compiler that meticulously examines your code, branch by branch, like a lumberjack inspecting a tree for the perfect cut. This interpreter analyzes your code's structure, evaluates expressions, and performs optimizations, all before runtime. It's a bit like a chess player planning their moves in advance, ensuring every step is calculated and efficient.

This approach gives compile-time Zig a lot of flexibility, allowing it to do the following:

- **Manipulate types**: Create, modify, and inspect types at will
- **Perform complex calculations**: Evaluate expressions and generate code ahead of time
- **Enforce constraints**: Validate parameters and ensure code correctness

It's a bit like a dynamic scripting language with static type safety, giving you the best of both worlds.

Runtime Zig: The speed demon

Runtime Zig, on the other hand, compiles directly to **native machine code**. This means that your code is translated into instructions that your computer's processor can understand and execute directly. It's like a race car driver hitting the gas pedal, with no time to waste on interpretation or analysis.

This approach gives runtime Zig a significant performance advantage, allowing it to do the following:

- **Execute quickly**: Run your program with minimal overhead
- **Interact with hardware**: Access memory, peripherals, and other system resources
- **Handle real-world events**: Respond to user input, network requests, and other external stimuli

It's the Zig you rely on to get things done, a systems programming language that's both powerful and efficient.

Having two different interpretation methods might seem like overkill, but it's actually a clever design choice. By using a tree-walking interpreter at compile time, Zig can perform complex metaprogramming and optimization tasks without sacrificing runtime performance. And by compiling to native machine code at runtime, Zig can execute your program with blazing speed and efficiency.

The golden rule for calling comptime functions

All arguments must be known at compile time. It's like ordering a custom-made suit; you need to provide your measurements up front, not after the tailor starts cutting the fabric. This means any values determined at runtime, such as user input or network responses, are off-limits.

Let's see this in action with some examples:

```
fn factorial(comptime n: u32) comptime_int {
    if (n == 0) {
        return 1;
    } else {
        return n * factorial(n - 1);
    }
}


const result = factorial(5); // Valid call, 5 is a compile-time constant
```

This works because 5 is a compile-time constant. The compiler knows its value up front, allowing it to execute `factorial(5)` at compile time.

```
var user_input = get_user_input(); // Runtime value
const result = factorial(user_input); // Invalid call
```

This fails because user_input is determined at runtime. The compiler can't execute factorial(user_input) at compile time since it doesn't know the value of user_input beforehand.

Understanding Zig's dual nature sets the stage for mastering its crown jewel: the type type. Think of type as the bouncer at an exclusive club—it decides who gets in and who doesn't. Let's explore why this gatekeeper is so crucial to Zig's design.

The type supertype: Compile time's bouncer

Remember that "two languages in one" thing we talked about? Well, the type supertype is like a strict bouncer at the compile-time club. It not only represents all types but also dictates when and where you can use them.

Another way to put this is that type is a special kind of value that represents a type itself. However, unlike regular values, types cannot be used as runtime values. Instead, they exist only at compile time (`comptime`). You can think of type as a meta-type that describes other types.

Compile-time exclusivity

The type supertype demands that all values involved in its operations be known at compile time. It's like a picky eater that only accepts ingredients that are pre-measured and ready to go. This means you can't use variables that are determined at runtime, such as user input or the result of a network request, when working with type.

```
const MyIntType = i32; // MyIntType is a type
```

In this example, `MyIntType` is a type that represents the integer type `i32`. You can use type to create generic functions or structures that work with any type.

Why restrict type to compile time? Simple:

- **Guarantees type safety**: All type-related operations resolve at compile time, preventing runtime errors
- **Maximizes performance**: Compile-time code optimizes away, leaving leaner binaries
- **Maintains clarity**: It is easy to distinguish between compile time and runtime code

Respect the bouncer. Any code using type must also run at compile time. Follow this rule, and you'll unlock Zig's full metaprogramming potential.

With the type supertype firmly in place, it's time to level up. Enter type functions—the architects of Zig's metaprogramming magic. These tools let you build custom types on demand, like a factory churning out bespoke parts. Let's see them in action.

Type functions: The type-generating powerhouses

Remember those "functions that return types" we mentioned earlier? Those are type functions, the architects behind Zig's unique approach to generics and compile-time type manipulation. They are like specialized factories, churning out custom-made types based on your exact specifications.

Building simple types

Before we jump into complex structures, let's start with a simple example. Need an array with a fixed size determined at compile time? Here's a type function:

```
fn FixedArray(comptime T: type, comptime size: usize) type {
    return [size]T;
}
```

This `FixedArray` function takes two `comptime` parameters:

- `T`: The type of elements the array will hold
- `size`: The number of elements in the array

It then returns a new array type with the specified size and element type. It's like a recipe that produces different cakes depending on the ingredients and the size of the baking pan.

Here's how you can use this type function:

```
const IntArray5 = FixedArray(i32, 5); // Creates a type for arrays of 5
i32s
const BoolArray10 = FixedArray(bool, 10); // Creates a type for arrays of
10 bools
```

This creates two new types, `IntArray5` and `BoolArray10`, each representing an array with a different size and element type. It's like having a set of cookie cutters that produce different shapes depending on the dough you use.

Leveling up: Creating structs

Now, let's take it up a notch and create a type function that generates structs. Imagine you need a struct with a single field, but the type of that field should be customizable at compile time. You can create a type function like this:

```
fn Pair(comptime T: type) type {
    return struct {
        begin: T,
        end: T,

        pub fn isBetween(this: @This(), other: T) bool {
            return this.begin <= other and other < this.end;
        }
    };
}
```

This `Pair` function takes a type parameter `T` and returns a new struct type with a single field named field of that type. It's like a blueprint that generates different houses depending on the materials you choose.

Here's how you can use this type function:

```
test "Pair of types" {
    const pairOfInts = Pair(i32){ .begin = 2, .end = 14 };
    std.debug.print("{d} {d} {any}\n", .{pairOfInts.begin, pairOfInts.end,
pairOfInts.isBetween(3)}) ;

    const pairOfFloats = Pair(f64){ .begin = 0.2, .end = 0.4 };
    std.debug.print("{d} {d} {any}\n", .{pairOfFloats.begin, pairOfFloats.
end, pairOfFloats.isBetween(0.22)}) ;
}
```

This creates two distinct struct types, `PairOfInts` and `PairOfFloats`, each with a different field type. It's like having a factory that produces different cars depending on the engine you choose.

Type functions provide a powerful mechanism for creating and manipulating types at compile time. They enable you to do the following:

- **Write generic-like code**: Create flexible and reusable code without the complexities of traditional generics
- **Perform compile-time type manipulation**: Generate and modify types based on compile-time parameters, pushing the boundaries of metaprogramming
- **Improve code clarity**: Separate type-related logic from runtime code, making your programs easier to understand and maintain

> **Type functions in the wild**
>
> Type functions are used extensively in Zig's standard library to provide generic data structures and algorithms. For example, the `std.ArrayList` type is a type function that takes a type parameter and returns an `ArrayList` type capable of storing elements of that type.

Now that we've built some impressive types, how do we inspect and understand them? Zig equips us with three trusty tools: `@typeOf`, `@typeInfo`, and `@Type`. Think of them as your magnifying glass, blueprint, and 3D printer for types. Let's dive in.

Tools of the trade: @typeOf, @typeInfo, and @Type

Feeling a bit like Alice tumbling down the rabbit hole in trying to grasp comptime? Fear not, because Zig provides you with three powerful built-in functions to navigate the wonderland of types: @typeOf, @typeInfo, and @Type. These are your trusty tools for understanding, inspecting, and even reconstructing types at compile time, allowing you to perform feats of metaprogramming that would make Houdini proud. While @typeOf helps you identify types and @typeInfo lets you peer under the hood, @Type acts as your 3D printer for types, bringing blueprints to life by dynamically constructing types from metadata. Together, they form Zig's ultimate toolkit for bending the rules of reality—or, at least, your code base.

@typeOf: The detective

@typeOf is a built-in function that returns the type of a given expression or variable. It can accept any number of expressions as parameters and will return the "peer type" (the most general type that all the expressions can be coerced into). It's like a detective that reveals the true identity of a variable, allowing you to make informed decisions based on its type.

Here's how it works:

```
const x: i32 = 42;
const y: f32 = 3.14;
const z = @TypeOf(x, y); // z is f32 because f32 is the peer type of i32
and f32
std.debug.print("{}\n", .{z}) ;
```

In this example, @typeOf(x, y) returns f32 because f32 is the common type that both i32 and f32 can be coerced into.

This is particularly useful when you want to determine the type of a variable or expression at compile time, allowing you to write more generic code.

@typeInfo: The magnifying glass

Now that you know who the mysterious figure is, it's time to delve deeper and understand their inner workings. That's where @typeInfo comes in. It's your magnifying glass for inspecting the intricate details of any type in Zig. It returns a value of type std.builtin.Type, which contains metadata about the type, such as whether it's an integer, float, struct, and so on. This allows you to perform introspection on types at compile time.

Here's how it works:

```
const info = @typeInfo(i32);
std.debug.print("Is integer: {}\n", .{info == .int}); // Prints: Is
integer: true
```

In this example, @typeInfo(i32) returns a std.builtin.Type value that describes the i32 type. You can then check whether the type is an integer by comparing it to .int. This value is a tagged union that can represent any type in Zig, including structs, arrays, pointers, functions, and even types themselves. It's like having X-ray vision that lets you see the internal structure of any type.

@typeInfo is often used in combination with @typeOf to inspect the structure of types at compile time.

@Type: Bringing types to life

Sometimes, you need to create a type based on a description or blueprint. That's where @Type comes in. It's your 3D printer for types, allowing you to construct types from std.builtin. TypeInfo values that are obtained from @typeInfo and reconstruct the original type from it. Essentially, it allows you to "reify" type information back into a usable type.

```
const type_info = @typeInfo(MyStruct); // Get the TypeInfo for MyStruct
// Modify the TypeInfo if needed, for example, add a new field
const MyModifiedType = @Type(type_info); // Create the modified type
```

In this example, @type(info) takes the std.builtin.Type value returned by @typeInfo(MyStruct) and reconstructs the MyStruct type from it.

@Type is particularly useful when you need to dynamically construct types based on runtime or compile-time conditions. For example, you could use @typeInfo to inspect a type, modify its properties, and then use @Type to create a new type based on those modifications:

```
const NewType = @Type(std.builtin.Type{
    .int = .{
        .signedness = info.int.signedness,
        .bits = info.Int.bits + 8,
    },
});
std.debug.print("NewType is now {}\n", .{NewType}); // NewType is now i40
```

Here, we modify the bit size of the i32 type to create a new type i40 using @Type.

Reflection and metaprogramming

These three functions (@typeOf, @typeInfo, and @Type) form the backbone of Zig's reflection capabilities. Reflection is the ability of a program to inspect and manipulate its own structure and behavior. In Zig, reflection is primarily achieved through these built-in functions, allowing you to write highly generic and flexible code.

For example, you can use @typeOf to determine the type of a variable, @typeInfo to inspect its properties, and @Type to reconstruct or modify types dynamically. This makes Zig particularly well suited to tasks such as serialization, deserialization, and other forms of code generation.

The following snippet demonstrates how to use comptime to generate a struct dynamically based on input arrays of field names and types. This is useful in scenarios where you need to define structs at compile time without hardcoding them:

```
fn generateStruct(comptime field_names: []const []const u8, comptime
field_types: []const type) type {
    var fields: [field_names.len]std.builtin.Type.StructField = undefined;

    for (field_names, 0..) |name, i| {
        fields[i] = .{
            .name = name[0..:0],
            .type = field_types[i],
            .default_value_ptr = null,
            .is_comptime = false,
            .alignment = @alignOf(field_types[i]),
        };
    }

    return @Type(std.builtin.Type{
        .@"Struct" = .{
            .layout = .auto,
            .fields = &fields,
            .decls = &.{},
            .is_tuple = false,
        },
    });
}
```

This function uses `comptime` to create a struct type with fields defined by the input arrays of names and types:

```
const MyStruct = generateStruct(
    &[_][]const u8{ "id", "name", "score" },
    &[_]type{ i32, []const u8, f32 },
    );


var instance = MyStruct{
    .id = 42,
    .name = "Zig Developer",
    .score = 95.5,
};
```

💡 **Quick tip:** Enhance your coding experience with the **AI Code Explainer** and **Quick Copy** features. Open this book in the next-gen Packt Reader. Click the **Copy** button (1) to quickly copy code into your coding environment, or click the **Explain** button (2) to get the AI assistant to explain a block of code to you.

```
                                           Copy      Explain
function calculate(a, b) {                  1          2
  return {sum: a + b};
};
```

🔒**The next-gen Packt Reader** is included for free with the purchase of this book. Scan the QR code OR go to https://packtpub.com/unlock, then use the search bar to find this book by name. Double-check the edition shown to make sure you get the right one.

We can go crazy and create dynamic database models or API response structures without manually defining each struct. Awesome, right? Reflection in Zig is like X-ray vision for your code—you can see through the shadows.

Armed with reflection tools and type functions, we're ready to tackle one last concept: anytype. This wildcard lets you write flexible, duck-typed code without sacrificing Zig's strict compile-time guarantees. It's the cherry on top of Zig's metaprogramming sundae.

anytype: The Swiss Army knife of types

The anytype keyword is a compile-time placeholder that can represent any type, making it ideal for creating generic functions. Unlike a concrete type, anytype defers type checking from the function's definition to its actual call site. This maintains Zig's type safety while providing flexibility.

For instance, you can write a single add function that works on both integers and floating-point numbers:

```
fn add(a: anytype, b: anytype) @TypeOf(a) {
    return a + b;
}
```

Here, add uses anytype to accept arguments of any type and returns their sum. The function works seamlessly with both integers and floating-point numbers:

```
const intResult = add(5, 10); // Works with integers
const floatResult = add(3.14, 2.71); // Works with floats
```

Duck typing

When you use anytype, you don't check against a predefined interface. Instead, the operations you perform on the anytype parameter become its required interface. Using a + b? The type must support addition. Calling a.len()? The type must have a len field. This contract is automatically verified by the compiler at the function's call site, giving you compile-time safety.

anytype is only allowed in function parameters because it is not a real type but a placeholder. This means you cannot declare variables of type anytype outside of function parameters.

Thus, there are key differences between anytype and type:

- anytype: Can represent any type, including the type itself. It is used to defer type logic into the function, where it can be dealt with imperatively at compile time.

- type: Represents a type itself, which exists only at compile time and cannot be used as a runtime value.

By deferring type logic into the function, anytype provides a way to handle a wide range of types dynamically, making it an essential feature of advanced Zig programming.

Common pitfalls: When types fight back

Now that you've met both type and anytype, let's explore the minefield of mistakes that trip up even experienced developers. Think of this as your "what not to do" survival guide, because nothing teaches you the rules quite like watching them explode spectacularly.

Mistake 1: Using anytype where type is required

The Crime Scene:

```
// This looks reasonable, right? WRONG.
fn createArray(comptime T: anytype, comptime size: usize) type {
    return [size]T;  // Compiler meltdown incoming
}
```

What went wrong: You tried to use anytype as a type parameter, but anytype is only allowed in function parameters, not in comptime type declarations. It's like trying to use a wild card in a game that demands specific suits.

The fix is as follows:

```
// Use 'type' for type parameters
fn createArray(comptime T: type, comptime size: usize) type {
    return [size]T;  // Happy compiler, happy life
}

// Usage
const IntArray = createArray(i32, 10);
var my_array: IntArray = undefined;
```

type is for when you need to manipulate types themselves. anytype is for when you want to accept any type, but let the compiler figure out what it is.

Mistake 2: Confusing compile time with runtime contexts

The Crime Scene:

```
fn processValue(value: anytype) void {
    const T = @TypeOf(value);
    if (T == i32) {  // This looks innocent enough...
        std.debug.print("It's an integer: {}\n", .{value});
    } else if (T == f32) {
        std.debug.print("It's a float: {}\n", .{value});
    }
    // Compiler: "I don't think so, buddy."
}
```

What went wrong: You're trying to do runtime branching based on compile-time type information. The compiler doesn't know how to generate code for this because the type is determined when the function is instantiated, not when it runs.

The fix is as follows:

```
fn processValue(value: anytype) void {
    const T = @TypeOf(value);
    comptime {
        if (T == i32) {
            std.debug.print("It's an integer: {}\n", .{value});
        } else if (T == f32) {
            std.debug.print("It's a float: {}\n", .{value});
        } else {
            @compileError("Unsupported type: " ++ @typeName(T));
        }
    }
}

// Or better yet, use switch for compile-time branching
fn processValueBetter(value: anytype) void {
    switch (@TypeOf(value)) {
        i32 => std.debug.print("It's an integer: {}\n", .{value}),
        f32 => std.debug.print("It's a float: {}\n", .{value}),
        else => @compileError("Unsupported type"),
    }
}
```

Why this matters: Type information exists at compile time, not runtime. If you need to branch based on types, make it a compile-time decision.

Mistake 3: The "everything should be anytype" trap

The Crime Scene:

```
// Overzealous use of anytype
fn add(a: anytype, b: anytype) anytype {
    return a + b;  // What could go wrong?
}


const result = add("Hello", 42);  // Surprise! Compiler explosion
```

What went wrong: anytype doesn't mean "magically make incompatible types work together." It means "accept any type, but the operation must still be valid for that type."

The fix is as follows:

```
// Be more specific about what you accept
fn add(a: anytype, b: @TypeOf(a)) @TypeOf(a) {
    return a + b;  // Both arguments must be the same type
}


// Or use constraints to be explicit
fn addNumbers(a: anytype, b: anytype) @TypeOf(a, b) {
    // This will only compile if both types can be added
    // and coerced to a common type
    comptime {
        const T = @TypeOf(a, b);
        if (!comptime isNumeric(T)) {
            @compileError("add only works with numeric types");
        }
    }
    return a + b;
}


fn isNumeric(comptime T: type) bool {
    return switch (@typeInfo(T)) {
        .Int, .Float, .ComptimeInt, .ComptimeFloat => true,
```

```
            else => false,
    };
}
```

anytype is powerful, but with great power comes great responsibility. Be explicit about what operations you expect to work.

Mistake 4: Forgetting about type coercion rules

The Crime Scene:

```
fn processNumbers(values: []anytype) void {  // Nope!
    for (values) |value| {
        std.debug.print("{}\n", .{value});
    }
}
```

What went wrong: You can't have a slice of anytype. A slice needs to know the concrete type of its elements at compile time.

The fix is as follows:

```
// Option 1: Generic function with concrete type
fn processNumbers(comptime T: type, values: []T) void {
    for (values) |value| {
        std.debug.print("{}\n", .{value});
    }
}
// Option 2: Accept individual values
fn processValue(value: anytype) void {
    std.debug.print("{}\n", .{value});
}
// Usage
const numbers = [_]i32{1, 2, 3, 4};
processNumbers(i32, &numbers);
// Or process one by one
for (numbers) |num| {
    processValue(num);
}
```

Mistake 5: Type parameter naming confusion

The Crime Scene:

```
fn createContainer(comptime type: type) type {  // Reserved keyword!
    return struct {
        value: type,  // This won't end well
    };
}
```

What went wrong: You used type as a parameter name, but type is a reserved keyword in Zig. It's like naming your dog "Dog"—technically possible, but confusing for everyone.

The fix is as follows:

```
fn createContainer(comptime T: type) type {
    return struct {
        value: T,

        pub fn init(val: T) @This() {
            return .{ .value = val };
        }
    };
}
// Usage
const IntContainer = createContainer(i32);
var container = IntContainer.init(42);
```

Pro tips for avoiding these traps include the following:

- **When in doubt, be explicit:** If you're not sure whether to use type or anytype, start with the more restrictive option and relax constraints as needed.

- **Use comptime blocks:** When working with type information, wrap your logic in comptime blocks to make your intentions clear.

- **Test your generics:** Create test cases with different types to make sure your generic functions actually work as intended.

- **Read the error messages:** Zig's compiler errors are usually quite helpful. When you see a type-related error, read it carefully. It often tells you exactly what went wrong.

- **Start simple:** Begin with concrete types, then generalize. It's easier to make something generic than to debug generic code that never worked in the first place.

Remember that types in Zig are like tools in a workshop. Use the right tool for the job, and you'll build something beautiful. Use the wrong tool, and you'll end up with a very expensive paperweight and possibly fewer fingers than you started with.

Now that we've explored how these types let you write flexible, duck-typed code that adapts to any situation, let's talk about the flip side of Zig's compile-time magic: managing the computational cost of all this power. While anytype and other comptime features give you incredible flexibility, they can sometimes push the compiler to its limits. That's where @setEvalBranchQuota, a tool to help you fine-tune the balance between compile-time complexity and performance, comes in.

comptime budgets: The branch quota

As you've seen, Zig's comptime allows you to execute code while your program is compiling. This is incredibly powerful, but it comes with a risk: what if you accidentally write an infinite loop in comptime code? The compiler itself would freeze, forcing you to kill the process.

To prevent this, Zig has a built-in safety mechanism: the **evaluation branch quota**. Think of it as a computational budget or a circuit breaker for the compiler. It puts a limit on the number of "backward branches"—essentially, loops and recursive function calls—that a single comptime block can execute. If the budget is spent, the compiler stops and reports an error, saving you from a frustrating freeze.

The override: What is @setEvalBranchQuota()?

For most comptime tasks, the default budget is more than enough. However, for advanced metaprogramming, you might have a legitimate, heavy computation that needs more resources. For these exact situations, Zig provides an override:

```
@setEvalBranchQuota(new_limit: u32) void
```

This built-in function allows you to increase the branch quota for a specific, trusted block of code. It's not a global setting; it applies only to the scope in which it's called, reflecting Zig's philosophy of local and explicit control.

You will almost never use this function proactively. The correct time to use it is when the compiler gives you the error: **evaluation branch quota reached**.

Imagine you want to generate a large lookup table of prime numbers at compile time. A function to do this might involve many thousands of loop iterations, easily exceeding the default quota:

```
fn generatePrimes(comptime limit: u32) []const bool {
    var is_prime = std.heap.allocator.alloc(bool, limit + 1) catch
```

```
unreachable;
    @memset(is_prime, true);
    is_prime[0] = false;
    is_prime[1] = false;
    var p: u32 = 2;
    while (p * p <= limit) : (p += 1) {
        if (is_prime[p]) {
            var i: u32 = p * p;
            while (i <= limit) : (i += p) {
                is_prime[i] = false;
            }
        }
    }
    return is_prime;
}


// Without increasing the quota, this compile-time call would likely fail.
const prime_lookup_table = comptime blk: {
    // We expect this to be computationally expensive, so we raise the
    budget.
    @setEvalBranchQuota(50000);
    break :blk generatePrimes(10000);
};
```

In this scenario, the generatePrimes function is a legitimate, heavy workload. By wrapping the comptime call in a block and using @setEvalBranchQuota, we are explicitly telling the compiler: "I know this looks like a lot of work, but it's intentional. Please allow it to proceed."

And there you have it. Zig's comptime isn't just a feature; it's a philosophy. By blending compile-time smarts with runtime speed, Zig empowers you to write code that's both clever and efficient. So go forth, brave programmer, and bend time to your will!

Speaking of speed and safety, let's shift gears from the time-bending magic of comptime to another cornerstone of high-performance programming: threads. If comptime is about bending the rules of time during compilation, threads are all about mastering concurrency at runtime. Ready to dive into the world of parallel execution? Let's untangle the complexities of Zig's threading model.

> **"Practice makes perfect"**
>
> Ready to put your metaprogramming skills to the test? Head over to the ch13 folder in our GitHub repository, where you'll find a hands-on tutorial that walks you through building a generic Stack data structure from scratch.

Threads in Zig: Herding cats with a laser pointer

Ever tried herding cats in an escape room? That's multithreading in Zig. You're dealing with raw OS threads. No handholding, no sugarcoating—just you and the chaos of parallel execution. If you've come from Go's goroutines or JavaScript's async/await playground, buckle up. Zig gives you the knife and says, "Don't stab yourself." But don't worry; by the end of this chapter, you'll know how to wield it like a seasoned dungeon master.

Spawning threads: Welcome to the Thunderdome

Let's start simple: spawning threads. In Zig, std.Thread.spawn is your gateway drug to concurrency. It's like summoning minions to do your bidding, but if you don't keep them in line, they'll burn down the castle.

Here's what it looks like:

```
const std = @import("std");

fn screamIntoTheVoid(steps: u8) void {
    for (0..steps) |_| {
        std.debug.print("A", .{});
        std.time.sleep(1 * std.time.ns_per_s); // Pause for dramatic
effect.
    }
    std.debug.print("!", .{}); // Finale!
}

pub fn main() !void {
    const thread = try std.Thread.spawn(.{}, screamIntoTheVoid, .{@as(u8,
5)});
    std.debug.print("Main thread here, sipping tea...\n", .{});
    thread.join(); // Wait for the minion to finish its tantrum.
}
```

What's happening here? The screamIntoTheVoid function is our toddler with a megaphone. We tell it how many "A"s to scream, and off it goes. Meanwhile, the main thread plays babysitter, printing messages and calling join() to ensure the toddler doesn't wander off mid-scream.

Here's the kicker: without join(), the program might exit before the thread finishes, leaving your toddler stranded in limbo. And trust me, abandoned toddlers are bad news; they tend to throw tantrums that crash your entire system.

Now that we've got our threads up and running, let's talk about something even scarier: sharing data between them. Because if you thought one screaming toddler was bad, wait until you unleash multiple toddlers on the same whiteboard.

Sharing data: Mutexes are your bouncers

Imagine a whiteboard where everyone writes at once, all with different colored markers. At first, it's organized. Then, chaos ensues. Threads are like toddlers fighting over the same toy. If you don't enforce some rules, your program will devolve into a cosmic horror devouring RAM.

Zig gives you two main tools for sharing data safely: mutexes and atomics. Both ensure thread safety, but they serve different purposes. Let's break them down.

Mutexes: The bouncers of your nightclub

Mutexes (short for "mutual exclusions") are like bouncers at a nightclub. They ensure only one thread gets access to shared data at a time. If another thread tries to barge in, it has to wait its turn.

Here's an example using std.Thread.Mutex:

```zig
const std = @import("std");

const Data = struct {
    mutex: std.Thread.Mutex = .{}, // The bouncer of your nightclub.
    counter: u32 = 0,
};

fn incrementCounter(context: ?*anyopaque) void {
    const data: *Data = @ptrCast(@alignCast(context.?)); // Casting: Zig's
trust fall.
    data.mutex.lock();
    defer data.mutex.unlock(); // Unlock even if you panic. Zig forgives,
but never forgets.
```

```
        data.counter += 1;
}


pub fn main() !void {
    var data: Data = .{};
    const threads = try std.heap.page_allocator.alloc(std.Thread, 2);
    defer std.heap.page_allocator.free(threads);

    for (threads) |*t| {
        t.* = try std.Thread.spawn(.{}, incrementCounter, .{&data}); //
Pass the data's address as a tuple.
    }
    for (threads) |t| t.join();

    std.debug.print("Counter: {d} (Pray it's 2)\n", .{data.counter});
}
```

Why does this work? Because mutexes serialize access to shared resources. Think of them as bathroom stalls—only one person gets in at a time. Lock before touching shared data, unlock afterward, and you'll avoid turning your program into a cosmic horror devouring RAM.

Mutexes are ideal in the following cases:

- You're protecting complex shared data structures (e.g., linked lists, trees)
- Multiple operations must be performed atomically as a group

For example:

```
data.mutex.lock();
data.counter += 1;
data.some_other_field -= 1;
data.mutex.unlock();
```

Atomics: The cheetahs of concurrency

If mutexes are bouncers, atomics are caffeinated cheetahs. They're faster, simpler, and perfect for lightweight synchronization tasks such as incrementing a counter. Instead of locking and unlocking, atomics perform operations directly on shared variables without blocking.

Here's the same example rewritten using `std.atomic.Value`:

```zig
const std = @import("std");


const Data = struct {
    counter: std.atomic.Value(u32) = std.atomic.Value(u32).init(0), //
Atomic counter.
};


fn incrementCounter(context: ?*anyopaque) void {
    const data: *Data = @ptrCast(@alignCast(context.?)); // Casting: Zig's
trust fall.
    _ = data.counter.fetchAdd(1, .seq_cst); // Atomically increment the
counter with sequential consistency.
}


pub fn main() !void {
    var data: Data = .{};
    const threads = try std.heap.page_allocator.alloc(std.Thread, 2);
    defer std.heap.page_allocator.free(threads);

    for (threads) |*t| {
        t.* = try std.Thread.spawn(.{}, incrementCounter, .{&data}); //
Pass the data's address as a tuple.
    }
    for (threads) |t| t.join();

    std.debug.print("Counter: {d} (Pray it's 2)\n", .{data.counter.load(.
seq_cst)}); // Load the counter with sequential consistency.
}
```

There are two key factors here:

- **Atomic operations**: The `fetchAdd` method increments the counter atomically, ensuring no race conditions occur

- **Memory ordering**: `.seq_cst` guarantees total ordering across all threads, making the behavior predictable and reliable

Atomics shine when you're working with simple, independent variables such as counters or flags, and also when performance is critical and you want to avoid the overhead of mutexes.

Now that we've covered sharing data, let's zoom out and ask the big question: when should you actually use threads? Spoiler alert—it's not always the answer. Threads are like RPG party members: powerful in the right scenarios but prone to tripping over each other if you're not careful. And speaking of tripping... let's talk about the multithreading pitfalls. Because even the most disciplined army of threads can devolve into chaos if you forget to lock the bathroom stall or accidentally summon a segfault demon.

Pitfalls: How to summon a segfault demon

Multithreading is a minefield. Use this checklist to keep your concurrent code sane and safe:

- **Data race:**
    - **What it is:** Two threads fighting over the same piece of data without a referee.
    - **The fix:** Protect all shared data with a mutex. No exceptions.
    - **Mantra:** Mutexes are the hand sanitizer of multithreading.

- **Deadlock:**
    - **What it is:** Thread A has a lock that Thread B needs, and Thread B has a lock that Thread A needs. A standoff.
    - **The fix:** Establish a global locking order and stick to it religiously.
    - **Mantra:** Always lock mutexes in the same order. No creative freelancing.

- **Lifetime issues:**
    - **What it is:** A thread tries to use data that has already been freed.
    - **The fix:** Ensure the parent thread waits for child threads to finish using `join()` before cleaning up.
    - **Mantra:** You allocated it, you attend its funeral. Make sure everyone else has paid their respects first.

Debugging concurrent code is like playing whack-a-mole blindfolded. Tools such as thread sanitizers can help, but nothing beats careful design and testing under varying loads. Speaking of performance, let's talk about how to avoid turning your program into a resource-hungry monster. Because while threads are powerful, they're not exactly free.

Performance considerations: Don't be a resource hog

Raw threads are powerful, but they're not free. Creating too many threads can overwhelm your system faster than a caffeine overdose. Instead, consider thread pooling, a technique where you reuse a fixed number of threads to execute multiple tasks sequentially.

This is a simple example:

```
const std = @import("std");

fn worker(slot: usize, task_id: usize) void {
    std.debug.print("Worker slot {d} executing task {d}\n", .{ slot, task_
id });
    // Simulate some work
    std.time.sleep(10 * std.time.ns_per_ms);
}


pub fn main() !void {
    const num_workers = 5; // fixed-size pool
    const num_tasks = 10; // total tasks to execute

    var threads: [num_workers]std.Thread = undefined;

    var next_task: usize = 0;
    while (next_task < num_tasks) {
        const remaining = num_tasks - next_task;
        const batch_size: usize = if (remaining < num_workers) remaining
else num_workers;

        // Dispatch up to num_workers tasks in this batch
        var i: usize = 0;
        while (i < batch_size) : (i += 1) {
            const task_id = next_task + i;
            threads[i] = try std.Thread.spawn(.{}, worker, .{ i, task_id
});
        }

        // Wait for current batch to finish before scheduling the next
tasks
```

```
        i = 0;
        while (i < batch_size) : (i += 1) {
            threads[i].join();
        }


        next_task += batch_size;
    }


    std.debug.print("All {d} tasks completed using {d} worker slots.\n",
.{ num_tasks, num_workers });
}
```

You should see a result like the following:

```
Worker slot 0 executing task 0
Worker slot 2 executing task 2
Worker slot 4 executing task 4
Worker slot 3 executing task 3
Worker slot 1 executing task 1
Worker slot 0 executing task 5
Worker slot 2 executing task 7
Worker slot 1 executing task 6
Worker slot 4 executing task 9
Worker slot 3 executing task 8
All 10 tasks completed using 5 worker slots.
```

This approach reduces overhead and improves scalability. Remember, threads are like RPG party members: you want a balanced team, not a mob of adventurers tripping over each other. Zig's threads are raw, unapologetic, and gloriously explicit.

Remember to grok your knowledge! Spawn threads, lock mutexes, and debug until your eyes bleed.

Now, if you'll excuse me, I need to go find some earplugs. Those screaming toddlers aren't getting any quieter.

So, you've tamed the feral threads, locked down your mutexes, and debugged enough segfault demons to last a lifetime. Congratulations! You're officially a multithreading initiate. But let's be honest: sometimes, even the most disciplined army of threads can't save you from the gnarly realities of low-level programming. What happens when you need to venture into the wilds of legacy code, third-party libraries, or that dusty old C library your boss insists on using?

Fear not! Zig doesn't just give you the knife; it also hands you a Swiss Army multitool for working with C. Whether you're calling C functions, embedding Zig in a C project, or wrapping a decades-old library in modern Zig goodness, Zig's C interop capabilities are here to save the day. Let's dive in and see how Zig bridges the gap between raw power and real-world pragmatism.

Interoperability with C: When you need to borrow someone else's tools (but make them work your way)

Ever duct-taped two LEGO sets together and called it a spaceship? Welcome to C interop. You'll glue Zig and C into a functional Frankenstein's monster without summoning the ghost of undefined behavior.

Don't worry if you're not fluent in C. I've got you covered! This section is designed to be accessible, regardless of your C proficiency. Think of it as a guided tour.

C: The cockroach of code (and why you'll learn to love/hate it)

C is the programming equivalent of a cockroach: it's been around since the Mesozoic era, it survives nuclear winters, and it lurks in every code base you'll ever touch. Need to talk to hardware? Use a decades-old driver? Zig's C interop lets you *embrace the chaos* without reinventing the wheel.

The real surprise is that Zig doesn't just tolerate C; it thrives on it. Rust, in its role as the neighborhood gentrifier, bulldozes the old C landscape to build shiny new condos (complete with exorbitant rent). Python, meanwhile, sublets a cramped, rent-controlled apartment and pretends the leaky plumbing doesn't exist. Zig, however, renovates the existing building, making it modern and functional without displacing everyone.

Before we dive into the practicalities of making Zig and C play nicely together, it's essential to understand the underlying rules of engagement. It's like learning the grammar of a language before trying to hold a conversation. That grammar, in the world of compiled code, is the ABI, or application binary interface. Let's explore this crucial concept, as it forms the foundation of all successful interoperation between Zig and C (or any other languages, for that matter). Understanding the ABI will prevent many headaches down the road.

ABI

Think of an ABI as the fundamental rulebook for how compiled code interacts at the lowest level. It dictates the in-memory layout of data (size, alignment, offsets), how symbols are named for linking, and, crucially, the calling conventions of functions—literally, how a function call works in binary. A stable ABI is what allows separately compiled libraries and executables, even those built with different compilers or on different machines, to play nicely together. This is the bedrock of foreign function interface (FFI), enabling code written in different languages to communicate. Zig, while not using a stable internal ABI itself, cleverly leverages C ABIs for its extern declarations, making it exceptionally good at talking to C (and, by extension, many other languages that also interface with C). This means Zig can seamlessly integrate with existing C code bases, leveraging the widely adopted standards of the C ABI for a particular target platform (CPU architecture and operating system). In essence, when you need predictable binary-level behavior for interoperability, Zig speaks fluent "C ABI."

@cImport: Your gateway to the C underworld

The @cImport intrinsic is Zig's Babelfish for C headers. Feed it a header, and it spits out Zig-compatible declarations. No wrappers, no tears.

So, how easy is it to actually use @cImport? Pretty darn easy. Check out this example:

```
const std = @import("std");
const c = @cImport({
    @cInclude("stdio.h");  // Yes, we're including stdio. No, we're not
sorry.
    @cInclude("time.h");   // For C's time functions—reliable as a
sundial.
});

pub fn main() void {
    _ = c.printf("Zig says: Hello from C's %s!\n", "printf");

    var tm: c.tm = undefined;
    const timestamp = c.time(null);
    _ = c.localtime_r(&timestamp, &tm);

    std.debug.print("\nToday's date (according to C): {d}-{d}-{d}\n", .{
        tm.tm_year + 1900,  // C counts years from 1900. Because why not?
        tm.tm_mon + 1,      // Months start at 0. January? More like
*Zeroth*uary.
        tm.tm_mday,
    });
}
```

Here's a quick explanation:

- @cImport: Your C-to-Zig translator. Handles headers like a champ, even if they're older than your parents.
- c.printf: Calls C functions as if they're native Zig. Warning: may cause existential crises in Go developers.
- C's Quirks: tm_year starts at 1900, tm_mon at 0. Zig won't judge—but it will side-eye.

To compile and run this code, you'll need to link against the C standard library (libc). This is because we're using C functions such as printf, time, and localtime_r, which are part of libc. You can do this by passing the -lc flag to the zig run command, like so:

```
zig run -lc cimport.zig
```

This command tells the Zig compiler to link the necessary C libraries when building and running your program. Without this flag, you'll likely encounter linker errors. Once you've run the command with the -lc flag, you should see the expected output, demonstrating the successful interaction between your Zig code and the C functions:

```
Zig says: Hello from C's printf!
Today's date (according to C): 2025-2-13
```

The -lc flag works for direct execution with zig run, but when using a build system, you need to explicitly tell the build process to link libc. This is usually done in your build.zig file using exe.linkLibC(); (where exe is your executable builder). This ensures that the necessary C libraries are linked when your project is built.

Understanding C

Ever find yourself staring at a chunk of C code that looks like it was written by a sleep-deprived compiler after a three-day bender? You know, the kind of code with so many nested pointers, casts, and macros that it makes your brain hurt? Well, before you reach for the strong stuff, consider Zig's translate-c command. It's like a Rosetta Stone for C, transforming that cryptic mess into (somewhat) readable Zig. It won't magically make the code good, mind you, but it'll at least give you a fighting chance of understanding what unholy machinations are at play. It is a great starting point. Think of it like this: when C gets hairy, unleash zig translate-c and watch the fur fly. You might just tame the beast and reveal the surprisingly simple (or horrifyingly complex) logic underneath. Play with it! You will discover code patterns.

Zig's @cImport built-in is quite distinctive in its design. It accepts an expression, but with a specific constraint: the expression can only consist of @cInclude, @cDefine, and @cUndef. Under the hood, this mechanism operates much like translate-c, seamlessly converting C code into Zig. It's a clever way to bridge the gap between the two languages without requiring manual intervention.

Now, let's break down the key players here:

- @cInclude: This function takes a path string and adds it to the list of includes. Think of it as Zig's way of saying, "Hey, I need this C header file, so let's make sure it's part of the compilation process."

- @cDefine and @cUndef: These functions handle the definition and undefinition of macros, respectively. If you've worked with C, you'll recognize this as the familiar dance of setting up and tearing down preprocessor directives.

What's particularly elegant about these functions is that they behave exactly as you'd expect if you were writing C code. There's no mental overhead or quirky deviations, just a straightforward, no-nonsense way to integrate C constructs into Zig. It's a thoughtful design choice that respects the conventions of C while leveraging Zig's modern capabilities.

Zig's interoperability with C is a two-way street. Not only can Zig call C, but C can also call Zig.

Calling Zig from C: Exporting your chaos

Want to inflict Zig on a C code base? Use export to expose functions like a food truck selling artisanal Zig tacos to C's bland function buffet. We're going to do this using Zig's export and callconv(.C) features. These are, respectively, Zig's way of saying, "Fine, I guess I can share this function," and "I'll try to speak your archaic dialect, C." Don't expect Zig to be happy about it, though. Zig prefers to talk to itself, in its own beautifully safe and predictable way. But we're not here for Zig's happiness, are we? We're here to make C dance to a slightly different, slightly Ziggier tune.

Let's illustrate this with a beautifully simple, yet utterly pointless, example: counting words in a string. Because, let's face it, C's string handling is about as elegant as a drunken hippo on roller skates.

```
const std = @import("std");

// Export the function for C compatibility
// Use C calling convention to match C's ABI
export fn count_words(str: [*:0]const u8) callconv(.C) u32 {
```

```
    var count: u32 = 0;
    var in_word: bool = false;
    var i: usize = 0;

    // Iterate over the string until the null terminator
    while (str[i] != 0) : (i += 1) {
        const c = str[i];
        if (std.ascii.isWhitespace(c)) {
            in_word = false;
        } else if (!in_word) {
            count += 1;
            in_word = true;
        }
    }

    return count;
}
```

Let's dissect this masterpiece of unnecessary complexity:

- `export fn count_words(...)`: This is Zig's grudging admission that, yes, this function can be called from outside. It's like putting up a "Beware of Dog" sign, but the dog is actually a fluffy poodle.

- `[*:0]const u8`: This, my friends, is a sentinel-terminated pointer. It's Zig's precise way of saying, "This is a pointer to a C-style string, and I swear it ends with a null byte (the 0)." If you're used to C's cavalier attitude toward string termination, this might seem overly cautious. But trust me, Zig's paranoia is your friend.

- `callconv(.C)`: Ah, the magic incantation. This tells Zig to use the C calling convention. Without this, you're in for a world of hurt, as Zig and C have very different ideas about how to pass arguments and manage the stack. Think of it as choosing between VHS and Betamax—you need to pick the right one, or you're going to have a bad time.

- u32: We're returning an unsigned 32-bit integer. Because consistency is for the weak, we're using a fixed-width type here, even though Zig could use usize. It's a best practice for FFI to avoid any platform-dependent surprises. Think of it as pre-emptively apologizing for any future confusion.

While on the C side, here's how it interacts with the Zig code:

```c
#include <stdio.h>
#include <stdint.h>

// Declare the Zig function with C linkage
extern uint32_t count_words(const char *str);

int main() {
    const char *example = "Zig is awesome";
    uint32_t result = count_words(example);
    printf("Word count: %u\n", result); // Output: Word count: 3
    return 0;
}
```

This code acts as the client that uses the Zig library:

- **Function declaration**: The extern keyword tells the C compiler that count_words is defined externally (in the Zig library)

- **String passing**: C strings (null-terminated char*) are passed directly to the Zig function, which expects [*:0]const u8

- **Result handling**: The Zig function returns a u32 (32-bit unsigned integer), which maps directly to uint32_t in C

This seamless interaction is possible because Zig and C share the same low-level memory model and data types.

They work together in two main phases. First in compilation, Zig code is compiled into a library (.so), and the C code is compiled and linked against this library. At runtime, C programs call the Zig function with a C string.

Pro tip: forgot callconv(.C)? Enjoy the fireworks. Zig defaults to its own calling convention, which C treats like a toddler reciting Shakespeare.

Playing nice with C: Structs, alignment, and the quest for interoperability (RPG edition)

Ah, the noble quest of making Zig and C play nice. A journey filled with danger, padding, and the occasional alignment trap. Picture yourself as a rogue, sneaking through the dungeons of low-level programming, where one wrong move in memory layout can summon the dreaded Segmentation Fault Dragon. Don't bother. I, your guide (with a dash of sarcasm and a love for roguelite metaphors), will light the way to interoperability. Let's dive in.

Extern structs: Your diplomatic passport to C

In the land of Zig, structs are free spirits, roaming memory as the compiler sees fit. But step into the realm of C, and you'll find a rigid, bureaucratic society that demands order. C expects structs to follow its ABI rules, a specific, predictable layout. Enter the extern struct, your diplomatic passport to this foreign land. By declaring an extern struct, you swear to follow C's memory layout rules, ensuring your data doesn't cause an international incident when crossing the border.

Think of it as learning the local customs before trading for magical artifacts (or, in this case, calling C functions). Without this, your structs might as well be speaking nonsense to C, leading to chaos, crashes, and the occasional existential crisis.

Alignment: The CPU's picky preferences

Now, let's talk about alignment, the CPU's version of being a picky eater at a five-star restaurant. CPUs like their data served on specific "plates"—addresses that are multiples of their preferred sizes. For example, a 4-byte float wants to start at an address divisible by 4. Serve it misaligned, and you'll get inefficiency, crashes, or worse—a CPU throwing a fit.

Zig, ever the gracious host, lets you specify alignment with the align keyword. It's like custom-ordering plates for your data, making sure the CPU eats in comfort. Ignore this at your own risk, because the CPU's wrath is swift and brutal.

Packed structs: The Tetris champions of memory

By default, the compiler prioritizes speed over size. To achieve this, it adds invisible bytes called padding between a struct's fields. It happens because CPUs can read data from memory addresses that are multiples of their word size (e.g., 4 or 8 bytes) much faster. Padding ensures that each field is aligned to an efficient boundary.

```
// This struct might take 8 bytes, not 5!
const MyStruct = struct {
```

```
    a: u8, // 1 byte
    // 3 bytes of invisible padding added here...
    b: u32, // 4 bytes
};
```

This alignment is a performance optimization that the compiler handles for you, making regular structs safe and easy to work with. Packed structs throw this convenience away in favor of absolute memory control.

Sometimes, you find yourself in a dungeon with severely limited memory, or maybe you're dealing with hardware that demands bit-level precision. In these tight spots, regular structs, with their padding and alignment quirks, are about as useful as a sword made of wet noodles. Enter packed structs, the Tetris champions of memory.

Packed structs eliminate padding, squeezing fields into the smallest possible space. Booleans take up a single bit, integers use their exact bit-width, and every byte is precious. This is perfect for network protocols, hardware interfaces, or any situation where memory is scarcer than a health potion in a roguelite. But beware: packed structs come with their own dangers, such as unaligned access penalties and the occasional compiler bug. Tread carefully, adventurer.

Bit-aligned pointers: Navigating the bitstream

When you're deep in the weeds of packed structs, you'll need bit-aligned pointers to navigate the chaos. These pointers are like specialized lockpicks, designed to access fields at exact bit offsets within tightly packed data. Without them, you're fumbling in the dark, trying to pull a single bit out of a sea of tightly packed bytes.

Bit-aligned pointers are your lifeline in this mess, making sure you can manipulate individual bits without summoning the dreaded Undefined Behavior Demon. Use them wisely, because they're both your salvation and your potential downfall.

To survive this quest, remember these golden rules:

- Use extern structs when dealing with C. It's the only way to make sure your data layout doesn't cause a diplomatic disaster.
- Respect alignment. The CPU is a picky eater, and misaligned data is like serving soup in a teacup.
- Embrace packed structs when memory is tight, but watch out for the risks. They're powerful but come with a cost.

- Master bit-aligned pointers. They're your key to navigating the bitstream without losing your mind.

And remember, adventurer: in the roguelite dungeon of low-level programming, every decision counts. Choose wisely, and may your structs always be aligned.

The perils of [*c]T: Zig's C pointer (and why you should (almost) never use it)

We've talked about pointers in Zig, the friendly *T for single items, the slightly stricter [*]T for arrays, and the ever-so-convenient slices []T. But lurking in the shadows, a relic of Zig's C interoperability, is the C pointer: [*c]T. This section is a cautionary tale, a "here be dragons" sign on your journey through Zig's pointer landscape.

Think of [*c]T as the wild west of Zig pointers. Unlike its more civilized cousins, [*c]T plays by C's rules (or lack thereof). This means a few things, and none of them are particularly good for your code's sanity:

- **Alignment anarchy**: Regular Zig pointers (*T, [*]T) are mindful of data alignment. They understand that certain types need to be placed at memory addresses that are multiples of their size (e.g., a 4-byte integer might need to be at an address divisible by 4). [*c]T throws this caution to the wind. It doesn't care about alignment, which can lead to performance penalties or even crashes on some architectures.

- **The null abyss**: Zig pointers are generally not allowed to be null (unless they're explicitly marked as optional with ?). This helps prevent the dreaded null pointer dereference, a classic source of C bugs. [*c]T, however, embraces the null. It can happily point to address 0, the digital equivalent of the void. If you try to dereference a null [*c]T that has been coerced to a non-optional Zig pointer, you will hit, hopefully, a runtime error.

- **Integer coercion chaos**: [*c]T can be freely coerced to and from integers. This might seem convenient, but it's a recipe for disaster. It allows you to do all sorts of pointer arithmetic shenanigans that can easily lead to memory corruption and unpredictable behavior. Regular Zig pointers have much stricter rules about arithmetic, promoting safety.

- **Coercion to other pointers**: [*c]T can be coerced to single (*T) and multi-item ([*]T) pointers. While the coercion itself exists, the value 0 is illegal.

So, given all these drawbacks, why does [*c]T even exist? It's primarily there for one reason: to interact with C code, especially code generated by zig translate-c. When Zig translates C code, it uses [*c]T to represent C pointers because it must match C's loosey-goosey pointer semantics.

However, and this is crucial: Outside of automatically translated C code, you should almost never use [*c]T directly in your Zig code. It's like bringing a chainsaw to a butter-carving competition—technically, it can cut things, but it's massive overkill and likely to cause a mess. Stick to the safer, more predictable Zig pointer types (*T, [*]T, []T, and their const variants) whenever possible. If you must interact with C code that uses raw pointers, carefully convert those [*c] T pointers to safer Zig pointer types as soon as possible, adding checks for null and alignment as needed. Treat [*c]T like a hazardous material—handle with extreme care, and only when absolutely necessary. Consider it a necessary evil, a bridge between the well-ordered world of Zig and the chaotic realm of C.

> **Honorable mention: zig cc and zig c++**
>
> Forget juggling multiple compiler installations and wrestling with cross-compilation toolchains. Zig's built-in zig cc and zig c++ commands are like having a universal translator for C and C++ code. These aren't just wrappers around Clang; they're fully integrated into Zig's build system, meaning you get effortless cross-compilation to various targets—all from a single Zig installation—and you benefit from Zig's caching system for faster builds. Essentially, zig cc and zig c++ turn the often painful process of building C/C++ for different platforms into a smooth, streamlined experience, making it a surprisingly powerful tool for projects that need to interface with C/C++ code, even if you're not primarily writing Zig.

This glimpse into C interop has hopefully sparked your interest, but be warned: we've only scratched the surface. The world of bridging Zig and C is *vast* and, at times, delightfully chaotic. Mastering it requires venturing deeper, perhaps even dedicating an entire series of books to this subject only.

Summary

You've taken significant strides toward becoming a Zig initiate. You explored comptime, Zig's compile-time powerhouse, which allows you to validate types, precompute values, and generate optimized code before your program even runs. Armed with this knowledge, you can now eliminate runtime errors and craft leaner, more efficient binaries.

Next, you dipped your feet into the chaotic yet thrilling waters of threading. You learned how to spawn threads, share data safely using mutexes and atomics, and navigate common pitfalls such as data races and deadlocks. With these tools, you're ready to start building concurrent systems that scale gracefully across multiple cores.

Finally, you bridged the gap between Zig and C, mastering the art of interoperability. From extern structs to packed memory layouts, you gained the expertise needed to interface with legacy code bases while preserving Zig's safety and performance guarantees.

You've unlocked the ability to write code that's safer, faster, and more adaptable. The compiler is no longer just a tool—it's your playground. As you move forward, remember: Zig isn't just a language; it's a mindset. And with these skills under your belt, you've conquered the core concepts, and now you're ready to join the ranks of Zig developers making a real impact. In the next chapter, we'll not only explore practical project ideas, but also discover where to find the community, what the future holds for Zig's grand plans, and whether its production users have found enlightenment or just a faster way to segfault.

Join us on Discord!

Read this book alongside other users, developers, experts, and the author himself.

Ask questions, provide solutions to other readers, chat with the authors via Ask Me Anything sessions, and much more. Scan the QR or visit the link to join the community.

`https://packt.link/deep-engineering-systemsengineering`

13

Real-World Zig

Congratulations! If you've made it this far, you've survived the gauntlet of Zig fundamentals—memory management, error handling, build systems, and all those delightful language features that make Zig both powerful and occasionally terrifying. But learning syntax and concepts in isolation is like studying sword techniques without ever facing an opponent. It's time to put everything together and build something genuinely useful.

In this chapter, we'll take a deep dive into FileGuard, a real-world file monitoring system built entirely in Zig. This isn't just another "Hello, World!" program with delusions of grandeur—it's a proper command-line tool that watches directories for changes, monitors file modifications, and reports what it finds. Along the way, you'll see how Zig's memory safety, error handling, and C interoperability features combine to create robust system software.

By the end of this chapter, you'll understand how to:

- Command-Line Tools: Automating Your Life (and Annoy Your Coworkers)
- Other Project Ideas: The Sky's the Limit (Or at Least the Memory Limit)
- Community Resources: Forums, Chat Rooms, and Other Dens of Iniquity (We Mean Knowledge)
- The roadmap: Zig's Future Plans (World Domination, Probably)
- Zig's Impact: Case Studies and Success Stories (From Humble Beginnings to Tech Giants) — Who's actually using this language in production, and have they lost their minds or found enlightenment?

Whether you're coming from garbage-collected language and wondering what all this "memory management" fuss is about, or you're a battle-hardened C++ veteran looking to escape template metaprogramming nightmares, the application of this chapter demonstrates why Zig is worth your attention. It's fast, it's explicit, and most importantly, it lets you sleep at night knowing your code isn't quietly leaking memory like a sieve.

So grab your favorite caffeinated beverage, clear your terminal, and let's build something worth showing off. Your journey from Zig novice to "that smug person who won't shut up about compile-time guarantees" starts now.

Technical requirements

All the code shown in this chapter can be found in the Chapter13 directory of our git repository:

https://github.com/PacktPublishing/Learning-Zig/tree/main/Chapter13.

Command-line tools: automating your life (and annoy your coworkers)

Let's face it: you didn't learn Zig to create yet another todo app with a fancy UI that crashes when someone sneezes near the server. No, you're here because you want to build tools that make the computer bend to your will—preferably from the comfort of a terminal window with a color scheme that makes your eyes bleed just a little less than the default.

Figure 13.1 – Terminal power: command-line tools bend computers to your will

Command-line tools are the bread and butter of a systems programmer's arsenal. They're how you'll automate away the soul-crushing tedium of your day job, impress your peers with your efficiency, and utterly confuse anyone who thinks computers are supposed to have "buttons" and "friendly interfaces." A well-crafted CLI tool is like a digital Swiss Army knife—compact, precise, and suspiciously satisfying to deploy at exactly the right moment.

And the best part? CLI tools written in Zig are blazingly fast compared to those bloated Python scripts everyone else is using. There's nothing quite like the smug satisfaction of watching your coworker's dependency-riddled monstrosity churn for 30 seconds while your Zig creation finishes in the blink of an eye. "Oh, is yours still running? Mine finished so long ago I had time to refactor it twice."

Enter FileGuard, our soon-to-be-created file monitoring system. No, this isn't some off-the-shelf utility you've never heard of—it's our very own creation that we'll build together, line by self-satisfied line. Is it going to revolutionize the software industry? Probably not. Will it make you feel like a digital demigod compared to the poor souls using batch files to track their changes? Absolutely.

FileGuard will detect when files are created, modified, deleted, or sneakily moved around. You could use it to monitor source code directories, track configuration changes, or set up tripwires for your coworkers who keep "borrowing" your carefully crafted scripts without attribution. In professional environments, FileGuard excels at practical tasks like helping DevOps teams detect configuration drift across environments, enabling security teams to monitor critical system files for unauthorized changes, or allowing development teams to track source code modifications in CI/CD pipelines. The tool's ability to distinguish between file moves and delete-create operations makes it particularly valuable for understanding the true nature of changes in complex deployment scenarios. And while similar tools exist in the wild, building our own gives us the perfect excuse to flex our Zig muscles without the pressure of creating the next billion-dollar startup.

So fire up your terminal emulator of choice, crack your knuckles dramatically (even though no one's watching), and let's build something that would make the UNIX philosophers proud—a tool that does one thing, does it well, and can be combined with other tools to rule your little corner of the computing universe.

FileGuard architecture: building your first real-world application

Before we start flooding our keyboards with code, let's take a moment to think about how our file guardian should be structured. After all, the difference between a "script kiddie" and a "systems programmer" is mostly about how much planning happens before the first line of code is written. And since you're reading a book with "Learning" in the title, I assume you're aiming for this.

Let's consider how we'll design FileGuard to be modular, efficient, and—dare I say it—elegant. A good architecture isn't just about making the computer happy; it's about not making future-you curse past-you's name every time you need to add a feature.

Resource Planning

FileGuard's memory footprint scales with the number of monitored files, as each requires storage for metadata including paths, timestamps, and file attributes. Memory usage increases notably when content hashing is enabled due to storing cryptographic checksums. CPU impact remains minimal during idle monitoring, with brief activity during directory scans that typically complete quickly on modern systems, though scan duration increases with directory size and depth. The primary performance consideration is disk I/O when content hashing is enabled, this feature substantially reduces scanning speed as it requires reading file contents but provides the most comprehensive change detection by catching modifications that don't affect file size or timestamps.

The file monitoring challenge

Let's understand what problem FileGuard actually solves. At its core, file monitoring seems simple. Just tell me when files change, right? But as with most "simple" problems in computing, the details make it deliciously complex.

The complexity starts with the fundamental differences in how operating systems handle file events. Linux provides *inotify* for efficient, kernel-level file system notifications, while macOS uses *kqueue*, and Windows relies on *ReadDirectoryChangesW*. Each system has different capabilities, limitations, and quirks—some provide granular event types, others require polling fallbacks, and each handles edge cases like network filesystems or high-frequency changes differently.

Rather than wrestling with these platform-specific APIs, FileGuard takes a different approach: periodic scanning with intelligent change detection, which works consistently across all platforms while remaining simple to understand and debug.

A proper file monitoring system needs to:

- Detect multiple types of changes: Files can be created, deleted, modified, or moved. Their permissions can change, or sometimes just their timestamps get updated without content modifications.

- Efficiently scan large directory structures: We can't afford to read every byte of every file on each scan if we want performance that won't make users contemplate their mortality while waiting.

- Filter out noise: Users rarely want to monitor every single file—they need ways to include only relevant files and exclude irrelevant ones.

- Detect moves/renames smartly: Is that a new file or just the same content with a different name? The difference matters.

- Report changes meaningfully: Raw data is useless without context and formatting that humans can understand.

We could solve this with naive approaches—reading every file's content on every scan would technically work—but that would be like killing a fly with a tactical nuke. Effective, yes, but with significant collateral damage to your CPU and RAM.

Design decisions: working smarter, not harder

How do we tackle these challenges efficiently? Here are the key architectural decisions that will guide our implementation:

1. **Two-Phase Change Detection**

   Instead of constantly rescanning everything, we'll use a two-phase approach:

   - Create a baseline index of file metadata (paths, sizes, timestamps, etc.)
   - On subsequent scans, create a new index and compare it to the baseline
   - Record the differences as changes
   - Update the baseline for the next scan

   This means we only need to read and store metadata, not entire file contents, making the process much faster.

2. **Inode Tracking for Move Detection**

    On UNIX-like systems (Linux, macOS), every file has an inode number, a unique identifier assigned by the filesystem that stays constant even when the file is renamed or moved. Windows uses a similar concept called *file IDs* or file reference numbers that serve the same purpose. By tracking these unique identifiers:

    - If a file disappears from location A but another file with the same *inode* appears at location B, we know it was moved, not deleted and recreated
    - This saves us from expensive content comparisons to detect moves
    - Zig's standard library abstracts these platform differences, so our code works the same way regardless of the underlying system

3. **Optional Content Hashing**

    For ultimate accuracy (at the cost of performance), we'll add an option to compute content hashes:

    - Defaults to off for performance reasons
    - When enabled, detects even subtle content changes that don't affect file size
    - Gives users control over the trade-off between speed and thoroughness

4. **Configurable Pattern Matching**

    Not all files are worth monitoring. We'll use glob pattern matching to:

    - Include only files matching specific patterns (e.g., ".zig", "config/")
    - Exclude files matching other patterns (e.g., ".tmp", "node_modules/")
    - Give users fine-grained control over what's monitored

Project structure: breaking it down

```
fileGuard/
├── build.zig          # Build configuration
├── build.zig.zon      # Dependencies
└── src/
    ├── main.zig              # Program entry point
    ├── file_metadata.zig     # File information tracking
    ├── file_index.zig        # Collection of file metadata
    ├── traversal.zig         # Directory walking
```

```
├── pattern.zig              # Glob pattern matching
├── change_detection.zig     # Identifying changes
├── config.zig               # Configuration structures
└── cli.zig                  # Command-line interface
```

Each module has a distinct responsibility:

- file_metadata.zig defines how we represent and track individual files
- file_index.zig manages collections of file metadata for efficient lookups
- traversal.zig handles walking directory trees according to configured rules
- pattern.zig implements file path matching
- change_detection.zig compares file indexes to identify what changed
- config.zig contains configuration structures for traversal and detection
- cli.zig processes command-line arguments and presents results
- main.zig ties everything together and provides the entry point

This separation of concerns makes the code more maintainable and testable. It also makes it easier to extend—if we wanted to add a GUI later, we could keep the core functionality and just add a new interface module.

The implementation roadmap

With our architecture mapped out, we'll implement FileGuard in these logical steps:

- Define the core data structures for file metadata and indexing
- Implement directory traversal with pattern matching
- Create the change detection logic
- Build the command-line interface
- Tie everything together in the main program
- Test and optimize the results

Let's start with the foundation—the structures that represent file information. In the next section, we'll dive into implementing `file_metadata.zig`, where we'll define how to capture and store information about individual files. This module forms the cornerstone of our entire system, so getting it right sets us up for success with everything that follows.

Implementing file metadata: the foundation of change detection

Before we can detect changes, we need a way to represent files and their attributes. This is trickier than it first appears. What exactly constitutes a "file" in a monitoring context? Is it just the path and contents? What about permissions, creation times, or those arcane extended attributes that might matter to some particularly picky application?

The answer is: it depends on what changes you care about. And since different users have different needs, our FileMetadata struct needs to be comprehensive enough to support various monitoring strategies without being bloated with rarely-used fields.

The FileMetadata struct: identity, state, and ownership

Let's define our metadata representation in file_metadata.zig:

```zig
const std = @import("std");
const fs = std.fs;
pub const FileMetadata = struct {
    md: fs.File.Metadata,     // File system metadata
    path: []const u8,         // File path
    inode: u64,               // Unique file identifier
    checksum: ?[]const u8,    // Optional content hash
    allocator: std.mem.Allocator, // Memory allocator
    // Methods will go here...
};
```

Each field serves a specific purpose:

- md: Zig's built-in File.Metadata structure, which encapsulates platform-specific file attributes and make our implementation agnostic
- path: The file's location in the filesystem
- inode: A unique identifier that helps us detect file moves (more on that later)
- checksum: An optional hash of the file's contents for detecting content changes
- allocator: The memory allocator responsible for any dynamically allocated memory

The beauty of using fs.File.Metadata instead of manually implementing everything is that it handles cross-platform differences for us. Whether you're on Linux, macOS, or Windows, the standard library abstracts away the platform-specific details like how permissions are represented or how timestamps are stored.

Think of it as delegating the mundane cross-platform headaches to the Zig standard library developers. They've already dealt with the "joy" of figuring out why Windows thinks timestamps should be measured from 1601 instead of 1970 like a sensible system. We just reap the benefits of their suffering.

Initializing file metadata: the birth of a tracking record

Now let's implement the initialization method:

```
pub fn init(allocator: std.mem.Allocator, path: []const u8, hash_content:
bool) !FileMetadata {
    const abs_path = try fs.realpathAlloc(allocator, path);
    errdefer allocator.free(abs_path);

    const file = try fs.openFileAbsolute(abs_path, .{});
    defer file.close();

    const md = try fs.File.metadata(file);
    const stat = try file.stat();
    var metadata = FileMetadata{
        .path = abs_path,
        .md = md,
        .inode = stat.inode,
        .checksum = null,
        .allocator = allocator,
    };
    if (hash_content) {
        metadata.checksum = try computeFileHash(file, allocator);
    }

    return metadata;
}
```

There's a lot happening here:

- We convert the provided path to an absolute path, which helps prevent confusion when the working directory changes.
- We open the file and retrieve both its standard metadata and its stat information (which includes the inode number).

- We initialize our FileMetadata structure with this information.
- If requested, we compute a hash of the file's contents.

Notice the errdefer statement after we allocate the absolute path. This is Zig's way of ensuring we don't leak memory if an error occurs—the path will be freed if any of the subsequent operations fail. It's like setting up a safety net for your memory that only activates when something goes wrong.

Memory management: the circle of life

Since we're allocating memory (for the path and potentially the checksum), we need a way to free it when we're done. Here's our cleanup method:

```
pub fn deinit(self: *const FileMetadata) void {
    self.allocator.free(self.path);
    if (self.checksum) |checksum| {
        self.allocator.free(checksum);
    }
}
```

This method frees any dynamically allocated memory we own. It's simple but crucial—without it, we'd leak memory like a sieve whenever we discard file metadata.

Notice we don't free md? That's because it's a simple value type that doesn't own any memory. The Zig standard library handles those details for us, another advantage of leveraging fs.File. Metadata.

Cloning metadata: sometimes you need a perfect copy

When comparing files over time, we need to keep the old metadata around while creating new metadata. That's where cloning comes in:

```
pub fn clone(fmd: FileMetadata) !FileMetadata {
    var new_metadata = FileMetadata{
        .path = try fmd.allocator.dupe(u8, fmd.path),
        .md = fmd.md,
        .inode = fmd.inode,
        .checksum = null,
        .allocator = fmd.allocator,
    };

    if (fmd.checksum) |cs| {
```

```
                new_metadata.checksum = try fmd.allocator.dupe(u8, cs);
        }

    return new_metadata;
}
```

This method creates a deep copy of a `FileMetadata` instance, duplicating any owned memory (the path and checksum) to prevent sharing allocations. It's like creating a genetic clone of a file reference, complete with its own independent memory.

Content hashing: when size and timestamp aren't enough

Sometimes, files can change in ways that don't affect their size or modification time. Maybe someone used a text editor that preserves those attributes, or maybe a cosmic ray flipped a bit (unlikely, but technically possible). For these cases, we need content hashing:

```
fn computeFileHash(file: fs.File, allocator: std.mem.Allocator) ![]const
u8 {
var hasher = std.crypto.hash.sha2.Sha256.init(.{});
// Use a 4KB buffer for reading
var buffer: [4096]u8 = undefined;

try file.seekTo(0);

while (true) {
    const bytes_read = try file.read(&buffer);
    if (bytes_read == 0) break;

    hasher.update(buffer[0..bytes_read]);
}


var hash: [32]u8 = undefined;
hasher.final(&hash);


const hex_hash = try allocator.alloc(u8, 64);
_ = try std.fmt.bufPrint(hex_hash, "{s}", .{std.fmt.
fmtSliceHexLower(&hash)});
```

```
return hex_hash;

}
```

This function:

- Initializes a SHA-256 hasher
- Reads the file in chunks to avoid loading it all into memory at once
- Updates the hash with each chunk
- Finalizes the hash and converts it to a hexadecimal string

The chunk-based approach is crucial for performance and memory efficiency. Imagine trying to hash a 10GB video file by loading it all into RAM first—your system would grind to a halt faster than a developer confronted with surprise scope creep.

Cross-platform considerations: the beauty of abstraction

One of the best features of our implementation is what's not there. We're not manually handling different timestamp formats between operating systems. We're not reimplementing permission bit interpretations for each platform. We're not juggling different file attribute APIs.

By relying on Zig's `fs.File.Metadata`, we get all that cross-platform compatibility for free. The standard library abstracts away the differences between:

- Windows, where timestamps are measured in 100-nanosecond intervals since January 1, 1601
- Unix-like systems, which use seconds and nanoseconds since January 1, 1970
- Different permission models across operating systems
- Various file attribute systems like Windows NTFS attributes versus Unix file modes

There's one area where platforms do differ significantly—inode numbers. On Unix-like systems, these are reliable unique identifiers that persist when files are moved or renamed. On Windows, we have to be more careful as the equivalent concept (file IDs) works slightly differently.

Using `md` for all this platform-specific metadata means our code stays clean and focused on the task at hand—file monitoring—instead of getting bogged down in OS-specific implementation details. It's like having a skilled translator who handles all the dialect differences while you focus on the actual conversation.

Putting it all together: the complete file metadata implementation

With all these pieces, our complete `file_metadata.zig` module gives us a robust way to capture, store, and compare file information across different operating systems. It's memory-safe, efficient, and handles all the cross-platform quirks through Zig's standard library.

This metadata foundation is the key to our entire monitoring system. Without reliable file information, we might as well be trying to spot differences in photographs taken with a potato camera.

Now that we have our file metadata implementation, we can move on to organizing these metadata records. In the next section, we'll build our `FileIndex` structure, which collects and organizes file metadata for efficient lookup and comparison. This index will form the backbone of our change detection system, allowing us to quickly determine what's changed in a directory between scans.

Building a file index: organizing your digital filing cabinet

Now that we can capture metadata for individual files, we need a way to organize this information. Imagine trying to monitor thousands of files by keeping individual metadata records in a massive unsorted pile—you'd spend more time searching for records than actually detecting changes. This is where our `FileIndex` comes in.

Think of `FileIndex` as the digital equivalent of a filing cabinet with a really enthusiastic librarian. It stores file metadata in a way that lets us quickly find information by path or by inode, determine whether files exist, and compare snapshots over time. Without this organization, our file monitoring would crawl along like a slug racing through molasses.

The FileIndex struct: a tale of two maps

Let's define our index structure in `file_index.zig`:

```
pub const FileIndex = struct {
    // Map from file paths to their metadata
    files: std.StringHashMap(FileMetadata),
    // Map from inodes to file paths (for detecting file moves)
    inodes: std.AutoHashMap(u64, []const u8),
    // Allocator for managing memory
    allocator: std.mem.Allocator,
    // Track path allocations separately
    path_storage: std.StringHashMap(void),

    // Methods will go here...
```

```
  };
```

The FileIndex contains two main data structures:

- files: A hash map that lets us look up file metadata by path
- inodes: A hash map that lets us look up file paths by inode number

This dual indexing is critical for our more advanced features. The path index is obvious—we need to know what files exist and their metadata. But the inode index is where things get interesting. By mapping inodes to paths, we can detect when a file has been moved or renamed rather than mistakenly reporting it as deleted in one location and created in another.

The path_storage might seem redundant—why track paths in a separate map? The answer lies in memory management. Since paths are used as keys in our main hash map, we need to keep track of which paths we've allocated so we can free them properly when the index is destroyed. It's like keeping a list of all the labels you've created for your filing cabinet drawers so you can remove them when you throw out the cabinet.

What the Heck is an Inode, Anyway?

Think of an inode as your file's secret identity card that the filesystem keeps in its underground bunker. While the filename is just the public alias your file uses when socializing with users, the inode is the actual unique ID number that the operating system uses to track the file behind the scenes.

When you rename a file, you're just changing its alias—like slapping a fake mustache on it—but the inode number stays the same. This is why we can detect moves: the file might be wearing a completely different disguise and hanging out in a new neighborhood, but its fingerprints (inode) remain identical.

Windows users: Your OS calls these "file IDs" instead because Microsoft apparently thinks "inode" sounds too much like "I, Node" — the autobiography of a JavaScript runtime.

Initializing the index: setting up shop

Let's start with the initialization method:

```
pub fn init(allocator: std.mem.Allocator) FileIndex {
    return FileIndex{
        .files = std.StringHashMap(FileMetadata).init(allocator),
        .inodes = std.AutoHashMap(u64, []const u8).init(allocator),
        .allocator = allocator,
        .path_storage = std.StringHashMap(void).init(allocator),
    };
}
```

This is straightforward. We initialize our hash maps with the provided allocator. Note that unlike many of our other functions, this one can't fail (it doesn't return an error union). This is because hash map initialization doesn't allocate any memory until you actually add items.

Cleanup: leaving no trace behind

When we're done with our index, we need to free all the memory it owns:

```
pub fn deinit(self: *FileIndex) void {
    // First free all metadata objects
    var it = self.files.iterator();
    while (it.next()) |entry| {
        entry.value_ptr.deinit();
    }

    // Free all path strings we've tracked
    var path_it = self.path_storage.keyIterator();
    while (path_it.next()) |path_ptr| {
        self.allocator.free(path_ptr.*);
    }

    // Free the hashmaps themselves
    self.files.deinit();
    self.inodes.deinit();
    self.path_storage.deinit();
}
```

This cleanup is more involved than you might expect. We need to:

1. Free all the FileMetadata objects in our index
2. Free all the path strings we've allocated
3. Free the hash maps themselves

Notice the order here—we free the contained objects before freeing the containers. It's like emptying the drawers of your filing cabinet before dismantling the cabinet itself. If we freed the hash maps first, we'd lose our references to the metadata objects and paths, creating a memory leak that would make your operating system quietly judge you.

Adding files: populating your index

Now let's implement the method to add files to our index:

```
pub fn addFile(self: *FileIndex, metadata: FileMetadata) !void {
    const cloned = try metadata.clone();
    errdefer cloned.deinit();

    const path_copy = try self.allocator.dupe(u8, cloned.path);
    errdefer self.allocator.free(path_copy);

    try self.path_storage.put(path_copy, {});
    try self.files.put(path_copy, cloned);
    if (cloned.inode != 0) {
        try self.inodes.put(cloned.inode, path_copy);
    }
}
```

Here's what's happening:

*   We clone the metadata to create an independent copy
*   We duplicate the path string for use as a hash map key
*   We track the path allocation for later cleanup
*   We add the metadata to our file index
*   If the file has a valid inode number, we add it to our inode index

The errdefer statements are our safety nets—if any allocation fails after we've already allocated something, we clean up what we've allocated so far. It's like having an automatic cleanup crew that only activates when things go wrong.

Lookup operations: finding your files

We need several methods to retrieve information from our index:

```
pub fn contains(self: *const FileIndex, path: []const u8) bool {
    return self.files.contains(path);
}


pub fn get(self: *const FileIndex, path: []const u8) ?*const FileMetadata
{
    return self.files.getPtr(path);
}


pub fn findByInode(self: *const FileIndex, inode: u64) ?[]const u8 {
    return self.inodes.get(inode);
}
```

These methods provide the core lookup functionality we need for change detection:

- contains tells us whether a file exists in our index

- get retrieves the metadata for a file by its path

- findByInode finds a file's path using its inode number

The findByInode method is especially important for move detection. If a file disappears from location A but we find another file with the same inode at location B, we know it was moved rather than deleted and recreated.

Cloning the index: sometimes you need a perfect copy

When monitoring files continuously, we need to keep a baseline index while creating a new one. After detecting changes, we replace the baseline with the new index. This requires a way to clone an entire index:

```
pub fn clone(self: *const FileIndex) !FileIndex {
    var cloned = FileIndex.init(self.allocator);
    errdefer cloned.deinit();

    var it = self.files.iterator();
    while (it.next()) |entry| {
        const original_metadata = entry.value_ptr.*;
```

```
        const metadata_clone = FileMetadata{
            .allocator = original_metadata.allocator,
            .path = try self.allocator.dupe(u8, original_metadata.path),
            .inode = original_metadata.inode,
            .md = original_metadata.md,                    .checksum = if
(original_metadata.checksum) |cs|
                try self.allocator.dupe(u8, cs)
            else
                null,
        };
        errdefer {
            if (metadata_clone.checksum) |cs| {
                self.allocator.free(cs);
            }
            self.allocator.free(metadata_clone.path);
        }

        const path_copy = try cloned.allocator.dupe(u8, metadata_clone.
path);
        errdefer cloned.allocator.free(path_copy);

        try cloned.path_storage.put(path_copy, {});

        try cloned.files.put(path_copy, metadata_clone);
        if (metadata_clone.inode != 0) {
            try cloned.inodes.put(metadata_clone.inode, path_copy);
        }
    }

    return cloned;
}
```

This is one of our more complex methods, but the idea is straightforward: create a new index and populate it with deep copies of all the metadata in the original index. The complexity comes from ensuring all the memory is properly allocated and tracked.

The careful memory management here is crucial. We're creating new allocations for every path and checksum, and we need to ensure they're all properly tracked and eventually freed. It's like making a photocopy of every document in your filing cabinet, including all the labels and folders.

Removing files: when it's time to say goodbye

We also need a way to remove files from our index:

```
pub fn removeFile(self: *FileIndex, path: []const u8) void {
    if (self.files.fetchRemove(path)) |removed| {
        if (removed.value.inode != 0) {
            _ = self.inodes.remove(removed.value.inode);
        }

        removed.value.deinit();

        _ = self.path_storage.remove(removed.key);
        self.allocator.free(removed.key);
    }
}
```

In this method:

- Removes the file entry from our file index
- If the file had a valid inode, removes it from our inode index as well
- Frees the metadata object
- Removes the path from our path tracking and frees it

Again, the order matters. We need to use the path to remove entries from the hash maps before freeing it. It's like needing the label to find the right drawer in your filing cabinet before you can remove the label itself.

Counting files: how big is your collection?

For reporting and debugging, it's useful to know how many files are in our index:

```
pub fn count(self: *const FileIndex) usize {
    return self.files.count();
}
```

This simple method returns the number of files in our index. It's surprisingly useful for sanity checks—if you're expecting thousands of files but only see a handful, something might be wrong with your traversal or filtering.

The power of dual indexing: path and inode lookups

One of the most powerful features of our FileIndex is the dual indexing by both path and inode. This dual approach gives us:

- Efficient Path Lookups: We can quickly check if a file exists and retrieve its metadata

- Move Detection: By looking up files by inode, we can detect when they've been moved or renamed

- Comprehensive Change Detection: We can find created, deleted, modified, and moved files efficiently

This dual indexing is what enables one of FileGuard's most impressive features—properly distinguishing between file moves and the delete+create operations that less sophisticated tools might report.

Memory management: the path tracking mystery explained

You might be wondering why we bother with the separate path_storage map when we already have paths in our files map. The reason is subtle but important: the paths are used as keys in the files map, and Zig's hash map doesn't give us an easy way to iterate through just the keys for cleanup.

By maintaining a separate map where paths are the keys and the values are simply empty structs (taking up no space), we can easily iterate through all the paths we've allocated when it's time to clean up. It's a small memory overhead for a significant simplification in our cleanup logic.

This approach demonstrates a common pattern in Zig programming—sometimes a little extra bookkeeping can make memory management much cleaner and more reliable.

This organized approach is what makes FileGuard fast and efficient. Instead of rescanning and reading entire directories on every check, we can build indexes and compare them—much like how a librarian uses their catalog to quickly find changes in a large collection rather than wandering the shelves.

Now that we have our files indexed, we need a way to populate this index by traversing directories and collecting file information. In the next section, we'll implement directory traversal with pattern-based filtering, allowing users to monitor exactly the files they care about.

Directory traversal: exploring your digital wilderness

Now that we have our file metadata and indexing structures, we need a way to actually find files to monitor. This is where directory traversal comes in—the digital equivalent of an expedition through your filesystem jungle, cataloging the flora and fauna (or in this case, documents and executables) we encounter along the way.

But not all explorers want to venture into every dark corner. Some might want to avoid the treacherous depths of "node_modules" or the mind-bending recursion of symbolic link loops. Others might only be interested in specific species of files, like rare .zig source files or the common .txt documents.

Our traversal.zig module handles this exploration with configurability that would make a GPS system jealous.

The TraversalConfig: your expedition parameters

Before diving into traversal code, let's define what options our explorers have. In config.zig, we'll define the configuration structure:

```
pub const TraversalConfig = struct {
    max_depth: ?usize = null,
    include_patterns: []const []const u8 = &.{"*"},
    exclude_patterns: []const []const u8 = &.{},
    hash_content: bool = false,
    follow_symlinks: bool = false,
    current_depth: usize = 0,
};
```

These options give us fine-grained control over our traversal:

- max_depth: How deep into the directory rabbit hole we're willing to go
- include_patterns: Which file types we're interested in (e.g., ".zig", ".txt")
- exclude_patterns: Which file types or directories to avoid (e.g., ".tmp", "node_modules/")
- hash_content: Whether to compute file content hashes (slower but more accurate)
- follow_symlinks: Whether to follow symbolic links (potentially dangerous, but sometimes necessary)
- current_depth: Internal tracking of how deep we currently are

Think of this as your expedition gear, the machete for cutting through undergrowth (pattern matching), the depth gauge for cave exploration (max_depth), and the trusty map that warns you about the dangerous symbolic link swamps that might leave you walking in circles until you run out of stack space and die.

Pattern matching: your file-finding filter

One crucial thing to do before we can traverse directories: we need a way to determine which files match our patterns. Let's implement the pattern matching in pattern.zig:

```zig
const c = @cImport({
    @cInclude("stdlib.h");
    @cInclude("fnmatch.h");
});

pub fn matches(pattern: []const u8, name: []const u8) bool {
    const patternC: [*c]const u8 = @ptrCast(pattern.ptr);
    const nameC: [*c]const u8 = @ptrCast(name.ptr);
    const rc: c_int = c.fnmatch(patternC, nameC, 0);
    return rc == 0;
}

pub fn matchesAnyPattern(patterns: []const []const u8, path: []const u8)
bool {
    for (patterns) |pattern| {
        if (matches(pattern, path)) {
            return true;
        }
    }
    return false;
}
```

Here we're leveraging C's fnmatch function to handle glob pattern matching. This is a perfect example of Zig's seamless C interoperability—why reinvent the wheel when decades of battle-tested pattern matching code is just an @cImport away?

The matches function checks if a single file path matches a single pattern, while matchesAnyPattern checks if a path matches any of a list of patterns. Simple, yet powerful.

The file filter: should we include this file?

With pattern matching in place, we can determine which files to include in our monitoring:

```
fn shouldIncludeFile(path: []const u8, config: *const TraversalConfig)
bool {
    // Exclusion patterns take precedence over inclusion patterns
    if (pattern.matchesAnyPattern(config.exclude_patterns, path)) {
        return false;
    }

    // Check if the file matches any inclusion pattern
    return pattern.matchesAnyPattern(config.include_patterns, path);
}
```

This function applies a simple rule: if a file matches any exclusion pattern, ignore it. Otherwise, include it if it matches any inclusion pattern. Exclusions always win—think of it as the bouncer at Club Filesystem checking the VIP blacklist before even looking at the general admission list.

The main traversal: your digital safari

Now for the main event—the directory traversal function:

```
pub fn traverseDirectory(
    index: *FileIndex,
    dir_path: []const u8,
    config: *const TraversalConfig,
) !void {
    // Open the directory
    var dir = try std.fs.cwd().openDir(dir_path, .{ .iterate = true });
    defer dir.close();

    // Iterate through directory entries
    var iter = dir.iterate();
    while (try iter.next()) |entry| {
        // Construct the full path
        const full_path = try std.fs.path.join(
            index.allocator,
            &[_][]const u8{ dir_path, entry.name }
        );
```

```zig
            defer index.allocator.free(full_path);

        // Handle different entry types
        switch (entry.kind) {
            .file => {
                // Check if the file should be included
                if (shouldIncludeFile(full_path, config)) {
                    // Get metadata and add to index
                    const metadata = try FileMetadata.init(
                        index.allocator,
                        full_path,
                        config.hash_content
                    );
                    try index.addFile(metadata);
                }
            },
            .directory => {
                // Check depth limit before recursing
                if (config.max_depth == null or config.current_depth <
config.max_depth.?) {
                    // Create a new config with incremented depth
                    var next_config = config.*;
                    next_config.current_depth += 1;

                    // Recursively process subdirectory
                    try traverseDirectory(index, full_path, &next_config);
                }
            },
            .sym_link => {
                if (config.follow_symlinks) {
                    // Handle symlinks (implementation omitted for
brevity)
                    // This would resolve the symlink and either process
the target file
                    // or recursively traverse the target directory
                }
            },
            else => {}, // Skip other types (pipes, devices, etc.)
```

```
            }
        }
    }
```

This function is the heart of our directory exploration:

- We open the directory and iterate through its entries
- For each entry, we construct its full path
- Depending on the entry type, we:
- For files: Check if they match our patterns and add them to the index if they do
- For directories: Recursively traverse them if we haven't hit our depth limit
- For symbolic links: Follow them if configured to do so
- For other types: Ignore them

The recursive approach is elegant but comes with a caveat—deep directory structures could potentially cause stack overflow if the recursion gets too deep. However, our `max_depth` configuration provides a safety valve to prevent this.

Handling symbolic links: the portals of the filesystem

Symbolic links deserve special attention because they can create loops in what's normally a tree-structured filesystem. If link A points to directory B, which contains link C that points back to A's parent, you've got yourself an infinite loop that would make recursion very unhappy.

Here's how we handle symbolic links (simplified):

```
.sym_link => {
    if (config.follow_symlinks) {
        const target_path = try dir.readLink(entry.name, &[_]u8{});
        const resolved_path = try std.fs.path.resolve(
            index.allocator,
            &[_][]const u8{ dir_path, target_path }
        );
        defer index.allocator.free(resolved_path);

        const target_stat = try std.fs.cwd().statFile(resolved_path);

        if (target_stat.kind == .directory) {
```

```
            if (config.max_depth == null or config.current_depth < config.
max_depth.?) {
                var next_config = config.*;
                next_config.current_depth += 1;
                try traverseDirectory(index, resolved_path, &next_config);
            }
        } else if (target_stat.kind == .file) {
            // Process target file (if it matches patterns)
            if (shouldIncludeFile(resolved_path, config)) {
                const metadata = try FileMetadata.init(
                    index.allocator,
                    resolved_path,
                    config.hash_content
                );
                try index.addFile(metadata);
            }
        }
    }
}
```

We first resolve the symbolic link to find its target, then check if that target is a directory or file. If it's a directory, we recursively traverse it; if it's a file, we process it like any other file.

The danger with symbolic links isn't just infinite loops—they can also lead to processing the same file multiple times under different paths. A more sophisticated implementation might track already visited inodes to prevent this, but for simplicity, we're accepting this potential duplication.

The traversal dance: how it all works together

Let's step back and see how these pieces work together:

- The user configures which files to monitor through inclusion and exclusion patterns
- Our traversal function walks the directory tree, respecting depth limits
- For each file encountered, we check if it matches our patterns
- If it does, we create metadata for it and add it to our index
- The result is a neatly populated index of all the files we care about

This selective approach is crucial for performance. Imagine monitoring a directory with thousands of files but only caring about a few dozen configuration files. By filtering during traversal, we avoid wasting time and memory indexing files we'll never monitor.

Performance considerations: traversal isn't free

Directory traversal can be expensive, especially when content hashing is enabled or when dealing with large directory structures. Here are some performance considerations built into our design:

- Selective Hashing: Content hashing is disabled by default and only performed when explicitly requested
- Depth Limiting: The `max_depth` option prevents traversing unnecessarily deep directory structures
- Pattern Filtering: We only process files that match our inclusion patterns and don't match exclusion patterns
- Deferred Cleanup: We use defer for path cleanup to ensure memory is freed even if errors occur

These optimizations ensure that FileGuard remains responsive even when monitoring large directory trees.

Our directory traversal system provides a robust way to explore filesystem structures and collect metadata about the files we care about. With configurable depth limits, pattern matching, and symbolic link handling, it's flexible enough to adapt to a wide range of monitoring scenarios.

Whether you're watching a handful of configuration files or tracking changes across an entire project directory, the traversal module efficiently collects just the information you need without wasting resources on files you don't care about.

With our file metadata, indexing, and traversal systems in place, we're ready to tackle the final piece of the puzzle—detecting changes between indexing runs. In the next section, we'll implement the change detection logic that identifies created, deleted, modified, and moved files, bringing our FileGuard tool to life.

Change detection: spot the differences in your digital world

So far, we've built a system to catalog files and their metadata. That's impressive, but it doesn't actually detect changes yet—it's like having thousands of security camera snapshots with no way to spot the differences between them. Now comes the fun part: building our change detection system.

When it comes to files, several types of changes can occur:

- Creation: A file that wasn't there before suddenly appears
- Deletion: A file that was there before vanishes into the digital void
- Modification: A file's contents change
- Movement: A file relocates to a different path
- Permission Changes: A file's access rights are altered
- Timestamp Updates: A file's timestamps change without content modification

Our job is to detect all these changes efficiently by comparing two file indexes—one from before and one from after. It's like playing the world's most tedious spot-the-difference game, except we're letting the computer do all the tedious work while we sit back and enjoy the results.

Defining change types: building your detective's notebook

Let's start by defining the types of changes we can detect in change_detection.zig:

```
pub const ChangeType = enum {
    created,     // File is new
    deleted,     // File no longer exists
    modified,    // File content has changed
    moved,       // File was moved or renamed
    permissions, // Permissions have changed
    timestamp,   // Timestamp has changed without content changes
};
```

This enum represents all the change types FileGuard can detect. It's the vocabulary of our change detection language—the difference between saying "the file changed somehow" and specifically identifying "the file was moved from location A to location B."

Representing changes: the FileChange struct

Next, we need a way to represent a detected change:

```
pub const FileChange = struct {
    // Type of change that was detected
    change_type: ChangeType,

    // Original path of the file (null for created files)
    old_path: ?[]const u8,

    // Current path of the file (null for deleted files)
    new_path: ?[]const u8,

    // Original metadata (null for created files)
    old_metadata: ?FileMetadata,

    // Current metadata (null for deleted files)
    new_metadata: ?FileMetadata,

    // When the change was detected
    timestamp: i64,

    // Allocator for memory management
    allocator: std.mem.Allocator,

    // Methods for initialization and cleanup
    // ...
};
```

Each FileChange instance represents a specific change to a file, capturing all the information we need to understand what happened.

The change journal: collecting your evidence

To collect multiple changes, we'll create a ChangeJournal:

```
pub const ChangeJournal = struct {
    // List of detected changes
    changes: std.ArrayList(FileChange),
```

```
    // Allocator for memory management
    allocator: std.mem.Allocator,

    // Methods for initialization, cleanup, and recording changes
    // ...
};
```

The journal is essentially a list of changes with methods to initialize, clean up, and record new changes as we detect them.

Detection configuration: customizing your detective work

Different users care about different types of changes, so we need a configuration struct:

```
pub const DetectionConfig = struct {
    // Enable timestamp monitoring
    monitor_timestamps: bool = true,

    // Enable size change detection
    monitor_size: bool = true,

    // Enable content hash comparison
    monitor_content: bool = false,

    // Enable permission change detection
    monitor_permissions: bool = false,

    // Enable move detection using inodes
    detect_moves: bool = true,
};
```

These options let users decide the trade-off between detection thoroughness and performance. For example, content hash comparison is expensive but catches subtle changes that size and timestamp monitoring might miss.

The main detection algorithm: finding your culprits

Now for the main event—the change detection algorithm. Let's break this down into manageable pieces.

First, we'll set up the function and start looking for deleted files:

```
pub fn detectChanges(
    old_index: *const FileIndex,
    new_index: *const FileIndex,
    config: *const DetectionConfig,
    journal: *ChangeJournal,
) !void {
    // Step 1: Find deleted files (in old but not in new)
    var old_iterator = old_index.files.iterator();
    while (old_iterator.next()) |entry| {
        const path = entry.key_ptr.*;
        const old_metadata = entry.value_ptr.*;

        if (!new_index.contains(path)) {
            // This file is in the old index but not the new one
            // It might be deleted or moved...
```

When a file isn't in the new index, we check if it might have been moved instead of deleted:

```
            if (config.detect_moves) {
                // Check if the file was moved (same inode appears
    elsewhere)
                if (old_metadata.inode != 0) {
                    if (new_index.findByInode(old_metadata.inode)) |new_
    path| {
                        // File was moved/renamed
                        const new_metadata_opt = new_index.get(new_path);
                        if (new_metadata_opt) |new_metadata_ptr|
                        try journal.recordChange(
                            .moved,
                            path,
                            new_path,
                            old_metadata,
                            new_metadata_ptr.*,
```

```
                );
                continue; // Skip recording as deleted
              }
            }
          }

          // If we got here, the file was truly deleted
          try journal.recordChange(
              .deleted,
              path,
              null,
              old_metadata,
              null,
          );
        }
      }
```

Next, we look for created and modified files:

```
    // Step 2: Find created and modified files (in new but maybe not in
old)
    var new_iterator = new_index.files.iterator();
    while (new_iterator.next()) |entry| {
        const path = entry.key_ptr.*;
        const new_metadata = entry.value_ptr.*;

        if (old_index.get(path)) |old_metadata| {
            // File exists in both - check for modifications
            try detectFileModifications(
                path,
                old_metadata.*,
                new_metadata,
                config,
                journal,
            );
        } else {
            // This file is in the new index but not the old one
            // It might be new or the destination of a move...
```

When a file is in the new index but not the old one, we check if it might be the destination of a move:

```
                    // Skip files already detected as moved
            var was_move = false;
            if (config.detect_moves and new_metadata.inode != 0) {
                // Check if this is the destination of a move operation
                if (old_index.findByInode(new_metadata.inode)) |_| {
                    was_move = true;
                }
            }

            if (!was_move) {
                // New file (not detected as moved)
                try journal.recordChange(
                    .created,
                    null,
                    path,
                    null,
                    new_metadata,
                );
            }
        }
    }
}
```

The magic here is in the move detection. By using inode numbers, we can detect when a file has simply been renamed or moved instead of being deleted and recreated. It's like recognizing that your friend is still the same person even if they've changed their name and moved to a new house.

Detecting file modifications: the devil in the details

When a file exists in both the old and new indexes, we need to check what (if anything) changed about it. Let's break this down by modification type.

First, we set up the function and check for content changes:

```
fn detectFileModifications(
    path: []const u8,
    old_metadata: FileMetadata,
    new_metadata: FileMetadata,
```

```
    config: *const DetectionConfig,
    journal: *ChangeJournal,
) !void {
    // Check content changes first (highest priority)
    if (config.monitor_content) {
        // If both have checksums and they don't match, content changed
        if (old_metadata.checksum != null and new_metadata.checksum !=
null) {
            if (!std.mem.eql(u8, old_metadata.checksum.?, new_metadata.
checksum.?)) {
                try journal.recordChange(
                    .modified,
                    path,
                    path,
                    old_metadata,
                    new_metadata,
                );
                return; // No need to check other modifications
            }
        }
    }
```

Content changes are the most significant, so we check them first. If the checksums don't match, we know the content has changed, and we don't need to check anything else.

Next, we check for size changes:

```
    // Check size changes
    if (config.monitor_size) {
        if (old_metadata.md.size() != new_metadata.md.size()) {
            try journal.recordChange(
                .modified,
                path,
                path,
                old_metadata,
                new_metadata,
            );
```

```
        return; // No need to check other modifications
    }
}
```

Size changes are also significant modifications, so if we detect one, we record it and don't bother checking permissions or timestamps.

Then, we check for permission changes:

```
// Check permission changes
if (config.monitor_permissions) {
    if (!std.meta.eql(old_metadata.md.permissions(), new_metadata.
md.permissions())) {
        try journal.recordChange(
            .permissions,
            path,
            path,
            old_metadata,
            new_metadata,
        );
    }
}
```

Permission changes are a distinct type of change, different from content modifications. If we detect a permission change, we record it as such, not as a general modification.

Finally, we check for timestamp changes:

```
// Check timestamp changes
if (config.monitor_timestamps) {
    // Focus on modification time
    const old_mtime = old_metadata.md.modified();
    const new_mtime = new_metadata.md.modified();

    if (old_mtime != new_mtime) {
        try journal.recordChange(
            .timestamp,
            path,
            path,
            old_metadata,
```

```
            new_metadata,
        );
    }
  }
}
```

Timestamp changes are the least significant type of change, but they can still be important in certain contexts, like detecting when a file has been touched without its content being modified.

The magic of move detection: inodes to the rescue

One of FileGuard's most impressive features is its ability to detect moved or renamed files. This is where our dual indexing (by path and by inode) really shines.

When we detect that a file has disappeared from its original location, we don't immediately conclude it was deleted. Instead, we check if any file in the new index has the same inode number. If we find one, we know the file was moved or renamed rather than deleted and recreated.

This distinction matters. Imagine you're monitoring source code files—knowing that a file was moved is far more informative than being told it was deleted in one place and created in another, especially when the content is identical.

The inode-based approach is elegant and efficient. It leverages the filesystem's own unique identifiers rather than trying to compare file contents, which would be much slower and less reliable.

With these components—change types, change records, the journal, the detection configuration, and the detection algorithms—we have a complete system for identifying what's changed in a directory between two scans.

This is the heart of FileGuard—the detective that spots what's changed while you weren't looking. Whether files are sneakily changing their contents, playing musical chairs with their locations, or simply vanishing into the digital ether, our change detection system will catch them in the act.

So far, we've built the complete monitoring engine: file metadata capture, efficient indexing with dual path/inode lookups, configurable directory traversal with pattern matching, and sophisticated change detection that can distinguish between creates, deletes, modifications, and moves.

We have a powerful foundation, but it's currently locked away behind function calls and data structures. What we need now is a bridge between this technical capability and the humans who want to use it.

In the next section, we'll build the command-line interface that transforms our monitoring algorithms into a practical tool, allowing users to configure monitoring behavior, customize output, and interact with FileGuard through familiar command-line patterns.

Building the command-line interface: making FileGuard user-friendly

We've built a powerful file monitoring engine, but without a usable interface, it's about as useful as a Ferrari with no steering wheel. To bridge the gap between our elegant file monitoring algorithms and the humans who want to use them, we need a command-line interface (CLI) that's both flexible and intuitive.

Creating a good CLI is trickier than it seems. You need to handle a multitude of options, validate user input, provide helpful error messages, and format output in a way that's both human-readable and potentially *machine-parseable*. It's the difference between a tool that makes users say "This is exactly what I needed!" and one that makes them question their career choices.

Let's dive into building the CLI for FileGuard, where we'll turn our powerful detection engine into a tool that actual humans can use without developing a twitch.

Command-line options: giving users control

First, let's define the options our CLI will support in `cli.zig`:

```
pub const CliOptions = struct {
    // Global options
    help: bool = false,
    verbose: bool = false,

    // Monitoring options
    include_patterns: []const u8 = "*",
    exclude_patterns: []const u8 = "",
    max_depth: ?usize = null,
    hash_content: bool = false,
    follow_symlinks: bool = false,
    monitor_timestamps: bool = true,
    monitor_size: bool = true,
    monitor_content: bool = false,
    monitor_permissions: bool = false,
    detect_moves: bool = true,
```

```
    continuous: bool = false,
    interval: u64 = 60,

    // More fields and methods...
};
```

This structure defines all the configuration options users can control. We provide reasonable defaults for each option, like monitoring timestamps and sizes but not content hashes (which are slower).

To make the CLI more user-friendly, we also define *shorthands* for commonly used options:

```
// Shorthands for command-line options
pub const shorthands = .{
    .h = "help",
    .v = "verbose",
    .i = "include_patterns",
    .x = "exclude_patterns",
    .d = "max_depth",
    .c = "hash_content",
    .s = "follow_symlinks",
    .t = "monitor_timestamps",
    .z = "monitor_size",
    .C = "monitor_content",
    .p = "monitor_permissions",
    .m = "detect_moves",
    .w = "continuous",
    .n = "interval",
};
```

These shorthands let users type -v instead of --verbose, saving precious keystrokes that can be better spent complaining about how slow other people's code is.

Parsing arguments: turning text into configuration

To parse command-line arguments, we'll use an external library called args. This saves us from writing a complex parser ourselves and lets us focus on the actual monitoring functionality.

Here's how we parse arguments in our run function:

```
pub fn run() !void {
    var gpa = std.heap.GeneralPurposeAllocator(.{}){};
    defer _ = gpa.deinit();
    const allocator = gpa.allocator();

    // Parse command-line arguments
    const args = try argsParser.parseForCurrentProcess(
        CliOptions,
        allocator,
        .print,
    );
    defer args.deinit();

    // Show help if requested
    if (args.options.help) {
        return showHelp(args.executable_name orelse "fileguard");
    }

    // Get the path to monitor (first positional argument, or default to
".")
    const path = if (args.positionals.len > 0) args.positionals[0] else
".";

    // More code...
}
```

This code:

- Sets up a general-purpose allocator for memory management
- Parses the command-line arguments into our CliOptions structure
- Shows help if the --help flag is provided
- Determines the path to monitor (defaulting to the current directory if none is specified)

Notice how we're using Zig's defer statement to ensure that resources are cleaned up properly, even if an error occurs during execution. This is one of Zig's most powerful features for writing robust code—it's like setting up dominoes that will automatically fall and clean up your mess when you leave the room.

Displaying help: guiding lost souls

When users pass the --help flag, we want to show them comprehensive documentation. Here's our showHelp function:

```zig
fn showHelp(program_name: []const u8) !void {
    const stdout = std.io.getStdOut().writer();

    try stdout.print("Usage: {s} [OPTIONS] [PATH]\n\n", .{program_name});
    try stdout.writeAll("A file monitoring system that detects and reports
changes to the console.\n\n");
    try stdout.writeAll("If PATH is not specified, the current directory
will be monitored.\n\n");

    try stdout.writeAll("Options:\n");
    try stdout.writeAll("  -h, --help                Show this help
message\n");
    try stdout.writeAll("  -v, --verbose             Enable verbose output\
n\n");

    // More options omitted for brevity...
}
```

Good help text is crucial for user experience. It's the difference between a user figuring out how to use your tool in seconds versus giving up and writing their own inferior version out of spite.

Running the monitor: the main event loop

With our configuration parsed and validated, we can now run the actual monitoring:

```zig
fn runMonitor(
    allocator: std.mem.Allocator,
    path: []const u8,
    options: CliOptions,
) !void {
    // First validate the path
    try validatePath(path);

    if (options.verbose) {
        std.debug.print("Monitoring {s} for changes\n", .{path});
    }
```

```
    // Resolve the real path
    const real_path = try std.fs.realpathAlloc(allocator, path);
    defer allocator.free(real_path);

    // Split the pattern strings into arrays
    const include_patterns = try splitPatterns(allocator, options.include_
patterns);
    defer {
        for (include_patterns) |pattern| {
            allocator.free(pattern);
        }
        allocator.free(include_patterns);
    }

    const exclude_patterns = try splitPatterns(allocator, options.exclude_
patterns);
    defer {
        for (exclude_patterns) |pattern| {
            allocator.free(pattern);
        }
        allocator.free(exclude_patterns);
    }

    // Set up configurations and baseline index
    // ...
}
```

This part of the function:

- Validates that the specified path exists and is accessible
- Resolves it to an absolute path
- Splits the include and exclude patterns
- Sets up proper memory management with defer statements

Next, we set up our traversal and detection configurations and create the baseline index:

```zig
    // Create traversal configuration
    const traverse_config = TraversalConfig{
        .include_patterns = include_patterns,
        .exclude_patterns = exclude_patterns,
        .max_depth = options.max_depth,
        .hash_content = options.hash_content,
        .follow_symlinks = options.follow_symlinks,
    };

    // Create detection configuration
    const detect_config = DetectionConfig{
        .monitor_timestamps = options.monitor_timestamps,
        .monitor_size = options.monitor_size,
        .monitor_content = options.monitor_content,
        .monitor_permissions = options.monitor_permissions,
        .detect_moves = options.detect_moves,
    };

    // Create baseline index
    std.debug.print("Creating initial baseline index...\n", .{});
    var baseline_index = FileIndex.init(allocator);
    defer baseline_index.deinit();

    // Traverse directory for baseline
    try traverseDirectory(&baseline_index, real_path, &traverse_config);

    if (options.verbose) {
        std.debug.print("Baseline index created with {d} files\n",
.{baseline_index.count()});
    }
```

Here we:

- Create a `TraversalConfig` from our CLI options
- Create a `DetectionConfig` from our CLI options

- Create a baseline index of files for comparison

- Traverse the directory to populate the baseline index

Finally, we enter the monitoring loop:

```
// Determine if we're doing continuous monitoring or a single check
const is_continuous = options.continuous;
const interval_ns = options.interval * std.time.ns_per_s;
var last_change_time: i64 = 0;

std.debug.print("Monitoring started. ", .{});
if (is_continuous) {
    std.debug.print("Will check every {d} seconds. Press Ctrl+C to
stop.\n", .{options.interval});
} else {
    std.debug.print("Will perform a single check.\n", .{});
}


// Monitor loop
while (!should_exit) {
    var current_index = FileIndex.init(allocator);
    defer current_index.deinit();

    // Traverse directory
    traverseDirectory(&current_index, real_path, &traverse_config)
catch |err| {
        std.debug.print("Error during directory traversal: {}\n",
.{err});
        std.debug.print("Will retry on next cycle\n", .{});
        if (!is_continuous) {
            return err;
        } else {
            std.time.sleep(interval_ns);
            continue;
        }
    };

    // Detect and report changes
```

```
        // ...

        // If not continuous monitoring, break
        if (!is_continuous) {
            break;
        }
        // Sleep for the interval
        std.time.sleep(interval_ns);
    }
```

This part:

- Determines whether to do continuous monitoring or a single check
- Enters a loop that continues until the program is terminated
- Creates a new index on each iteration
- Traverses the directory to populate the current index
- Handles errors gracefully
- Sleeps between iterations if continuous monitoring is enabled

Reporting changes: making results human-readable

Once we've detected changes, we need to report them to the user in a readable format:

```
// Create a change journal
var change_journal = ChangeJournal.init(allocator);
defer change_journal.deinit();

// Detect changes
try detectChanges(&baseline_index, &current_index, &detect_config,
&change_journal);

// If changes were detected
if (change_journal.count() > 0) {
    const timestamp = std.time.timestamp();

    std.debug.print("\n=== Changes detected at {d} ({d} changes) ===\n\n",
.{
        timestamp,
        change_journal.count(),
```

```
    });

    // Print each change
    for (change_journal.changes.items) |change| {
        printChange(change, allocator) catch |err| {
            std.debug.print("Error printing change: {}\n", .{err});
        };
    }

    std.debug.print("\n", .{});
    last_change_time = timestamp;

    // Update baseline by creating a fresh copy of current_index
    const new_baseline = try current_index.clone();
    baseline_index.deinit();
    baseline_index = new_baseline;
} else {
    if (options.verbose) {
        std.debug.print("No changes detected at {}\n", .{std.time.
timestamp()});
    }
}
}
```

This code:

- Creates a change journal to collect detected changes
- Runs the change detection algorithm
- Reports any detected changes in a nicely formatted way
- Updates the baseline index to the current state for the next iteration

The actual printing of changes is handled by a separate function:

```
fn printChange(change: FileChange, allocator: std.mem.Allocator) !void {
    const stdout = std.io.getStdOut().writer();
    const old_path = change.old_path orelse "unknown";
    const new_path = change.new_path orelse "unknown";

    switch (change.change_type) {
        .created => {
```

```
            try stdout.print("[{d}] CREATED: {s}\n", .{
                change.timestamp,
                new_path,
            });
        },
        .deleted => {
            try stdout.print("[{d}] DELETED: {s}\n", .{
                change.timestamp,
                old_path,
            });
        },
        // Other change types...
    }

    // Show additional details for certain change types
    // ...
}
```

This function formats each change in a way that's easy for humans to read, with timestamps and detailed information about what changed. For complex changes like modifications, it shows exactly what aspects of the file changed (size, content, etc.).

Error handling: when things go wrong

A robust CLI needs to handle errors gracefully. Let's look at how we validate the path to monitor:

```
fn validatePath(path: []const u8) !void {
    var dir = std.fs.cwd().openDir(path, .{}) catch |err| {
        switch (err) {
            error.FileNotFound => {
                std.debug.print("Error: Path '{s}' does not exist\n",
.{path});
                return error.PathNotFound;
            },
            error.AccessDenied => {
                std.debug.print("Error: Access denied to path '{s}'\n",
.{path});
                return error.AccessDenied;
            },
```

```
        else => {
            std.debug.print("Error: Unable to access path '{s}':
{}\n", .{ path, err });
            return err;
        },
    }
};
dir.close();
}
```

This function tries to open the directory and provides specific error messages depending on what went wrong. It's much more user-friendly than just letting the program crash with a generic error.

Similarly, our directory traversal error handling in the monitoring loop ensures that temporary failures (like a file being locked) don't cause the entire monitoring process to fail in continuous mode.

With all these pieces, our CLI provides a complete and user-friendly interface to FileGuard's functionality. Users can:

- Configure which files to monitor through inclusion and exclusion patterns
- Control how deeply to traverse directory structures
- Choose which types of changes to detect
- Run either a one-time check or continuous monitoring
- Get clear, readable reports of detected changes

The CLI transforms FileGuard from a collection of algorithms into a useful tool that real people can use to solve real problems.

Beyond the basics: professional CLI features

So, let's say you've gone from "Hey, I'm learning Zig!" to "This file monitoring tool is going straight into our mission-critical production pipeline!" faster than you can say "resume-driven development." Before you slap this adorable pet project onto your company's servers and subsequently update your LinkedIn profile to "seeking new opportunities," consider adding these features:

- Output Formats: Support for machine-readable formats like JSON or CSV, because Dave from DevOps will absolutely lose it if he has to parse stdout with regex again
- Logging: Writing changes to actual log files instead of stdout, which mysteriously disappears the moment you need to prove it wasn't your tool that deleted the CEO's presentation

- Notifications: Sending alerts via email, Slack, or carrier pigeon so you can be woken up at 3 A.M. when someone modifies a temp file

- Filters: More sophisticated filtering of reported changes, because nobody needs 500 alerts about `.DS_Store` files changing

- Integration Hooks: Running custom commands when changes are detected, like automatically triggering your "polish resume" script when critical files vanish

Remember, there's a fine line between "impressive weekend project" and "reason for the all-hands emergency meeting on Monday." These enhancements might just be the difference between your colleagues thinking "what a useful tool" and "who authorized this catastrophe?"

Now that we've implemented the command-line interface, we've completed all the major components of our FileGuard tool. In the next section, we'll tie everything together with our main program and discuss the broader context of building command-line tools in Zig.

Tying it all together: the main program and beyond

We've built all the individual components of our FileGuard system—file metadata tracking, indexing, directory traversal, pattern matching, change detection, and the command-line interface. Now it's time to bring them all together in the `main.zig` file, the orchestrator that turns these components into a cohesive application.

Compared to the complexity of our other modules, `main.zig` is refreshingly simple:

```
// imports ommitted for brevity
pub fn main() !void {
    // Run the CLI
    try cli.run();
}
```

The simplicity of `main.zig` is a testament to good modular design. Each component has a clear responsibility, and they interact through well-defined interfaces. This approach makes the code easier to understand, test, and maintain.

While our `main.zig` orchestrates the application at runtime, the unsung heroes of our project are `build.zig` and `build.zig.zon`—the conductors that orchestrate how our code becomes an executable in the first place. These files represent Zig's approach to build systems and dependency management, and they're worth understanding as deeply as the code they compile.

Building and wrangling dependencies

Let's start with build.zig, the file that tells Zig how to build our application:

```zig
const std = @import("std");
pub fn build(b: *std.Build) void { const target =
b.standardTargetOptions(.{}); const optimize = b.standardOptimizeOption(.
{});
const exe_mod = b.createModule(.{
    .root_source_file = b.path("src/main.zig"),
    .target = target,
    .optimize = optimize,
});

const exe = b.addExecutable(.{
    .name = "fg",
    .root_module = exe_mod,
});
exe.linkLibC();
exe.root_module.addImport("args", b.dependency("args", .{
    .target = target,
    .optimize = optimize,
}).module("args"));
b.installArtifact(exe);

// Additional build steps for testing and running...

}
```

Look at what our build file does:

- Defines the build target (architecture and OS)
- Sets optimization levels
- Creates a module from our source code
- Defines an executable with our module as its root
- Links with the C library (for our fnmatch pattern matching)
- Adds the external args dependency
- Installs the resulting artifact

All this, and it's still more readable than your average package.json file that's somehow accu-
mulated 8,742 dependencies since lunchtime.

Now let's look at build.zig.zon, the file that manages our external dependencies:

```
{
    .name = .zig_file_guard,
    .version = "0.0.1",
    .fingerprint = 0x3112a747329a3960, // Changing this has security and
trust implications.
    .minimum_zig_version = "0.14.0",
    .dependencies = .{
        .args = .{
            .url = "git+https://github.com/ikskuh/zig-args?ref=master#9425
b94c103a031777fdd272c555ce93a7dea581",
            .hash = "args-0.0.0-CiLiqv_NAAC97fGpk9hS2K681jkiqPsWP6w3ucb_
ctGH",
        },
    },

    .paths = .{
        "build.zig",
        "build.zig.zon",
        "src",
        "README.md",
    },
}
```

This is Zig Object Notation (ZON), Zig's answer to JSON but with fewer quotes and more sanity.
Our build.zig.zon file specifies:

- Basic project metadata (name, version)
- The minimum Zig version required
- External dependencies with precise versioning
- Project paths to include in distributions

The dependency system deserves special attention. Notice how we're not just saying "give me the latest zig-args" or "any version that's kinda-sorta compatible." Instead, we specify an exact commit hash. This is Zig's approach to reproducible builds—if it worked once, it should work forever, without mysterious "it worked yesterday" issues that send developers into existential crises.

The hash value ensures the downloaded code matches exactly what we expect. It's like having a bouncer check ID at the door, except this bouncer has perfect memory and can spot a fake from across the room while blindfolded.

Unlike some languages where the build system feels tacked on as an afterthought (looking at you, languages that rely on third-party package managers), Zig's build system is an integral part of the language experience. It's elegant evidence that the same principles of explicitness and clarity that make Zig code good also make Zig builds reliable.

So the next time someone shows you their 500-line webpack.config.js or their Gradle script that somehow requires differential equations to understand, you can smile smugly and show them your sleek, comprehensible build.zig file. Just try not to be too insufferable about it.

Building and running FileGuard: from code to executable

With our code complete, we can build FileGuard using Zig's built-in build system:

```
zig build
```

This command compiles all our code into a single executable, which we can then run:

```
./zig-out/bin/fileguard </path/to/monitor>
```

To enable continuous monitoring with custom options:

```
./zig-out/bin/fileguard --continuous --interval=5 --include-patterns="*.
zig,*.md" </path/to/monitor>
```

For our ADHD friends, they do not need to recollect everything. Use the help command instead:

```
./zig-out/bin/fileguard --help
```

The compilation and execution process are seamless thanks to our build.zig file, which defines how all our components fit together, and which external dependencies (like zig-args) are needed.

Extending FileGuard: the road to professional use

While our current implementation is functional, there are several ways it could be extended for more professional use:

- Database Backend: Store file metadata and change history in a database for long-term analysis.
- Web Interface: Add a web-based dashboard for visualizing and exploring file changes.
- Plugin System: Allow users to write custom plugins for specialized processing of detected changes.
- Distributed Monitoring: Support monitoring files across multiple machines with centralized reporting.
- Security Enhancements: Add checks for suspicious changes that might indicate security breaches.

These extensions would transform FileGuard from a learning exercise into a genuinely useful tool for system administrators, developers, and security professionals.

Other project ideas: the sky's the limit (or at least the memory limit)

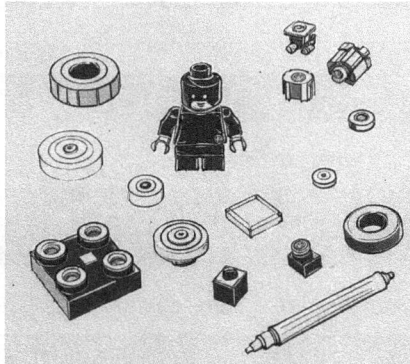

Figure 13.2 – The spare parts of productivity: build something that matters

Now that you've built FileGuard, you might be wondering what other practical projects you could tackle with Zig. Rather than suggesting you build the next operating system kernel or quantum computing simulator (because, let's face it, you've got actual work to do between burnouts), here are some down-to-earth project ideas that might actually help with your day-to-day developer life:

- Command-Line Search Tool: Create a faster, more intuitive version of grep or find that doesn't require consulting man pages every single time. Focus on common search patterns you use daily and make them dead simple.

- Log Parser/Analyzer: Build a tool that slices and dices those 10GB log files that everyone ignores until production crashes. Parse specific formats (nginx, Apache, custom app logs) and extract the actually useful information from the sea of debug noise.

- Development Server Watcher: Create a file-change-based development server that automatically recompiles/restarts your application when source files change - but one that doesn't consume all your CPU cores like it's mining cryptocurrency in the background.

- Configuration Validator: Build a tool that parses and validates your sprawling configuration files (JSON, YAML, TOML) before you push that broken config that takes down production at 2 A.M. on a Saturday.

- Directory Synchronizer: Create a tool that intelligently syncs directories without the complexity of rsync's 500 command line options that nobody fully understands. Perfect for keeping development environments in sync.

- Markdown Converter: Build a **blazing-fast** markdown-to-HTML converter that doesn't require downloading half the npm registry. Great for documentation generation or static site content.

- JSON/XML Processor: Create a command-line tool for querying and transforming JSON or XML data without having to remember arcane jq syntax or write throwaway Python scripts.

- Text Manipulation Toolkit: Build a Swiss Army knife for the types of text transformations you do every day - counting words, replacing patterns, extracting columns from tabular data, or normalizing whitespace.

- Simple HTTP Client: Implement a focused HTTP client for the specific APIs you work with regularly, with built-in formatting and common operations, so you don't have to craft the same curl commands over and over.

- Build Artifact Cleaner: Create a tool that reclaims precious disk space by intelligently cleaning up old build artifacts, *node_modules* directories, nix packages, and other development detritus that somehow consumes 200GB of your disk.

These projects are perfect for Zig because they benefit from its speed (faster tools = less waiting), minimal dependencies (no "left-pad" disasters), and precise error handling (because tools should tell you what went wrong rather than just exploding mysteriously).

Best of all, each of these ideas solves an actual problem you probably face weekly, if not daily. Unlike those "build your own database engine" tutorials that leave you with code you'll never use again, these projects create tools that earn their keep in your development workflow.

And hey, when your coworker's Go binary is still warming up while your Zig tool already finished the job, you'll experience that special kind of smugness that only comes from using half the memory in a quarter of the time.

Community resources: forums, chat rooms, and other dens of iniquity (we mean knowledge)

Building real-world projects inevitably leads to questions, challenges, and the occasional head-scratching moment when you're staring at an error message that might as well be written in ancient Sumerian. This is where the Zig community becomes invaluable.

The Zig community, while smaller than those of more established languages, is exceptionally helpful and knowledgeable. Here are some key resources for when you need help or want to learn more:

- Zig Showtime: A video series by Loris Cro (VP of Community at the Zig Software Foundation) and guests, showcasing Zig projects and features.

- The Zig Discord Server: The most active hub of the Zig community, with channels for beginners, language design discussions, and project showcases.

- The Ziggit Forum: A dedicated forum for Zig discussions, ideal for longer-form questions and debates.

- Zig on GitHub: The main repository where Zig development happens, with extensive issue discussions and documentation.

- r/Zig: The Zig subreddit, where users share projects, articles, and questions.

These resources can help you overcome challenges in your Zig projects and connect with other developers who share your interest in the language.

Contributing to Zig: open-source development for the greater good (and your resume)

After building your own projects, you might be interested in contributing to Zig itself or to the ecosystem of libraries and tools around it. This is a fantastic way to deepen your understanding of the language and give back to the community.

Contributing opportunities include:

- Core Language Development: Working on the Zig compiler, standard library, or language features.
- Documentation Improvements: Enhancing Zig's documentation to make it more accessible to newcomers.
- Package Development: Creating and maintaining libraries that extend Zig's capabilities.
- Tooling Development: Building tools that improve the Zig development experience.
- Education and Advocacy: Writing articles, creating tutorials, or speaking about Zig to help others learn.

Even small contributions can make a big difference, especially in a growing language like Zig. And yes, open-source contributions do look good on your resume—they demonstrate both technical skills and the ability to collaborate in a distributed team.

The roadmap: Zig's future plans (world domination, probably)

Zig is still evolving, with significant developments planned for future releases. Understanding this roadmap can help you align your learning and projects with where the language is headed.

Key areas of ongoing development include:

- Self-Hosted compiler: Moving from the current C++-based compiler to one written entirely in Zig.
- Package manager: Developing a robust solution for dependency management.
- Improved memory management: Expanding the options for managing memory in different contexts.
- Enhanced interoperability: Making it even easier to work with code in other languages.
- Performance optimizations: Continuing to refine the compiler for faster compilation and execution.

- Concurrency: A new Async I/O implementation.
- A language server protocol that deals with `comptime`.

These developments will make Zig even more powerful and user-friendly, expanding the range of projects where it's the optimal choice.

Zig's impact: case studies and success stories (from humble beginnings to tech giants)

Despite its youth, Zig is already making inroads in various domains, from embedded systems to web services. Looking at these success stories can provide inspiration and validation for your own Zig projects.

Notable examples of Zig in the wild include:

- Bun: A JavaScript runtime and toolkit built with Zig that emphasizes performance and developer experience.
- MachEngine: A game engine built with Zig that leverages the language's performance and control.
- TigerBeetle: A distributed financial accounting database written in Zig, designed for high throughput and reliability.
- Zig in Embedded Systems: Various projects using Zig for embedded development, taking advantage of its small runtime and precise control (e.g.: microzig).
- Zig in WebAssembly: Projects that compile Zig to WebAssembly for high-performance web applications.

These examples demonstrate Zig's versatility and its potential to excel in domains where performance, control, and reliability are crucial.

Summary

> *Your Zig journey has just begun*

Building this program is just the first step in your journey with Zig. You've seen how to structure a real-world application, manage memory explicitly, interact with the filesystem, and create a user-friendly interface. These skills form the foundation for more ambitious projects.

As you continue exploring Zig, remember that the greatest strength of any language is its community. Don't hesitate to share your projects, ask questions, and contribute to the ecosystem. Your experiences and insights are valuable, even (or especially) when you're still learning.

So, what will you build next? A database engine? A game? A compiler? Yet another enterprise CRUD? The possibilities are limited only by your imagination and the occasional compiler error that makes you question why you're doing that to you. But with each project, your understanding will deepen, and your ability to harness Zig's power will grow.

Welcome to the world of real Zig development—where explicitness is a virtue, performance is a priority, and each allocation has a home to return to.

Consider yourself initiated (and hopefully there will be no need to call `deinit()`).

Unlock this book's exclusive benefits now

UNLOCK NOW

Scan this QR code or go to `https://packtpub.com/unlock`, then search this book by name.

Note: Keep your purchase invoice ready before you start.

14

Unlock Your Book's Exclusive Benefits

Your copy of this book comes with the following exclusive benefits:

- ☁ Next-gen Packt Reader
- ✦ AI assistant (beta)
- 📖 DRM-free PDF/ePub downloads

Use the following guide to unlock them if you haven't already. The process takes just a few minutes and needs to be done only once.

How to unlock these benefits in three easy steps

Step 1

Have your purchase invoice for this book ready, as you'll need it in *Step 3*. If you received a physical invoice, scan it on your phone and have it ready as either a PDF, JPG, or PNG.

For more help on finding your invoice, visit `https://www.packtpub.com/unlock-benefits/help`.

> **Note:** Did you buy this book directly from Packt? You don't need an invoice. After completing Step 2, you can jump straight to your exclusive content.

Step 2

Scan this QR code or go to `https://packtpub.com/unlock`.

On the page that opens (which will look similar to *Figure 14.1* if you're on desktop), search for this book by name. Make sure you select the correct edition.

Figure 14.1 – Packt unlock landing page on desktop

Step 3

Once you've selected your book, sign in to your Packt account or create a new one for free. Once you're logged in, upload your invoice. It can be in PDF, PNG, or JPG format and must be no larger than 10 MB. Follow the rest of the instructions on the screen to complete the process.

Need help?

If you get stuck and need help, visit https://www.packtpub.com/unlock-benefits/help for a detailed FAQ on how to find your invoices and more. The following QR code will take you to the help page directly:

Note: If you are still facing issues, reach out to customercare@packt.com.

\<packt>

packtpub.com

Subscribe to our online digital library for full access to over 7,000 books and videos, as well as industry leading tools to help you plan your personal development and advance your career. For more information, please visit our website.

Why subscribe?

- Spend less time learning and more time coding with practical eBooks and Videos from over 4,000 industry professionals
- Improve your learning with Skill Plans built especially for you
- Get a free eBook or video every month
- Fully searchable for easy access to vital information
- Copy and paste, print, and bookmark content

At www.packtpub.com, you can also read a collection of free technical articles, sign up for a range of free newsletters, and receive exclusive discounts and offers on Packt books and eBooks.

Other Books You May Enjoy

If you enjoyed this book, you may be interested in these other books by Packt:

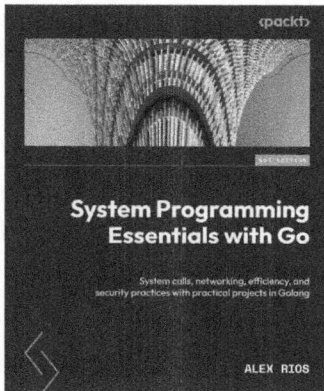

System Programming Essentials with Go

Alex Rios

ISBN: 978-1-80181-344-0

- Understand the fundamentals of system programming using Go
- Grasp the concepts of goroutines, channels, data races, and managing concurrency in Go
- Manage file operations and inter-process communication (IPC)
- Handle USB drives and Bluetooth devices and monitor peripheral events for hardware automation
- Familiarize yourself with the basics of network programming and its application in Go
- Implement logging, tracing, and other telemetry practices
- Construct distributed cache and approach distributed systems using Go

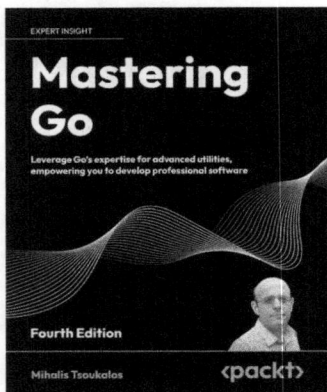

Mastering Go - Fourth Edition

Mihalis Tsoukalos

ISBN: 978-1-80512-264-7

- Learn Go data types, error handling, constants, pointers, and array and slice manipulations through practical exercises
- Create generic functions, define data types, explore constraints, and grasp interfaces and reflections
- Grasp advanced concepts like packages, modules, functions, and database interaction
- Create concurrent RESTful servers, and build TCP/IP clients and servers
- Learn testing, profiling, and efficient coding for high-performance applications
- Develop an SQLite package, explore Docker integration, and embrace workspaces

Packt is searching for authors like you

If you're interested in becoming an author for Packt, please visit authors.packt.com and apply today. We have worked with thousands of developers and tech professionals, just like you, to help them share their insight with the global tech community. You can make a general application, apply for a specific hot topic that we are recruiting an author for, or submit your own idea.

Share your thoughts

Now you've finished *Learning Zig*, we'd love to hear your thoughts! Scan the QR code below to go straight to the Amazon review page for this book and share your feedback or leave a review on the site that you purchased it from.

https://packt.link/r/1835085121

Your review is important to us and the tech community and will help us make sure we're delivering excellent quality content.

Index

www.ingramcontent.com/pod-product-compliance
Lightning Source LLC
Chambersburg PA
CBHW081220220326
41598CB00037B/6839

* 9 7 8 1 8 3 5 0 8 5 1 2 7 *